CIVIC
RITUAL IN
RENAISSANCE
VENICE

CIVIC
RITUAL IN
RENAISSANCE
VENICE

EDWARD
MUIR

PRINCETON UNIVERSITY
PRESS

PUBLISHED BY PRINCETON UNIVERSITY PRESS, PRINCETON NEW JERSEY
IN THE UNITED KINGDOM: PRINCETON UNIVERSITY PRESS, CHICHESTER, WEST SUSSEX

LIBRARY OF CONGRESS CATALOGING IN PUBLICATION DATA WILL BE FOUND ON THE
LAST PRINTED PAGE OF THIS BOOK

PUBLICATION OF THIS BOOK WAS ASSISTED BY A GRANT FROM THE PUBLICATIONS
PROGRAM OF THE NATIONAL ENDOWMENT FOR THE HUMANITIES

THIS BOOK HAS BEEN COMPOSED IN VIP ALDUS

PRINCETON UNIVERSITY PRESS BOOKS ARE PRINTED ON ACID-FREE PAPER
AND MEET THE GUIDELINES FOR PERMANENCE AND DURABILITY OF THE
COMMITTEE ON PRODUCTION GUIDELINES FOR BOOK LONGEVITY OF THE
COUNCIL ON LIBRARY RESOURCES

PRINTED IN THE UNITED STATES OF AMERICA

10 9 8 7 6 5 4

FOR
ANNETTE

CONTENTS

CONTENTS

LIST OF FIGURES

ACKNOWLEDGMENTS

The second section of chapter seven, entitled "The Funeral and Coronation of the Doge," is a revised and amplified version of an article first published as "The Doge as *Primus Inter Pares:* Interregnum Rites in Early Sixteenth-Century Venice," in *Essays Presented to Myron P. Gilmore*, edited by Sergio Bertelli and Gloria Ramakus, Florence, 1978, 1:145–60. I wish to thank "La Nuova Italia" Editrice, Florence, for permission to republish the essay here. In revising this section, I have benefited from the comments and criticisms of Robert Finlay, Felix Gilbert, and Donald Queller, who have led me to modify my views somewhat on the actual powers of the sixteenth-century doges.

In the course of researching and writing this book, I have enjoyed aid and encouragement from several sources, which deserve my thanks. I thank first of all my mother for introducing me to *Tosca* and Titian, thus determining my bent toward things Italian, and my father for cheerfully helping me through the lean years of graduate school and research in Venice. While writing my dissertation, I spent an invigorating year as a fellow at the Harvard University Center for Italian Renaissance Studies at Villa I Tatti, Florence, with a stipend from the Committee to Rescue Italian Art. Our hosts, Sheila and the late Myron Gilmore, created a congenial community that will always be fondly remembered. Since then, I have received a summer stipend from the National Endowment for the Humanities and a Research Fellowship for Recent Recipients of the Ph.D. from the American Council of Learned Societies, for which Syracuse University graciously granted me a semester's leave. Over the years numerous acquaintances, colleagues, and friends have made suggestions, passed on references, pointed out my stupidities, and provoked me to revise my interpretations. I must thank William Brown, Peter Burke, Demetrios Constantelos, Paul Grendler, Deborah Howard, Norman Land, Christopher Lloyd, Oliver Logan, William Lubenow, Michael Mallett, Margaret Marsh, Reinhold Mueller, Kenneth Pennington, James

Powell, Guido, Ruggiero, and James Williamson. Olga Puma-
nová of the Národní Galerie, Prague, kindly provided me with
a photograph of the Andrea Michieli ("il Vicentino") painting
in the episcopal residence of Litoměřice (Leitmeritz), Bohemia.
In Venice the informed help of the personnel of the Archivio di
Stato, Biblioteca del Museo Civico Correr, Biblioteca Nazionale
Marciana, Biblioteca Querini Stampalia, and Fondazione Giorgio Cini solved many of my problems; Dottoressa Maria Fran-
cesca Tiepolo has earned my special regards for her generosity
in guiding me through the Archivio di Stato. Richard Trexler's
advice on various theoretical and practical problems in the interpretation of ritual has been invaluable. A constant intellectual companion over the last seven years who has listened to
my inchoate ideas and read and commented on scattered bits
and pieces of this book, David R. Edward Wright has influenced
my thinking in many subtle and, I am sure, unrecognized
ways. At Princeton University Press Joanna Hitchcock, R. Mir-
iam Brokaw, and especially William Hively made my manuscript a book. My study of Venetian civic rituals began as a
paper for a seminar led by Donald Weinstein; he has remained
an unflagging guide, a mentor in the highest sense of the word,
and will ever be *il miglior fabbro*. My wife, Annette, merits
more credit than a simple dedication. She helped in the research, especially in the tedious reading of the fifty-eight volumes of Marin Sanuto's diaries, tendered suggestions and criticisms at every stage, taught me how to write what I meant,
and held me to her uncompromising standards. I hope this book
may be a worthy offering.

May 1980   E.M.

ABBREVIATIONS

ASF   Archivio di Stato, Florence
ASV   Archivio di Stato, Venice
BMV   Biblioteca Nazionale Marciana, Venice
MCV   Biblioteca del Museo Civico Correr, Venice
ONV   Österreichische Nationalbibliothek, Vienna
SUL   Syracuse University Library, Syracuse, New York

A NOTE ON DATING

All dates are given in the new style unless they are followed by
the abbreviation m.v., which stands for *modo veneto*. The
Venetian style was to date the beginning of the year from
March 1.

CIVIC
RITUAL IN
RENAISSANCE
VENICE

INTRODUCTION

On a spring afternoon in 1972, my wife and I sat at a table in front of the minuscule neighborhood bar in Campo San Cassiano, a drab but sunlit square in the working-class district of Venice where we had by then lived for nine months. My wife, ever attracted to kindly old ladies, struck up a conversation with two stout grandmothers who were enjoying their afternoon aperitif at the table next to us. We talked of Venice. In dialect punctuated by demands for the barman to supply the correct Italian words, the women told us about life in the parish where each had lived her entire eighty-odd years. One teased the other about the wanderlust that had caused her to move one street away from her birthplace and about the exotic taste that had influenced her to marry a *straniero*, a "foreigner" from Padua, some twenty miles distant. The other in turn lamented abandonment by her children, who had all moved to the Lido, fifteen minutes away by boat. It was clear that the parish was the extent of their world: one had never been to the mainland; the other had bothered to visit Piazza San Marco only a few times in her life. Their quiet parish was a place of great antiquity, their church's obscure patron saint protected his flock, the Virgin's presence was real, and the grandmothers knew who belonged with them and who did not. Their sense of space was narrow and confined; but their knowledge of their place was intimate, their satisfaction with it complete, their love of it total.

On a different continent two years later, I discussed with my own octogenarian grandfather the impending fall of Richard Nixon. In canvassing the various political opinions of his generation, my grandfather mentioned that one of his relatives, a retired dentist living in a small town in rural Utah, claimed that Nixon was clearly God's chosen vicar on earth, since all Presidents were elected according to the divinely ordained practices of the Constitution. For this dentist, Nixon's persecutors in their attempts to unseat him had thus become instruments of the Devil. This rather extreme opinion was, to be sure, a naive and antiquated notion of the theory of the divine right of rulers, but I suppose more than one of my grandfather's compatriots shared this belief. For the dentist, the incumbent and the office were inseparably bonded; the sanctity of the office had suffused the man, Richard Nixon.

The convictions of the Venetian grandmothers and the Utah dentist attest to the continued existence of two fundamental patterns of thought—mentalities, if one will—that seem little altered by short-term events and that persist through the very long dimension of time measured by millennia.[1] My informers disclosed, in the first case, parochialism—the affective identification of the self with a particular, geographically defined place—and, in the second, a belief in the sacred nature of institutions and leaders, an attitude that invests things and persons political with a mystical aura, distinguishing them from mundane structures and from ordinary mortals. These two mentalities, of course, were even more widespread during the Renaissance.

It has long been supposed that the glorification of civic life in Renaissance Italy flourished best under conditions of urban independence and republican political activity. In Italy from at least the time of Coluccio Salutati and Leonardo Bruni, *la vita civile* stood for an ideology about civilization and about life itself, an ideal that proposed that only complete immersion in the affairs of one's community and one's city could lead to a superior life and to a sense of satisfaction and completion.[2] Even today, for the citizens of many Italian towns, the responsibility, commitment, and group identification that is associated with membership in a local community reaches far beyond parochialism: community life is often seen as the very essence of *civiltà*.[3] And for Italians *civiltà* is a word more manifold with

[1] Fernand Braudel, "History and the Social Sciences." My thinking about the units of historical time has been further stimulated by the comments Immanuel Wallerstein made at the symposium on "Historical and Sociological Perspectives on Change and Continuity" at the Maxwell School Day, Syracuse University, November 30, 1977.

[2] Perhaps the most notable among the large number of studies that reflect this point of view are those by Hans Baron, *The Crisis of the Early Italian Renaissance,* and by William J. Bouwsma, *Venice and the Defense of Republican Liberty.*

[3] Sydel Silverman, *Three Bells of Civilization.*

affective meanings than its much abused English translation, "civilization."

In Renaissance Venice, a particularly glittering temple to *civiltà*, an intense community life seems to have been fostered by an intricate design of civic rituals, which succeeded in melding parochialism and the tendency to hold certain offices and institutions sacred into an unusually vibrant and durable civic patriotism. In the great cycle of civic rituals may be read a story created by the Venetians about their own political and social world. And beyond this, in the rituals and their accompanying legends may lie a clue to the rise of a republican political ideology often called "the myth of Venice," which endures as Venice's lasting contribution to the political ideals of the Western world.

Civic ritual in Venice was a peculiar hybrid of liturgical and ceremonial elements, taken from diverse sources, that prospered in the Venetian community. These regular communal affairs reveal an indigenous civic identity and ideology based upon a broad consensus about social values. Civic rituals were commentaries on the city, its internal dynamics, and its relationship with the outside world. In commenting upon civic realities, the rituals illustrated an ideal arrangement of human relationships, created a homily that stimulated or altered some formal political and social ideas, and provided a medium for discourse among the constituent classes and between the literate elite and the masses.[4] Although civic rituals often served the rulers' interests, they were not just propaganda and did not pass messages only in one direction. The study of civic ritual might, therefore, allow one to discover changes and continuities over a long period of time in the self-perceptions of a large social group.

The historian of civic ritual attempts to decipher complexly evolved patterns of behavior. Civic time is the first consideration. It appears that feast days in Venice and the events they commemorated, the commune's designation of new feast days and its obliteration of others, and a particularly Venetian use of

[4]Cf. Natalie Zemon Davis, "Some Tasks and Themes in the Study of Popular Religion," p. 318.

the liturgical calendar supplied an important temporal frame for Venetian civic life. Second, the historian pursues the notion of civic space as it was expressed in rituals. The Venetian regime's creation of certain specialized ritual territories and processional routes, its recognition of ritual centers and borders in the city, and its maintenance or suppression of ritual relationships between the central authority and the geographical subdivisions of the city—the neighborhoods and parishes—indicate an increasingly political use of space. Third, he looks for changes in the aggregate number and frequency of rituals over a specific period of time. The results of such a search might test the commonly asserted hypothesis that modernity and ritual are incompatible and that the rise of the modern world was accompanied by a decline in ritual. Fourth, the historian seeks evidence for the "laicization" or "secularization" of ritual. Laicization, in this context, refers to the replacement of ecclesiastics with laymen as ritual specialists and as spiritual instructors. Secularization implies not the old Burckhardtian notion that a secular world view was opposed to and replaced a religious one, but rather, in the words of Donald Weinstein, ". . . the transfer of the scene of religious ritual from reserved monastic or ecclesiastical space to public, civic space . . . [and] the religious legitimation of formerly worldly and temporal activities and institutions."[5] In Venice there was an ancient tendency to attribute holiness to secular leaders; hence this study tries to identify which secular institutions in Venice became sacred, and when. The peculiar legalisms found in ceremonies are a fifth concern. In numerous medieval and Renaissance examples, legal and "constitutional" precepts and precedents found expression in ceremony long before they were written down in formal codes; and Venice, it seems, was indeed no stranger to the habit of ceremonial law. Sixth, the historian of civic ritual investigates how ceremonies may reveal the citizens' own sense of their city's relations with the outside world, relations that the Venetians saw by and large in imperial terms. A seventh inquiry traces the emergence, suppression, or alteration in the

[5]Donald Weinstein, "Critical Issues in the Study of Civic Religion in Renaissance Florence," pp. 266–67.

ritual representation of specific social groups. In Venice one finds that the legally defined social classes, the patrilineal family, age groups, and women all shared varying degrees of ritual recognition that marked their place in the political and social organization of the city. And last, the historian of civic ritual must attempt to compare the ideas he finds represented in rituals with those transmitted in other ways, as in literature, formal political thought, and the visual arts.

The following text offers a detailed deciphering of Venetian civic ritual, beginning with a discussion of the myth of Venice. The mythology will be familiar to most Italian Renaissance scholars, particularly to Venetian specialists; but Part One is organized to show a kaleidoscopic image of the myth of Venice as our point of view shifts from the perspectives of the Venetians themselves, their contemporaries, and their admirers and critics at home and abroad to those of modern historians and students of ritual. Part Two describes the legends and rituals inherited by the Renaissance Venetians, especially those who lived in the sixteenth century, although there are numerous excursions, when possible, into earlier periods. Here one finds that the Renaissance republican ideology germinated from the medieval civic liturgy. Part Three focuses on the ceremonies that involved the doge, the princely but republican head of Venetian government, and, in order to define the structure of the Venetian commonwealth, analyzes the political and social functions of public ceremony as celebrated in the sixteenth century.

The meaning of civic rituals no doubt changed in the centuries between their inception and the sixteenth century, but, sadly, the existing documents do not allow a comprehensive study of such mutations.[6] This book must therefore offer a somewhat limited interpretation of the Venetian rituals and legends as known during the Cinquecento. Whenever possible I have relied directly on the testimony of contemporary Venetians; when the Venetians were mute, I have sought the opinions of foreigners; when these too have failed, I have offered

[6]This opinion is confirmed by Gina Fasoli, "Liturgia e cerimoniale ducale," 1:261.

hypothetical interpretations consonant with the political and social assumptions of the period. In addition, I have tried, wherever appropriate, to elucidate social functions and mentalities of which the Venetians were no doubt unconscious. Even the Venetians themselves did not always agree on the precise meaning of discrete rites and, in particular, offered variant versions of the origins of rituals; so in most cases I have used the official interpretations of civic ritual found in state papers and patrician commentaries. Finally, though I have deliberately sought the voices of the opposition and the alienated, I have found little evidence of a counter-ideology that had a wide following in Venice. Instead I have found that throughout the sixteenth century civic rituals presented a carefully arranged portrait of a remarkably well-ordered society, a large and convincing tableau that unfolded the myth of Venice.

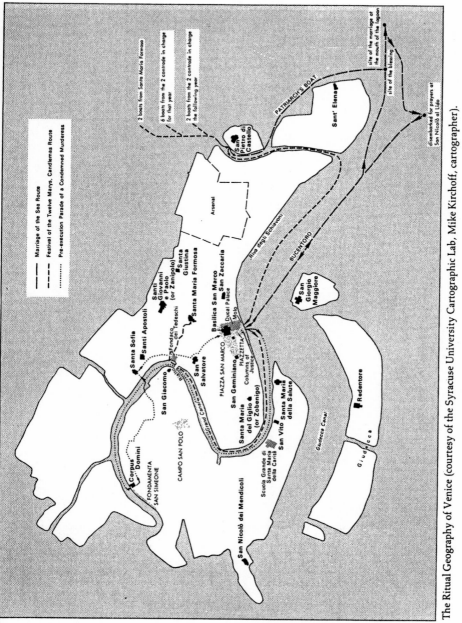

The Ritual Geography of Venice (courtesy of the Syracuse University Cartographic Lab, Mike Kirchoff, cartographer).

PART ONE

MYTH AND RITUAL

Sun-girt city, thou hast been
Ocean's child, and then his queen;
Now is come a darker day,
And thou soon must be his prey.
— Shelley, *Lines Written Amongst
the Euganean Hills*

In order to make up our minds we must know how we
feel about things; and to know how we feel about things
we need the public images of sentiment that only ritual,
myth, and art can provide.
— Clifford Geertz, *The Interpretation of Cultures*

ONE

THE MYTH OF VENICE

THE MEANING OF THE MYTH

In an act of communal genius, late medieval and Renaissance Venetians intertwined the threads of parochialism, patriotism, and the ideal of *la vita civile* to weave their own sort of republican, popular piety. In this endeavor Venice anticipated Rousseau's warning in the *Contrat sociale* that a state, if it is to endure, must enlist not only the interests of men but their passions as well. Venice endured as a republic while its neighbors did not, thus achieving for itself an international reputation as a state in which the interests and passions of the citizens were almost mystically bound to the system of government. Until its capture by Napoleon, in 1797, Venice had been an independent community for nearly a millennium; for the last five hundred years of its sovereignty, it had been a republic under the continuous rule of a hereditary patriciate that styled itself as a nobility. During that period of independence the Venetian patriciate created social and political institutions so outwardly stable, harmonious, and just that the tensions inherent in any community seemed to be contained in Venice, and self-interest subordinated to the common good. The fundamental problem of the historians of Venice since then has been to separate outward appearance from reality, to uncover from the veneer of propaganda and mythology the actual social and political structure of the city.

Burckhardt painted the classic, if somewhat misleading, portrait of Venice. Contrasting the dynamic restlessness and creativity of Florence with the stagnant repose and traditionalism of Venice, he depicted Venice as a strange and mysterious creation formed without turbulent divisions of political parties, with exceptional concern for citizens in need, and with mutual acceptance of common interests between rulers and subjects. Burckhardt attributed Venice's political success more to the virtue imposed on the citizenry than to the institutions of government themselves: "No state, indeed, has ever exercised a greater moral influence over its subjects, whether abroad or at home."[1] In some sense Burckhardt was misled by Renaissance rhetoric about Venice, which rather more often took the form of righteous sentimentality than the shape of precise fact.

Today much of what Venetians and their admirers declaimed about Venice sounds too self-serving, too daintily melodious to be considered accurate; yet these words do reveal much about the Venetian point of view, the Weltanschauung of a people whose city was to have a tremendous influence on the imagination and aspirations of other Europeans. The Venetians were fond of writing about themselves, praising their city and its institutions. But, as is often the case in patriotic matters, the parvenu citizen, the adopted foreigner, or even the conquered subject was as often responsible for articulating the values of civic patriotism as was the citizen of ancient lineage; what someone born in a city takes for granted, an outsider often discovers like one newly converted to a religious creed. In Florence, another city noted for its civic values, it took a man from Arezzo, Leonardo Bruni, to trace the ideal of civic life for the natives; and it took a Ferrarese, Savonarola, to transform the civic myth into a millenarian promise.[2] Venice, too, was served by *stranieri*.

Praise of Venice during the Renaissance invariably began with applause for its unparalleled beauty and urban charm as a city quite literally built upon the sea. An emissary from Friuli, Cornelio Frangipane, in a characteristic oration to Doge Francesco Donà (1545–53) once lauded Venice as incomparably beautiful to see, marvelous to contemplate, secure, peaceful, and rich; on another occasion he added that, after Paradise, Venice was the best place in the universe.[3] An ambassador from

---

[1]Jacob Burckhardt, *The Civilization of the Renaissance in Italy*, p. 89. His views on Venice cover pp. 82–95.

[2]Baron, *Crisis of the Early Renaissance*; Donald Weinstein, *Savonarola and Florence*.

[3]"In somma è tale, che non è cittade al mondo piu bella da vedere, ne piu meravigliosa da contemplare, ne piu secura da habitare, ne piu commoda da

Belluno, Paolo Novello, in his oration to the doge cleverly transported the seven marvels of the ancient world to a Venetian setting, listing among Venice's seven "miracles" its openness to the sea (a metaphor for its political liberty), the protection afforded by the Lido, and its physical setting on the water. The urban wonders in Novello's discourse metamorphosed into images of Venice's political and historical traditions, as if Venice's destiny had been foreordained by its relationship with nature.[4] Venice's natural beauty, always a point of civic pride, was heightened by striking architecture, imposing public monuments, and the vast Piazza San Marco. As in other Italian cities, building projects in Venice were often expressions of communal values and devotion. The identification of Venice in the arts and in rhetoric with its picturesque qualities, as in the sixteenth-century iconography that symbolized the city as the sea-born Venus, was an unchanging feature of the Venetians' perpetual encomium to their city. Many of the cultural preoccupations of the Renaissance, especially the humanists' emphasis on rhetorical hyperbole and the Neoplatonic belief that outward beauty was a sign of inward virtue, encouraged the cultivation of pleasant appearances; so to many Renaissance minds a stunning cityscape alone gave proof of a well-arranged political and social order.[5]

---

riposare, ne verso di se piu ricca, piu magnifica, piu di uina. O Vinetia ricetto di libertà, tempio di religione, vero albergo di pace, & di tranquillitade. O Illustre domicilio di gloria, ò dignissima sede d'Imperio, ò grande, antica, & veneranda cittade, madre di tanti Heroi, sii felice, sii beata, sii eternamente regnante." The oration was published by Francesco Sansovino, *Delle orationi recitate a principi di Veneti nella loro creatione da gli ambasciadori di diverse città . . .* , fol. 6r. The other citation is from Cornelio Frangipane, *In laude di Venezia*, p. 16. Cf. the anonymous *Fantasia composta in laude de Veniesia*, Venice, 1582, in the Biblioteca Nazionale Marciana, Venice (hereafter BMV), misc. 2619/11. Major victories usually prompted a flood of new works in this genre. In the Marciana I have counted well over one hundred titles of lauds, *canzone, rime,* and descriptions of the battle or victory celebrations that were printed immediately after the Venetian victory in 1571 against the Turks at Lepanto. A cursory examination of them revealed that they usually relied on the most traditional and conservative patriotic themes to express the exhilaration produced by the victory.

[4]Novello's oration was published by Sansovino, *Delle orationi recitate a principi,* fols. 31v–32r.

[5]Edward Muir, "Images of Power."

Likewise, the outward show of religious faith in Venice led panegyrists to argue that Venice was exceptionally pious. Not only did the city harbor the body of the Evangelist Mark, but it gloried in numerous churches, in patronage of religious orders, in charity to the poor, in unflagging opposition to the infidel Turks, and in devout processions.[6] These works were, of course, everywhere encouraged by Catholic dogma as a means to attain salvation, but to the civic-minded Venetians such extraordinary devotion proved Venice a chosen city of God, a city infused with grace. According to the fifteenth-century Venetian humanist, Giovanni Caldiera, the cardinal virtues—Faith, Hope, and Charity—underlay the republican virtues; so obedience to the state was metaphorically obedience to the will of God.[7] Thus, in Venice patriotism equaled piety. The Venetians' conception of themselves as a chosen people, in consequence, was always revealed in their attachment to certain sacred institutions, such as the state church, housed by the basilica of San Marco, and the republic itself, and rarely in the chiliastic forms that swept Florence during the Savonarola mania and many other cities during times of political tension or social upheaval.[8] Belief in Venice-as-the-chosen-city and adherence to the historical institutions of the republic enabled the Venetians to withstand the tremendous forces for change, including the temptations of millenarian enthusiasm, that ravaged the rest of Italy during the late fifteenth and sixteenth centuries. Instead, the Venetians cautiously accepted the legacy of their social order, their special place in the divine plan, and so transcended the outcome of *événements*. Venice's first contribution to European political thought was, therefore, a conservative example of the long-term preservation of so-called divinely ordained institutions.

In addition to esteeming the beauty and religiosity of Venice, characteristics derived simply from its geographical setting and from its most public demonstrations of communal faith, parti-

[6]Cornelio Frangipane in Sansovino, *Delle orationi recitate a principi,* fol. 6r.

[7]Margaret L. King, "Personal, Domestic, and Republican Values in the Moral Philosophy of Giovanni Caldiera," pp. 559–65.

[8]Weinstein, *Savonarola and Florence;* Norman Cohn, *The Pursuit of the Millennium;* Michael Barkun, *Disaster and the Millennium.*

sans admired Venice's liberty, peacefulness, and republican form
of government. For the Venetians "liberty" was a matter not of
personal freedom, but rather of political independence from
other powers. According to Frangipane, the Venetians had
never been anyone's subjects, since they were by nature rulers
over others—"peroche soli per natura signoreggiano."[9] Venice's
historical pretentions to liberty were given their best exposition
in Scipione Feramesca's 1640 treatise on the diplomatic precedence of Venice over the imperial electors, in which Feramesca
claimed Venice to be the only republic ever born in freedom,
comparing it to Athens, Sparta, Rome, Florence, Lucca, Genoa,
and unnamed others. He further asserted that the independence of Venice had been recognized by numerous emperors
and popes and that its liberty and power had been upheld by
the *virtù* of its rulers, rights *(ragioni)*, laws, and customs *(consuetudine)*.[10] Venice's *libertà* was consequently an ideological
inheritance, a gift of fortune that the Venetians had valued and
preserved, and a political fact that the two great claimants to
universal sovereignty, the pope and emperor, had been forced to
recognize.

The city's liberty, Venetian apologists were anxious to demonstrate, coexisted with domestic harmony and respect for the
territory of its neighbors, never with military might or aggres-
sion. Yet Venetians also loved to boast of their imperial posses-
sions, obtained undeniably by war. A sixteenth-century English
traveler to Venice, William Lithgow, reconciled this apparent
contradiction by observing that

> The *Venetians*, howsoever of old, they have bene great
> warriours; they are now more desirous to keepe, then

[9]Sansovino, *Delle orationi recitate a principi*, fol. 5v. Cf. Frangipane, *In
laude di Venezia*, p. 12.

[10]"Sola questa Serenissima Republica già nacque libera ne altro simil'esempio
di libertà cred'io, che pop'addirsi, se non quella Libertà, che nacque all'ora, che
nacque il Mondo." Scipione Feramesca, "Discorso delle ragioni della Serenissima Republica sopra gl'Elettori dall'Imperio in materia di precedenza," first
piece in the bound vol. "Discorsi di precedenza officii e feste, 1597–1794,"
BMV, MS Italiano VII, 1743 (7802). The quote is on fol. 2v. Also see fols. 8v–
17v. Another copy of the MS is in the Biblioteca del Museo Civico Correr,
Venice (hereafter MCV), MS P.D. 701c/II (n. 9). The work is dated 1640.

inlarge their Dominions, and that by presents and money, rather than by the sword or true valour, so whatsoever they loose by battell, it is observed, they recover again by treatise.[11]

The Venetians, who were less cynical about this supposed proclivity toward bribery, argued that they had inherited a clement approach to foreign affairs.[12] They contrasted their experience to the fate of the Romans, who, although great, valorous, and victorious warriors, had nonetheless suffered from the domestic turmoil and political instability created by their dependence on overly powerful armies. The Venetians had preferred intelligent negotiation, prudence, and temperance.[13] As the Venetians often boasted, whoever lived in Venice was free from the sufferings of war, from its mental anquish, fear, and economic ruin; shops and homes were secure from both plundering troops and tax collectors; and the absence of factions liberated the republic from internal treacheries. As the saying went, "non est vivere extra Venetiis."[14] The ancient Venetians, according to one author, had even introduced a style of dress for men that encouraged gravity of bearing, modesty, and a quiet demeanor; if clothes make the man, then long trousers made the Venetian a lover of peace.[15] Through such reasoning, specious or not, Venice became the Most Serene Republic, La Serenissima.

[11]William Lithgow, *The Totall Discourse, of the Rare Adventures, and Painfull Peregrinations of Long Nineteene Yeares Travayles, from Scotland, to the Most Famous Kingdomes in Europe, Asia, and Africa*, pp. 39—40.

[12]Frangipane in Sansovino, *Delle orationi recitate a principi*, fol. 7v.

[13]"Ne men vittoriosa questa ben ordinata Republica la quale usando il valore, ove è bisogno di forza, l'intelletto & prudentia, ove è necessario il consiglio, è ridotta a tanta altezza, che non ritrova inimico, in tanto ardor di guerre, non è chi ardisca di offenderla, nel colmo de gli odii è da tutti amata & riverita, talmente che si puo dir con verità nel grembo suo riposarsi & la guerra & la pace non teme la guerra, non la desidera, non provoca, non è provocata, quello procede da animo temperato, questo dalla fortezza, & gagliardezza sua." Oration by Pietro Godi in ibid., fol. 27r—v. In contrast Lithgow, *The Totall Discourse*, p. 41, pictures the Venetians as the heirs of the Romans.

[14]Girolamo Priuli, *I diarii*.

[15]Girolamo Bardi, *Delle cose notabili della città di Venetia, libri III*, p. 16.

THE MYTH OF VENICE

The rather ambiguous Venetian attitudes about peacefulness and serenity were, however, little more than shadows of the more substantial institutional forms of the republic. Controlled by a hereditary caste of some 2,500 nobles, Venice became the most famous living example in early modern Europe of the advantages gained from government by a thoughtful few. Admiration for the Venetian republic largely took two forms, in praise either for the wisdom embodied in Venice's political institutions or for the devoted civic service practiced by the patrician rulers. The government consisted of a disciplined corps of magistrates, who usually held office for short terms of a few months or a year. Since 1297, when its membership rolls had been definitively drawn up, the Great Council, consisting of all noblemen over twenty-five, served as the electorate, voting to select magistrates for the other judicial, administrative, and legislative offices of the republic.[16] In effect the Great Council delegated the responsibility of government to other bodies, principally the Senate, which was the real center of political life in Venice.[17] The Collegio of the Senate, composed of the doge, his counselors, and three standing committees whose members were known as *savii*, handled the day-to-day business of the

[16] The simplest reference on the Venetian constitution is Andrea da Mosto, *L'Archivio di Stato di Venezia*, especially 1:21, 22– 23, 25– 26, 29– 31, 34– 38, 52– 55, 63– 64. A more detailed description is available in Giuseppe Maranini, *La costituzione di Venezia dopo la serrata del maggior consiglio*. The best analysis of the decisive constitutional events of 1296– 97 is Frederic C. Lane, "The Enlargement of the Great Council of Venice." Some young men between the ages of twenty and twenty-five were selected by lot each year for membership in the Great Council. Gasparo Contarini, *De magistratibus et republica Venetorum libri quinque*, pp. 19, 22; English version, pp. 16, 19– 20. On the question of age qualification for the Great Council and the means of evading the rules see John Easton Law, "Age Qualification and the Venetian Constitution." Membership figures for the Great Council are given in James Cushman Davis, *The Decline of the Venetian Nobility as a Ruling Class*, p. 58.

[17] "The whole manner of the commonwealths government belongeth to the senate." Contarini, *De magistratibus et republica Venetorum*, p. 65, English version, p. 68. The Senate consisted of 60 regular and 60 supplementary *(zonta)* members, but nearly all of the other important office-holders were entitled to attend Senate meetings in an *ex officio* capacity, so that by the 1520s there were some 220 members. Contarini, *De magistratibus et republica Venetorum*, p. 63; English version, p. 66.

Senate. The duties of the *savii* encompassed diplomatic, colonial, military, naval, and ceremonial matters.[18] At the pinnacle of the Venetian hierarchy stood the doge, a prince elected for life whose statutory powers came from his ceremonial prerogatives and his position as chairman of the Great Council, Senate, Collegio, and the Council of Ten. Symbolically, he was the sovereign of Venice; legally, he was merely the *primus inter pares* of the patrician class; but practically he could wield whatever power his own ability and political connections provided.[19] The Council of Ten stood somewhat apart from the hierarchy of offices but was proverbially powerful. With its secret funds, system of anonymous informers, police powers, and broad judicial mandate over matters of state security, the members of the Council of Ten, along with those of the Collegio, rotated offices among themselves and constituted the inner circle of oligarchical patricians who, in effect, ruled the republic.[20] The only other nobles besides the doge who were granted a lifetime right to their office were the procurators of San Marco, who marshaled substantial economic power as administrators of endowments given to the basilica and considerable political influence as members of the Council of Ten.[21] For Venetians and their foreign admirers, the strength of the government of Venice lay principally in this legalistic, yet severely aristocratic, hierarchy of offices.

[18]Decisions made in the Collegio pertaining to official ceremonies from the sixteenth century to the fall of the republic are found in the MS series, Archivio di Stato, Venice (hereafter ASV), Collegio Cerimoniali.

[19]On the political powers of the doges see Robert Finlay, *Politics in Renaissance Venice*, pp. 109–62.

[20]The Council of Ten was founded in 1310 to investigate the conspiracy of Baiamonto Tiepolo and Marco Querini, but the Council's permanent powers were not confirmed until 1455. Consisting of ten ordinary members and until 1582 of a *zonta* of some fifteen or twenty additional members, the Council of Ten was composed of senior senators chosen by the Great Council to serve for terms of one year without the possibility of re-election to the succeeding term. Mosto, *L'Archivio di Stato*, 1:52–55.

[21]The Procuratoria was traditionally composed of nine members; after 1516 additional procuratorships were sold for increasingly huge sums—12,000 to 100,000—ducats until at one point there were as many as forty procurators. Ibid., 1:25–26. Also see Reinhold C. Mueller, "The Procurators of San Marco in the Thirteenth and Fourteenth Centuries."

THE MYTH OF VENICE

A well-ordered system of magistracies, however, was insufficient to maintain political stability without an auxiliary ethic of political service. In 1527 Marco Foscari outlined this ethic in a report, or *relazione,* to the Senate, delivered on his return from a diplomatic mission to Florence. He argued that good and true senators strengthen themselves in three ways: "ut intelligant, ut explicent, ut ament rempublicam." Intelligence and good rhetoric were important, but for Foscari they were valueless unless accompanied by a "love of the republic" that was simple, perfect, and filial, not servile. Filial love was the love sons gave their father despite the demands he placed on them; it was the love of a dog which returned to his master even when beaten and abused. In the same way citizens should give their republic unqualified love, notwithstanding any inconvenience encountered in its service or any offense committed by its ministers.[22] This civic ethos of meekness, humility, and faithful service permeated much Venetian discourse about the state. Although the ethic of virtuous service may have been, like most moral ideals, more honored in the breach than in the observance, it was central both to how the Venetians thought of themselves and to how foreigners developed their impressions of the Venetians. In the Venetians' civic ethic historians like Burckhardt found the "moral influence" that was a reason for Venice's political triumph.

Venice's historical reputation for beauty, religiosity, liberty, peacefulness, and republicanism modern scholars call "the myth of Venice." This catalogue of attributes constituting the myth is not just the creation of latter-day scholars, however; the Renaissance Venetians acknowledged the same myth in their visual arts, musical lyrics, poetry, official and popular history, humanist works, and above all in ritual and pageantry.[23] In the myth of Venice parochial sentiments that cut across class lines

[22]"Relazion fatta per Marco Foscari nell'eccellentissimo Consiglio di Pregadi della Legazion de Fiorenza, con qualche cosa adiuncta da lui nel scrivere essa legazione, 1527," in *Relazioni degli ambasciatori veneti al Senato,* ed. Arnaldo Segarizzi, Scrittori d'Italia series, Bari, 1916, 3:4.

[23]Bernard Berenson, *The Italian Painters of the Renaissance,* p. 16; Millard Meiss, "Sleep in Venice;" Ellen Rosand, "Music in the Myth of Venice"; Antonio Medin, *La storia della repubblica di Venezia nella poesia;* Gaetano

met with the elite ideal of the civic life. Although the myth is typically studied as a creation of the Quattro- and Cinquecento, Petrarch was clearly aware of its rudiments in 1364, when he wrote his description of the Venetian celebration of a victory in Crete.

> The august city of Venice rejoices, the one home today of liberty, peace and justice, the one refuge of honorable men, the one port to which can repair the storm-tossed, tyrant-hounded craft of men who seek the good life. Venice—rich in gold but richer in fame, mighty in her resources but mightier in virtue, solidly built on marble but standing more solid on a foundation of civil concord, ringed with salt waters but more secure with the salt of good counsel![24]

For the Venetians such passages became sacred texts of their mythic heritage, a spiritual and emotional heritage that was made intellectual and historical in the writings of men like Gasparo Contarini and Paolo Sarpi.

Studying the "myth of Venice" in modern times has often meant attempting to sort out, from a puzzling set of beliefs that were not necessarily true and from an enigmatic series of events that are not historically verifiable, what was "reality." Not surprisingly, the results of such study have sometimes been contradictory. And hence the most successful path in the pursuit of the elusive myth of Venice has been its study as an ideology. From at least the sixteenth century the myth presented a fascinating vision of possibilities that made many foreigners consider Venice a city like no other in the world. Venice, its myth, and its ideology contributed importantly to what William Bouwsma has called "the political education of Europe." In his opinion, ". . . Venice represented in the modern world the central political values of Renaissance republicanism,

---

Cozzi, "Cultura, politica e religione nella 'pubblica storiografia' veneziana del '500"; Paul F. Grendler, "Francesco Sansovino and Italian Popular History, 1560–1600"; Muir, "Images of Power."

[24]Francesco Petrarch, *Letters*, p. 234. Cf. Poggio Bracciolini, *In laudem rei publicae Venetorum*, in *Opera omnia*, ed. Riccardo Fubini, Turin, 1966, 2:925–37.

which she made available to the rest of Europe in a singularly attractive and provocative form."[25] More vital than the fossilized memory of Athens or Rome or an utopian dream, antimonarchists in Europe and colonial America found in the living Venice an example that justified their cause. But more importantly, the myth represents the world view of a particularly cohesive community, an index of cultural symbols from which can be read the peculiarly Venetian mentality.

HISTORIOGRAPHY OF THE MYTH

Differing interpretations of the myth of Venice have usually resulted from an emphasis on different periods of Venetian history. For Hans Conrad Peyer and Gina Fasoli the myth originates in Venice's possession of the relics of Saint Mark, who came to personify Venetian *communitas*. According to Fasoli, the myth was born on the day in 827 or 828 when Doge Giustiniano Particiaco accepted the body of Saint Mark as a gift from two local merchants, who had smuggled it out of Moslem-controlled Alexandria. Tailoring the relationship between Saint Mark and Venice by the pattern of Saint Peter and the Papacy allowed the Venetians to claim by the late eleventh century that a mystical bond linked Saint and city so inextricably that each had taken on the other's attributes and qualities.[26] In the chronicle of John the Deacon, which became the source in all Venetian historiography for the notion of Venice as an ethical-spiritual commonwealth, the bonding with Saint Mark made Venice a "free" *res publica* under the rectorship of the doge.[27]

Venice subsequently became one of the most praised of medieval Italian cities: Saint Peter Damian recognized it as an

[25]William J. Bouwsma, "Venice and the Political Education of Europe," p. 445.

[26]Hans Conrad Peyer, *Stadt und Stadtpatron in mittelalterlichen Italien*, pp. 8–62; Fasoli, "Nascita di un mito"; idem, "Comune veneciarum," p. 486. Fasoli identifies a two-faced myth that is actually a list of descriptive qualities rather than a pseudo-historical narrative. One face emphasized the magnanimous, heroic, generous, liberal, and powerful aspects of Venetian rule, and the other, proclaimed by the enemies of Venice, depicted the tyranny, vileness, and impotence of the upstart Venetians.

[27]Fasoli, "Comune veneciarum," p. 486.

apostolic seat and a daughter of Rome, Emperor Henry IV
visited and applauded it, and Pope Gregory VII acknowledged
its liberty. Furthermore, Saint Mark served as the consummate
symbol of Venetian dominion; when the Venetians conquered
Crete in 1211, they imposed a political cult of Saint Mark on
the subject peoples by demanding the recitation of lauds to the
doge on Saint Mark's Day. Springing from these remote traditions, the myth of Venice, Fasoli argues, matured by the middle
of the fourteenth century into a civic cult of mystical patriotism.[28]

Other developments point to the fourteenth century as crucial in the creation of a Venetian civic consciousness. The gradual restriction of the powers of the doges during the late thirteenth century and the reform of the Great Council in 1297,
which permanently defined the closed, hereditary patriciate,
enabled the Venetian republic to resist to a certain extent the
destructive extremes of factional discord and political violence
that plagued other Italian city-republics during the fourteenth
century.[29] Turning away from its Byzantine orientation in the
fourteenth and early fifteenth centuries, Venice looked toward
Italy and the West for artistic inspiration and began to portray
itself as a "New Rome," the true heir of both the ancient
Roman Republic and Empire.[30] At this point, however, the

[28]Fasoli, "Nascita di un mito"; idem, "La coscienza civica nelle 'laudes civitatum' "; Ernst H. Kantorowicz, *Laudes Regiae*, p. 154.

[29]Stanley Chojnacki notes, however, that there was indeed considerable turmoil among Venetian patricians in the early and middle decades of the fourteenth century; see his "Crime, Punishment, and the Trecento Venetian
State." On the political transformation of the republic during this period see
the following works by Frederic C. Lane: "At the Roots of Republicanism,"
"Medieval Political Ideas and the Venetian Constitution," "The Enlargement of
the Great Council," and *Venice*, pp. 86–117, 172–87, 256–73. Lane notes
that there was no theoretical background for the 1297 republican reforms. In
fact, the first Italian republican theorist was Ptolemy of Lucca. Charles T.
Davis, "Roman Patriotism and Republican Propaganda."

[30]Galienne Francastel, "Une peinture anti-hérétique à Venise?"; Guido Piovene, "Anacronismo della Venezia quattrocentesca"; D. S. Chambers, *The Imperial Age of Venice, 1380–1580*, pp. 12–30. Frederic Lane has referred to the
change as the "turn westward." Lane, *Venice*, pp. 202–72. On the artistic
theme of Venice as a New Rome see Deborah Howard, *Jacopo Sansovino*, pp.
2–7, and Michelangelo Muraro, "La scala senza giganti." On the general

myth of Venice was, inchoate and lacked a theoretical exposition, which was achieved only when the analytic rhetoric of the humanists clothed Venetian institutions in neoclassical dress and made them appear as if they were living models of ancient ideals. The definitive form of the myth, as it is commonly understood by historians, was hence fashioned in the fifteenth and especially the sixteenth centuries.

The most influential of the fifteenth-century Venetian humanists was Bernardo Giustiniani, who drew liberally from the treçento chronicles of Andrea Dandolo and Lorenzo d'Monaco to compose his *History of the Origin of Venice*. Giustiniani contended that, as the Roman Empire dissolved, God led a favored few to a refuge on the lagoon, making the Venetians lineal heirs of Roman greatness. Giustiniani's polished Latin exhortations that his contemporaries emulate the virtue of the founding fathers established the form for most humanistic treatments of the Venetian past.[31] Marin Sanuto's rambling corpus in the *volgare*, which lacks Giustiniani's humanist rigor, confirms that Giustiniani's views closely conformed to the attitudes of an average though unusually voluble Venetian patrician. Besides the famous diaries that Sanuto compiled in anticipation of writing a history of the contemporary affairs of Venice, he produced a history of the doges that traced the process of their acquiring independence and sovereign authority for Venice.[32] At approximately the same time these two men were writing, Venetian leaders recognized the importance of disseminating the myth in a more active way, and official writers were appointed to pen Latin histories that echoed the position of the rulership on the issues of diplomacy and war. From these fawning pages the Venetians emerged, not unexpectedly, as selfless pursuers of peace against covetous enemies and as loyal subjects of a government of just laws promulgated by virtuous leaders.[33] By the early decades of the sixteenth

---

phenomenon of New Romes see William Hammer, "The Concept of the New or Second Rome in the Middle Ages," and Robert Lee Wolff, "The Three Romes."

[31]Patricia H. Labalme, *Bernardo Giustiniani*, pp. 247–304.

[32]Marin Sanuto, *Le vite dei dogi*, and idem, *I diarii*.

[33]Cozzi, " 'Pubblica storiografia' veneziana." For some important corrections

century, the language of humanism had transformed the traditional myth of a holy city protected by Saint Mark, independent from all foreign powers, into a coherent political ideology
that was classical in its derivation. Venetian councils, for instance, were now seen as evolved forms of Roman institutions.
All this invigorated the myth, for as Europeans groped for
stability they fitfully sensed the possibility that the accepted
models of ideal government were practicable in a real republic.

During the sixteenth century, however, members of the
Venetian ruling class witnessed a number of events that could
lead them only to question the efficacy of their own traditions.
News of two events arrived in Venice in 1499, precipitating a
social malaise: one report lamented that the Turks had defeated
the Venetian fleet at Zonchio and the other, a letter from Alexandria, revealed that three ships under the Portuguese flag
had arrived in Aden and Calicut in search of spices. With the
naval defeat the Venetians lost their claims to many Greek and
Albanian cities vital to the eastern trade of La Serenissima,
and, according to Frederic Lane, Venice's leaders thenceforth
abandoned their commitment to naval supremacy.[34] Although
it was a century or more before Venice experienced a permanent
economic loss as a result of the Portuguese adventure, the star-
tling news that it had been outflanked in the campaign to secure
the lucrative pepper traffic eroded domestic confidence in Venice's traditional domination of the Levant trade.[35]

But events much closer to home triggered the deepest par-
oxysm of insecurity. The Venetian expansion on the *terraferma*, particularly in Romagna after the death of Cesare Borgia, aroused fears among the other powers that Venice sought
to establish an Italian empire and influenced France, Spain, the
Holy Roman Empire, the Papacy, and various Italian states to
form the League of Cambrai against Venice. On May 14, 1509,
the forces of the league routed the entire Venetian army at

---

of Cozzi's article see Felix Gilbert, "Biondo, Sabellico, and the Beginnings of
Venetian Official Historiography."

[34]Frederic C. Lane, "Naval Actions and Fleet Organization, 1499–1502."
and idem, *Venice*, p. 242.

[35]Donald Weinstein, *Ambassador from Venice*, pp. 9–10.

Agnadello. Soon most of Venice's mainland domain from Brescia to Padua declared for the enemy, and Venice prepared for a siege that never came.[36] Divisions within the league and seven years of war saved Venice and returned most of its former territories, but not before the pressures of war wrought a permanent change in the composition of the ruling group and forced the Venetian nobility to re-examine its political beliefs.

Choosing a political emphasis different from the mystical one of Fasoli and Peyer, a large group of scholars including Federico Chabod, Franco Gaeta, Alberto Tenenti, Felix Gilbert, and Gaetano Cozzi find the events of the turn of the century, particularly the War of the League of Cambrai, to be the catalysts for a new exposition of the myth of Venice. Chabod characterizes Venetian diplomacy during the first three decades of the sixteenth century as fundamentally misconceived and therefore miscalculated: the Venetians failed to recognize that after the 1490s, when France invaded Italy and occupied Milan and when the Turks more vigorously renewed their hostilities on several fronts, the diplomatic game changed. No longer could the Italian cities conduct their affairs independently from those of the Valois and Hapsburgs, who were ambitious to dominate Italy; nor could Venice, surrounded by enemies, hope to influence European events as it had Italian ones. In response to diplomatic failures, the Venetians retreated into the comfort of the myth, which seemed to grow, according to Chabod, in an inverse proportion to the decline of Venice's actual political power.[37] Although Franco Gaeta recognizes that a variety of authors over a period of several centuries contributed to the myth, he insists that without the stimulus of the War of the League of Cambrai not only would the myth have been less urgently espoused, it would never have developed at all. For Gaeta, the myth was

[36]Nicolai Rubinstein, "Italian Reactions to Terraferma Expansion in the Fifteenth Century"; Felix Gilbert, "Venice in the Crisis of the League of Cambrai"; Federico Chabod, "Venezia nella politica italiana ed europea del Cinquecento"; Lane, Venice, pp. 242–45; Lester J. Libby, Jr., "The Reconquest of Padua in 1509 According to the Diary of Girolamo Priuli"; Robert Finlay, "Venice, the Po Expedition, and the End of the League of Cambrai, 1509–1510."
[37]Chabod, "Venezia nella politica del Cinquecento."

neither an utopian dream nor an elaborate subterfuge of a ruling class wishing to further its power, but rather a loose collection of beliefs that the Venetians universally accepted. Gaeta, in
fact, discerns three different myths: Venice as the republic of a
mixed government, as the commonwealth of liberty, and as the
gallant city. The "republic of a mixed government" myth claimed
that the Venetian institutions of Great Council, Senate, and
doge constituted an ideal combination of democracy, aristocracy, and monarchy. The "commonwealth of liberty" myth alluded both to Venice's freedom from foreign powers and to its
alleged security from domestic tyranny. Lastly, the myth of
"the gallant city" arose in response to Venice's dramatic cityscape and to its toleration of libertine amusements.[38] Alberto
Tenenti is more the *annaliste* in his argument: according to
him, the Turkish wars and the War of the League of Cambrai
altered the Venetians' "sense of time," expressed in their feeling
that in the future Venice would endure all trials because of its
"liberty." Even if it were destroyed, the world would require
another such defender of the ideal of liberty.[39]

More convincing and precise analyses of the influence of war
and diplomatic failures on Venetian society have come from
Felix Gilbert and Gaetano Cozzi, who are less concerned with
reinterpreting the elusive myth than with finding demonstrable
structural changes in the patriciate. Gilbert has discovered a
growing divergence of interests between the majority of nobles
in the Great Council and a small, wealthy elite from the Senate,
among whom the most powerful offices were shared and rotated. Their greater wealth and expanded control of the bureaucracy, resulting largely from the War of the League of Cambrai,
allowed these oligarchs to consolidate their power and to ignore
the ever more alienated lesser nobles.[40] Cozzi sees a similar
shift in the relative power of the republic's two major judicial
bodies, the *avogadoria di comun* and the Council of Ten, whose
jurisdiction overlapped. The *avogadoria*, which had tradition-

[38]Franco Gaeta, "Alcuni considerazioni sul mito di Venezia."

[39]Alberto Tenenti, "The Sense of Space and Time in the Venetian World of
the Fifteenth and Sixteenth Centuries," pp. 17–37.

[40]Gilbert, "Venice in the Crisis," especially p. 290. Cf. Bouwsma, *Venice
and Republican Liberty*, pp. 95–161.

ally guaranteed legal equality to all nobles, gradually lost its
jurisdiction to the Council of Ten, which protected the interests
of the oligarchy. The results were a decline in equality before
the law, "that linchpin of the republican regime," a strengthening of the principle of authority, and a rigid execution of the
penal laws, which all indicate to Cozzi that, despite its zeal, the
oligarchy's hold on power was indeed precarious.[41] In Venice
such power struggles and accompanying structural changes did
not, as in so many other Italian cities, result in institutional
changes—a fact that enormously enhanced the republic's image
of constitutional stability. The more the republic fell under the
domination of a small faction and the more a rigid authoritari-
anism subverted the legal equality of the patricians, the more
heralded were the balanced harmony of the republic's institutions and the egalitarian justice of the courts. According to this
view, the humanist examination of the republic was an attempt
to understand frightening social and political changes by recalling the example of a lost past.

The actual influence of the events of the early Cinquecento
on attitudes about Venice is illustrated in the contrasting views
of two sixteenth-century writers, Luigi da Porto and Gasparo
Contarini. Da Porto, a Vicentine nobleman, kept a political and
philosophical diary in which he recounted the events in the
Veneto during the War of the League of Cambrai. According to
his account, the members of the league attacked Venice because
they were envious of the *bellezza* and richness of its dominion
and because they wished to humble the pride (*alterigia*) of the
Venetians, who were aiming for an Italian empire. Da Porto
presented two contrasting images of Venice: one was the usual
laudatory myth of Venice's good government, liberty, and peace;
but the other was a sarcastic indictment of its tyranny, insensi-
tivity to provincial interests, inefficiency, and corruption. Im-
plicit in the contradiction was a subtle critique of Venetian policy. On the whole da Porto remained loyal to Venice, but he
doubted in particular Venice's commitment to the liberty of
other Italian cities and questioned even the freedom within the
confines of the lagoon. In the end, da Porto's view was cyclic,

[41]Gaetano Cozzi, "Authority and the Law in Renaissance Venice," pp. 293–
95, 305–307, 325–37, 338.

fatalistic, and traditional: if the Venetians were to survive, they must return to the superior mores of their forefathers.[42] Such a position was probably quite common in the Veneto after the 1520s, but it had little influence on the formal enunciation of the myth of Venice.

That enunciation was left to the more optimistic and reform-minded humanist, Gasparo Contarini, who, along with Andrea Navagero, Giambattista Egnazio, and Andrea Mocenigo, reinterpreted Venetian history and politics based on republican and traditional themes.[43] Contarini, who became a leading Erasmian cardinal and papal legate to the Diet of Regensburg in 1541, considered spiritual renewal and good government as inseparable: the qualities of a virtuous bishop were those of a good citizen, and no reordering of the Church was possible without sympathetic political leadership. Rather than an art of pragmatic calculation, politics was, for Contarini, a form of philosophy and thus had a moral purpose. The problems after the War of the League of Cambrai (and possibly his meeting with Thomas More in 1521) spurred Contarini to seek the same kind of moral renaissance for the Venetian republic that he sought for the Roman Church; and, just as he had turned to the biblical accounts of the apostolic Church as examples for religious revival, he found inspiration for political regeneration in the legends of the foundation of Venice.[44] His *De magistratibus et republica Venetorum*, which was widely read in Italian, French, and English translations, became one of the standard analyses of Venetian government. The source of Gaeta's "mixed government myth," Contarini credited Venice's political stability to its perfectly balanced combination of the forms of govern-

---

[42]Luigi da Porto, *Lettere storiche dall'anno 1509 al 1528*, pp. 26, 29, 46; Achille Olivieri, " 'Dio' e 'fortuna' nelle *Lettere storiche* di Luigi da Porto," pp. 271–73; Charles Jerome Rose, "The Evolution of the Image of Venice (1500–1630)," pp. 152, 191–93.

[43]Lester J. Libby, Jr., "Venetian History and Political Thought after 1509," p. 8.

[44]Felix Gilbert, "Religion and Politics in the Thought of Gasparo Contarini"; idem, "The Date of the Composition of Contarini's and Giannotti's Books on Venice"; Myron P. Gilmore, "Myth and Reality in Venetian Political Theory;" James Bruce Ross, "Gasparo Contarini and His Friends"; and idem, "The Emergence of Gasparo Contarini."

ment, explaining that in order to protect the republic from the
dangers of factionalism there were prohibitions against groupings and thus against cabals of relatives in the Senate and other
magistracies, and in order to ensure mature and sober judgment
there was a requirement that older men fill the most important
offices.[45] Despite an occasional hyperbole—for example, that
"the mixed government of Venice" was "rather framed by the
hands of the immortal Gods, than any way by the arts, industry, or invention of men"—Contarini believed the Venetian
government a creation of wise ancestors, human artifice, and
human virtue.[46] From this proposition arose a dilemma: Was
the *virtù* of Venice's rulers a quality inherent in them; that is,
did they *ex natura* act for the common good rather than for
private advantage? Or was there something in the institutions
themselves that called forth communal *virtù?* Contarini sided
with the second alternative—the Venetians were fortunate to
possess laws that eliminated passions and led men to rational
decisions. J. G. A. Pocock has observed that in *De magistratibus*
Contarini assumed the existence of "artificial angels," or "men
. . . not wholly rational [who] functioned as members of an
institutional framework which was."[47] This model of Venetian
government significantly enlightened the political discourse of
Europe: the nature of man could not be changed, but laws and
institutions could be copied, guaranteeing, many hoped, a polity guided by reason.[48]

Contarini and his humanist colleagues did not coin the political ideology of Venice; they merely codified and made more
coherent the myths that had for centuries formed the mentality of the patriciate. These myths were so interwoven with the
Venetians' perception of their place in the world that many an

[45]Felix Gilbert, "The Venetian Constitution in Florentine Political Thought,"
pp. 468–70; J. G. A. Pocock, *The Machiavellian Moment,* p. 327; Rose, "Evolution of the Image of Venice," p. 114; Contarini, *De magistratibus et republica
Venetorum,* English version, pp. 64, 67.

[46]Pocock, *The Machiavellian Moment,* pp. 320–21.

[47]Ibid., p. 324.

[48] Brian Pullan, "The Significance of Venice," pp. 455–56. Cf. the oration
made by Giangiorgio Trissino to Doge Andrea Gritti, published in Sansovino,
Delle orationi recitate a principi, fol. 1v.

ambassador known for his common sense in diplomatic matters nevertheless revealed in his *relazione*, the official résumé of his mission, the most blind bias toward Venetian traditions.[49]

If the crises of the early decades of the sixteenth century encouraged Contarini to mine the Venetian tradition for spiritual and political rejuvenation, the events of the 1570s and early 1580s, according to William Bouwsma, forced many patricians to defend republican liberty even more adamantly. During the sixteenth century there was what Bouwsma styles a dialectical struggle between the forces of secular, man-centered Renaissance republicanism, on the one hand, and ecclesiastical, God-centered medieval (and ultimately Counter-Reformation) monarchism, on the other. Venice emerged from this struggle as the best example of a secular, republican alternative to the resurgent papal monarchy The victory of the combined Catholic forces over the Turks at Lepanto in 1571 and the bloodless coups of 1582 and 1583, which Bouwsma claims enervated the Council of Ten and replaced the coalition of older, wealthy families with a regime of younger, activist senators, called the *giovani*, precipitated a renewed interest in republicanism. As a result, Venice ended its passive isolation and initiated an anti-papal defense of its system of government. Paolo Paruta, as the supposed spokesman for the *giovani*, set forth a plan that was meant to translate republican beliefs into policy and action. For example, Paruta urged a pacifistic policy on his government by recalling Venice's long commitment to peaceful diplomatic methods.[50] Like Bouwsma, Angelo Baiocchi sees Paruta's polit-

---

[49] Felix Gilbert, "Venetian Diplomacy before Pavia," and Gilmore, "Myth and Reality," pp. 437–39.

[50] Bouwsma, *Venice and Republican Liberty*, pp. 162–292, 417–82. Bouwsma's interpretation of the reforms of 1582 and 1583 is a thought-provoking examination of the view offered by Aldo Stella, "La regolazione delle pubbliche entrate e la crisi politica veneziana del 1582." Martin John Clement Lowry has criticized these works by demonstrating that the *giovani/vecchi* dichotomy of special importance to Bouwsma's thesis did not correspond to any meaningful political division within the nobility, that there were no major changes in the actual personnel occupying the most powerful offices before and after 1582, that Paolo Paruta was not a member of any identifiable political group let alone the ideological spokesman for a party, and that Doge Nicolò da Ponte—according to Bouwsma the *giovani's* leader in the destruction of the

ical thought as an essentially conservative attempt to defend the values of the aristocracy and the structures of the republic by emphasizing that *virtù* could survive only in political freedom.[51] Paruta, however, in his failure to think through the consequences of his ideas, in his conviction that political affairs were inherently ambiguous, and in his refusal to accept raison d'état, only nudged Venetian thought toward ideological opposition to papal Rome.[52]

The full expression of such opposition awaited both the controversies accompanying the papal interdict against Venice in 1606 and 1607 and the pen of Fra Paolo Sarpi, who wrote as the official apologist of the republic. The interdict represented a papal challenge to Venice's authority to legislate and administer justice for all its subjects, both lay and clerical. Sarpi turned this jurisdictional struggle into ideological combat over the separation of civil and ecclesiastical power, countering the hierarchical tenets of the Papacy with an appeal for civil liberty.[53] Sarpi sculpted the myth of republican liberty into its most evolved ideological form, fashioning an essentially civic and narrowly aristocratic ethic into a manifesto that was adopted by anti-monarchists throughout the western world.

At the hands of the humanists and their intellectual heirs, the myths of Venetian government thus became an ideology of republicanism. Although the myth and the ideology were certainly Venetian creations, they did not necessarily mirror Venetian life. To avoid being misled about Venice, as Burckhardt apparently was, one must look beyond rhetoric into what is known about the realities of Renaissance Venice.

---

zonta of the Council of Ten (pp. 229–30)—actually tried to save the *zonta*. Lowry, "The Reform of the Council of Ten, 1582–3." Lowry's arguments are supported by the findings of William Archer Brown, "Nicolò da Ponte," pp. 145–58. Other important criticisms of the Bouwsma thesis include Paul F. Grendler, *The Roman Inquisition and the Venetian Press, 1540–1605*, pp. 26–27, n. 4, and Renzo Pecchioli's review of *Venice and Republican Liberty* in *Studi veneziani* 13 (1971):693–708.

[51] Paruta's *giovani* affiliation did not determine his ideology, according to Angelo Baiocchi, "Paolo Paruta."

[52] Bouwsma, *Venice and Republican Liberty*, pp. 270–91.

[53] Ibid., pp. 417–82.

MYTH AND REALITY

As one might expect, not all Venetian writing about the city
was rhapsodic praise, for Venice did have its native critics. Perhaps the most perceptive critique of Venetian government came
from Domenico Morosini, a local patrician who began his *De
bene instituta re publica* in 1497 and died some two months
before the Venetian disaster at Agnadello. In order to reproach
contemporary Venetian magistrates, Morosini imagined an ideal
republic with Venetian institutions but also with utopian practices that contrasted sharply, for instance, with Venice's imperial expansion onto the *terraferma* and its ruthless pursuit of
riches. Perceiving avarice and greed as the agents of decline,
Morosini proposed to exclude merchants from government,
since they seemed to be under the spell of self-interest; he also
advocated that the powers of the Great Council be curtailed to
the election of only minor officials, that the electoral responsibility for the most influential offices be transferred to the Senate, and that the authority of the doge be further circumscribed. The effect of these changes, Morosini hoped, would be
an oligarchical form of government and an end to electoral
corruption.[54] Morosini's position was by no means radical and
in several ways anticipated the structural realignment in the
patriciate identified by Gilbert and Cozzi. *De bene instituta* was
even to some degree a foretaste of the disappointment with
Venetian diplomatic blunders after Cambrai.

The confusion of the early decades of the sixteenth century
understandably drew forth philippics against the policies of the
Senate. In 1514, when the Friuli erupted with rebellions exac-
erbated by war, Sanuto reported that one morning, spread
along the Merceria, the principle commercial street in Venice,
appeared handbills reading, "Enough is enough, to death with
a sack of these tyrannical Venetian thieves!" Investigating the
incident immediately, the Council of Ten discovered that the
disturbance was apparently related to the pending execution of

---

[54] Morosini criticized both the Great Council for being too crowded and the
dogeship for being too dangerous. Gaetano Cozzi, "Domenico Morosini e il *De
bene instituta re publica*," and idem, "Authority and the Law," pp. 301–302.

a seditious Friulian priest.[55] Others who condemned Venice's policies chose their words more judiciously but still revealed a deep discontent with the republic. In his official history of the Cambrai years, Pietro Bembo alleged that the failure of his class to defend, support, and protect the state had been treason; he duly passed sentence on an entire generation of patricians, demanding punishment for the guilty.[56] After the defeat at Agnadello, the diarist Girolamo Priuli bitterly castigated his noble compatriots for their arrogance and lamented the vice that he averred had provoked divine retribution.[57]

Throughout the century occasional attempts at reform and random literary diatribes impeached the reputation of the republic. By 1582 opposition to the *vecchi*, the oligarchical clique that monopolized the higher offices and especially the Council of Ten, coalesced around a group of senators referred to as the *giovani*. Lacking a coherent program of their own, the *giovani* mutinied by obstructing the nomination of candidates for the Council of Ten's *zonta*, a supplementary council of forty to fifty members, whose decision-making powers rivaled those of the Senate itself. The victory of the *giovani* meant that the insti-

[55] "Damatina, hessendo stà questa note et questa matina per Marzaria et verso San Lio trovade molte polize in terra, che erano stà butate di mala sorte a riuna e danno di nui zentilhomeni, sussitando i populi contra de nui con parole scrite, come dirò di soto, e tra li altri sier Alvise Barbaro qu. sier Piero ne trovae molte e Vasallo capitanio e altri, e fo portade a li Cai del Consejo di X . . . i qual Cai andono in Colegio et mostrono ditte polize, et fo parlato molto di gran rebeli è in questa terra, e che uno solo havia fato tal cossa. Però non parse di dar taja, nè mostrar di far di tal stima alcuna. Il tenor di le polize è questo: 'Su su a la morte, a sacho de questi ladri tyranni venitiani.' " Sanuto, *I diarii*, 18:44–45.

[56] Rose, "Evolution of the Image of Venice," p. 117.

[57] Gilbert, "Venice in the Crisis," pp. 274–75. For very different reasons Alessandro Caravia, an author with Protestant sympathies, attacked the pomp, ceremony, and ritual in Venetian life as useless vanities. He especially denounced the Scuola Grande di San Rocco for wasting money that rightfully belonged to the poor and for the indecorous behavior of its members at processions. *Il sogno dil Caravia*, Venice, 1541, pp. 160–78, in BMV, misc. 1890/7. His Protestant position is fully revealed in his work, *La morte de Giurco e Gnagni*, n.p., n.d., in BMV, misc. 1945/31. See also Vittorio Rossi, "Un aneddoto della storia della riforma a Venezia."

tutional strength of the Council of Ten ultimately declined and
that the appearance of power reverted to the Senate; nevertheless the same men still occupied the principal offices. The ad-
justment of institutions masked the fact that there was no real
change.[58]

Divisions within the nobility continued to grow during the
late sixteenth and early seventeenth centuries, giving rise to
another internal crisis in 1628–29. This time the poorer, politically impotent nobles in the Great Council followed a renegade
member of the oligarchy, Renier Zeno. In 1625 Zeno, who had
championed some poor nobles in a tax dispute with the *savii* of
the Collegio, was exiled for his interference. Upon his return to
Venice, Zeno, supported by his coalition in the Great Council,
impugned the oligarchy and particularly Doge Giovanni Corner
with criticisms contrasting Venice's myth of justice and equality
before the law to the gross corruption of the doge and his
cronies. Specifically, Zeno cited Corner's nepotism in fixing his
sons in high governmental and diplomatic posts as a violation
of his oath of office, the *promissione ducale*. After an assassi-
nation attempt on Zeno in which the doge's son was implicated,
the Great Council refused either to elect the oligarchy's candidates to the Council of Ten or to return the retiring members
of the Council to the Senate. Meanwhile, the oligarchy closed
ranks around the doge. The impasse ended only when a moderate party led by Nicolò Contarini intervened and forced Zeno
to retire from active politics. The moderates also suggested that
a commission be formed to reform the Council of Ten. Again
nothing changed. The episode, however, did reveal the disparity
between real injustice and inquality and the canons of the myth
of Venice. In his *History of the Council of Ten*, written after
the events of 1628–29, Zuan Antonio Venier described Venice
as a political society on the brink of dissolution, torn by struggles between rich and poor patricians and ruled by an anachronistic elite. And still Venier himself had supported the moderates, choosing thereby to preserve the reputation of Venetian

[58] Lowry, "Reform of the Council."

magnanimity and the power of the government at the expense of genuine equality and freedom within the aristocracy.[59]

There is increasing evidence, in addition to these attacks on their policies, that many patricians were hardly sober, self-sacrificing servants of their city. Stanley Chojnacki notes that two centuries of dissension separated the closing of the Great Council in 1297 and the formation of the sixteenth-century myth: during the fourteenth century there were three major conspiracies against the state, and nobles frequently defied the law openly and violently.[60] By the sixteenth century improvements in policing and in administering justice discouraged similar attempts to intimidate the government, but did not guarantee that Venetian nobles would practice self-abnegation for their *patria*. According to Donald Queller, patricians were often reluctant to accept the burdensome charge of offices and embassies. Frequent legislation attests to the attempts of some nobles to avoid election by fleeing abroad or to Murano. Others paid fines in lieu of service or found in the electoral procedures flaws or loop-holes by which to escape office; or, in order to become ineligible for posts, they even claimed to have violated laws themselves. Queller discounts the fame of the Venetian diplomatic service: it was compromised, he claims, by recruitment problems, financial difficulties, conflicts of interest, and serious breaches of security. During and after the War of the League of Cambrai, Venice engaged in a desperate policy of financing military payrolls through simony, which menaced the electoral system; and the wartime confidence and loyalty of the subject people flagged when nobles refused to pay back-taxes or to join the military service. The increase of embezzlement among officeholders and the infamous *broglio*, by which poor nobles sold their votes to the highest bidder, further tarnished the reputation of the republic. Even the ducal processions, which were supposed to illustrate Venetian social harmony, were often disrupted by quarrels over precedence, late arrivals, and disorderly

[59] Charles J. Rose, "Marc [sic] Antonio Venier, Renier Zeno and 'The Myth of Venice.' " Cf. Gaetano Cozzi, *Il Doge Nicolò Contarini*, pp. 224–83.

[60] Chojnacki, "Crime and the Venetian State."

conduct among the members of the participating sodalities. In pointing out such reprehensible acts, Queller scorns "the false cult of adulation of Venetian patriotism and statecraft" and claims that too many scholars have studied the litany of the myth rather than actual behavior.[61] It is clear that Venetian patricians were not a higher order of mortals, less susceptible than others to greed, self-interest, and laziness. But, even if one assumes that corruption naturally cohabited with Venetian institutions, the republic was still comparatively stable, many Venetians still believed in the myth with religious fervor, and the Venetian example still impressed foreigners.

The patricians, however worthy or irresponsible, were not the only privileged members of Venetian society. Contarini, who praised the exemplary behavior of his fellow nobles, said that Venice maintained harmony among the classes because the patricians guaranteed equality before the law and set aside certain offices for the *popolo*.[62] By *popolo* he here referred to the small class of *cittadini*, a lower-level hereditary elite (hardly a middle class, since their position was defined by law rather than by wealth), who had special economic, social, and bureaucratic privileges that opened for them careers in the permanent civil service, the lower echelons of the diplomatic corps, the law, notarial offices, trade, and medicine.[63] Unlike the patriciate, the *cittadine* class was somewhat open to outsiders: any immigrant who had settled in Venice for a prescribed period, engaged in an honorable trade, and paid his taxes on time and in full could apply for *cittadine* status. Some of the *cittadini* belonged to a select subgroup, the *cittadini originarii*, who were members of established families that boasted of generations spent in government service as secretaries of the major councils, notaries in the chancellery, and diplomatic envoys.

[61] Donald E. Queller, *Early Venetian Legislation on Ambassadors*; idem, "The Civic Irresponsibility of the Venetian Nobility"; and idem, "The Development of Ambassadorial *Relazioni.*" The quote is on p. 174.

[62] Libby, "Venetian History and Political Thought," p. 19.

[63] Brian Pullan, *Rich and Poor in Renaissance Venice*, pp. 99–100; Eric Cochrane and Julius Kirshner, "Deconstructing Lane's *Venice,*" p. 327; Contarini, *De magistratibus et republica Venetorum*, p. 127; English version, pp. 141–42; Donato Giannotti, *Libro de la republica de Vinitiani*, fol. 16r–v. The

At the apex of the *cittadine* hierarchy was the grand chancellor, who was prominent in many civic ceremonies and had ceremonial precedence over all noble magistrates except the doge and his relatives, the ducal counselors, and the procurators.[64] The grand chancellor received an elaborate formal investiture of his office and a public funeral, wore distinctive purple robes *al modo ducale*, was privy to official secrets, and was leader of his class; or, as Contarini put it, he was "the Prince of the common people."[65] The grand chancellor, as superintendent of the ducal chancellery, had the right of appointing secretaries to the various councils, the task of keeping government records, and the privilege of attending the meetings of government councils. As professional bureaucrats who held their posts for years, the *cittadini* secretaries were probably more familiar with the day-to-day details of government than were the nobles, who typically held office for only a few months. The expertise of the *cittadini* gave them considerable influence and prestige, and many of them thus had a genuine stake in the established regime and shared in an ethic of civil service.[66]

Also reserved for the *cittadini* was the leadership of the Scuole Grandi, the five (and, after 1552, six) rich and prestigious confraternities that gave relief to the poor, administered charitable endowments, provided manpower for galleys, sup-

---

material on the *cittadini* that follows has been derived from Pullan, *Rich and Poor in Venice*, pp. 99–108.

[64] Pullan is incomplete on this point. *Rich and Poor in Venice*, p. 103. See Mosto, *L'Archivio di Stato*, 1:219. In 1618–19 there was a dispute over precedence between the grand chancellor and the relatives of the doge; justifications for the honorable position of the grand chancellor were adduced by Scipione Feramesca, "Discorso sopra la pretentione di precedenza fra li figliuoli et frettelli de doge, con il cancelier grande di Venetia," MCV, MS P.D. 701c/II (n. 9).

[65] Contarini, *De magistratibus et republica Venetorum*, p. 129; English version, pp. 143–44; Felix Gilbert, "The Last Will of a Venetian Grand Chancellor," pp. 502–11.

[66] Pullan, *Rich and Poor in Venice*, pp. 103–4. Regarding a *cittadine* secretary sent to England in 1603 to secure restitution of Venetian goods captured by English pirates, Sir Henry Wotton reported, "Carlo Scaramella must return home for want of nothing but nobility, being otherwise esteemed one of their ablest instruments." Logan Pearsall Smith, *The Life and Letters of Sir Henry Wotton*, 1:319.

ported hospitals, paid for the tableaux vivants for public processions, and patronized the arts. Priests, nobles, and non-*cittadini* artisans were excluded from positions of responsibility in
the Scuole Grandi, although not from membership itself. The
cittadini on the executive committees of the Scuole Grandi had
considerable financial resources to control as well, and the government often charged them with transmitting its commands
to the lower classes.[67]

The role of the *cittadine* elite in the permanent civil service
and in the Scuole Grandi has often been adduced in explanations of the supposed tranquility of Venetian class relations.
Giovanni Botero associated the Scuole Grandi with the maintenance of social order and repeated the commonplace that the
Scuole Grandi offered an honorable compensation to those
wealthy or ambitious persons who were excluded by law from
the political rights of the patriciate.[68] Comparing the dignity of
the guardians of the Scuole Grandi among the *cittadini* with
that of the procurators among the nobility, Gasparo Contarini
described the proverbial social harmony of Venice:

> such honours doe the plebians of eyther sort attaine unto
> in this commonwealth of ours, to the end that they should
> not altogether thinke themselves deprived of publike au-
> thority, and civile offices, but should also in some sort
> have their ambition satisfied, without having occasion ei-
> ther to hate or perturbe the estate of nobilitie, by which
> equall temperature of government our common wealth
> hath attained that, which none of the former have, though
> otherwise honorable and famous, for from the first begin-
> ning till this time of ours it hath remained safe and free
> this thousand and two hundred years, not only from the
> domination of Straungers, but also from all civile and in-
> testine sedition of any moment or weight, which it hath

[67] The Scuole Grandi—Santa Maria della Carità, San Giovanni Evangelista,
Santa Maria Valverde della Misericordia, San Marco, San Rocco, and after
1552 San Teodoro—were each legally entitled to admit between 500 and 600
regular members. Pullan, *Rich and Poor in Venice*, pp. 33–34. Pullan's discussion of the Scuole Grandi covers pp. 33–193.

[68] Botero, *Relatione della republica venetiana*, pp. 42, 97–98, 107–8. Cf.
Pullan, *Rich and Poor in Venice*, pp. 75–117.

not accomplished by any violent force, armed garrisons, or fortified towers, but onely by a iust and temperate manner of ruling, insomuch that the people do obey the nobilitie with a gentle and willing obedience, full of love and affection, and farre from the desire of any straunge change.[69]

Contarini continued with a commonly used metaphor to explain how the Venetian forefathers had framed the commonwealth in imitation of a perfected human body: the nobility were the eyes, seeing all and directing the actions of the body; the plebians (Contarini here placed together the *cittadini* and the *popolani*) were the lower, more menial limbs, following the orders of the eyes. Yet there was reciprocity: the eyes and limbs depended on each other for survival.[70]

Luigi da Porto offered a different and probably more accurate view of the *cittadini*. First, he reported that the *cittadini* differed in their opinions about the nobility: some hated the patricians, but they were few and "of little determination"; most had only recently come to Venice and were so enamored of their trading rights that they were steadfast partisans of the nobility; many others had no interest in a political life alien to them.[71] Second, da Porto assigned to the ruling nobles themselves an attitude of condescending arrogance toward the *cittadini*. In a speech that da Porto attributed to Doge Leonardo Loredan (1501–21), the nobles are pictured as bearing all of the risks of government, whereas the subject classes, with few responsibilities, taste the fruits of good government. Loredan denied that the noble magistracies produced any profit for their incumbents and claimed that the positions reserved for the *cittadine* class, especially the secretariate in the chancellery, bore great honor and indeed influence.[72] Although Brian Pullan's recent studies seem to indicate that the privileges the nobility offered to the

---

[69] Contarini, *De magistratibus et republica Venetorum*, p. 131; English version, p. 146.

[70] Ibid., pp. 133–34; English version, pp. 148–49.

[71] Rose, "Evolution of the Image of Venice," p. 167; Porto, *Lettere storiche*, p. 128.

[72] Rose, "Evolution of the Image of Venice," pp. 168–73.

cittadini were enough to purchase their loyalty and to assuage their desire for political power, so little is known about individual *cittadini* that a conclusion about their careers and attitudes cannot be drawn.

More anonymous still is the great mass of Venetian plebians, which did not enjoy *cittadine* status but which nonetheless, when compared with other sixteenth-century urban populations, seems to have been unusually quiescent. Other than an occasional bread riot or some demonstrations against unpopular doges, there were few acts of mass violence in Venice during the sixteenth century, and upper-class dissidents were not able to incite the lower orders to revolt. Many historians wonder why this was the case. Some scholars have contended that Venice was virtually a police state, where the *popolani* shouldered a heavy tax burden, were abused by the courts, and were oppressed by the Council of Ten.[73] Alberto Tenenti has characterized the *popolani* after the fifteenth century as "hardly more than a spineless multitude," alienated from the government, tied to their rulers by little more than immediate advantage, and deprived of the "cultural myths" enjoyed by the patriciate.[74] Indeed there seems to be considerable evidence of a growing divergence between the classes during the sixteenth century as the patricians put greater emphasis on aristocratic privilege at the expense of communality.[75] The voicelessness of the *popolani* may in part have been due to the heterogeneity of a population made fluid by immigration and thus lacking the social resources for effective organization.[76] Frederic Lane, however, cites a different set of reasons. Noting that there was no permanent garrison of troops to intimidate the population, Lane attributes the loyalty and obedience of the governed to

[73] Cochrane and Kirshner, "Deconstructing Lane's *Venice*," p. 328.

[74] Tenenti, "Sense of Space and Time," pp. 19–21.

[75] Muir, "Images of Power"; Cf. Ugo Tucci, "The Psychology of the Venetian Merchant in the Sixteenth Century."

[76] Porto recognized this to be the case in the sixteenth century. Rose, "Evolution of the Image of Venice," p. 167. Although his study, "Citizenship and Immigration in Venice, 1305 to 1500," covers an earlier period, Stephen Richard Ell confirms the hypothesis that the Venetian social structure was made fluid by immigration. Cf. David Herlihy, "The Population of Verona in the First Century of Venetian Rule."

the maintenance of a steady food supply, to the egalitarian attitude of the courts, which of course did not mean equality of economic or political opportunity, to the defusing of class tensions by the parish organizations, and to the prevalence of pageants and festivities that gave the *popolani* a sense of belonging.[77]

The guilds were also an important organ of social and economic control. The patrician government always carefully regulated the guilds so that they never achieved the political power the guilds had in Florence and so that the government could control the economy. The guilds, however, had the right of appeal to several different governmental agencies that were, according to Richard Tilden Rapp, highly responsive to the guildsmen's demands.[78] Paul Grendler's study of the Venetian bookmen, who usually found patrician voices willing to defend the guild's economic interests against Inquisitorial censorship, likewise rejects the thesis that credits successful governmental oppression for the guild workers' tranquility.[79]

The question of why the *popolani* were so uncharacteristically passive in Venice cannot yet be answered with much certainty. As Brian Pullan has noted, the humble people of Renaissance Venice have left little evidence of why they chose, consciously or unconsciously, to acquiesce to "so rigid, so exclusive, and so neurotically watchful a regime."[80] Pullan quite sensibly contends that the causes of stability in Venice are inevitably a matter of speculation since, in contrast to rebels who make demands and offer alternatives, those who passively or even resentfully obey leave no record of their thoughts. Even though he is the scholar with the most comprehensive knowledge of Venetian social history, Pullan is in the end forced to return to elements of the myth of Venice to explain its unusual stability. For Pullan, Venice had a mixed constitution. And as soon as one accepts the premise that the "body politic" in Venice meant only the small hereditary patriciate, "who were the

[77] Lane, *Venice*, pp. 271–73.
[78] Richard Tilden Rapp, *Industry and Economic Decline in Seventeenth-Century Venice*, especially pp. 15–16, n. 2.
[79] Grendler, *The Roman Inquisition*.
[80] Pullan, "The Significance of Venice," p. 462.

Venetian state in microcosm," then Contarini's explanation of
the republic as a "mixed constitution" becomes plausible. Second, Pullan observes that Venice had a substantial middle class.
Persons of middling wealth, whether of noble or *cittadine* status, could gain compensatory salaries in public service; conversely, the burden of financing prestigious offices was so great
that even the very rich often had their wealth trimmed. In
effect, those most able to support the splendor of the state did
so: "the courtiers themselves paid for the court." Third, Pullan
explains that Venice excluded clerics from positions of political
influence. Although other Catholic powers did this as well, in
Venice it was a natural defense against curial attempts to use
spiritual weapons in temporal disputes.[81] The result was a finely
structured regime that did not guarantee the good behavior of
nobles or citizens, yet usually satisfied enough of their needs to
retain their loyalty, and that jealously guarded its authority
from any potential threat.

The Myth Abroad

Different from lifeless classical models and elusive utopian
dreams, Renaissance Venice had a particular allure for foreigners interested in ideal government: only here was republican
ideology bedfellow with a real, observable commonwealth.[82]
Whether seduced or repulsed, foreigners found Venice worthy
of debate. The notion that the Venetian constitution was ideal
cannot be attributed to the Venetians alone, for it also grew
from a dialogue among fifteenth-century humanists who worked
in a pan-Italian setting. One of them, Pier Paolo Vergerio, first
adumbrated Venice's government as "mixed" when he suggested
the aristocratic republic was particularly well constructed because the government also had some democratic and monarchical features. In the early fifteenth century George of Trebizond, who was patronized by the influential Venetian patrician
Francesco Barbaro, first noted the analogy between the Venetian constitution and the republic outlined in Plato's *Laws*, a

[81] Ibid., pp. 453–61.
[82] Cf. Angel A. Castellan, "Venecia como modelo de ordenamiento politico
en el pensamiento italiano de los siglos XV y XVI," p. 13.

work in which Plato argued that successful government must contain elements of the one, the few, and the many. It could not be accident, Trebizond reasoned, that two things should be so alike; the Venetians should thus honor Plato as their lawgiver just as the Athenians had claimed Solon and the Spartans Lycurgus. Almost a century later Contarini's *De magistratibus* made a system of Trebizond's observations.[83]

In Italy the Venetian example particularly intrigued the Florentines, whose city-state was another with a strong republican tradition. The Florentine courtship of the Venetian ideal began after 1410, when debaters repeatedly upheld Venice as the only city other than Florence capable of supporting republicanism; in the acrimonious debates over fiscal reform held between 1422 and 1427, for example, Florentine advocates of a *catasto*, or tax census, encouraged their fellow citizens to emulate the Venetian example.[84] Left with a flaccid, ineffectual constitution after the fall of the Medici regime in 1494, the politically insecure Florentines turned anew for inspiration to the Venetian myth, attractively translated into humanist terminology by such writers as Francesco Patrizi, Poggio Bracciolini, Marc Antonio Sabellico, and Francesco Negri.[85] Before 1494, their work had elicited praise for Venice only from the Medici circle of *primati*, who appreciated the aristocratic nature of Venetian government. But after Piero de' Medici's ignominious escape from Florence, the circle of admirers broadened, and the Venetian constitution was more openly discussed. It was used to justify two major reforms: in 1494 the establishment of the Great Council and a new electoral system for offices, and in 1502 the extension of the office of the standard-bearer of justice to a lifelong term. These two reforms served quite opposite purposes: the 1494 action purportedly broadened democratic

[83] Gilbert, "The Venetian Constitution in Florentine Political Thought," pp. 468–70.

[84] Gene Brucker, *The Civic World of Early Renaissance Florence*, pp. 317–18, 444–46, 464; David Herlihy and Christiane Klapisch-Zuber, *Les Toscans et leurs familles*, p. 56.

[85] Gilbert, "The Venetian Constitution in Florentine Political Thought," pp. 464–65; Renzo Pecchioli, "Il 'mito' di Venezia e la crisi fiorentina intorno al 1500."

participation in government, whereas the 1502 revision tightened the aristocratic hold on Florence.[86] Savonarola embraced the 1494 amendments and called in his sermons for more laws to regulate the moral and spiritual life of Florence so that the city might become a New Jerusalem; in preparing plans for the government he urged that the Venetian constitution be used as the model. The friar encouraged the emulation of Venice primarily because he believed that an electoral system and a Great Council would eliminate civic dissension and assure domestic peace; but he may also have been under the influence of the *primati,* who feared even more radical reforms and who thought the Venetian system would support aristocratic privilege. Ultimately, however, the Florentines' dalliance with the Venetian prototype during the Savonarola years seems fragile and fugitive when compared with their enthusiasm for Savonarola's own prophetic promises.[87]

The great transformation in Florentine political thought, indeed the very origins of modern political thought itself, postdated Savonarola; it arose from discussions held in the gardens of Bernardo Rucellai (the Orti Oricellari) from 1502 to 1506. The unprecedented historical and psychological method of treating political questions developed at the meetings in the Orti was adopted by the three great Florentine investigators of Venice: Niccolò Machiavelli, Francesco Guicciardini, and Donato Giannotti. Machiavelli participated in some of the discussions about Venice held at the Orti after Bernardo Rucellai's death in 1514; but, ever the advocate of wide citizen engagement in government, he dissented from the general admiration of its aristocratic structure and developed some of the most cogent criticisms against it. His dislike of Venice was manifold. The Venetians were at the same time arrogant and timid; having proven at Agnadello that their power was illusory, they remained overly ambitious, insolent, and avaricious. Venice had

---

[86] Gilbert, "The Venetian Constitution in Florentine Political Thought," pp. 470–78.

[87] Weinstein, *Savonarola and Florence,* pp. 30, 151–56, 248–61, 308; Gilbert, "The Venetian Constitution in Florentine Political Thought," pp. 479–80; Pocock, *The Machiavellian Moment,* pp. 111–13.

neither a mixed nor a democratic constitution, but was dominated rather by an aristocracy prone to abuse its power and especially offensive in its "effeminate" decadence. Machiavelli far preferred Genoa as a constitutional exemplar, for the Genoese system, which depended on a citizen-militia, ensured military power in a way the Venetian system, with its reliance on mercenaries, could not. And in politics military power is all that finally counts.[88]

Doubting that Machiavelli's ideal of the citizen-militia was still practical for Florence, Guicciardini, a *primato* himself, respected the stability a disarmed few were able to preserve in Venice. Like Machiavelli, Guicciardini gave little credit to the idea that Venice had maintained a balance of the three forms of government. He saw instead an aristocratic edifice; but, since *virtù* was for him an attribute of only a select elite anyway, he considered that this feature recommended itself. Guicciardini esteemed the principle of selecting the doge for life both because the dogeship required an experienced leader and because the restriction of the doge's authority protected liberty; on the other hand, he criticized the Venetian election system because it failed to eliminate private intrigues and alliances.[89] More balanced than Machiavelli's critique, Guicciardini's *Dialogo del Reggimento di Firenze* reflects, on the whole, the aristocratic interpretation of the Venetian constitution that had for decades tempted Florence's *primati*.

Donato Giannotti, a republican from the generation following Machiavelli and Guicciardini, wrote the most comprehensive study of the Venetian constitution by a Florentine. Opposed to the revived Medici regime of 1512–27 and well acquainted with Venice, Giannotti was at once an admirer of Machiavelli and of Venice; in his *Libro de la republica de Vinitiani* (1525–26) he advocated that Florence return to a citizen-

[88] Felix Gilbert, "Bernardo Rucellai and the Orti Oricellari"; idem, "Machiavelli e Venezia"; Nicola Matteucci, "Machiavelli, Harrington, Montesquieu e gli 'ordini' di Venezia," pp. 337–49; Pocock, *The Machiavellian Moment,* pp. 185–86; Rose, "Evolution of the Image of Venice," pp. 13–46.

[89] Pocock, *The Machiavellian Moment,* pp. 181–271, especially pp. 256–63. Cf. Rose, "Evolution of the Image of Venice," pp. 47–107.

militia and yet imitate the best features of Venetian government.[90] Giannotti rejected the hopeful rhetorical claim of Trebizond that Venice should revere Plato as its hero-legislator. His
keener sense of history led him to argue that Venice's political
institutions resulted from its leaders' pragmatic reflections on
past experience; he thought Venice ought to be venerated not
for the miraculous wisdom exercised in its founding but for its
long history of stability.[91] The ruling class in Venice, which
became a permanent aristocracy of birth after the reform of the
Great Council in 1297, had treated the poor well, thus earning
the loyalty of the lower classes. It had also established a complex electoral routine of nominating and voting that, in Pocock's
words, "mechanized virtù": by alternating elections and lotter-
ies, the system mixed the elements of choice and chance in a
way that presented each voter with a clear set of alternatives
and freed him from factional influences.[92] Giannotti's book
came to rival Contarini's De magistratibus as the most popular
source for information about Venetian government, and therefore the differences between the two books became important.
Contarini, encumbered by an Aristotelian model, had described
Venice as a society with two classes, noble and plebian; Giannotti, in contrast, was more accurate in sketching the three
legal classes of Venice—noble, cittadine, and commoner.[93]
Giannotti, furthermore, shed Contarini's concept of Venice's
mixed constitution and, accenting the exclusiveness of the nobility, introduced the metaphor of a pyramid to describe the
ascending hierarchy of offices: Great Council, Senate, Collegio,
and doge.[94] As a result of the differing viewpoints of Contarini

[90] Pocock, The Machiavellian Moment, pp. 272–73, 306; Randolph Starn,
Donato Giannotti and His "Epistolae," pp. 18–22.

[91] Pocock, The Machiavellian Moment, pp. 280–81, 319.

[92] Giannotti, Libro de la republica de Vinitiani, fol. 20r–v; Pocock, The
Machiavellian Moment, pp. 279–85.

[93] Giannotti, Libro de la republica de Vinitiani, fol. 21r–v; Gilmore, "Myth
and Reality," p. 7.

[94] "Et se voi considerate bene la rendono simile ad una piramide. La quale si
come voi sapete ha la basa larga, poi à poco à poco si ristringe, et finalmente in
un punto fornisce." Giannotti, Libro de la republica de Vinitiani, fol. 23r; Cf.
Gilmore, "Myth and Reality," p. 436, and Pocock, who notes that Giannotti,
elsewhere in his work, seems to accept the mixed government theory of the
Venetian constitution. The Machiavellian Moment, p. 286.

and Giannotti, the Venetian constitution became equivocal: Was Venice a mixed government, or was it an aristocracy?[95] The very ambivalence of the model contributed to its magic. What could be more delightful than a political paragon that was kaleidoscopic? Turned slightly this way or that, the Venetian constitution could become almost anything one wanted or needed it to be.

The Venetian and Florentine literature offered the greatest store of ideas about the republic of Venice; added to this, however, was what Gina Fasoli has called the "anti-myth" of Venice, which was largely the product of foreign propaganda characterizing the Venetian regime and its policies as tyrannical, vile, and militarily impotent.[96] Certainly Machiavelli had furthered this anti-myth, but it can be traced back to at least the *Dragmalogia de eligibili vitae genere* of Giovanni Conversino da Ravenna, who was active in Padua between 1390 and 1405 and whom Hans Baron has called "in age and significance the Salutati of Padua." Conversino's work was a comparative study of republics and tyrannies. He considered the latter a superior form of government: assuming that the prince's interest corresponded to the general interest, a tyranny might eliminate passions and violence. He recommended this form over that of republics like Venice, which were inefficient and indecisive.[97]

Venetian territorial expansion onto the *terraferma* during the fifteenth century further aggravated anti-Venetian feelings in Italy; Venice was often chastised for its unlimited desire to dominate others and for its ambitions to gain an Italian empire in imitation of ancient Rome.[98] The anti-myth survived Venice's drubbing in the War of the League of Cambrai and resurfaced throughout the sixteenth and seventeenth centuries whenever a foreign power ran afoul of Venetian *superbia*. The most notorious work in this vein was the early seventeenth-century *Squintinio della libertà veneta*, which documented a historical case against Venice's claims to liberty, revealing that Venice was founded under the jurisdiction of others, that it had

[95] Pocock, *The Machiavellian Moment*, p. 100.
[96] Fasoli, "Nascita di un mito."
[97] Baron, *Crisis of the Early Renaissance*, pp. 134–45.
[98] Rubinstein, "Italian Reactions to Terraferma Expansion."

been under the suzerainty of various emperors, and that the
nobles had destroyed the rights of the *popolo*, rendering them
subjects and not free citizens.[99]

The anti-myth was most prominent in monarchical France,
where Venetian ideas had small chance of countering the dominant absolutist tendencies of late sixteenth- and seventeenth-
century political thought. It was most coherent in the writings
of Jean Bodin, the seminal theorist of sovereignty. Bodin's reputation as an original thinker stemmed in large part from his
refutation of a favorite Renaissance truism, namely, that the
optimal state had a mixed government. In this task Bodin's
target was the work of Gasparo Contarini; Bodin insisted that
Venice had an aristocratic constitution and that its stability was
an illusion. The whole concept of a mixed state offended Bodin's
idea of sovereignty, which, by definition indivisible, could be
found only in one place, in one institution. Bodin accordingly
devised a new metaphor for Venetian government, a series of
concentric circles with gradually increasing diameters: in the
central circle was the doge; at the outside, the holder of supreme power—the Great Council. The Venetian state in this
image was unitary, and the various councils represented not
different forms of government, as Contarini had suggested, but
merely served different functions. Believing aristocracy always
less stable than monarchy, Bodin attacked Venice's reputation
for social control; if Venice were indeed stable, it was due to the
patricians' distribution of rewards to the people and to their
equality before the law, not to Venice's form of government.[100]
Bodin's argument was historically sophisticated and theoreti-
cally consistent, but the bias in his version reveals how thoroughly the *idées fixes* of those who examined Venice shaped
and reshaped the image of its government.

[99] "Gli Cittadini e popolari di Venetia non tengono maggior libertà di quello
tenga qual si voglia Città soggetta." *Squintinio della libertà veneta, nel quale
si adducono anche le raggioni dell'Impero Romano sopra la città & signoria di
Venetia*, p. 75. Also see Tommaso Campanella, *Antiveneti*.

[100] Elio Gianturco, "Bodin's Conception of the Venetian Constitution and
His Critical Rift with Fabio Albergati"; Gilmore, "Myth and Reality," pp.
440–42.

In Poland, the myth of Venice received a more sympathetic hearing, since there were numerous ties between Venice and Poland—a common enmity against the Turk, mutual commercial interests, and Polish students at the University of Padua. Two early seventeenth-century works on Venice, by Paul Palczowski and Christopher Warszewicki, account for the spread of Venetian constitutional ideas among the Polish nobility. Deriving their ideas in the main from Contarini's *De magistratibus*, Polish political writers and parliamentary debaters often cited the Venetian mixed constitution as a model for reform at Cracow and praised in particular the system of councils, the methods of balloting, the scrutiny of potential candidates' qualifications for office, and the limitation on the powers of the doge. After the death of Sigismund II in 1572 Polish kings, like the doge, were elected for life, with no rights to dynastic succession, and were forced to swear a *pacta conventa* in emulation of Venice's restrictive *promissione ducale*. Poland's similar history of aristocratic domination encouraged the habit of borrowing from its southern sister; the anonymous Polish author of the *Libera respublica qual sit* pointed out that there had been only three true republics—Rome, Venice, and Poland (Poland, of course, was greatest because it was largest)—and that in Venice and Poland the nobility enjoyed exclusive political rights.[101] In their struggle to repress the ever-encroaching kings and to strengthen the republic of the *szlachta*, the Poles recurrently turned to the political enticements of Venice's aristocratic regime.

England's interest in Venice was long-standing, but it grew more intense during the Jacobean, Caroline, and Commonwealth periods. An Irish Franciscan, Simon Fitz-Simon, gave the British Isles their first detailed account of northern Italy, one charged with superlatives, after his pilgrimage to Egypt and Palestine in 1323. He began a tradition of paying homage

---

[101] Bronisław Biliński, "Venezia nelle peregrinazioni polacche del Cinquecento e lo *Sposalizio del Mare* di Giovanni Siemuszowski (1565)," pp. 289–90; Karol Koranyi, "La costituzione di Venezia nel pensiero politico della Polonia," p. 206 and passim.

to Venice's sumptuous religious relics and magnificent processions, a tradition continued by William Wey, who made pilgrimages in 1458 and 1462, and by the anonymous chronicles of the pilgrimage of Sir Richard Guylforde (published in 1511). Venice, in the eyes of these visitors, exhibited an almost oriental splendor.[102] William Thomas, who visited Venice in the 1540s, published the first English eulogy of Venice's political traditions in his *History of Italy:* ". . . their principal profession is liberty, and he that should usurp another should incontinently be reputed a tyrant, which name of all things, they cannot abide."[103]

For Englishmen, at least, liberty became the essential quality of Venetian political life. In the late sixteenth century, travelers, including Richard Torkington, Fynes Moryson, and Thomas Coryat, continued to return with tantalizing accounts of life in Venice; in fact, John Hale has argued that a common motive among Elizabethan and Jacobean Englishmen for journeying to Italy was to study the Venetian constitution, although one might observe that the traveler in Jonson's *Volpone,* Sir Politick Would-Be, researched courtesans more than constitutions. English translations of Guicciardini's *Storia d'Italia* and in 1599 of Contarini's *De magistratibus* disseminated even more comprehensive information about Venetian government, so that by the seventeenth century a peculiarly British vision of Venetian life entered the literary and cultural milieu of educated Englishmen. Sarpi's works as well were so extensively quoted, copied, alluded to, adapted, controverted, and explicated in England that they nearly became an English literary tradition in and of themselves. Shakespeare had a greater acquaintance with and interest in Venice than he had for any other Italian city; his plays confess knowledge of the details of its government, mercantile interests, cityscape, and architecture. And in *Volpone* Jonson contrasted the shoddy morals of some of his characters with the impartiality of the Venetian courts that judged them; he saw the Venetian state as a moral bridle for the intemperate passions of the Italians.[104]

[102] George B. Parks, *The English Traveler to Italy,* pp. 579–85.

[103] William Thomas, *The History of Italy (1549),* p. 72.

[104] Fynes Moryson, *Itinerary Containing his Ten Yeeres Travell,* pp. 74–90;

THE MYTH OF VENICE

To reach its full appeal in England, however, the Venetian political ideal required the relative freedom in publishing and the interest in alternatives to monarchy that accompanied the Puritan Revolution. Two works of the Cromwellian period recommended the Venetian example: James Howell's *S.P.Q.V., a Survey of the Signorie of Venice, of Her Admired Policy, and Method of Government, &c, with a Cohortation to All Christian Princes to Resent Her Dangerous Condition at Present* (London, 1651), and James Harrington's *Oceana*, published in 1656 and dedicated to Cromwell. Howell's combined encomium and history, which relied almost exclusively on Paolo Sarpi as his unacknowledged source, recapitulated the mythical attributes of Venice's beauty, freedom, and wise government. His proem creates images of Venice's sovereign impregnability with a number of sexual metaphors and puns meant, one supposes, to insinuate, though crudely, the city's many feminine charms.

UPON THE CITTY AND SIGNORIE OF VENICE

Could any State on Earth Immortall be,
Venice by Her rare Government is she;
Venice Great Neptunes Minion, still a Mayd,
Though by the warrlikst Potentats assayed;
Yet She retaines Her Virgin-waters pure,
Nor any Forren mixtures can endure;
Though, Syren-like on Shore and Sea, Her Face
Enchants all those whom once She doth embrace,
Nor is ther any can Her beauty prize
But he who hath beheld Her with his Eyes:
These following Leaves display, if well observed,
How she so long Her Maydenhead preserved,
How for sound prudence She still bore the Bell;

Thomas Coryate, *Crudities*, 1:427; J. R. Hale, *England and the Italian Renaissance*," p. 29; Ben Jonson, *Volpone*; Richard H. Perkinson, " 'Volpone' and the Reputation of Venetian Justice"; Bouwsma, "Venice and Europe"; Zera S. Fink, "Venice and English Political Thought in the Seventeenth Century"; idem, *The Classical Republicans*, pp. 28–51; John Leon Lievsay, *Venetian Phoenix*, p. 181; Horatio F. Brown, "Shakespeare and Venice" and "Cromwell and the Venetian Republic," in his *Studies in the History of Venice*, 2:159–80, 296–321.

Whence may be drawn this high-fetched parallel,

Venus and Venice are Great Queens in their degree,
Venus is Queen of Love, Venice of Policie.[105]

Inspired, if not poetically, by a visit to Venice in 1634 or
1636, Harrington, the serious political thinker of the two, attempted in his utopian plan for England to overcome Machiavelli's objections to the Venetian example. He hoped for a polity
that would employ an armed citizenry in the cause of unlimited
expansion, as in ancient Rome; and yet it should enjoy stability
and liberty through an institutional equilibrium, as did Venice.
Harrington most valued the secret ballot, the rotation of offices, and the mixed nature of Venetian government, all of
which he thought curtailed the power of the rich. His advocacy
of popular government was limited, however, by a desire to
preserve the rule of an enlightened patriciate, a bias that gives
his work an elegantly sophistical character in utter opposition
to the tone of Howell's.[106] Oceana was widely read throughout
the following century, providing Englishmen and colonial
Americans the example of Venice cast in utopian form.

Even after the Restoration, curiosity about Venetian republicanism remained high: John Hale has counted at least ten
books published between 1668 and 1672 that were concerned in
some way with the constitution of Venice. Never in this period
did the English contemplate Florence as they did Venice. And
in America William Penn, influenced by Harrington, adopted
the secret ballot in draft plans for the colonial constitutions of
Pennsylvania and New Jersey, as security against corruption.[107]
Indeed, throughout the Western world, during times of political uncertainty, the Venetian ideal was particularly attractive to
moderate reformers who hated tyranny but who were fright-

[105] As quoted in Pullan, "The Significance of Venice," p. 453; also see Lievsay, Venetian Phoenix, pp. 94–97.

[106] Matteucci, "Machiavelli, Harrington, Montesquieu," pp. 349–59; Pocock, The Machiavellian Moment, pp. 333, 392–94.

[107] Hale, England and the Italian Renaissance, pp. 29–32, 40–42; Fink,
"Venice and English Political Thought"; idem, The Classical Republicans, pp.
28–51; H. F. Russell-Smith, Harrington and His "Oceana," pp. 37–38, 170–
71.

ened by the prospects of a popular democracy; none of these reformers, however, had a very precise understanding of the Venetian constitution. On the other hand, the image Venice offered was enough of a Siren that many enemies of the Renaissance republican tradition felt obliged to rebut the claims of Venice's partisans. Bodin did. And even Montesquieu, who thought that liberty and social stability were inconsistent political objectives, exerted himself to prove that Venice was actually a despotic republic where the only freedom was that of cavorting, with harlots.[108]

Abroad, the myth of Venice had a life of its own, a life so engaging that it could command men from the Florence of Savonarola to the Philadelphia of William Penn. In so doing, the myth has obscured to this very day the actual personality of its mistress.

FROM MYTH TO RITUAL OR FROM RITUAL TO MYTH?

Patriotic myths, of course, occur in many cultures throughout history. During the three centuries before Savonarola, the Florentines indulged in a myth that made Florence a daughter of Rome, the favored home of a messianic second Charlemagne, and the millennial New Jerusalem of the Elect. In Ferrara, the Este fabricated a despotic myth of their antique origins, nobility, and political virtues, a myth designed to glorify further a
. city that already prided itself on its physical beauty, social stability, neutral diplomacy, and peaceful nature. Even little San Marino's survival as an independent republic while much of the rest of Italy slid into political decadence after the fifteenth century was remarkable enough to engender a myth of San Marino's perpetual liberty. The medieval French, claiming to live in a mystical *terra sancta* and to be God's Chosen People, went so far as to allege that "God couldn't get along without France"; and modern Americans persist in imagining that their country's "youthfulness" endows it with invincibility and innocence.[109]

[108] Matteucci, "Machiavelli, Harrington, Montesquieu," pp. 360–69.

[109] Weinstein, *Savonarola and Florence*, passim; Werner L. Gundersheimer, *Ferrara*, pp. 69, 73, 279–81; Aldo Garosci, "La formazione del mito di San Marino"; Joseph Strayer, "France"; C. Vann Woodward, "The Aging of America."

Historians attempt to use myths such as these as guides to the inherited symbols and mentalities of a particular culture in order to find out how the members of that culture perceived the world and whether these perceptions remained static or changed. In this kind of study there are two traps that the historian must avoid. Obviously one must become neither emotionally nor intellectually captive to the myths themselves, which sometimes by their very nature appeal to a psychological level deeper than the rational. Through myths history can achieve a personal and spiritual significance that it might not otherwise attain: Christ and Mohammed were historical figures, but their importance lies in the myths that grew from their life stories. Second, and less obviously, one must recognize that a myth is no less real than the empirical facts of economic and social history. Consequently, the objective in studying myths is not just to winnow the historic grain of truth from the chaff of legendary falsehood, but to trace the history of myths as a manifestation of human ingenuity and as a way of gleaning collective mentalites. As Leo Marx has put it, "To understand a society and culture as a whole, we must recognize how profoundly it is affected by the way its people perceive the world (including, of course, themselves); and yet, at the same time, we must recognize how untrustworthy these perceptions may be."[110]

If myths may thus be read as sets of stories that might reveal assumptions about man, nature, and the divine, one may seek in the myth of Venice, to borrow the phrasing of the anthropologist Clifford Geertz, a Venetian reading of Venetian experience, a story they told themselves about themselves. The myth's function then, if myth can ever be reduced to anything so simple, is not just to reinforce status discriminations, such as keeping the lower classes in their place, nor is it just to maintain group loyalties; its function is to make a "meta-social commentary" on the whole matter of organizing people around certain institutions, which then control the major part of col-

[110] Marx's comments on "The Aging of America," by C. Vann Woodward, p. 599; Cf. Francesco Lanzoni, *Genesi svolgimento e tramonto delle leggende storiche*, p. 258.

lective existence.[111] The student of myth in this sense tries to discover where "high thought" and "low thought" meet, to integrate theology and legends, and to unite symbols of the unconscious mind with manifestations of the conscious.[112] Using this approach, one can argue that Venice's traditional communal myths fostered the republican ideology that burgeoned in the sixteenth century but still recognize that the Venetian ideology came to have a life of its own as a cutting transplanted to foreign soil. Ideology here means, first, the particular ideas and beliefs shaped by and for the Venetian patricians in their efforts to preserve their hegemony over the institutions of government, and second, the neoclassical constructs humanists used to describe those institutions.[113] Ideology, hence, was the exclusive possession of a politically or educationally advantaged group, whereas myth, distinct from ideology, was at least potentially the communal property of every member of the society.

A truth at one time almost universally acknowledged was that ritual is in some way a cognate of myth. But the exact nature of that relationship was a problem universally debated. Since the publication of Sir James Frazer's *The Golden Bough*, there have been several standard theories. Frazer's own theory of ritualism derived myth and the folklore and literature based on myth from antecedent rituals. He preferred the study of rituals to that of myths because to him ritual was more conservative, less mutable, and far less apt to be manipulated consciously or unconsciously; rituals therefore came closer to the essential truth he so assiduously sought.[114] Other scholars have

[111] Clifford Geertz, "Deep Play: Notes on the Balinese Cockfight," in his *The Interpretation of Cultures*, pp. 412–53, especially p. 448. Cf. E. P. Thompson, "Anthropology and the Discipline of Historical Context."

[112] Cf. Jeffrey Burton Russell, *The Devil*, p. 42.

[113] I am following here the distinction between myth and ideology developed by Ben Halpern, " 'Myth' and 'Ideology' in Modern Usage."

[114] Robert Ackerman, "Frazer on Myth and Ritual," pp. 115, 126; Cf. Erving Goffman, *The Presentation of Self in Everyday Life*, pp. 250–51. In this book I do not follow Jack Goody's distinction between ritual as "a category of standardized behaviour (custom) in which the relationship between the means and the end is not 'intrinsic,' i.e. is either irrational or nonrational" and

preferred an alternative view of ritual as a kind of dramatic illustration of mẏth. In either theory myth and ritual are considered two different ways of expressing the same thing. Claude Levi-Strauss, in contrast, argues that the homology between myth and ritual is not very precise and in some cases does not even exist; for him it is best to see myth and ritual as particular illustrations of a more general relationship, which is not mechanical but dialectical.[115] If such is the case, it becomes essential for the historian to pursue with great care the meanings contemporaries attributed to particular myths and rituals; although general theories help one ask better questions of the evidence, they do not provide ready answers to those questions.

This difficulty exists because most social science theories about ritual are notably ahistorical. To a large degree such theories emphasize how rituals function to reduce intra-group violence, to serve as communal bonding systems, to communicate shared values, to underline the exclusiveness of cultural units, and to assign an emotional value to handed-down customs.[116] Such an approach tells much about social stability and cultural

ceremony as "those collective actions required by custom, performed on occasions of change in the social life. Thus a ceremonial consists of a specific sequence of ritual acts, performed in public." "Religion and Ritual," p. 158. All of the rites discussed herein are on the one hand public and collective and on the other directed simultaneously toward divinity and society. The necessary distinction is not a functional one—rites directed toward the supernatural or toward the public—or one between the sacred and the profane, both of which in the Venetian case provided mutual validation, but a social-political one between the ritual performers, that is, priests or secular magistrates. Priests performed rituals; so did magistrates on occasion, but they also participated in essentially legalistic and constitutional ceremonies. Ritual thus becomes an inclusive term describing stylized, formalized, regularized, repetitive actions of many sorts, and ceremony refers to those actions having a peculiarly, distinctively, and exclusively political character. I would not wish to offer this as a generalized definition, but merely as one useful for this study.

[115] Claude Lévi-Strauss, "Structure and Dialectics," in his Structural Anthropology, pp. 229–38.

[116] See the papers by Sir Julian Huxley, K. Z. Lorenz, E. H. Erikson, and V. W. Turner in Sir Julian Huxley, ed., A Discussion on Ritualization of Behaviour in Animals and Man, pp. 249–72, 273–77, 337–50, and especially pp. 521–22. Cf. Victor W. Turner, The Ritual Process, and Geertz, "Ritual and Social Change: A Javanese Example," in his Interpretation of Cultures, pp. 142–69, especially p. 144.

equilibrium, but little about the processes of historical change
or the discontinuitiés between society and culture. It is least
satisfactory in explaining how rituals change in meaning; for,
as historians of early modern Europe know, the very festivals,
such as carnival, that on one occasion functioned to preserve
the social order by channeling energy into ritualized violence
and role reversals could, on another, incite revolts that threatened that very order.[117] The leading historical scholar of ritual,
Johan Huizinga, defines ritual as the pursuit of serious play,
which in his mind is the living principle of all civilization; but
even Huizinga failed to discover a handy philosopher's stone to
transmute the base metal of ritual to the gold of civilization.[118]
One must rely rather on the alchemist's onerous technique—
empirical research.

Tracing the conversion of ritual into civilization itself, or
making rites subject to theoretical generalization, is so difficult
mainly because ritual is an inherently local phenomenon. Even
in the Christian Europe of the Later Middle Ages, when the
Church attempted to enforce uniformity in its own rites, most
feasts existed at best on a provincial or diocesan level. The
Roman Church offered merely a skeletal structure around
which localities arranged a calendar of feasts.[119] Besides the
liturgical rites, each town in France, for example, had at least
one annual festival in which the town itself was represented by
a venerated statue, a triumphal cart, a civic banner, or something else to which the citizens displayed their reverence and
loyalty, usually in a public parade. These communal festivals
informed strangers and inhabitants alike of the town's power,
grandeur, and well-being, and they disappeared only when the
process of political centralization made them appear embarrassing.[120] From circa 1200 to the Reformation there was an infla-
tion of ritual in Europe: simple mystery plays and penitential
processions grew into the magnificent pageants of the High
Renaissance. This transformation accompanied the rise of polit-

[117] Yves-Marie Bercé, Fête et révolte."

[118] Johan Huizinga, Homo Ludens, pp. 100–101.

[119] Edith Cooperrider Rodgers, Discussion of Holidays in the Later Middle
Ages, p. 16.

[120] Bercé, Fête et révolte, pp. 96–125.

ical sophistication and concern for propagandistic display on the part of the Renaissance states; many Italian cities, particularly during the sixteenth century, either permanently set aside large areas of public space as festive stages or altered, temporarily but radically, the visual aspect of existing streets and piazzas for triumphs and ceremonial entrances.[121]

Venice was a city especially well known for the number and splendor of its public ceremonies. In Defendente Sacchi's famous work on the festivals of the medieval Italian city-states, eighteen percent of the festivals discussed—more than in any other city—took place in Venice.[122] In 1364 Petrarch marveled at the good order and flourish of the victory celebrations he witnessed in Piazza San Marco; in the late fifteenth century the Milanese pilgrim Pietro Casolo recorded that after a Venetian ceremony both the French and Milanese ambassadors commented that neither of their sovereigns had ever held such a pompous festival, and Casolo himself was amazed at what he saw.[123] Centuries later, Burckhardt portrayed the ceremonial reception the Venetians gave to the Princess of Ferrara in 1491 as something belonging to fairyland.[124] The reputation of the Venetian rituals was such that all over Europe during the Renaissance the very name of Venice could conjure images of extravagant public display. In attempting to find a fitting description for the Lord Mayor of London's cortege in 1610, Christianus, the Prince of Anhalt, invoked the distinction of Venice, declaring that no other state or city in the world accompanied the election of its magistrates with as much magnificence as Venice, which on this occasion the City of London nearly equaled.[125]

---

[121] André Chastel, "Le lieu de la fête."

[122] Defendente Sacchi, *Delle condizione economica, morale e politica degli italiani ne' tempi municipali. Sulle feste, e sull'origine, stato e decadenza de' municipii italiani nel medio evo.*

[123] Petrarch, *Letters*, pp. 234–39; Pietro Casolo, *Viaggio a Gerusalemme*, p. 109.

[124] Burckhardt, *Civilization of Renaissance Italy*, pp. 421–22.

[125] Quoted by Jean Robertson, "Rapports du poète et de l'artiste dans la preparation des cortèges du Lord Maire (Londres 1553–1640)," p. 270.

Even after the fall of the republic in 1797, the repute of the traditional Venetian rituals was so great they remained the subject of considerable interest. Giustina Renier Michiel, a daughter of a patrician family, published in six volumes *Le origine delle feste veneziane* (Milan, 1817), the most extensive exposition of Venice's myths and public rituals ever written, a work that went through numerous editions in the nineteenth century and was translated into French. In fervently patriotic prose, Michiel wove together most of the historical and legendary Venetian traditions. Other nineteenth-century Venetians such as the scholars Giuseppe Tassini and Pompeo Molmenti kept the clichés of the myth in circulation by describing Venice's great ceremonies. Molmenti, for example, associated the festivals of the republic with the maintenance of social harmony.

> The people, to compensate themselves for political nonentity, drowned the thought of their lost liberties in the delight of public spectacles which served to display all the pomp of vast riches; and mid the universal gaiety they remained both quiet and smooth-tempered. Rarely even in such a crowd did quarrels spring up; one seldom saw threatening gestures or heard insults exchanged. . . . The whole movement of Venetian life recalled the gaiety of a happy family.[126]

For Molmenti the rituals of the republic may have ceased, but the myth was still very much alive.

[126] Pompeo G. Molmenti, *Venice*, 3:91. The revised Italian edition of the same work is *La storia di Venezia nella vita privata dalle origini alla caduta della repubblica*. Tassini's work on festivals is *Feste, spettacoli divertimenti e piaceri degli antichi veneziani*. The only major work on festivals in recent years is Bianca Tamassia Mazzarotto, *Le feste veneziane*. This book is not a comprehensive historical study of festivals, but a discussion of a series of eighteenth-century paintings by Gabriel Bella in the Pinacoteca Querini Stampalia in Venice.

PART TWO

AN INHERITANCE OF LEGEND AND RITUAL

To write history is so difficult that most historians are forced to make concessions to the technique of legend.
— Erich Auerbach, *Mimesis*

Saint Mark, to his cost, and perhaps in vain, discovers late that he needs to hold the sword and not the book in his hand.
— Niccolò Machiavelli, *Tercets on Ambition*

AN ESCAPED TROJAN
AND A TRANSPORTED
EVANGELIST:
AUSPICIOUS BEGINNINGS

The Legends of the Origins of Venice

Francesco Lanzoni, the Italian folklorist, pointed out the common practice among medieval peoples of fabricating pseudo-histories of themselves. Since it was often expedient to claim primacy in the eyes of God or to be considered the Chosen People, many false documents—protocols, wills, statutes, collections of laws and canons, trial records, letters, histories, chronicles, annals, saints' lives, and autobiographies—were accordingly forged to prove a people the first to convert to Christianity or a town the first to support a bishop. Many of the early legends thus invented slipped from collective memory, some remained only formulas in elite literature, and others, such as the donation of Constantine, fell victims to the historical techniques of Renaissance humanists and their heirs. But many more, surviving both time and attack, continued to excite the imaginations of peoples well into modern times. In many cases local legends became official dogma, and to criticize them was to compromise the state. In the seventeenth century in Switzerland any book that questioned the authenticity of the legend of William Tell was publicly burned, and in Venice a tract that controverted the alleged antiquity of Venetian independence from Byzantium suffered a similar fate.[1]

In Italy legends commonly surrounded the foundation of a city or the genesis of a family or people, and such legends were

---

[1] Lanzoni, *Genesi delle leggende storiche*, especially pp. 76–77, 169–70, 245–57.

often subject to political fashions. In the early fifteenth century, the traditional imperial myth that soldiers of Julius Caesar had first settled Florence was replaced by a more acceptable notion that Florence had been founded during the Roman Republic. Even more ardent republican sentiments led Leonardo Bruni to insist that Florence was originally an Etruscan city-republic.[2] From the thirteenth to fifteenth centuries the Este claimed two myths, one that they were descendants of Trojan princes and the other that their ancestors were settlers from Carolingian France; by the 1560s, however, they asserted in concert with contemporary custom that they stemmed from a noble family of republican Rome.[3]

The Venetians likewise entertained several legends about their origins: in one category were stories that traced the lineage of the ancient settlers of the lagoon; in a second were tales that explained when and why these settlers left the mainland to live in the inhospitable marshes. Most of the legends in the first group proposed that the early Venetians came either from Gaul, a descent that affirmed the affection and diplomatic ties between Venice and France, or from Troy, a heritage that transfused Venetian blood with the nobility of the aristocratic Trojan warriors who had supposedly found refuge in Venetia after the sack of their city. In his highly patriotic fifteenth-century history of Venice, Marc Antonio Sabellico defended the Gallic theory, even though his precursor, Bernardo Giustiniani, the first serious humanist historian of the origins of Venice, had found a way to reconcile both traditions.[4] Most writers, however, used the Trojan theory exclusively, a practice long popular in the Veneto. In the late thirteenth century Martin da Canal reported that the Trojans had built all the cities from Hungary to the Adda River (which flows into Lake Como), including the mother-city of Venice, Aquileia.[5] The 1292 chronicle of Marco

[2] Pocock, *The Machiavellian Moment*, p. 52.

[3] Gundersheimer, *Ferrara*, pp. 19–20.

[4] Labalme, *Bernardo Giustiniani*, p. 262; Agostino Pertusi, "Gli inizi della storiografia umanistica nel Quattrocento," pp. 318–19, 331. Bardi offered a third theory in affirming that the first Venetians came from "Paflagonia." *Delle cose notabili*, p. 4.

[5] Martin da Canal, *Les estoires de Venise*, p. 6.

describes the destruction of Troy, the escape to Italy of Trojan nobles under the leadership of Antenor, and the settling of Padua.[6] Both writers were, of course, appending details to the passage in the *Aeneid*—then accepted as authentic history— that referred to Antenor's displaced band of Trojans as the founders of Padua.[7] Official support of the Trojan myth in Venice often fluctuated according to existing diplomatic relations between the two cities, until Padua finally came under inexorable Venetian domination in the early fifteenth century. A sixteenth-century Latin poem by Semusovio, a Pole, describes tapestries in the apartments of the doge that depicted the Trojan origins of the Venetians, and, in a seventeenth-century history of the confrontation between Emperor Frederick Barbarossa and Pope Alexander III, the author attributes to Barbarossa a speech in which the Venetians and Trojans are explicitly compared.[8]

The attractions of the Trojan myth are easy to see. The Trojans were widely interpreted as a people who had never paid tribute to anyone and who had been willing to abandon even their city in order to preserve their freedom. Trojan roots gave the Venetians a claim both to great antiquity, therefore pri-

---

[6] BMV, MS Italiano XI, 124 (6802), fol. 4r-v.

[7] Antenor potuit, mediis elapsus Achivis,
Illyricos penetrare sinus atque intima tutus
regna Liburnorum et fontem superare Timavi,
unde per ora novem vasto cum murmure montis
it mare proroptum et pelago premit arva sonanti
hic tamen ille urbem Patavi sedesque locavit
Teucrorum et genti nomen dedit armaque fixit
Troia, nunc placida compostus pace quiescit.

Virgil, *Aeneid* 1.242–49. For a typical example of the Venetian adaptation of this story see Marc Antonio Sabellico, *Le historie vinitiane*, fols. 2r–4v. Cf. Pietro Giustiniano, *Dell'historie venetiane*, pp. 3–5. Bardi argued that the Trojans settled Antenorida, later called Altino, not Padua, which was settled by Patavio, the king of the Veneti. *Delle cose notabili*, p. 4.

[8] Biliński, "Venezia nelle peregrinazioni polacche," p. 269. Barbarossa's speech to his son Otto reads, "Gli disse non haver dubitatione, che un'altro sforzo sarà apparecchiato per rinfrancar la fatta perdittione, galee armarò contra de Venetiani, che li disfarò come furo Troiani." Brandimarte Franconi Ferrarese, *Historia di Papa Alessand. III et di Fedrico Barbarossa imperatore*, no pagination.

macy, and to the purest noble blood, untainted by intermarriage with barbarians. The Venetians, moreover, were not alone as aspirants to this glorious past: others, besides the Este, that celebrated Trojan ties were Mantua, Modena, Piacenza, Parma, Imola, Pisa, Prato, Fiesole, Paris, France, Brittany, the Visconti, and, of course, Rome.[9]

Once the noble origins of the Venetian people were established, the myth-makers had to explain the migration from the fertile plains of the *terraferma* to the barren lagoon. One popular saga in this second category of legends claimed that during the Italian campaign of Attila many refugees from Venetia fled to the sparsely populated islands in the peaceful lagoons at the head of the Adriatic. Bernardo Giustiniani wrote that among these immigrants were nobles from Padua whom God had chosen to found a new city that would become the heir to a justly punished Rome.[10] The eventual success of Pope Leo I in halting Attila's conquest of Italy added a religious, perhaps even miraculous, element to the events.[11] Attila thus achieved an important niche in Christian history, and the Venetians so astutely developed and preserved the story of Venice's founding by refugees from Attila that the episode became part of the modern European mythical heritage. In 1622 Sir Henry Wotton described the origins of Venice in a letter to the Marquess of Buckingham and thereby revealed the mythic use of the Attila legend.

How they came to be founded in the midst of the waters I could never meet with any clear memorial. The best and most of their authors ascribe their first beginnings rather to chance or necessity, than counsel; which yet in my opinion will amount to no more than a pretty conjecture intenebrated by antiquity, for thus they deliver it: they say that among the tumults of the middle age, when nations went about swarming like bees, Atylas, the great captain

[9] Lanzoni, *Genesi delle leggende storiche*, p. 77.

[10] Labalme, *Bernardo Giustiniani*, pp. 265–66. In a letter to the doge of Venice dated 1077, Pope Gregory VII said that the liberty of the Venetians came from their roots in the Roman nobility. C. Davis, "Roman Patriotism and Republican Propaganda," p. 428.

[11] Roberto Cessi, *Le origini del ducato veneziano*, p. 15.

of the Hunnes, and scourge of the world (as he was styled) lying along with a numerous army at the siege of Aquileia, it struck a mighty affrightment and confusion into all the nearer parts. Whereupon the best sort of the bordering people out of divers towns, agreed either suddenly, or by little and little (as fear will sometimes collect, as well as distract) to convey themselves and their substance into the uttermost bosom of the Adriatick Gulf, and there possessed certain desolate islets, by tradition about seventy in number, which afterwards (necessity being the mother of art) were tacked together with bridges, and so the city took a rude form, which grew civilized with time, and became a great example what the smallest things well fomented may prove.

They glory in this their beginning two ways. First, that surely their progenitors were not of the meanest and basest quality (for such having little to lose had as little cause to remove). Next, that they were timely instructed with temperance and penury (the nurses of moderation). And true it is, that as all things savour of their first principles, so doth the said Republic (as I shall afterwards show) even at this day; for the rule will hold as well in civil as in natural causes.[12]

The Attila myth survived even the republic: during the Austrian occupation of Venice in the nineteenth century, Verdi chose the Attila legend for an opera that slipped *risorgimento* propaganda past the censors of the modern "Huns." Although such legends make good propaganda and good theater, they are not history. According to Roberto Cessi, even though Attila's armies tramped through Venetia and besieged Aquileia, his men were warriors, not settlers, and most of the effects of their ravaging were temporary; so, even if a considerable number of people did indeed abandon their homes on the *terraferma* for the safety of the lagoon, there was no reason for them not to return after the barbarians had passed. Despite some visible scars from the invasion, which invited succeeding generations

[12] Smith, *Sir Henry Wotton*, 2:256.

to credit the .legends, Aquileia remained the metropolis of the region, and the rise of Venice had to wait for later developments.[13]

Legends, unlike history, can not tolerate ignorance, and so legend-makers invented whatever details seemed necessary to command belief. A myth was commonly dressed with many "facts"—names, dates, descriptions, numbers killed in battle, motives, words spoken—so as to confound refutation. In the Middle Ages this craving for detail often took the form of providing the exact time and place for the foundation of a city. Jerusalem made its beginning 366 years after the flood, 2,023 after creation, and 1,941 before Christ; in Naples the first stone was placed on stone 2,804 years after the creation, 20 after the fall of Troy, and 408 before the founding of Rome.[14] The Venetians likewise sought a precise date for the inception of their city, and an auspicious one at that. To this purpose another legend arose, which in many ways contradicted the Attila myth. The standard version of this second legend about the movement from the *terraferma* to the lagoon is found in the chronicle of a Paduan doctor, Jacopo Dondi, who probably wrote between 1328 and 1339. Dondi recounts that at about noon on March 25, 421, a group of Paduans founded a city at *Rivum altum* in the Venetian lagoon and designated three notables with the title of consul to rule it.[15] For the date of March 25, Dondi relied on the Venetian ceremonial practice, which went back to possibly the eleventh century, of marking the beginning of the year on the day of the Annunciation.[16] Dondi's version of the legend caused controversy, however, because it appeared to offer primacy to Padua, after 1405 a subject city of Venice;

[13] Cessi, *Le origini del ducato veneziano*, pp. 15–16.

[14] Lanzoni, *Genesi delle leggende storiche*, pp. 23, 25–33.

[15] Jacopo Dondi, *Liber partium consilii magnifice comunitatis Padue*, part of the Liber Tabularum or the Liber A., fol. 165v in the Archivio Civile of the Museo Civico, Padua. In the published edition by Vittorio Lazzarini (see Bibliography, "Primary Sources," s.v. Dondi), note especially pp. 1264–65. The portion regarding the foundation of Venice is also published in Roberto Cessi, ed., *Documenti relativi alla storia di Venezia anteriori al mille*, 1:1–2. Also see Ezio Franceschini, "La cronachetta di Maestro Jacopo Dondi," especially p. 970.

[16] Antonio Niero, "I santi patroni," p. 79.

but the date of March 25 proved too auspicious for the Venetians to abandon, and instead they tended to edit out references to Padua. The date of March 25, 421, was more or less official in Venetian historiography; it appears in the works of Martin da Canal (who preceded Dondi), Andrea Dandolo, Bernardo Giustiniani, Marin Sanuto, Marc Antonio Sabellico, and Francesco Sansovino.[17]

March 25, of course, was charged with ritual significance. As the first month of the Roman year, March was associated in the time of Ovid (Fasti 3.11.78) with the legends of the founding of Rome and with the springtime renewal of nature.[18] Christianity further enriched the connection between fertility and the month of March by celebrating the Annunciation, the moment at which Christ's spirit entered Mary's womb and became incarnate, on the day of the Vernal Equinox on the Julian calendar, March 25. Thus, in Venice the founding day of the city was mystically conjoined with the founding of Rome, the beginning of the Christian era, the annual rebirth of nature, and the first day of the calendar year.[19] Venetians were completely aware of the mystical significance of this date, which Sabellico detailed.

Some say that where the church of Saint Mark now stands was the starting point for the building [of Venice], and nearly all agree that the beginning was on the twenty-fifth of March. Whatever the case, if we would just consider some of the excellent works which have been per-

[17] Canal, Les estoires de Venise, p. 6; Niero, "I santi patroni," p. 79; Francesco Sansovino, Venetia città nobilissima et singolare, fols. 342v–43v. The date March 25, 421, also appears in the anonymous pamphlet Feste di palazzo et giorni ne'quali sua serenità esce di quello, under the heading "Marzo," in MCV, Op. P.D. 71. The pamphlet can be dated from internal evidence as between 1656 and 1727.

[18] Also see Plutarch, Romulus, pp. 3ff., and W. Warde Fowler, The Roman Festivals of the Period of the Republic, pp. 33–65. Plutarch offered the theory that Rome was founded in April.

[19] Until 1797 Venetians used three different systems of dating: notaries used March 25 as the beginning of the year; public acts and official documents were dated from March 1; documents destined for circulation outside the Venetian dominions and nearly all private records after circa 1520 were dated from January 1. A. Cappelli, Cronologia, cronografia e calendario perpetuo dal principio dell'era cristiana ai giorni nostri, p. 16.

formed on that day, there will be no doubt that [there was]
nothing established on that day which is not great and
marvelous, [for as] the sacred letters affirm for the perpetual glory of mankind, on that same day the omnipotent
God formed our first ancestor. Likewise, [on that day,] the
son of God was conceived in the womb of the Virgin.[20]

Francesco Sansovino avowed as well that this providential
founding meant that the Venetians had inherited the rights of
ancient Rome. The Annunciation, moveover, became such a
favorite Venetian religious and political theme that it appeared
in relief on the facade of the basilica of San Marco, and it joined
Saint Mark and Saint Theodore at the base of the Rialto
Bridge.[21] In comparison to the Attila myth, the narrative of the
beginning of Venice on March 25 became the more powerful,
influential, and popular, not only because of its greater intrinsic
symbolism, but also because it was one of the two founding
legends incorporated into official ceremony. The Annunciation
Day procession and high mass in San Marco permanently
bound the destiny of Venice to the veiled will of God, the
harmony of nature, and the imperial authority of Rome.[22]

In addition to the legends of noble ancestors and of the timely
founding of the city, a few sparse accounts of early Venetian life
encouraged Renaissance Venetians to idealize their simple, pure
beginnings in much the same way that Protestant reformers
imagined the perfection of the primitive Church. The sense of

[20] "Dicono alcuni, che dove e hora la chiesa di san Marco fu il principio di
tanta fabbrica, & tutti quasi si accordano, che tale principio fosse a xxv. di
Marzo. Per laqual cosa, se noi volemo considerare alcune opere eccellenti in
cotal giorno essere state fatte, non sara dubbio a creder che niuna cosa in quel
giorno ha principio, laqual non sia grande & maravigliosa, & è perpetua
gloria delle cose humane le sacre lettere affermano in quel medesimo giorno
l'omnipotenti Dio haver formato il nostro primo parente. Similmente che
esso figliuol d'Iddio fu nel ventre della Vergine conceputo." Sabellico, Le
historie vinitiane, fol. 3v. Cf. Labalme, Bernardo Giustiniani, p. 267.

[21] Sansovino, Venetia, 1604, fols. 342v–43v; Niero, "I santi patroni," pp.
79–80; Otto Demus, The Church of San Marco in Venice, pp. 126–35.

[22] Sansovino, Venetia, 1604, fols. 342v–43v; Giustina Renier Michiel, Le
origine delle feste veneziane, 1:5–64. Michiel associated the March 25 celebration with the Venetian struggle with Pepin in the early ninth century. This
connection was not made in the sixteenth century.

continuity in Venetian history was particularly profound, and sixteenth-century Venetians saw in their city's beginnings auguries of their own political truths.[23] In the description of the lagoon by Cassiodorus (537–38) the humanist historians discovered a vision of a virtuous primitive life: small wooden boats plied the waters of a vast, nearly deserted lagoon, whose inhabitants existed by hunting, fishing, and bartering salt. Cassiodorus said that the line of islands enclosing the lagoon from the sea created a "permanent tranquil security."[24] Venice's legendary, independence at its birth from both the Empire and the Roman Church, added to its security and peacefulness, perpetuated the notion of Venetian liberty. In the sixteenth century Gasparo Contarini contrasted the founding of Venice, accomplished through the collective pursuit of "onore," "chiarezza," and "virtù" by its settlers, with the founding of Athens, Lacedaemon, and Rome by a single hero-legislator. Venice's independent foundation was thus the source of its stability.[25] Although in his *Second Treatise of Government* (par. 102, ll. 3–6) John Locke differed from Contarini in his view of the origin of Rome, Locke nevertheless emphasized the importance of a foundation in freedom: ". . . who will not allow that the *beginning* of *Rome* and *Venice* were by the uniting together of several Men free and independent one of another, amongst whom there was no natural Superiority or Subjection." By the Renaissance, when the historical awareness of Venetians was most keen, the .mythical origins of Venice had a profound influence on the development of a republican political ideology.

Modern historians, however, have rejected much of this idealized picture of early Venice. In the view of Roberto Cessi, the search for the date and circumstances of Venice's foundation and independence is wrongheaded, since Venetian autonomy was not simply a local development but part of the long dissolution of the Byzantine Empire. He argues that the supposed autonomy recorded by Cassiodorus was an illusion and that the

[23] Cf. the comments by Fasoli, "Comune veneciarum," p. 474.
[24] M. A. Cassiodorii, *Epistulae variae*, 1:12, no. 24, reprinted in *Documenti anteriori al mille*, pp. 2–4. Cf. Gian Piero Bognetti, "Natura, politica e religioni nelle origini di Venezia," p. 3.
[25] Pocock, *The Machiavellian Moment*, pp. 322–23.

major migrations to the lagoon occurred not in the fifth but in the sixth and seventh centuries, as a result of the Lombard conquest of the Friuli, Padua, Treviso, and Vicenza. Furthermore, he rejects the favorite claim of Venetians—that Roman nobles figured in the migration to Venice—by demonstrating that the early Venetians, unlike the Romans, conceived of nobility as a title gained only by holding political office, not as a social distinction. In fact, the first proposals to limit by law those who could be elected to office came as late as 1286.[26]

Gradual independence came to Venice in the eighth century, when Constantinople accepted the first *duces* elected by local will alone. In 810 the political center of the lagoon was transferred to its present site at Rialto, and by 840 the Carolingian emperors had recognized the autonomy of the *ducato*. In the tenth century Rialto consolidated its administrative authority over the other lagoon towns, and by the eleventh Venice had begun its physical expansion as a city, its commercial adventures to the Levant, and its transformation of the *ducato* into a commune.[27] Venice, well on its way to becoming the Most Serene Republic, needed only a device by which it might maintain the institutional and procedural continuity necessary for a stable, peaceful mercantile environment. That device became the civic liturgy, an annual succession of feast days and ceremonial occasions conducted by the patrician rulers of Venice.

THE FESTIVE CALENDAR

Machiavelli observed that "Men in general make judgments more by appearances than by reality, for sight alone belongs to everyone, but understanding to few. Everyone sees what you appear to be, few know what you are, and those few do not dare to contradict the opinion of the many who have the majesty of the state to defend them; and in the actions of all men, and most of all of princes, from whom there is no appeal, one must

[26] Cessi, *Le origini del ducato veneziano*, pp. 18–32, 323–39.

[27] Fasoli, "Comune veneciarum," pp. 477–85, 490–91; Carlo Guido Mor, "Aspetti della vita costituzionale veneziana fino alla fine del X secolo," pp. 125–27.

consider the end result."[28] It is dangerous for the prince to be weak, but worse to look so. One way Machiavelli suggested that the prince might strengthen his own public presence was to follow the Roman formula of providing *circenses* for the plebians: "He should . . . , at appropriate times of the year, keep the people occupied with festivals and shows."[29] In the strict observance of the festive church calendar and in the elaboration and enrichment of certain feasts for the purposes of state, the prince best obeyed Machiavelli's dictum. The prince was, in effect, enjoined to imitate a truth that perceptive priests, if not dogmatic theologians, had long understood; as E. P. Thompson has put it, ". . . to the degree that the ritual calendar year chimes in with the agrarian calendar, the authority of the Church is strengthened."[30] The state likewise enhanced its authority when it could insinuate its own special rites into the agrarian calendar. Yet such a civic liturgy was not just a calculated political gesture but also a communal celebration of civic values and a dramatic revue of society in all its constituent parts. In this sense public spectacles were more than a popular diversion: like the chorus in a Greek play, the civic liturgy commented on the roles of the actors in community life. On the basis of this commentary, Machiavelli averred, men understand and judge the state.

Calendrical rites, which anthropologists tend to distinguish from the life-crisis rites that define the biological or status transitions of an individual, nearly always embrace large groups or whole societies that must adapt to seasonal changes. Performed at well-delineated times in the agricultural year, calendrical rites ease the transition from scarcity to plenty, as at harvest feasts, or from plenty to scarcity, when winter hard-

---

[28] "E li uomini in universali iudicano più alli occhi che alle mani; perchè tocca a vedere a ognuno, a sentire a pochi. Ognuno vede quello che tu pari, pochi sentono quello che tu se'; e quelli pochi non ardiscano opporsi alla opinione di molti, che abbino la maestà dello stato che gli defenda; e nelle azioni di tutti gli uomini, e massime de' principi, dove non è iudizio a chi reclamare, si guarda al fine." *Il Principe* 18.5.

[29] "Debbe, oltre a questo, ne' tempi convenienti dell'anno, tenere occupati e populi con le feste e spettaculi." *Il Principe* 21.7.

[30] Thompson, "Anthropology and Historical Context," p. 51.

ships are magically anticipated.[31] Calendrical rites are thus buffers against the potential of chaos; with these rites the superior claims of group over individual interests are emphasized, and the cohesiveness of society is, in theory, reinforced. If life-crisis rites define the idiosyncratic, the personal, and the biological, then in contrast calendrical rites proclaim the communal, the universal, and the eternal. All rituals help individuals and societies confront potentially confounding change, since a ritual can recognize, define, explain, and thus control change. In the European historical context, as we have noted, there were exceptions to this anthropological model; in Venice, however, there was a remarkable consistency in the ways public rituals supported and strengthened communal stability.

The Venetians, of course, adopted in outline the liturgical calendar of Christianity, which flowered from the grafting of the pre-agrarian lunar calendar of the Hebrews to the solar calendar of the Romans. The results of this grafting can be seen in the two distinct cycles of the Christian liturgy: the Easter cycle of movable feasts, derived from the lunar dating of the Hebrew Passover; and the Nativity cycle of fixed feasts, reckoned from the dating of Christ's birth on the twenty-fifth day of the tenth month of the Julian solar year.[32] The ritual commemoration of the life of Christ in the liturgy kept time with the passing of the seasons, and thus the mission of Christ, relived each year in the Church's feasts, became as much a part of the universal order as the waning and waxing of the moon or the apparent movements of the planets. Through ritual, Christianity became as natural as Nature itself.

Other than using the dating conventions of Roman Christianity and celebrating the major feasts at the same time as other Western Christians, the Venetian calendar was a purely local creation owing little even to Byzantium for its distinctive character. The Venetians neither directly copied rites nor at first competed with Constantinople in imperial splendor; Byzantine

[31] Turner, *The Ritual Process*, pp. 168–69.

[32] *The Catholic Encyclopedia*, s.v. "Calendar"; F. L. Cross, ed., *The Oxford Dictionary of the Christian Church*, s.v. "Calendar," "Ascension," "Epiphany," "Advent," "Candlemas," "Pentecost," and "Whitsunday." E. O. James, *Seasonal Feasts and Festivals*.

traditions may have governed the taste and style of early Venetian ceremonies without determining the details of individual rites, but by the fourteenth century local influences were entirely dominant.[33] Venice had its own particular liturgy called the *patriarchino*, adopted from the patriarchate of Grado, which had in turn taken it from Aquileia. Although its local variations made it a liturgy like no other, the *patriarchino's* greatest debt was to the Gregorian calendar, for it had no particular affinities to the calendar of Alexandria or Constantinople. The offices of the *patriarchino* were usually longer than in other rites, the doge himself could give a *benedictio* in it, and changes in the rite normally came at the behest of the doges, who kept an absolute authority over the liturgy of San Marco. The *patriarchino*, therefore, was especially subject to political influences. Until the fifteenth century the rite was practiced throughout Venice, but in 1456 a papal brief, requested by Patriarch Maffeo Contarini, abolished it everywhere except in San Marco; so the *patriarchino* became the exclusive liturgy of the doge and Signoria—a liturgy of state.[34]

Just as the Christian ceremonies relived the history of Christ, the Church, and the saints, the Venetian liturgy re-enacted the history of Venice, so that secular history and legend became as sacred as the biblical mysteries. The liturgy sanctified the past and nurtured belief in the moral order of the *res publica:* what was peculiarly Venetian was associated with what was universally Christian or eternally natural, thus blending patriotism and faith.

The dates of the annual celebrations in Venice corresponded either to feast days on the Roman calendar of saints' days or to events in Venetian history, and they fell into four distinct groups: those which honored a saint, Saint Mark in particular; those which recalled the visit to Venice of Pope Alexander III in 1177 and the gifts with which he supposedly honored the doge; those which marked important events in Venetian history, such as the victory at Lepanto; and those which illustrated the rights, obligations, and limitations of the doges and other of-

[33] Fasoli, "Liturgia e cerimoniale ducale," pp. 275–76, 292–93.

[34] Antonio Pasini, "Rito antico e cerimoniale della basilica." The details of the liturgy can be found in BMV, MS Latin III, 172 (2276).

AUSPICIOUS BEGINNINGS

fice-holders. From the thirteenth to the sixteenth centuries, moreover, Venetian annual celebrations became more complex and more frequent; the conception of civic time came increasingly to rely on ritual performances.[35]

Pax Tibi Marce Evangelista Meus

The cult of Saint Mark was the nucleus of Venetian civic consciousness. In the civic liturgy Saint Mark personified the Venetian polity, and his cult as expressed in legend and ceremony recorded and preserved for the collective memory dramatic precedents in the history of the community. Silvio Tramontin has argued, for example, that the four major Venetian legends about Saint Mark were allegories for political events, constitutional principles, or stages in the historical development

---

[35] In contrast to Venice, the Florentines associated all the days save one on their republican festive calendar with the intercession of a saint. Richard C. Trexler, "Ritual Behavior in Renaissance Florence," p. 134. The earliest list of Venetian feast days is *Kalendarium Venetum saeculi XI.* See Silvio Tramontin, "Il 'Kalendarium' veneziano." In the thirteenth century Martin da Canal found twelve annual festivals worthy of discussion. *Les estoires de Venise,* pp. 247–63. By the end of the fifteenth century Marin Sanuto recognized twenty important days. *Le vite dei dogi,* pp. 86–91. The official ceremonial book of the Collegio lists sixteen annual events that required the participation of the doge and Signoria during the sixteenth century and also shows that the number of events varied greatly from year to year. ASV, Collegio Cerimoniale 1, fol. 11r–v. Other lists, which include many of the locally celebrated saints' days, name twenty-nine, sixty-nine, and seventy-eight annual days of ceremonial importance. See, respectively, BMV, MS Latin III, 172 (2276), fol. 54r–v; MCV, Cod. Cicogna 2992/1 28, fols. 1r–5v; and MCV, MS Donà delle Rose 132/6, fols. 139r–143v. Comparing a number of sources, I have found at least eighty-six different days that, by the end of the sixteenth century, had some ceremonial importance for the republic. Sansovino distinguished between the ten holidays requiring a full procession comprised of the doge, Signoria, and the display of the ducal symbols and the four holidays conducted without the symbols and musicians. *Venetia,* 1604, fols. 330v, 243v–45v. Seven of these fourteen days also required the participation of the Scuole Grandi, clerical congregations, and orders of regulars, and it was on these occasions that tableaux vivants and musical performances were likely to be appropriate. BMV, MS Latin III, 172 (2276), fol. 55v. Cf. Rosand, "Music in the Myth of Venice," p. 516.

of the *res publica veneta*.[36] The Evangelist's cult was perhaps the most important element contributing to the continuity in Venetian mythology, and the Venetian liturgy intensified the moral and mystical resonance of the cult.

A Venetian legend claimed that Saint Mark stopped at the lagoon while evangelizing in Italy and that this visit forged an inseparable bond between Saint and city. The definitive account appeared in Doge Andrea Dandolo's fourteenth-century *Chronicon venetum*.[37] Saint Peter sent Mark and a companion, Hermagoras, to proselytize Aquileia; surprised by a squall on their return to Rome, Mark and his companions sought shelter in the placid lagoon where the major rivers of the Veneto found an outlet to the sea. Their boat came to rest at a small island (the very one upon which the city of Rialto would later be established), where Mark debarked to spend the night. In a dream an angel came to the frightened Evangelist and proclaimed, "Pax tibi, Marce. Hic requiescet corpus tuum." The angel reassured Mark that he still had much to accomplish for Christ and described to him the glorious city that refugees would someday build on the spot where he lay, the honor they would render to his relics, and the many gifts God would grant them through Mark's intercession. Later writers revised the story to add that the future inhabitants of the desolate isle would be a superior breed of men, ever dedicated to *virtù* and *pietà*; or, as Sansovino described Saint Mark's influence, ". . . under his custody the Empire of this people must grow and forever survive for the good of mankind."[38]

[36] Silvio Tramontin, "Realità e leggenda nei racconti marciani veneti." There is a bibliography of studies regarding Saint Mark in Venice on p. 35. Peyer, *Stadt und Stadtpatron*, pp. 8–24; Silvio Tramontin, "Breve storia dell'agiografia veneziana."

[37] The account that follows has been taken from Tramontin, "Realità e leggenda," pp. 45–46. The Andrea Dandolo text is edited by E. Pastorello in *Rerum Italicarum Scriptores*, 2d. Bologna, 1938, 12:10. Other versions include the "Cronaca di Marco," BMV, MS Italiano xi, 124 (6802), fol. 5v. and Sansovino, *Venetia*, 1663, pp. 506–7.

[38] ". . . sotto la sua custodia, l'Imperio di questa natione dovesse crescere, & mantenersi perpetuo per salute del genere humano." Sansovino, *Venetia*, 1663, p. 505. Cf. Giovanni Stringa, *Vita di S. Marco evangelista, protettore invitissimo della serenissima republica di Venetia, con la traslatione, & apparitione del sacro suo corpo; fatta nella nobilissima chiesa, al nome suo dedicata*, pp. 23–24.

This fable is without historical foundation. There is no contemporary ot biblical evidence of an evangelical visit by Saint
Mark to Aquileia or to anywhere in Venetia, nor did his cult
appear in the region until long after his death. The story seems
to have been a thirteenth-century fabrication designed to justify the theft of Saint Mark's relics by claiming the transfer
pre-ordained.[39] The early Christian churches in the area, none
of which date from before the mid-third century, were devoted ·
to other saints, and, as late as the sixth century, Venantius
Fortunatus reported that Saint Fortunatus was the greatest
treasure of Aquileia, just as Saint Mark was the glory of Egypt.
Saint Hermagorus, whose cult was closely linked to that of
Saint Mark, did not appear in the Aquileian calendar until the
fifth century or become the city's patron until the eleventh
century. The first mention of Saint Mark as founder and a
patron of the Christian church in Aquileia is in the Lombard
chronicle of Paul the Deacon (783– 86).[40] But at the end of the
eighth century, Paulinus, the patriarch of Aquileia, wrote of
Saint Mark as the founder of the diocese, a claim that gave the
patriarch immense prestige and that supported Aquileian pretensions to autonomy from Rome and, at the Synod of Mantua
in 827, to primacy over the rival patriarchical seat at Grado. By
the ninth century, then, Saint Mark was well established in the
region as a symbol of local privilege. From Aquileia the cult
migrated to Grado, the "New Aquileia," and eventually, after
the acquisition of the Saint's remains, to Venice.

Venetians claimed that the transfer, or *translatio*, of Mark's
body from Alexandria to Venice, in 827 or 828, secured the
Saint's patronage. According to the legend, ten Venetian ships
on a voyage to the East were blown off course and forced to
seek refuge from a storm in the Arab-controlled port of Alexandria. The sources emphasize that the visit was involuntary,

[39] Cf. the comments on the justification of relic thefts by Patrick J. Geary,
Furta Sacra, pp. 140– 42.

[40] Paul the Deacon wrote of Saint Mark's evangelical trip to Aquileia: "Mar-
cum vero qui praecipuus inter eius discipulos habebatur, Aquileiam destinavit,
quibus cum Hermagoram suum comitem Marcus praefecisset, ad beatum Pe-
trum reversus, ab eo nihilominus Alexandriam missus est." Quoted by Silvio
Tramontin, "San Marco," p. 48.

because there was an imperial decree in effect at the time that
prohibited Christians from trading with Saracens. Among the
merchants who debarked in Alexandria were two tribunes,
Buono da Malamocco and Rustico da Torcello, who became
friendly with a monk named Staurizio and a priest called Theodore, both of whom were from the Christian church that har- ·
bored the remains of Saint Mark.[41] Fearing that the Moslems
might destroy the Christian shrines, Theodore proposed that
the two Venetians rescue the body from danger, and in reply
Buono and Rustico recalled the story of Mark's conversion of
Aquileia and Venetia, argued that "hence we are his eldest
sons," and declared Venice the Evangelist's proper home.[42] With
the promise of a handsome reward from the doge, Theodore
and Staurizio helped the Venetians smuggle the body past the
Arab customs inspectors by covering it with pork, whose very
sight disgusted the Moslems. They replaced Mark's body with
another clad in the Saint's vestments. On the voyage home
Saint Mark saved the ship from running aground while the
crew slept, and he defended the ship's company from an attack
of demons; these miracles verified the authenticity of the relics
now in Venetian possession.[43] Expecting punishment for having
visited an Arab country, Buono and Rustico sent word ahead
from Istria that they would give the body to Doge Giustiniano
Particiaco in exchange for a pardon, but the doge was so overjoyed at the news about the relics that he not only pardoned
but richly rewarded the two pious merchants. With a majestic
procession the religious and secular authorities received the

[41] This account of the *translatio* of Saint Mark is based primarily on Tramontin, "Realità e leggenda," pp. 46–48; Cf. Michiel, *Le origine delle feste
veneziane*, 1:63–83, and Geary, *Furta Sacra*, pp. 107–15, for an account based
on the earliest sources. Martin da Canal differs in several details from this
synopsis. *Les estoires de Venise*, pp. 16–20. A sixteenth-century version that
conforms to the account given here is by Giorgio Dolfin, "Cronica di Venezia
dall'origine sua fino all'anno 1458," BMV, MS Italiano VII, 794 (8503), fols.
47r–48r.

[42] In other accounts the Venetians first proposed the removal of Saint Mark's
body. Canal, *Les estoires de Venise*, p. 18, and Geary, *Furta Sacra*, pp. 113–
14.

[43] For an account of the miracles see Canal, *Les estoires de Venise*, pp. 18–
20, and Dolfin, "Cronica," BMV, MS Italiano VII, 794 (8503), fols. 47v–48r.

body, which affirmed its holiness by performing several miracles in the Ducal Palace. Soon Saint Mark completely displaced all other saints as Venice's palladium.

Whether or not the body of Saint Mark or some other relic was actually transferred to Venice in 827 or 828 is incidental to the history of the legend, but it is an issue that still engages some historians. Silvio Tramontin, the most prominent scholarly advocate of the veracity of the *translatio*, cites two favorable bits of evidence: a Frankish monk, Bernard, reported after a late ninth-century pilgrimage to the Holy Land that the body of Saint Mark, no longer in Egypt, had been taken to Venice; and a provision in Doge Giustiniano Particiaco's will ordered that a basilica be built in honor of Mark.[44] The earliest recounting of the transfer story itself, however, is in a tenth-century codex, and Antonio Niero notes that an Egyptian tradition has the Evangelist's head still in Alexandria in the thirteenth century.[45] The eyewitness account of the opening of Saint Mark's tomb in 1809 is likewise inconclusive: although the investigators did find a pulverized skeleton, the other objects placed in the grave dated from the eleventh century.[46] As with many celebrated relics, the evidence is so contradictory that verification is impossible and, moreover, not necessarily important for modern historiography.

Far more important are the uses of the legend. The *translatio* supposedly occurred within a generation of Pepin's attempt in 810 to conquer Venice by sacking Malamocco, which was then the capital, and the subsequent removal of the ducal government to Rialto. One scholar has suggested that the *translatio* was a political invention of Doge Giustiniano Particiaco; it obscured the spiritual authority of Grado in order to force the patriarch to abandon his Frankish alliance and to move his seat

[44] Tramontin, "San Marco," pp. 54–56. The passage in Doge Particiaco's will regarding the basilica reads, "Quidquid exinde remanserit de lapidibus et quidquid circa hanc [p]e[tram] iacet et de casa Theophilato de Torcello hedifficetur basilicha beati Marci evangeliste, sicut supra imperavimus." Cessi, ed., *Documenti anteriori al mille*, p. 96.

[45] On the tenth-century codex see Geary, *Furta Sacra*, p. 114; Antonio Niero, "Reliquie e corpi di santi," pp. 192–94.

[46] Jacopo Filiasi, *Memoria sopra il corpo di S. Marco*, pp. 54–56.

to the Realtine Islands, where the doge could better control him.[47] Indeed, the *translatio* legend clearly accords the gift of Saint Mark's body to Doge Particiaco rather than to a particular church or prelate, a fact that forged the permanent spiritual union between the doges and the Saint and that made Mark's cult a political concern. In a similar interpretation, Patrick Geary emphasizes that Doge Particiaco acquired the body as a conscious political challenge to the Franks, who at the Synod of Mantua had supported Aquileia's patriarch over Grado's. In addition to countering Carolingian influence, the decision to remove the Evangelist Mark to Rialto had the secondary advantage of reducing Byzantine dominance in the city by substituting the "Italian" Evangelist Mark for the Greek soldier Theodore as the personal patron of the doge.[48] Nelson McCleary argues that Particiaco's primary purpose was to unify the Venetian towns and islands around a religious center that was directly under his own tutelage, thus undermining the patriarchates of both Aquileia and Grado.[49] Hans Conrad Peyer, in contrast, sees the *translatio* as merely a local manifestation of a phenomenon common to many of the small Italian states left as residue after the breakdown of Byzantine domination. While he concedes that the Particiaci doges probably used their possession of the evangelical relics to gain spiritual sovereignty over Grado, Peyer notes that in many of the formerly Byzantine cities dominion correlated with the possession of the mortal remains of a saint-protector who guarded the citizens from attack and who sanctioned communal independence.[50] Any attempt to explain the exact motives or combination of motives behind the supposed transfer is largely guesswork, but it seems probable that, whether or not Doge Particiaco actually planned the acquisition in advance, he was quick to recognize the tremendous political and spiritual potentialities of Saint Mark's body. The *translatio* provided the Venetians with a highly placed intercessor and, at

[47] See Tramontin's comments on the thesis of Gfrörer. "San Marco," p. 56.

[48] Geary, *Furta Sacra*, pp. 108–11.

[49] Nelson McCleary, "Note storiche ed archeologiche sul testo della 'Translatio Sancti Marci,' " p. 224.

[50] Peyer, *Stadt und Stadtpatron*, pp. 9–11. Cf. Tramontin, "San Marco," p. 56.

the same time, declared the independence of Venice; as Gina
Fasoli put it, the "myth of Venice" was born on the very day
Doge Particiaco accepted the body.[51] In the eleventh century
the Venetian liturgical calendar added a commemorative mass
to be sung in San Marco on January 31, and thus the *translatio*
story became a permanent fixture in the civic ritual of Venice.[52]

As possessors of the Evangelist's body, the Venetian *duces*
modeled their relationship to Mark on that of the popes' to
Saint Peter. Just as the popes had inherited the authority of
Peter, so had the Venetians inherited that of Mark. The popes
were autonomous; therefore so should be the Venetian state. In
the cult of Saint Mark religious and civic values became inseparable; the idea that Venice had a divine destiny culminated in
the thirteenth-century legend of the angelic prophecy given to
Mark while he rested at the Rialto.[53] In political thought the
patronage of Saint Mark created the basis for a theory, to use
the terminology coined by Walter Ullmann, of a descending
political authority in which the *potestas* granted by God was
transferred through Mark to the doge.[54]

In the Renaissance the rituals of Saint Mark's feast day, April
25, perpetuated both the mystical bond between Saint Mark
and the doge and the conception of descending authority. On
the eve of Saint Mark's Day a vespers procession of the doge,
high magistrates, musicians, and bearers of the ducal symbols
marched from the Ducal Palace to San Marco, where at the
singing of the Magnificat the doge lighted a white candle on the
high altar in honor of the Evangelist. This act renewed the
spiritual bond between the Saint and the city and reiterated the
doges' central role in the Saint's cult.[55] Commentators noted
that in 1177 Pope Alexander III gave the white candle to the

[51] Fasoli, "Nascita di un mito."

[52] Canal, *Les estoires de Venise*, p. 20; Sanuto, *Le vite dei dogi*, p. 89;
Tramontin, "San Marco," p. 59.

[53] Tramontin, "Realità e leggenda," pp. 36–44, 53–54; idem, "San Marco,"
pp. 47–52; Niero, "I santi patroni," pp. 82–83; Fasoli, "Nascita di un mito,"
pp. 451–52; McCleary, "Translatio Sancti Marci," pp. 224–31.

[54] Walter Ullman, *Principles of Government and Politics in the Middle Ages.*

[55] Sansovino, *Venetia*, 1663, p. 507; Sanuto, *Le vite dei dogi*, p. 90; ASV,
Collegio Cerimoniale 1, fol. 8v; BMV, MS Latin III, 172 (2276), fol. 53r.

doge, thus implying that the popes had recognized the doges' special relationship with the Saint. The ceremony, however, was not exclusively ducal. The law required several of the guilds— along with the Scuole Grandi, the most important non-noble organizations—to join the procession and to offer candles, as had the doge, for the Evangelist. The gifts not only revealed the broad social base of devotion to Saint Mark but also signified the "feudal" ties of the guilds to the doge: in a seventeenth-century description of the ceremony Nicolò Doglioni named four guilds that were obliged "to offer some wax candles signifying a recognition of vassalage."[56] The annual homage to Saint Mark thereby provided an additional dramatic opportunity for statecraft: on a public and sanctified stage the doge ritually enacted his lordship over the plebian institutions of Venice.

The same principle of making political relationships explicit governed the ceremonies at the high mass sung in honor of Mark on the following day. For example, the doge and papal nuncio confessed simultaneously to the officiating priest in order to avoid the quarrels over precedence that Venetian pretensions to administrative independence from the Papacy were bound to provoke. And after the services, while they were passing in review before the dignitaries, Scuole Grandi members gave specially decorated candles to the doge, his wife, the nuncio, the foreign ambassadors, the ducal counselors, and the entire assembled secular and religious hierarchy down to senators, bishops, and abbots.[57] In this procession the confraternities also displayed their most prized relics, including the miraculous cross of the Scuola di San Giovanni Evangelista, a thorn

[56] "Ad offerire alcuni Torci di cera come senso per ricognitione di Vasalaggio. . . ." Nicolò Doglioni, Le cose notabili et maravigliose della città di Venetia, p. 263. The four guilds were the pittori, fabri, pellizzari, and "quei che fan panni di setta." One of the capitoli of the Mariegola (incorporation regulations and statutes) for the painters' guild required the members to offer two candles, each worth five lire, every year on the eve of Saint Mark's Day. MCV, MS P.D. 606c/III, fol. 9. Also see Sanuto, I diarii, 20:139.

[57] Sansovino, Venetia, 1663, pp. 507–8. The procession also included guildsmen, but they did not give candles on this occasion. The guilds that participated varied considerably from year to year, but the sartori were usually present. Sanuto, I diarii, 30:169, 41:219, 44:552; Doglioni, Le cose notabili, p. 263.

from the crown of Christ, a finger of Saint Roch, and the episcopal ring of Saint Mark.[58] As a legal obligation, the distribution of candles signified—if one can make an inference from Doglioni's comments about the guildsmen's gifts of candles—the similar ties of "vassalage" of these sodalities to the nobility and, of course, the Scuole Grande members' reverence toward Saint Mark.[59] Feudal terminology and ritual homage combined in this instance to define the social relationship between the subordinate classes and the nobility, and the definition was made in a hallowed context that could imply only a divine sanction of the status quo.

Just as the *translatio* represented in allegory the political unification of the lagoon under the doges and the initial stages of Venetian independence from Byzantium, the legend of the apparition or *inventio* of Saint Mark was an allegory of the consummation of Venetian political autonomy.[60] The church built by the Particiaci doges to house Saint Mark's body burned in 976 during a revolt against Doge Pietro IV Candiano. Because the doges had feared thieves, only a few trusted officials knew the precise location of the Evangelist's relics; after the fire the spot was altogether forgotten. Despite numerous searches beneath the new church built on the same site by Doge Domenico Contarini (1043–71), the body remained lost until 1094, when, as a final resort, Doge Vitale Falier ordered the bishop to declare a communal fast lasting for three days and ending with a solemn procession on the fourth day, June 25.[61] The fervent devotion of the populace during the procession was said to have evoked a miracle, for during the high mass a portion of a column made from pieces taken from the old basilica gradually moved, revealing the body of Saint Mark, which filled the air

[58] Sanuto, *I diarii*, 30:169.

[59] The Scuole spent a total of 209½ lire for wax for Saint Mark's Day, according to the list in BMV, MS Latin III, 172 (2276), fol. 78v. The amount spent for the candles given to different officials varied considerably.

[60] The account of the *inventio* of Saint Mark that follows is based primarily on Tramontin, "Realità e leggenda," p. 55–57. An early account of the legend is in Canal, *Les estoires de Venise*, p. 218.

[61] Michiel, who presents a slightly different version of this legend, claims that the search was prompted by a pilgrimage made to the basilica by Emperor Henry V. *Le origine delle feste veneziane*, 3:128–46.

with a sweet odor.[62] The body was left on public display for the edification of the faithful until a crypt was ready for it and until the new basilica was consecrated on October 8, which also became an annual feast day.[63] Although the full legend and the annual holiday were creations of the second half of the thirteenth century, Tramontin has argued that the story may be an embellishment of an actual event. During the building of a new basilica, the body (if it had not been lost in the fire) would have been exhumed from the old tomb and probably put on display until the new crypt was built.[64] Added to the *inventio* story in the fourteenth century was the detail of Saint Mark extending his arm out from the column, and in the sixteenth-century versions a pastoral gold ring appeared on the protruding hand.[65]

The cult of Saint Mark required such an apparition legend, if for no other reason, in order to imitate the pattern that medieval hagiographers had established for important saints' afterlives: a martyrdom (*passio*), a transferral (*translatio*), and a rediscovery of relics (*inventio*).[66] For the Venetians the miraculous rediscovery of Saint Mark's body signified not only the re-establishment of the material and magical bonding between Saint and city but also the efficacy of the communal procession itself as a ritual act, for it was the penetential procession that had brought about the saintly miracle. In addition, the apparition allegorized the culmination of the Venetian struggle for independence from Byzantium by re-asserting Saint Mark as a symbolic alternative to the Byzantine protector-saints. The date of the apparition is important, since the Venetians' desire to rise above the Byzantine heritage may have been stimulated by the Byzantine emperor's desperate circumstances after his defeat at the hands of the Seljuk Turks at Manzikert in 1071, the same circumstances that eventually led Pope Urban II to call for

[62] Cf. Tramontin, "San Marco," p. 57.

[63] Sanuto, *Le vite dei dogi*, p. 89.

[64] Tramontin, "Realità e leggenda," p. 57. On the dating of the legend and of the feast see G. Monticolo, "L'apparitio Sancti Marci ed i suoi manoscritti," pp. 112–30; McCleary, "Translatio Sancti Marci," p. 232; Demus, *The Church of San Marco*, p. 13, n. 41.

[65] Monticolo, "L'apparitio Sancti Marci," pp. 128–30.

[66] Tramontin, "Realità e leggenda," p. 57.

the First Crusade in 1095. Thereafter, the cult of Saint Mark became a fundament of the Venetian colonial system and was used as part of a conscious imperial policy: in 1211 Doge Pietro Ziani demanded that the Cretans sing lauds to the Venetian doge each year on Christmas, Easter, Saint Titus's Day (the Cretan apostle and patron), and Saint Mark's Day. The forced inclusion of Saint Mark's Day in the Cretan liturgical calendar constituted, according to Ernst Kantorowicz, the imposition of the Venetians' local "diety" upon a conquered people.[67]

The June 25 ceremonies dedicated to the *inventio* paralleled those of Saint Mark's Day, April 25, except that on this occasion the clerical congregations and the religious orders joined the Scuole Grandi in paying the homage of candles to the doge and other magistrates. In describing this rite no commentator applied the feudal terms used to interpret the April 25 gift of candles, but it is clear that the ceremony was an act of submission to the doge on the part of the ecclesiastical establishment and signified the spiritual dominion of the secular authority. As on Saint Mark's Day the procession was an occasion for the public display of the relics associated with Saint Mark, including a book said to be written in the Saint's own hand and his gold bishop's ring, proudly carried in a sumptuous tabernacle by the members of the Scuola Grande di San Marco.[68]

The origin of the episcopal ring of Mark was the subject of two mutually contradictory tales that illustrate ways in which the essentially civic and political cult of Mark inspired the pious imagination of Venetians. The older story was the more famous and seemingly the one preferred in official circles. On February 25, 1341, during a fierce winter storm, a stranger approached an old fisherman who was trying to save his boat and gear from damage. Ignoring the gaffer's fearful protests, the stranger ordered him to row to the island of San Giorgio (see map) where boarded a second stranger, who commanded the boatman to row even farther—to San Nicolò on the island of the Lido. There a third mysterious stranger appeared and directed the

[67] Kantorowicz, *Laudes Regiae*, p. 154.
[68] Sanuto, *I diarii*, 18:296, 24:405–6, 58:372; Sansovino, *Venetia*, 1663, p. 515; Michiel, *Le origine delle feste veneziane*, 3:136–37.

fisherman to row to the mouth of the lagoon, where the boatman and his three passengers spied a terrible ship of demons
who were causing the storm. The combined invocations of the
three strangers, now revealed as Saint Mark, Saint George, and
Saint Nicholas, dispatched the demons, rendering the lagoon
again placid. The awed fisherman returned each saint to the
spot where he had met him. When Saint Mark debarked, he
gave his gold ring to the old man, instructing him to present it
to the doge. The fisherman obeyed and received a pension from
the doge as a reward.[69] An obvious allegory of the threefold
protection of the city by the Evangelist Mark, the soldier
George, and the sailors' helper Nicholas, the mildly suspenseful
story confirmed the city's saintly favor and the doges' inheritance of the ecclesiastical prerogatives of Mark. The conception
of descending political authority is somewhat confused in this
legend since Saint Mark chose to bequeath his ring to the doge
through an intermediary chosen from the people, who voluntarily turned it over to the doge, implying that his "episcopal"
power was somehow contingent upon popular consent. In the
fourteenth century the doge's coronation ceremony still echoed
this same idea of communal consent by requiring that a newly
elected doge be presented to the assembled populace for its
approval. The confusion between descending and ascending
lines of authority, or more accurately the blending of them, is
typical of the constitutional ideas embodied in Venetian ritual
.and reflects the hodge-podge historical accumulation of sometimes contradictory precedents that one should expect in a city
where no revolution or reform of sufficient magnitude ever
cleared away overworn traditions.

The other legend of the gift of Saint Mark's ring was of
sixteenth-century origin and never as popular as the fisherman
story. According to Giovanni Stringa's account of the apparition
of Saint Mark, when the body miraculously appeared in the
column and extended its hand the crowd noticed a gold ring on
a finger of the Saint.[70] Many in the congregation desired the
ring; the doge, bishop, and others tried to pull it off the hand,

[69] Tramontin, "Realità e leggenda," pp. 57–58.
[70] Stringa, *Vita di S. Marco*, pp. 85–89.

but to no avail, since the Saint did not wish them to have it. Among those present was one Domenico Dolfin, a pious man extremely devoted to Saint Mark, who, wishing for the ring more than any of the others, prayed with such fervent devotion that he fell ill. Seeing this, Saint Mark was convinced that Dolfin deserved the ring above all others, and accordingly a voice from the column spoke to Domenico: "Take the ring, take it; it is permitted that this nobleman pull the ring from the finger, and after it is off he will be the free and absolute possessor and owner of it."[71] Dolfin did so, and his family kept the ring until a Lorenzo Dolfin gave it to the Scuola Grande di San Marco, which thereafter carried it in the June 25 procession in memory of the apparition. Other than the ring's reputation for healing the infirm, there is no contemporary evidence implying that the Dolfin ring was accorded any particular mystical or political significance.[72] Like the ring given to the fisherman, this ring was a token of ecclesiastical jurisdiction, but there is no claim that the Dolfin family or the Scuola Grande di San Marco inherited any jurisdictional rights, as was the case when the fisherman gave the ring to the doge. It did not particularly bother the Venetians to have several rings in their mythology, and in fact a third legend (discussed in the next chapter) traced yet another ring, with which the doge married the sea, to a gift of Pope Alexander III. Each ring legend signified something different. Whereas the fisherman's tale accorded the doge Saint Mark's episcopal prerogatives and whereas the Alexander gift, as we shall see, offered a papal confirmation of the doge's ecclesiastical jurisdication and Venice's imperial ambitions, the Dolfin story merely asserted the on-going intercession and miracle-working powers of Saint Mark and perhaps provided the Dolfin patriline with a family myth that distinguished it from others.

Through their celebration in annual holidays, in mosaic representations on the walls and ceilings of San Marco, and undoubtedly in oral tradition, the legends of Saint Mark wedded

[71] "Prendi l'Anello, prendi; permisse, che il Nobil'huomo dal dito glielo cavasse, e poscia di quello ne fusse libero, & assoluto possessore, e padrone." Ibid., pp. 86–87.

[72] Monticolo, "L'apparitio Sancti Marci," p. 130.

popular piety and civic patriotism into one cult. In his book on the saints, Gabriele Fiamma, a fifteenth-century canon regular of San Marco, summarized the conventional Venetian attitude toward the cult when he said, "I was born a Venetian and live in this happy homeland, protected by the prayers and guardianship of Saint Mark, from whom that Most Serene Republic acknowledges its greatness, its victories, and all its good fortune."[73] The cult fully dominated Venetian piety by the eleventh century, when the *inventio* of Mark's relics—in the words of Peyer, a "state miracle"—confirmed God's preference for the established form of ducal government. Thereafter, the Evangelist came gradually to signify far more than the privileges of the doges, until finally he came to personify the republic and to represent the entire civic corpus: in the ensuing centuries, as the doges lost their powers of lordship, ultimate authority became increasingly abstract and was invested in the mystical person of Saint Mark.[74] In addition, the Saint Mark cult had an institutional dimension of great economic and social significance. Not only was the basilica a state church and the artistic center of the city, but also the trustees for San Marco's endowment, the procurators, were by the thirteenth century Venice's most important source of credit, executors of private testaments, guardians for orphans, administrators of private trusts, and financial advisors. The procurators became a substitute paterfamilias with public responsibilities for preserving the family structure of patrician families; wealthy benefactors frequently left their entire patrimony to be managed by the procurators, thus attesting to their faith in the stability of the state. As Rheinhold C. Mueller has observed, "There was little dichotomy between private wealth and public policy."[75]

[73] "Son nato Veneziano e vivo in questa felice patria, difesa dall' orationi e dal presidio di S. Marco, da cui reconosce quella Serenissima Repubblica le grandezze, le vittorie e tutte le felici avventure sue." Quoted in Tramontin, "San Marco," p. 64.

[74] Peyer, *Stadt und Stadtpatron*, especially p. 15. Cf. Tramontin, "San Marco," p. 62. For a view that sees the Saint Mark cult as a fortuitous tie to papal authority rather than as a symbolic challenge to it, see Guglielmo Biasutti, *La tradizione marciana aquileiese*.

[75] Mueller, "The Procurators of San Marco," p. 220. Also see Demus, *The Church of San Marco*.

With such a total political, religious, and economic commitment to his cult, Saint Mark not surprisingly became synony-
mous with the Venetian republic.

SAINTS THEODORE, GEORGE, AND NICHOLAS

The Venetians prided themselves in their hagiolatry, and the
crown of saint-worship was the possession and veneration of
numerous relics. About all that William Wey, the fifteenth-
century English pilgrim to the Holy Land, recorded of his stay
in Venice was the abundance of sacred relics found there; his
list was long and impressive.[76] In the seventeenth century,
when most of the official designations of patron saints were
made, in addition to Saint Mark Venice listed as principal patrons the Virgin Annunciate and Lorenzo Giustiniani (the first
patriarch of Venice) and sixteen saints as secondary patrons.[77]
Many of the saints and beatifieds revered in Venice were of local
origin—such as Saint Pietro Orseolo, a tenth-century doge
who retired to a monastery to follow Saint Romuald—or had
relics housed in Venice, or were associated with some particular
event in Venetian history, such as Saint Marina, who was given
credit for the recovery of Padua in 1509, and Saint Roch, whose
adoration became official policy after the plague of 1576.[78] During the crusades, in particular, the remains of numerous saints
were stolen, bought, or transferred from the East to new homes
in the churches of Venice. Earlier Byzantine influences in Venice made the new Eastern cults seem less exotically oriental;
there were, for example, a large number of churches dedicated
to Old Testament prophets in Venice, as was common in Eastern

---

[76] William Wey, *The Itineraries . . . to Jerusalem, A.D. 1458 and A.D. 1462;
and to Saint James of Compostella, A.D. 1456,* p. 53. For a list of relics removed
to Venice see Nicole Hermann-Mascard, *Les reliques des saints,* pp. 368–69.

[77] Niero, "I santi patroni," p. 78.

[78] Ibid., pp. 87–88; Giovanni Musolino, "Feste religiose popolari," pp
224–25; Giovanni Musolino, A. Niero, and S. Tramontin, *Sainti e beati veneziani,* p. 105.

Christianity but comparatively rare in Western.[79] Yet, Venetian hagiolatry was more Roman than Byzantine: of the 160 saints pictured in the mosaics of San Marco, most are Western in origin.[80] Consequently, the idea of a Venice more Byzantine than Italian seems mere romance.

The possession of relics, in most instances acquired centuries after the end of Byzantine control over Venice, took on singular political importance in Venice, especially in the cases of three secondary saints whose hagiography contributed to civic mythology.[81] Saint Theodore was the most important of the three, but the history of his cult is a chronicle of confusions. The Venetian Theodore, who shared with Saint George the iconographical designation as an armor-clad warrior slaying a dragon, was possibly a fusion of two early Christians: one was a soldier martyred at Amasea in Pontus whose feast day was November 9, and the other a general of Heraclea whose feast day was February 7.[82] In 1096 the body of Saint Theodore of Amasea was brought to an unknown repository in Venice; that of Saint Theodore of Heraclea arrived in 1267 and was deposited in the church of San Salvatore (see map).[83] When the Senate declared in 1450 that on November 9 each year a ducal procession be formed in honor of Saint Theodore, the destination was to be San Salvatore; thus, on the feast day of one Theodore, the

[79] Silvio Tramontin, "Influsso orientale nel culto dei santi a Venezia fino al secolo XV," and Antonio Niero, "Culto dei santi dell'antico testamento," p. 157.

[80] Silvio Tramontin, "I santi dei mosaici marciani," especially pp. 135, 152.

[81] This section will be concerned only with those saints who had a place in the annual round of civic rituals and became important to the civic cult. For other saints honored in Venetian ritual see chapter 6.

[82] *Bibliotheca Sanctorum*, s.v. "Teodoro, soldato, santo, martire ad Amasea," by Agostino Amore and Maria Chiara Celletti, 12:238–42. Cf. Lucy Menzies, *The Saints in Italy* p. 428. On the legends associated with Saint Theodore see Hippolyte Delehaye, *Les légendes greques des saints militaires*, 1975, pp. 11–43.

[83] Andrea Dandolo, *Chronicon venetum*, col. 336; Niero, "I santi patroni," pp. 91–92; Musolino, "Feste religiose popolari," p. 230. The Theodore transfers and the revival of the cult in 1450 contradict the claim that "the Byzantine warrior was allowed to vanish entirely in the restoration [of Saint Mark] of 1094." Geary, *Furta Sacra*, pp. 111–12.

relics of the other were revered.[84] The 1450 decree of a *festum solemnis* for Saint Theodore seemed to indicate a revival of interest in the saint who, according to local tradition, had preceded Saint Mark as the local patron; and indeed the cult continued to receive special attention during the following century, culminating in 1552 when the Scuola di San Teodoro, founded as a scuola piccola in the thirteenth century, was elevated to the status of a Scuola Grande.[85] This elevation gave the devotees of Saint Theodore a position in all the great civic processions.

If the largely fourteenth-century sources can be believed, Saint Theodore was the first protector-saint of the Venetian *dux* at the time when the *dux* was still a Byzantine military commander of a province, for whom Theodore would have been a symbol of the sovereignty of Constantinople. The first ducal chapel at the new governmental seat of Rialto was built and dedicated to Theodore in or before 819 by a wealthy Greek named Marco, who was often confused in Venetian lore with a more famous sixth-century general of the same name. But after the *translatio* of Saint Mark the first patron saint lost his place of importance, and his chapel disappeared or was incorporated into the more imposing basilica of San Marco. In the basilica mosaics, the two representations of Theodore as a soldier placed him as a counterpart to Saint George. Memory of him as the first protector was de-emphasized if not erased.[86] As an unwanted reminder of Venice's early subjection to the superior authority of Byzantium, it is likely that Saint Theodore was relegated to the status of a minor saint until the slow eclipse of Byzantine power in the fourteenth and fifteenth centuries resolved and made irrelevant any political problem with his cult.

[84] MCV, Cod. Cicogna 2043, fol. 31; Nicolò Trevisan, "Cronaca veneta dalle origine al 1585," BMV, MS Italiano VII, 519 (8438), fol. 262v (new foliation); Sanuto, *Le vite dei dogi*, p. 89. As late as 1448 the relics of Theodore of Amasea were still highly honored and were still distinguished from those of Theodore of Heraclea. See a description of a ducal procession to San Nicolò al Lido in Giorgio Dolfin, "Cronica di Venezia," BMV, MS Italiano VII, 794 (8503), fol. 302. Cf. Demus, *The Church of San Marco*, p. 22, n. 74.

[85] Pullan, *Rich and Poor in Venice*, p. 34.

[86] Demus, *The Church of San Marco*, pp. 21–22. Cf. Tramontin, "I santi dei mosaici marciani," p. 142.

The possibility has been raised, however, that the tradition of Saint Theodore as the first patron of Venice is pure canard. Antonio Niero rejects the belief that Saint Theodore was the first protector, argues that the earliest sign of his cult in Venice comes from the tenth century, and suggests that the tradition of Saint Theodore as the first palladium arose during the War of Chioggia, fought against Genoa between 1377 and 1381.[87] Indeed, Theodore, the warrior saint, may have been re-elevated in the late fourteenth century as a foil to Genoa's soldier-patron, Saint George, and to provide Venice with a military protector different from George. Theodore was not by then the iconographic competition to Mark that he had been even the century before, when Saint George, rather than Theodore, was chosen for a relief prominently placed on the west facade of San Marco. But Theodore's star was rising even before the Genoese wars, for in 1329 his statue was placed atop one of the two columns in the Piazzetta of the Ducal Palace, making him an equal partner to Mark in guarding this distinguished entrance by sea to the political and religious center of the Venetian dominion.[88] Probably only excavations for the chapel of Saint Theodore that reputedly preceded San Marco could determine whether the early *duces* did, after all, honor Saint Theodore and then later expunge all traces of his patronage in favor of Saint Mark, or whether the tradition of his initial protection was the invention of some later period. At any rate, by the sixteenth century he was widely believed to have been the first patron and was thus a political and military symbol second only to Mark, superior even to George, and the object of official ritual devotions consisting of an annual ducal procession.[89]

Respect for Saint George was nonetheless of long standing in Venice, and although he never received the official recognition accorded to Theodore, George was important in art and mythology. Like Theodore he was a saint made much of in Constantinople, but, unlike Theodore, he attained immense popularity in the West, becoming the patron of England, Catalonia,

---

[87] Niero, "I santi patroni," pp. 92–93.
[88] Demus, *The Church of San Marco*, pp. 22, 133–34.
[89] On the procession see Sanuto, *Le vite dei dogi*, p. 89.

Aragon, Portugal, and more than a hundred Italian cities.[90] His cult, one of the oldest in Venice, probably came from Ravenna, and he was the object of homage by the Particiaci doges, who had a *sacellum* built for him sometime before 829; the Particiaci's choice of Saint George may have served their anti-Carolingian, pro-Byzantine policies as did Saint Mark: one scholar suggests that naming the island opposite the Ducal Palace (see map) after Saint George identified the strait of water in between with the Dardanelles, at the time also named after George, and thus made a metaphor for Venice's Byzantine connection.[91]

Saint George's cult spread in the eleventh and twelfth centuries. The mosaics in San Marco picture him in three places standing next to Theodore and once as a solitary soldier; in the thirteenth century the procurators of San Marco chose to commission for the west front of the basilica a relief of Saint George as a parallel to a Greek relief of the soldier Saint Demetrius, brought to Venice in the spoils of the Fourth Crusade; and it was Saint George who figured among the triad of protectors in the fourteenth-century fable of the fisherman and the ring.[92] In 1462 the Senate ordered the captain of the sea or any other official in the Aegean to procure "by prudent means and without violence" the famed relic of the head of Saint George; this commission accomplished, the head was deposited in the monastic church of San Giorgio Maggiore, where in 1971 Kenneth Setton rediscovered it in a cupboard.[93] Besides the monks of San Giorgio, a scuola of Dalmatians (San Giorgio degli Schiavoni) made the soldier-saint their patron; and for them Vittore Carpaccio executed the famous cycle of paintings on Saint George's life. By the sixteenth century, however, the Venetians honored Saint George principally because they possessed a famous relic. Saint George was a popular protector of Venice, to be sure, but he was not an official patron, nor had he any longer

[90] Kenneth M. Setton, "Saint George's Head," pp. 2–4. On the Greek legends regarding Saint George see Delehaye, *Les légendes greques*, pp. 45–76.

[91] Carlo Candiani, "Antiche titoli delle chiese," pp. 111–31.

[92] Tramontin, "I santi dei mosaici marciani," p. 143; Demus, *The Church of San Marco*, pp. 126–35.

[93] Setton, "Saint George's Head," pp. 9–10.

a capacity for political symbolism comparable to that of Saint Mark and Saint Theodore. This fact was apparent in the absence of any civic ritual devoted exclusively to Saint George.

As patron of sailors, Saint Nicholas had a sinecure in the maritime republic. The cult of Saint Nicholas spread in the West after citizens of Bari rescued the saint's relics from Myra in 1087, an act that consequently turned their city into a pilgrimage center. Venetians made a second raid on Myra in 1116 and claimed to have brought back the true remains of Nicholas, but they were never able to convince the rest of the world that their relics were more authentic than those of Bari.[94] Patrick Geary explains these two transfers and the Venetian *inventio* of Saint Mark in 1094 as manifestations of the commercial competition between Bari and Venice for control of the transport and marketing of Apulian grain, and in fact the two earliest accounts of the Barian transfer emphasize that the Barians were initially moved to steal Saint Nicholas' remains by rumors that the Venetians were planning to do so themselves.[95] The acquisition of the body of Saint Nicholas implied that his protection and favor would be granted to the possessor, an important factor in competition over shipping lanes. Saint Nicholas in the end divided his favor: Bari became the goal of pilgrims, but Venice captured the commerce. As was the case with the cults of Saints Mark and Theodore, the legend of the Saint Nicholas transfer was closely tied to the secular history of the Venetian commune. The Venetians placed their relics in a monastery on the Lido (see map), which had already been built in 1053 in honor of Saint Nicholas.[96] Nicholas was widely popular among the sea-going populace of Venice: he appeared seven times, always in prominent places, in the San Marco mosaics; he was the third protector-saint in the legend of the fisherman and

---

[94] Geary, *Furta Sacra*, pp. 115–27; Adriaan D. DeGroot, *Saint Nicholas*, pp. 31–35; Charles W. Jones, *Saint Nicholas of Myra, Bari, and Manhattan*, pp. 172–209. Also see idem, *The Saint Nicholas Liturgy and its Literary Relationships (Ninth to Twelfth Centuries)*.

[95] Geary, *Furta Sacra*, pp. 124–27; Jones, *Saint Nicholas of Myra, Bari, and Manhattan*, pp. 83, 177, 194.

[96] Tramontin, "I santi dei mosaici marciani," p. 137; Musolino, "Feste religiose popolari," p. 218.

the ring; and he was honored in official rites and in a parish festival.

The doge and civil magistrates revered Nicholas twice a year. First, the church of San Nicolò al Lido was from the eleventh century the location of an annual rite of *benedictio* to propitiate the sea.[97] There is nothing to indicate that the ceremony was at first any more than a simple invocation of Saint Nicholas to protect Venetian sailors and a benediction of the Adriatic with holy water, but when the *benedictio* rite evolved into the elaborate Ascension Day marriage of the sea, discussed in the next chapter, a pilgrimage visit to San Nicolò was retained. The ritual homage the patriarch and the doge paid at the monastic church signified perhaps that Saint Nicholas himself officiated over the marriage of the doge and the sea. Until 1172 the location of San Nicolò was also the site where citizens assembled to acclaim the new doges, and the monastery there was used throughout the Renaissance as a banquet hall for departing captains general. San Nicolò al Lido was gradually transformed from a center of peculiar religious and political significance, rivaling San Marco and the Ducal Palace, to the gateway and border of the city. In his protection of the Venetians at sea and his patronage of the doge and captain general, Saint Nicholas complemented and balanced Saint Mark, both in his spiritual functions and in the urban location of his major shrine.

The second official annual occasion was on December 6, the feast day of Saint Nicholas, which was commemorative as well as solicitous of the saint's favor. Doge Enrico Dandolo, the hero of the fabled conquest of Constantinople in 1204, died before he could return to Venice for his triumphal reception; so his successor, Pietro Ziani, had a chapel built in the Ducal Palace in memory of the blind warrior, dedicated it to Saint Nicholas, and decreed that every year on December 6 the doge and Signoria hear a mass sung there.[98] If the chapel dedication is an indication, Saint Nicholas seems to have been credited with the success of Venetian naval exploits, and it became an obligation

[97] Samuele Romanin, *Storia documentata di Venezia*, 1:281; Lina Padoan Urban, "La festa della Sensa nelle arti e nell'iconografia," p. 312.

[98] Michiel, *Le origine delle feste veneziane*, 2:139–91; MCV, MS Venier P.D. 517b, under heading "Decembre."

of the doge to offer prayers to Nicholas in order to retain the saint's favor. The Saint Nicholas chapel was the only one within the walls of the Ducal Palace that hosted an annual ducal cere-monial visit and thus had an affinity—albeit a relatively minor one—to the doge's other private chapel, the basilica of San Marco. For the ducal and ecclesiastical establishment Saint Mark and Saint Nicholas formed a "binomial mystery," a dual protectorship that signified Venetian independence and rights over the sea lanes and symbolized, in addition, what Roberto Cessi has identified as the concrete political relationship be-tween the doge and the patriarch.[99] In representing the city's evangelical heritage and its maritime destiny, the pairing of Saint Mark and Saint Nicholas was similar to the pairing of the doge and patriarch, who stood respectively for the political and ecclestiastical authority mystically unified in the Venetian res publica. From a theoretical and a practical point of view, these two partnerships were unequal: both Saint Nicholas and the patriarch possessed divine rights and privileges, but their au-thority never matched that of Saint Mark or the doge. Hence, the primacy of the political hierarchy in all aspects of life was again enunciated in a sanctified context; and the doge's atten-dance at mass in the Saint Nicholas chapel not only confirmed his political concern for the Nicholas cult but adopted the cult for the magnification of the doge and republic.

Saint Nicholas also enjoyed popular religious devotions that had intriguing parallels to the ducal ceremonies. The parish of San Nicolò dei Mendicoli (see map) was one of the poorest in Venice (a condition echoed in the name mendicoli) and was almost exclusively populated by fishermen, who annually elected a parish chief called the "doge of the Nicolotti." The name is significant since it offers both a popular imitation of elite polit-ical terminology and an index of the extent to which the saint's cult reached the common people. After each new plebian doge was elected, he proceeded to the parish church of San Nicolò dei Mendicoli, where he knelt before the altar of the saint to swear loyalty to the parish. The parish priest formally consigned to

[99] Cessi's work on this point is cited and discussed in Tramontin, "I santi dei mosaici marciani," p. 137.

him a standard depicting Saint Nicholas, and a Te Deum was sung. The following day the patrician doge honored the doge of the Nicolotti in a formal reception. Throughout the year at public festivals the doge of the Nicolotti was allowed to dress in scarlet satins and in the seventeenth and eighteenth centuries to wear the wig and cap of a gentleman.[100] Unfortunately, the extant information on this popular ceremony is, to my knowledge, entirely from the early modern period, so there is no record of when the practice began. The populace of Venice, however, had been divided sometime before the sixteenth century into factions of Nicolotti and Castellani, who on some holidays fought pitched battles with fists and sticks for the possession of a bridge; thus the institution of the doge of the Nicolotti may have signified official recognition of an ancient geographical division of the populace. The imitation of an elite political institution was common in late medieval and Renaissance Europe, where Lords of Misrule held sway on festive occasions; yet the doge of the Nicolotti was not elected in jest or as a burlesque of elite practices, as was the custom elsewhere at carnival time. To what degree the doge of the Nicolotti was anything more than a ceremonial representative of the parish is unknown, but his office shows that the lower classes were neither unaware of the charm and political symbolism of the annual ducal ceremonies nor ignorant of the significance of a ducal investiture.

The Saint Nicholas honored by the Venetian fisherfolk was, after the Virgin, one of the most universally popular saints in the Middle Ages.[101] Several legends portray Nicholas as a maritime saint, saving sailors from peril in a storm, rescuing drowning men, or walking on the waves to calm a storm; but he was often called on to provide help in other emergencies. He was credited with providing dowries for poor marriageable girls, giving babies to barren couples, and succoring children; in short he was, according to Adriaan De Groot, the guardian

[100] Musolino, "Feste religiose popolari," p. 219.

[101] The monuments to Saint Nicholas in Europe surely number in the thousands. Meisen's quite incomplete list of monuments in France, Germany, and the Low Countries enumerated 2,137 items. Jones, *Saint Nicholas of Myra, Bari, and Manhattan*, p. 3.

of the entire process of human reproduction and family growth, from courtship and procreation to the protection of vulnerable offspring. De Groot sees the combination of fertility and maritime themes as particularly fortuitous in psychological terms, since there are analogies between the emergencies of shipwreck and childbirth: both are moments largely out of human control when life hangs in the balance; only a safe arrival in port or parturition brings relief of tension and suffering. Fertility symbolism was clearly woven into the very fabric of the Saint Nicholas cult; yet another aspect of Saint Nicholas was that he gave without demanding anything in return—he did not have to be propitiated like a harsh Neptune—and thus he symbolized the higher power of giving in any social relationship. His other patronates of transport, communication, trade, baking, and moneylending (bread and money "grow") conform to this complex of helping, giving, and ensuring fertility.[102] In Venice these elemental functions, so obviously important to the populace, were fully recognized in the governmental attention to Saint Nicholas's cult epitomized by the homage rendered to him at the Ascension Day marriage of the sea ceremonies; and the popular cult, so alive with fertility associations, was made an institution with the doge of the Nicolotti. There was in this case complete harmony between popular desires and elite priorities.

THE LEGENDS of the founding of Venice and the ceremonies for saints' feast days catechized sixteenth-century Venetians about their city's noble foundation in freedom, about its divinely ordained military and maritime destiny, about ducal rights to authority over ecclesiastical institutions, and, most of all, about Venice's autonomy from other powers in the world. None of these ideas belonged only to Venice; any city or country, of

---

[102] De Groot, Saint Nicholas, pp. 108–9, 152–60, 163, 177. A mythic figure as historically important and as widely popular as Saint Nicholas must not be reduced to a single set of symbolic and pyschological significances; thus, De Groot's thesis should be taken with extreme caution. I have abstracted some of his observations here because they seem to elucidate better the Venetian cult of Saint Nicholas, but one should be fully aware that, for other places and times, this fertility interpretation may be artificial.

course, could. and usually did pretend to special divine favor through hagiography. And, although there was a singular concordance in the sixteenth century between Venice's liturgical and hagiographical heritage and its political ideals, discerning scholars of the times were less likely to be convinced than were their ancestors. They needed to find a more historically grounded justification for Venice's far-reaching claims, a supporting argument based on human rather than mystical sources. That support was to be found in the gifts of Pope Alexander III.

THREE

A GRATEFUL POPE
AND A DOWERED BRIDE:
IMPERIAL PREROGATIVES

THE DONATION OF POPE ALEXANDER III

The ducal *trionfi,* that is, the gifts of Pope Alexander III, symbolized Venice's jurisdictional autonomy. According to the tradition accepted in the sixteenth century, Pope Alexander III
gave these *trionfi* to Doge Sebastiano Ziani in 1177 to repay
him for his role in the struggle between the pope and Emperor
Frederick Barbarossa. Frederick's expedition against the towns
of Lombardy and Tuscany alarmed the pope, who was ever
antagonistic to imperial interference in Italian affairs; therefore, fearing capture by the German knights, Alexander fled
and, in disguise, sought refuge among the ". . . pious, generous, and humble Venetians, lovers of virtue and good Christians."[1] Alexander spent his first night in Venice outside the
door of San Salvatore, then moved to Santa Maria della Carità
(see map), where a pilgrim recognized him and reported his
presence to the doge. Doge Sebastiano Ziani unhesitatingly offered to protect the pope and to mediate in the dispute with the
emperor. In thanks for the doge's support, Pope Alexander con-

---

[1] [Pope Alexander] "Montete in barca poi con vigoria, / per gionger quanto
prima a la cittade / dove risciede la gran Signoria, / saggia gentil, & piena di
bontade, / credendo, che la gran malinconia / ch'havea nel cor sia estinta per
pietade, / di generosi, & humil Venetiani, / amator di virtuosi, & buon
Christiani." Ferrarese, *Historia di Papa Alessand III,* no pagination. The best
sources for the donation story are BMV, MS Italiano IX, 28 (6301), and BMV,
MS Italiano VII, 728 (8070); Biblioteca Nazionale, Florence, MS Magliabec-
chiana XXV, 8, 273, col. 2; MCV, I, 383 (1497), fols. 25v ff.; and the poem by
Pietro de' Natali. All are published in O. Zenatti, "Il poemetto di Pietro de'
Natali sulla pace di Venezia tra Alessandro III e Federico Barbarossa." Cf.
Marcus Paschalicus, *Orationes due Marci Paschalici philosophiae et theologiae
doctoris. Altera de scientiarum laudibus. Altera vero de Veneta sponsaliorum
maris ratione,* and Tramontin, "Realità e leggenda," p. 57.

ceded to Ziani and his successors the first of the *trionfi,* the
right to carrý a white candle in processions on major feast days
as a "sign of noble honor" and as a token of the pope's love.[2]
When Doge Ziani commissioned two envoys to approach Barbarossa in Pavia, he sealed their orders with wax; but the pope
wished the wax seals to be exchanged for something more dignified and thus granted the doge the privilege of using lead
seals in imitation of papal practice.[3] Barbarossa, having answered the ambassadors' entreaties with threats of death to all
Venetians unless (according to one source) they surrendered the
pope in irons, commanded his son, Otto, to lead a fleet of some
seventy-five galleys against Venice.[4] Ziani steadfastly prepared
a much smaller fleet to defend the pope and city. As Doge Ziani
embarked for battle, Alexander invested him with a sword,
symbolic of the justice of the doge's cause, and assured salvation

[2] "Agiongendo quel [Pope Alexander] disse: 'Figliol franco, / questo a te
dono et a' toi subcessori, / che mai per tempo alcun non venga manco, / ma
sempre quel portate in vostri honori / vele processione et feste grande, / o sia
vostre persone dentro o fori.' " Zenatti, "Il poemetto di Pietro de' Natali," p.
142. "Donòno el cirio biancho el nobel duca / et a so' sucessori in tute
bande. / E vol che quelo seco senpre duca, [i]'n segno de fede vera e puri-
tade, / et che nel mondo questo tal relucha." Appendix I in Zenatti, "Il poemetto di Pietro de' Natali," pp. 176–77. "Come alla Chiesa il Papa fù arri-
vato, / un cereo bianco egli si fece dare, / e quello dopò al Duce ha
presentato, / che la festa di San Marco il die portare, / & esso il prese, hav-
endosi inchinato, / e' l Papa disse, ciò s'hà da stimare, / come per segno di
notabile honore, / e farà ancora segno del mio amore." Ferrarese, *Historia di
Papa Alessand III,* no pagination. Ferrarese blames the entire confrontation on
the forgeries of a false cardinal and is hence far less anti-imperial than the
other writers.

[3] Some of the sources make the new seals of gold or silver. Zenatti, "Il
poemetto di Pietro de' Natali," p. 146. The following quotations are from
Zenatti. "Vedendo el papa la comissione / sigelata cum cera, cum
fervore / subito volse far provixione / che 'l doxe havesse sua bola
pendente / d'oro, d'arzento e de tuta raxone." Appendix I, p. 167. "Volendo la
credenza in carta dare, / bollandola con ciera, immantanente / il papa in-
pronpte di metal fe' fare, / qual oggi vedi s'usa; e tal consente / pria
s'inprontasse, ma non col favore / fanno li tre ch'oggi bollan pendente." Appendix II, p. 186. " 'Io [Pope Alexander] voio che questa letera sia bollada con
bolla de plombo, sula qual sia da un ladi misier san Marcho e lo doxe apresso,
e dal'oltro ladi sia scrito el nome del doxe; cossì como vien bollade le mie letere
con bolla de plumbo e con misier sen Piero entro.' " Appendix III. p. 194.

[4] Ibid., p. 194.

to all who touched it.[5] The Venetians, victorious despite their inferior numbers, captured Otto and a number of imperial barons, whom Doge Ziani presented to the pope as captives. As a reward the pope gave Ziani a gold ring and the right to marry the sea as a token of the doge's "lordship of the sea" and "in sign of perpetual dominion."[6] Otto came from his prison to the pope and implored that he be allowed to return to his father to counsel him to relent; then, as the pope's vassal, Otto persuaded Barbarossa to sign a formal peace treaty.[7] Consequently, on Ascension Day, 1177, Frederick and Alexander were reconciled at San Marco, where the emperor kissed the pope's feet; in memory of the peace Alexander granted a plenary indulgence to all those who in the future visited San Marco on Ascension.[8]

The peace secured, Alexander set sail for Ancona in the company of Barbarossa, Ziani, and various Venetians. When they landed, the citizens of Ancona appeared with two umbrellas—

[5] "Una spada poi in li [Pope Alexander] fece dare, / e quella benedì con propria bocca / ciascuno che con quella haura a toccare / giù di galea convien che trabocca, / e tutti gli altri haverete a superare, / onde alli nostri il Paradiso tocca, / chi morirà andarà in santa gloria, / prego il Signor, che vi doni vittoria. / La spada li fù data per segnale, / che i Principi a venire la portasse, / il Duceando contra l' Imperiale, / & ordinò ch'ogn'un s'apparecchiasse, / l'armata già come s'havesse l'ale, / l'aere, e la terra parea che tremasse, / e ad ogni qualitade di persone / diè il Papa santo la benedittione." Ferrarese, *Historia di Papa Alessand III*, no pagination.

[6] Zenatti, "Il poemetto di Pietro de' Natali," p. 148.

[7] Ibid., pp. 170–71.

[8] Barbarossa: "Quale più piace a vostra santitate / et de voi duce, [l'] è buon metter la falça, / si ch'el se taglia tutte le mal note / erbe cressute de falsa semença, / et le buone rimanga ben netate.' / Dato a cotal parole audiença / questi maestri: 'Che te par de fare? / Che 'l padre meo sia ala vostra presença, / el qual per modo alcun non vol restare / ch'el non attenda ben de far l'acordo, / che 'l m'à promesso: a voi sta el dimandare / Ma per vostra honorança ve aricordo, / che ne la ecclesia de miser san Marco / il sia conçato cotanto discordo. / Quivi gl'imperator stenderà l'arco / dela mala vogliença per lui tolta / contra de voi, aleviando el carco.' " Ibid., p. 157. The account of the reconciliation in Martin da Canal is far more acerbic. *Les estoires de Venise*, p. 40. On the indulgence Pope Alexander granted see "Dell'origine et accresimento della città di Venetia et isole della lagune principiato dell'anno CCCCXXI et molte altre cose notabili fino l'anno MDLVI," Syracuse University Library (hereafter SUL), Ranke MS 69, fol. 72r.

insignia of princely distinction—as gifts for the pope and emperor, but Alexander refused to accept his until a third umbrella was provided for the doge.[9] Later, as the party approached Rome, city officials met them with eight banners and long silver trumpets, which Alexander gave to Ziani as an additional honor.[10] Doge Ziani, with his newly acquired *trionfi*—the white candle, lead seals, sword, gold ring, umbrella, eight banners, and silver trumpets—entered the Holy City, and at Saint John Lateran the pope solemnly confirmed the privileges and honors he had bestowed on the basilica of San Marco, the commune of Venice, and the doge.[11]

This legend did at least veil some historical truths. An English witness to the signing of the peace, one Nicholas of Dunstable, recounted the events with great attention to visual detail—but mentioned nothing of the papal gifts to the doge.[12] There was, in fact, neither a naval victory nor even a naval battle; in 1176 the Lombard League defeated the imperial army at the battle of Legnano. Venice did not actively participate in the war and was so equivocal in choosing sides that San Marco was chosen as a neutral place for the peace negotiations. The doge's role as a mediating prince at the peace talks in San Marco, however, contributed significantly to the prestige of his office and to the genesis of the legend. The peace marked the

[9] "E qui l'onbrela el papa al doxe dona / e a so' sucessori, e cuscì porta / a tute feste, come el vero sona." Appendix I in Zenatti, "Il poemetto di Pietro de' Natali," p. 177. "Giunti in Ancona, il popol lor insenna / a presentarli onbrelle due, ma il papa / un' altra terminò che 'l dogie inpenna, / et sempre per memoria innanzi i capa." Appendix II in Zenatti, "Il poemetto di Pietro de' Natali," p. 190.

[10] "Questo anchora al doxe se ge dona, / per più magnificar: trombe d'arzento, / che avanti senpre la festa li sona." Appendix I in ibid., p. 177. "In Roma giunti, al papa è presentato / di sol quattro colori otto vexili, / scorgon delli elementi un doppio stato, / con trono uno e tube otto argentee e brilli, / le qual tantosto il papa largì al duca / per preminentie di futuri stilli." Appendix II in ibid., p. 190.

[11] Pope Alexander: " 'Mo ch'io som in la mi seça, io ve confermo tute le perdonançe e le honorançe ch'io ve ò concedude ala gliexia de misier sen Marco et a vu' et al comun de Veniexia como a fioli dela santa mare Gliexia.' " Appendix III in ibid., p. 198.

[12] Rodney M. Thomson, "An English Eyewitness of the Peace of Venice, 1177."

failure of the German emperors to assert political control over northern Italy, a reality that explains the anti-imperial tone of the story. Despite their reluctance to defend Italian liberty and papal honor, the Venetians did not come away from the peace empty-handed: Frederick allowed Venetian traders a complete exemption from imperial tolls throughout the Holy Roman Empire, and Pope Alexander transferred the ecclesiastical jurisdiction over Dalmatia to the patriarch of Grado, an act that furthered Venetian dominion over the Adriatic.

During the late twelfth century Venice was subject to recurring threats from Constantinople, Norman Sicily, and Hungary, as well as from the German Empire; so the legend may also represent the successful elimination of all of these threats to Venetian independence. In a sense then, the imperial and papal concessions and the failure of Barbarossa to establish hegemony in northern Italy signaled the full assertion of Venetian lordship over the Adriatic. The symbolic gifts in the legend may, furthermore, represent the effort Venice began to make at that time to impose treaties legalizing its dominance over the area.[13] Pope Alexander's legendary grant to Doge Ziani of the right to marry the sea, therefore, may have symbolized a particular political situation, but one somewhat different from that described in the legend told in later centuries.

Elements of the legend existed in the thirteenth century, but they were inchoate. Bonincontro de' Bovi's 1317 narration of the legend is the oldest extant version.[14] By 1319 there was a fresco cycle depicting the peace in the chapel of San Nicolò in the Ducal Palace, and the story also appeared in Doge Andrea

[13] Lane, *Venice*, pp. 57–58; William H. McNeill, *Venice*, pp. 26–28.

[14] Zanetti, "Il poemetto di Pietro de' Natali," p. 123. Zanetti argues (p. 122, n. 1) that there were probably paintings of the event in the Ducal Palace during the thirteenth century. This opinion is confirmed by a sixteenth-century source that states that the Senate "deliberandosi cinquanta anni doppo, che si dipingesse ne muri della Sala del maggior Consiglio, tutto il successo di quella guerra." Girolamo Bardi, *Vittoria navale ottenuta dalla republica venetiana contra Othone, figliuolo di Federico primo imperatore; per la restitutione di Alessandro terzo, pontefice massimo, venuto à Venetia*, p. 30. An ellipsis in the MS of Martin da Canal's *Les estoires de Venise*, p. 40, prevents us from knowing what parts of the legend other than the gift of the umbrella were current in 1275.

Dandolo's mid-fourteenth-century chronicle. The definitive, fully developed source, however, is the poem composed in 1381 or 1382 by Pietro de' Natali, the bishop of Equilio (Iesolo).[15] Members or persons in the employ of the governing Venetian establishment wrote all the fourteenth-century accounts; thus the legend as retold above was probably a late invention, officially asserted for political reasons some time after Venice had conquered Constantinople and firmly established mastery over the eastern Mediterranean, and it appealed to Venetians because it flattered not just the aristocratic doge but them all. Paintings, chronicles, histories, and inscriptions referred to the legendary gifts, but as late as 1485 it was possible for a Venetian writer to recount the events of the 1170s and to discuss Frederick Barbarossa's Italian campaign without mention of the Alexandrine gifts.[16] Evidently some skepticism was still possible. By the sixteenth century, nevertheless, the story of Alexander III's gift to Doge Ziani had become official dogma, and when paintings were planned to replace those destroyed in the 1577 fires in the Hall of the Great Council, the inclusion of the legend in a cycle of history paintings was hardly a striking innovation (see figures 1–4).[17] The legend became the standard historical justification for the Venetians' jurisdictional privilege and their special devotion to the Holy See. On the eve of the famous interdict against Venice of 1606–7, a dispute between the Venetian ambassador and Pope Clement VIII degenerated into a quarrel over the whole history of Venetian-papal relations. When Clement charged Venice with having stolen papal lands in the Romagna and denied the Venetians' long loyalty to the Papacy, the ambassador countered with the story of Doge Ziani's service to Alexander III. Even though the pope ridiculed

[15] Zanetti, "Il poemetto di Pietro de' Natali," pp. 105–26.

[16] Dolfin, "Cronica di Venezia," BMV, MS Italiano VII, 794 (8503), fol. 68r–v. For a list of the sources defending the legend see Cornelio Frangipane, Per la historia di Papa Alessandro III publica nella sala regia à Roma, & del maggior consiglio à Venetia. Allegatione in iure.

[17] These paintings, still in place, are described and interpreted by Girolamo Bardi, Dichiaratione di tutte le istorie, che si contengono ne i quadri posti novamente nelle sale dello scrutinio, & del gran consiglio, del palagio ducale della serenissima republica di Vinegia. Also see Staale Sinding-Larsen, Christ in the Council Hall, pp. 21–29.

the account as mere myth, the Venetians, at least, still accorded the story great respect.[18]

Each of Pope Alexander's gifts came to be interpreted as a symbol of a distinct ducal privilege or of a specific attribute of the Venetian polity. The gifts together affirmed Venice's piety, devotion to the Church, and freedom from imperial supervision; the *trionfi* were carried in all major ducal processions, and many of them were common iconographical attributes of Venice in paintings and sculpture.

Only by a characteristic transmutation, however, did the white candle come to depict the true and pure faith of the Venetians. Long before the legendary gift of Alexander, bishops and popes had a candle carried before them in religious processions as a symbol of respect, and a candle-bearer also preceded the Byzantine emperors in a triumph or in an entrance to a city.[19] The candle probably did first appear as a ducal symbol in the 1170s, as the legend would have it, but for entirely different reasons than those given. Without first obtaining the papal permission necessary to destroy a consecrated church with impunity, either Doge Vital II Michiel or Sebastiano Ziani dismantled the chapel of San Geminiano to enlarge the piazza in front of San Marco. For this neglect the pope anathematized the doge and removed the anathema only when the doge agreed to rebuild the church and to commit himself and his successors to an annual penitential visit to the new San Geminiano. At the processional visit each year the parish priest of San Geminiano, standing on the location of the old church, recalled the purpose of the visit, reminded the doge of his obligation to return the following year, and gave him a candle to be used in all the ducal processions for the coming year.[20] Through the introduction of

[18] Grendler, *The Roman Inquisition*, p. 252.

[19] Fasoli, "Liturgia e cerimoniale ducale," p. 273.

[20] Ibid.; Sanuto, *Le vite dei dogi*, pp. 90, 298–99; ASV, Collegio Cerimoniale 1, fol. 8r; Sansovino, *Venetia*, 1663, pp. 109, 496–97; Michiel, *Le origine delle feste veneziane*, 1:43–52; MCV, MS Venier P.D. 517b, under heading "Ottava di pasqua"; BMV, MS Latin III, 172 (2276), fols. 52v–53r; Emmanuele Antonio Cicogna, *Delle inscrizioni veneziane*, 4:5, 8, n. 1; Doglioni, *Le cose notabili*, pp. 47–48. Tassini calls the original church, destroyed to make room for the enlarged piazza, San Allorquando. *Feste, spettacoli*, p. 77.

1. *(top)* Leandro Bassano, *Pope Alexander III Gives the White Candle to Doge Sebastiano Ziani in San Marco.*   2. *(bottom)* Francesco Bassano, *At the Point of Departing with the Armada against Barbarossa, Doge Sebastiano Ziani Receives the Sword from Pope Alexander III.*

3. *(top)* Andrea Michieli, called "il Vicentino," *Doge Sebastiano Ziani Presents Otto to Pope Alexander III and Receives the Ring with Which He Celebrates the Marriage of the Sea Every Year.*   4. *(bottom)* Girolamo Gambarato, *Accompanied by Frederick Barbarossa and Doge Sebastiano Ziani, Pope Alexander III Arrives at Ancona and Gives to Ziani a Golden Umbrella.*

the Alexander III legend, the candle, originally a symbol of penitence, was deliberately transformed into an insigne of honor, privilege, and faith.

In the ducal processions the chaplain of the doge or an acolyte carried the white candle, and it was understood to be an accessory of the doge himself; if for some reason the doge did not participate in a procession, the candle was not carried. Sansovino said that the candle recalled the promise of the doges to obtain peace for the Papacy and symbolized the *patronia* of the doge over the basilica of San Marco.[21] One sixteenth-century writer reported that the candle showed how God had "illuminated" Doge Ziani and how Ziani had abolished darkness in the world when he had acted on behalf of Pope Alexander.[22] Another said all of the gifts "showed that by means of their aid, kindness, virtues, [the Venetians] freed the Church of God from so many misfortunes, which had hung over it, so that not only the Roman Church but all of Italy must be always obliged [to them]."[23] The candle, therefore, identified the doge as the patron and protector of the Church, both the Roman Church through his defense of Pope Alexander and the Venetian Church through his proprietorship of San Marco.

The Venetians were correct in pointing out that the use of lead seals was a mark of particular distinction. Venice was the only maritime republic in Italy that did not follow the chancellery practices of the communes in using wax seals for official documents but imitated instead the fashion of the popes, Byzantine emperors, Italian dukes, and Norman princes. The Venetian use of lead or occasionally gold or silver seals was a practice reserved for the highest authorities, a sign of quasi-sovereignty. It has been suggested that the Venetians adopted the Byzantine imperial style of lead seals when they considered

[21] Sansovino, *Venetia*, 1604, fol. 321v.

[22] Pope Alexander to Doge Ziani: "Io vi di questo Cerio imp[re]mese de Sume, acciò Iddio vi illumini, et che colui, che è le tenebre, & da voi sia illuminado." SUL, Ranke MS 69, fol. 70v.

[23] "Dimostrò la Chiesa d'Iddio essere stata liberata dalle tante calamità, che gli soprastavavo, mediante gli aiuti loro, alla bontà, & virtù de' quali non solo bisognava, che la Chiesa Romana, ma l'Italia tutta fosse per sempre obligata." Bardi, *Vittoria navale*, p. 30.

themselves emancipated from Byzantium, but the earliest examples of the lead seals are from the mid-twelfth century, much later than the Venetian emancipation, and the earliest Venetian official documents, dating from between 1090 and 1108, lack such seals. The oldest lead seal comes from the period of Doge Pietro Polani (1130–48) and thus clearly precedes the supposed donation by Alexander III. Despite its inability to explain the origin of Venetian lead seals, however, the legend's widespread acceptance gave Venice great prestige, a prestige illustrated by the Florentines' request to Pope Alexander V (1409–10) for a grant to employ lead seals "just like the Venetians obtained from Pope Alexander III."[24] The lead seals, like the sword, umbrella, banners, and trumpets, were primarily symbols of a political sovereignty that elevated Venice above the other incorporated communes.

In the accounts of Pope Alexander's gifts, the sword was generally said to signify that the doges were true sons of the Mother Church, had defended her honor against the *superbia* of the emperor, and thus were endowed with a sense of true justice.[25] But in the course of time, emphasis came to be placed

[24] Giacomo Bascapè, "Sigilli della repubblica di Venezia," pp. 93–95. Cf. *Traité du gouvernement de la cité et seigneurie de Venise*, 2:272–73.

[25] "In quel giorno cum voluntà [de] pura / el papa donò al doxe quela spada / che avanti lui se porta; et ozi dura / cotal usanza, et cuscì se vada / senpre portando i suo' successori, / come se vede, per ogni siada; / e felo cavalier cum sumi honori, / cum tuti i successori che li monta / et qui' che po' verano per tut'ori; / et questa spada, segondo se conta, / significa iusticia per raxone." Appendix I in Zenatti, : "Il poemetto di Pietro de' Natali," pp. 168–69. "E in segnio di giustizia li largiva / la spada che à un sol taglio, e quella 'i cigne / con propria mano e si llo benediva: / 'Qual cavalier di Cristo, a chiu il cuor spigne / libertà, carità e vero amore / della giustitia, u' por tutto t'alligne, / et certo spera, avrai sommo vigore / di conculcar la superbia canina / del nimico Ferigo, a suo dolore!' " Appendix II in Zenatti, "Il poemetto di Pietro de' Natali," pp. 186–87. Pope Alexander: " 'Tuo' questa spada, fiol de la santa Gliexia, e va' a combater seguramente con questa spada, la qual io conciedo a ti et a tuti li tuo' sucessori, che la diebia portar.' " Appendix III in Zenatti, "Il poemetto di Pietro de' Natali," p. 195. Pope Alexander: "Così come i figlioli della S[an]ta Madre Giesia vano à Combater p[er] la Rason, combata queste Spada seguram[en]te che Iddio concederà Vittoria, et all'hora li Cinse la Spada, et benedillo condetto. Il Popolo et disse ciaschuno, che anderà à combatter p[er] la S[an]ta Madre Giesia Cattolica contro l'Imperador siano assolti di colpa, e di pena de tutti li suoi peccati." SUL, Ranke MS 69, fol. 70v.

almost exclusively on the sword as a symbol of justice. The sword was the most ancient of the ducal symbols; by the end of the ninth century and probably earlier the Venetian *dux*, the provincial representative of Constantinople, acquired the Byzantine title of *spatharius* and later *protospatharius*, and the sword probably served as an insigne for both titles.[26] As the position of the doges changed in the ensuing centuries, the sword gradually changed from an exclusively ducal emblem to a symbol for the justice of the republic. In the visual arts a female personification of Justice holding a scale and sword ranked second only to the winged lion of Saint Mark as a symbol of the republic. In sixteenth-century ducal processions, the sword was the specific insigne of the judicial magistracies; usually the sword was carried by a nobleman scheduled to serve abroad as a provincial *podestà* or captain, and hence charged with bringing Venetian justice to the subject peoples. If no one fitting that description was available, one of the *giudici del proprio* (judges of civil cases in the first instance) carried it. The symbolic bond between these officials of justice and the sword was so strong that when the ducal *trionfi* including the sword were excluded from a procession, as was the case on Giovedì Grasso, then a *guidice del proprio* did not participate in the procession; likewise, if for any reason he was absent, the sword was eliminated. On one occasion, the procession for the Sunday of the Apostles in 1514, when the sword appeared despite the absence of a *giudice del proprio*, Marin Sanuto was outraged, confiding to his diary "That *de jure* one cannot carry the sword without the giudice del proprio, because he is the podestà of Venice in criminal affairs."[27] The sword's double-edged symbolism—as a papal gift to a prince who made peace and as an epitome of a legal system that promoted equality before the law and social concord—accorded well with the republic's design to present itself as harmonious. That the republic embraced the

[26] Peyer, *Stadt und Stadtpatron*, p. 63; Agostino Pertusi, "Quedam regalia insignia," pp. 82–93.

[27] "Che *de jure*, non si pol portar spada senza Zudexe di proprio, perche quello è podestà di Venexia in criminal." Sanuto, *I diarii*, 18:149. Also see Sansovino, *Venetia*, 1604, fols. 317r, 322r, and MCV, MS Venier, P.D. 517b, under heading "avertimenti generali."

principle of justice was an idea so pervasive that even one of La Serenissima's most adamant critics, Jean Bodin, grudgingly admitted that in Venice one could find, if not the best form of government, at least just and equitable courts.[28]

The umbrella came to typify both Venice's independence from the German Empire and the Papacy, as well as its sovereignty. The Venetian doges may have displayed an umbrella or baldachin as a personal attribute as early as the struggle between Frederick Barbarossa and Alexander III, since it was at about that time that baldachins were first used in English and Spanish coronations.[29] Martin da Canal, who first reported the gift of the umbrella but recorded that it was presented in Venice, not at Ancona, claimed that the pontiff explained to Doge Ziani that he was giving it "Because I have found no other son of the holy Church except for you."[30] The later sources, which added the detail of the pope's demand for a third umbrella from the citizens of Ancona, emphasized that previously only the pope and emperor had enjoyed such a dignity and that Barbarossa protested when Alexander conceded to Ziani and his successors the right to walk under an umbrella.[31] The umbrella was an ". . . honor which without any doubt rendered the doge similar to kings" and which denoted the doge a third potentate of the world equal in authority to pope and emperor.[32] This was an honor indeed, and one that offered stout underpinnings to

---

[28] Gilmore, "Myth and Reality," pp. 440–42.

[29] Pertusi, "Quedam regalia insignia," pp. 87–88.

[30] Pope Alexander: "Porce que je ne trovai autre fil de sainte Yglise fors que toi, veul je que tu portes onbrele enci con je fais." Canal, Les estoires de Venise, p. 40.

[31] Pope Alexander: " 'O, è la terça? e se la non de xè, fila trovar per misier lo doxe.' e misier lo imperador disse: 'Misier, el no è plu che do segnori al mundo che diebia portar questa ombrella, çoè vu' e mi. e vu' volé ch'el doxe de Veniexia sia el terço segnor? parme stranio.' e misier lo papa li respoxe: "Çiò è che misier lo doxe sia una cossa con nu', perçò voio ch'elo ebia ombrella como nu'.' e cossì fo dada la umbrella a misier lo doxe et ali suo' sucessori.' " Appendix III in Zenatti, "Il poemetto di Pietro de' Natali," pp. 197–98. Cf. SUL, Ranke MS 69, fol. 72v, and Bardi, Dichiaratione di tutte le istorie, fol. 38v.

[32] The quote is from Sansovino, Venetia, 1604, fol. 322v. Also see SUL, Ranke MS 69, fol. 73r.

the elevated conception the Venetians had of their city's freedom.

The legend of Doge Ziani's entrance into Rome and the Alexandrine gifts of banners and silver trumpets from the Roman officials were patterned after a king's advent into a city; such a reception for a doge implied that he was similar in status to an anointed king. The Frankish kings and the German emperors, for their part, adopted ceremonial entrances imitating the entry of the exarch of Ravenna into Rome. Thirty miles out of the city, judges and officials of Rome carrying their banners met the visitor and conducted him to Saint Peter's, where he met the pope and higher clergy. The king's advent was a combination of an imperial Roman triumph and the Christian Advent, whose prototype was Christ's Palm Sunday entrance into Jerusalem as king of the Jews; thus, the liturgical images of the Advent transformed a king into the likeness of Christ, and a terrestrial city into another Jerusalem.[33] The Venetians did not extend their interpretation of Doge Ziani's entrance into Rome this far, but they were concerned to draw a parallel between the honors extended to kings and emperors at their entrance into Rome and those granted the doge. The legendary gifts confirmed the Venetians' interpretation. The silver trumpets were simply a well-known regal dignity to which the Venetians never attributed a peculiarly Venetian significance, as they did to the umbrella and the banners. The instruments were adopted somewhat later than the other *trionfi* and are first mentioned in the 1229 *promissione ducale* of Doge Jacopo Tiepolo. A typical comment about them came from Donato Giannotti: "I shall not speak about the music, for it is common to all the princes of Italy."[34] The Venetians were concerned to have their doge appear like a prince, and the trumpets helped create a consonant image.

The banners (*vexillum triumphale*), on the other hand, were rich with symbolic meaning. The use of banners may have

[33] Ernst H. Kantorowicz, "The 'King's Advent' and the Enigmatic Panels in the Doors of Santa Sabina," pp. 210–16.

[34] Giannotti, *Libro de la republica de Vinitiani*, fol. 65r–v. Also see Pertusi, "Quedam regalia insignia," pp. 11, 91, and Sansovino, *Venetia*, 1604, fol. 321v.

come from Byzantium; they appeared in the West by the end of the tenth century, when they were introduced into the liturgy to signify the triumph of Christ and later that of the saints. Their introduction may have implied that the Church's initial resistance to the symbols of warfare was on the wane. They appeared in Venice about the year 1000, when Doge Pietro II Orseolo, in launching a campaign against the Croats and Narentans in Dalmatia, assembled a fleet at Olivolo in order to receive a victory standard from Bishop Dominicus. On the way the expedition stopped at Grado, where the patriarch bestowed on the doge a second victory banner that bore the image of Saint Hermagoras, the patron of Grado. The Venetians henceforth carried into battle a saint's banner, by the thirteenth century invariably emblazoned with the winged lion of Saint Mark.[35] Wherever they appeared in Christendom, the banners of saints were initially religious symbols, "pledges of divine protection and victory" that implied no legal privileges or enfeoffment but indicated that a holy war had been declared. They became the exclusive privilege of the bishop or abbot charged with the particular saint's church, and the investiture of a saint's banner elevated the pursuit of warfare above the petty level of a struggle for worldly power. The ritual manifestation of an attachment to the saint, therefore, was more important than the standard itself. Venetian doges frequently received banners before embarking on military missions; in fact Pope Calixtus II bestowed the *vexillum beati Petri* on the doge for the crusade of 1122.[36] Before a campaign in later centuries, when doges superintended a bureaucracy rather than an army, the patriarch invested a banner of Saint Mark on the doge, who in turn transferred it to the newly elected captain general.

In the ducal processions there were four different colors of *trionfi* banners: white stood for peace, red for war, dark blue for a league, and violet for a truce; the current state of Venetian military affairs determined which color was carried first. The

[35] Pertusi, "Quedam regalia insignia," pp. 88–91; Carl Erdmann, *The Origin of the Idea of Crusade*, pp. 35–47; Percy Ernst Schramm, *Herrschaftszeichen und Staatssymbolik*, p. 860.

[36] Erdmann, *Idea of Crusade*, pp. 51–52, 186–87.

banners continued to serve as a religious sanction for war or, as a matter of fact, for whatever situation the Venetians found themselves in; but by the late sixteenth century the banners' importance extended considerably beyond a straightforward sign of saintly favor. Francesco Sansovino explained that for his contemporaries the standards demonstrated that the rulers of Venice were absolute and unrestrained by any worldly power.[37] So again a ducal symbol was transformed to serve as an insigne of sovereignty.

The Alexandrine gifts constituted a symbolic complex that expressed the religious and political doctrines most important to the Venetian community. The *trionfi* not only symbolized Venice's dedication to the Papacy, the doge's status as a prince equal to popes and emperors, Saint Mark's protection of Venetian military conquests, and the Venetian espousal of the principles of justice, but also, by means of the legend, proclaimed to the world that a pope had recognized and praised these traits. The Alexander legend so permeated Venetian culture that it was accepted as the single most important source for civic feasts, ceremonies, and symbols. On Thursday of Holy Week, for example, the doge and his closest retainers were rowed in the ducal *piatti* to San Giacomo di Rialto (see map) to enjoy the indulgence granted by Pope Alexander, as tradition held, to those who visited the church on that day.[38] Again, on April 3, the doge and magistrates went to Santa Maria della Carità in pursuit of an Alexandrine indulgence.[39] The candle the doge lighted for Saint Mark on his feast day was reputedly a donation of Pope Alexander.[40] Finally, Alexander's most famous and richly symbolic gift, the ring and the right to marry the sea, became the centerpiece of a great communal ritual that, more

[37] "Significano parimente Imperio assoluto senza alcuna superiorità." Sansovino, *Venetia*, 1604, fol. 321v.

[38] MCV, MS Venier, P.D. 517b, under heading "Settimana Santa"; Sansovino, *Venetia*, 1604, fol. 348v; 1663, pp. 519–20; and Doglioni, *Le cose notabili*, pp. 72–73.

[39] MCV, MS Venier, P.D., 517b, under heading "Aprile"; Doglioni, *Le cose notabili*, p. 47; Michiel, *Le origine delle feste veneziane*, 1:305–29.

[40] Sansovino, *Venetia*, 1663, p. 507; Sanuto, *Le vite dei dogi*, p. 90; ASV, Collegio Cerimoniale 1, fol. 8v; BMV, MS Latin III, 172 (2276), fol. 53r.

than anything else, pronounced the imperial designs of the Venetians.

THE MARRIAGE OF THE SEA

The most telling metaphor for Venetian dominion was a sexual one. A city so immersed in fertility ritual, so concerned with cosmetic appearances, was bound to take advantage of the most seductive imagery. The marriage between the city and the sea propagated just that. This marital image has been preserved in the romantic memory of a Venice now lost.

> Once did She hold the gorgeous east in fee;
> And was the safeguard of the west: the worth
> Of Venice, the eldest Child of Liberty.
> She was a maiden City, bright and free;
> No guile seduced, no force could violate;
> And when she took unto herself a Mate,
> She must espouse the everlasting Sea.[41]

Wordsworth, unfortunately, had his genders switched; for essential to understanding the marriage is the point that the doge was the husband of a maritime bride, who as the female partner was naturally and legally subject to the male.

A ritual blessing of the Adriatic probably dates from Doge Pietro II Orseolo's expedition to Dalmatia in about the year 1000, which first introduced the victory banners and established Venetian control of the northern Adriatic. Orseolo set sail on Ascension Day, and afterward his victories were recalled every year on that day, when the bishop of Olivolo, accompanied by the doge and citizenry, blessed the sea (a *benedictio*).[42] Although this annual blessing may have merely made official a

[41] William Wordsworth, "On the Extinction of the Venetian Republic," in *Wordsworth: Poetical Works*, ed. Thomas Hutchinson, revised by Ernest De Selincourt, Oxford, 1969, ll. 1–8.

[42] Michiel, *Le Origine delle feste veneziane*, 1:169–79; Romanin, *Storia documentata di Venezia*, 1:281; Urban, "La festa della Sensa," p. 312; Kantorowicz, *Laudes Regiae*, p. 147. Dates given for the expedition vary from 997 to 1000.

rite commonly performed at the beginning of the sailing season in many sea-going communities, the blessing from this time on acquired local political significance as an expression of dominion.[43] Orseolo demanded that, in Dalmatian liturgical rites, lauds be sung to the Venetian doge immediately after the acclamation of the Byzantine emperor, an innovation that must have eventually facilitated the transfer of allegiance from Constantinople to Venice.[44] The introduction of the *benedictio* as an official Venetian ritual occurred at the same time as the adoption of saints' banners in warfare and ducal lauds in the liturgy, and all three practices had a quasi-imperial connotation. In the mid-eleventh century, the bishop began to stage the *benedictio* from San Nicolò al Lido and to add prayers to Saint Nicholas as part of the rite. By 1267, when Martin da Canal described the ceremony, a *desponsatio*, or matrimonial covenant, between the doge and the sea had been grafted onto the *benedictio*, creating a composite rite and establishing the rudiments for the marriage of the sea, or the Sensa festival.[45] This significant transformation was probably a response to the heightened concern for Venice's own imperial image that followed the conquest of Constantinople in 1204. As the new lord of "a quarter and half a quarter" of the Byzantine Empire, the doge required a proper ritual manifestation of his newly acquired dominion, and the marriage of the sea constituted the quintessential imperial rite. In the thirteenth century there remained a vague aura of paganism about the Sensa rites since they seemed, despite the Christian elements, to resemble too closely a sacrifice to Neptune; Salimbene de Adam, in fact, explained the marriage as an ancient idolatry.[46] The Ascension rites came to be the center of

[43] Cf. Fasoli, "Liturgia e cerimoniale ducale," p. 274.

[44] Kantorowicz, *Laudes Regiae*, pp. 147–51.

[45] "Et li prestre qu' est aveuc monsignor li dus beneïst l'eive et monsignor li dus gete dedens la mer un anel d'or." Canal, *Les estoires de Venise*, p. 250. Cf. Urban, "La festa della Sensa," pp. 312–14.

[46] "Simili modo [the previous passage described the gold rose the Pope gave each year] dux Veneciarum cum Venetis suis cum anulo aureo in die Ascensionis Domini marè desponsat, partim causa solatii et deductionis, partim ex quadam ydolatrie consuetudine motus, qua Neptuno sacrificant Veneti, partim ad ostendendum quod Veneti dominium maris habent. Postea piscatores qui volunt (quia aliter non coguntur) denudant se, et aleo pleno ore, quod postea

a vast spring festival complete with public entertainments, a fifteen-day fair, and an Alexandrine indulgence given visitors to San Marco. Large, often unruly crowds of foreigners came to Venice for the occasion, and by the sixteenth and seventeenth centuries the Sensa festival inaugurated the theater season, which lasted until July.[47] One can be certain, therefore, that thousands witnessed the ritual every year.

In the sixteenth century the marriage of the sea was the carefully orchestrated apogee of the state liturgy. At dawn on Ascension Day the doge's cavalier in charge of ceremonial preparations determined whether the sea was calm emough for a procession of boats; if it was, he obtained the ceremonial ring (the *vera*) from the officials of the Rason Vecchie and announced the beginning of the Sensa.[48] After mass was sung in San Marco the doge, high magistrates, and foreign ambassadors boarded the Bucintoro, the doge's ceremonial galley decorated with figures of Justice and the insignia of the republic. As they were rowed out onto the lagoon (see map), the chapel choir of San Marco sang motets, and the bells of the churches and monasteries under the patronage of the doge began ringing.[49] Near the convent of Sant' Elena, the patriarch of Castello, in his flat-boat (*piatto*) bedecked with banners, joined the procession of vessels, which usually included thousands of gaily adorned pri-

spargunt, descendunt in profundum maris ad anulum inquirendum. Et quicumque illum invenire potest, absque ulla contradictione possidet illum. De hac materia dicit Psalmista: *Qui descendunt mare in navibus, facientes operationem in aquis multis, ipsi viderunt opera Domini et mirabilia eius in profundo* [italics in original]. Et nota quod Neptunus a poetis et gentilibus dicitur deus maris." Salimbene de Adam, *Cronica*, pp. 822–23. The passage is dated 1285.

[47] Urban, "La festa della Sensa," pp. 330–41. For an example of jousts held during the Sensa festival of 1497 see Sanuto, *I diarii*, 1:614. On the theater season see Girolamo Priuli, "Diario," Österreichische Nationalbibliothek, Vienna, ex Foscarini Cod. 6229, b. 3, fol. 307v. A microfilm copy of this MS is on deposit in the Fondazione Giorgio Cini, Venice.

[48] *Cerimoniale solenne nel giorno dell'ascensione per lo sposalizio del mare che compivasi al doge di Venezia tratto dal codice inedito che serviva di norma all'ultimo cavaliere del doge*, pp. 9, 12.

[49] The best discussion of the history and décor of the Bucintoro is in Urban, "La festa della Sensa," pp. 317–29. On the bell ringing see MCV, Cod. Cicogna 2991/1.20, fol. 3r.

vate gondolas, barges hired by the guilds, pilot boats (peote)
fitted out by companies of young noblemen, and galleys manned
by sailors from the Arsenal. The religious rites of benedictio
took place on the patriarch's boat: two canons began by singing,
"Hear us with favor, O Lord," to which the patriarch answered
three times, "We worthily entreat Thee to grant that this sea
be tranquil and quiet for our men and all others who sail upon
it, O hear us"; the patriarch blessed the waters, and the canons
sang an Oremus. The patriarchical boat then approached the
ducal Bucintoro, from which the primicerio, the head priest of
San Marco, thrice intoned, "Sprinkle me, Lord, with hyssop
and marjoram." Next, while his boat circled the Bucintoro, the
patriarch blessed the doge with holy water, using an olive
branch as an aspergillum.[50] When the party reached the mouth
of the lagoon, the place where a break in the Lido opened Venice
to the Adriatic, the actual marriage ceremony took place. At a
signal from the doge the patriarch emptied a huge ampulla
(mastellus) of holy water into the sea, and the doge, in turn,
dropped his gold ring overboard saying, "We espouse thee, O
sea, as a sign of true and perpetual dominion."[51] After the
marriage ceremony the doge and his guests stopped at San
Nicolò al Lido for prayers and a banquet that lasted until
evening, others returned to feast at home, and the pilgrim and
merchant galleys bound for the East, the first of the season,

[50] "Exaudi nos, Domine, cum propiciis"; "Ut hoc mare nobis et omnibus in
eo navigantibus tranquillum et quietum concedere digneris te rogamus, audi
nos"; "Asperges me, Domine, ysopo et mundabar." Urban, "La festa della
Sensa," pp. 314–15. Cf. ASV, Collegio Cerimoniale 1, fol. 8v; BMV, MS
Latin III, 172 (2276), fol. 53r–v; Sansovino, Venetia, 1663, pp. 500–502.
Urban, p. 315, says that the patriarch climbed aboard the Bucintoro to bless
the doge. The official ceremonial book, however, reads, "movens se cum navic-
ula sua, quae ad latus dextrum steterat Bucentauri, circuit navem ipsam Du-
calem, spargendo in D. Ducem, et omnes aquam benedictam." ASV, Collegio
Cerimoniale 1, fol. 8v.

[51] "Desponsamus te Mare, in signum veri perpetuique dominii." Sansovino,
Venetia, 1663, p. 501. Cf. Michiel, Le origine delle feste veneziane, 1:187. In
other sources, however, there is no mention of the phrase, "Desponsamus te
Mare." ASV, Collegio Cerimoniale 1, fol. 8v. Cf. Urban, "La festa della Sensa,"
p. 315.

5. Giacomo Franco, *On Ascension Day the Doge in the Bucintoro Is Rowed to the Marriage of the Sea.*

made their way under the protection of the bishop's blessing and the plenary indulgences received at San Marco.[52]

[52] For examples of pilgrim ships waiting until after the marriage of the sea to depart, see Pero Tafur, *Travels and Adventures, 1435–1439*, pp. 33, 47, 156, 159, 162.

IMPERIAL PREROGATIVES

IN EXPLAINING the Sensa ceremonies to themselves, sixteenth-century Venetians recalled the legend of Pope Alexander III, a story that tended to emphasize three aspects of the ceremony: the ring as a token of papal grace, the marriage as a symbol of Venetian dominion, and the blessing as an act of propitiation. Francesco Sansovino, a writer of popular history, recounted that when Pope Alexander gave Doge Ziani the ring after the Venetian victory, he said, "Take this, O Ziani, which you and your successors will use each year to marry the sea, so that posterity knows that the lordship of the sea is yours, held by you as an ancient possession and by right of conquest, and that the sea was placed under your dominion, as a wife is to a husband." The pope added, according to Sansovino, that the ceremony would protect sailors and consecrate the waves as a cemetery for those lost at sea.[53] The marriage ring, or *vela*, was distinct from the episcopal ring of Saint Mark referred to in the previous chapter; the *vela* recalled the pope's sanction of Venetian maritime dominion and even signified, according to some sources, that Alexander had invested Doge Ziani with the Adriatic as a fief.[54] The essential political point, then, was that in marrying the sea the doge established his legitimate rights of domination over trade routes and over the lands lapped by the waters of the Adriatic. But the ring made manifest much else as well. Rings figure prominently in folklore, chivalric literature, mythology, and the visual arts, and so any particular ring could have had numerous levels of meanings in different

---

[53] "Ricevi questo o Ziani, col quale tu, & tuoi suoi successori, userete ogni anno di sposare il mare. Accioche i posteri intendino, che la Signoria d'esso màre, acquistata da voi per antico possesso, & per ragion di guerra è vostra. Et che il mare è sottoposto al vostro Dominio, come la moglie al marito." Sansovino, *Venetia*, 1663, p. 501; also see pp. 498–500. In another sixteenth-century account Pope Alexander gives the ring to Doge Ziani and says, "Così come li huomeni sposano le Donne in segno di vero matrimonio. Così voglio che voi, et sucessori vostri sposino el Mar ogn'anno nel giorno dell'Ascension in Memoria di questa Vittoria, accioche in tutto el Mondo sia noto." Then Pope Alexander made the doge the "Cavalier de tutto el Mar Adrian." SUL, Ranke MS 69, fol. 71r. Cf. Ferrarese, *Historia di Papa Alessand III*, no pagination; Bardi, *Delle cose notabili*, p. 40; Doglioni, *Le cose notabili*, pp. 41–42; Zenatti, "Il poemetto di Pietro de' Natali," pp. 148, 175, 188–189, 195.

[54] Michiel, *Le origine delle feste veneziane*, 1:187.

contexts. The circular unity of the ring, for example, usually symbolized joining, continuity, eternity, and fertility.[55]

The marriage of the sea was so richly symbolic precisely because it imitated a universal and socially meaningful contractural relationship. In Venetian law the husband was the *padrone* of his wife: his authority was considered to be the most ancient, preceding the authority of fathers over children, masters over servants, and princes over subjects; and it was supported by the divine law of the Bible and the civil law of Rome. Scripture, by saying a wife should be a companion, not a slave, in theory moderated the harshness of the Roman civil law, which included the precept that the husband, in consultation with his wife's relatives, had full power to punish his spouse for adultery or libertine acts. The Roman wife, on the other hand, had no rights against a husband even if his adultery could be proven. Whatever moderation there was under Christianity, the supreme position of the male remained.[56] Venetian women owned their dowries as their share of their natal patrimony, but husbands could legally invest their wives' dowries as they saw fit.[57] In applying their legal conception of marriage to territorial dominion, the Venetians created an unequal ritual partnership wherein they would protect subject territories, exercise supreme authority over them, and enjoy the income from the subjects' fisc in the same fashion that the husband administered his wife's dowry.

[55] Cf. Mikhail Bakhtin, *Rabelais and His World*, p. 243. In a letter accompanying a gift of four rings to Richard the Lionhearted in 1198, Pope Innocent III explained that the rings' " . . . form, number, and material all have a message: the king should harken to this secret meaning *(mysterium)* rather than to the mere value of the precious metal and stones of the jewel. The round form and the gems were to remind him of eternity, the number four of the *constancia mentis*, the gold of *sapientia*. The pope offered a symbolic interpretation for every piece and for every stone of the present. The jewels thus, 'correctly' understood, constituted a veritable ethical vademecum, strengthening the heart of the king and reminding him of the duties of a Christian prince." J. M. Bak, "Medieval Symbology of the State," p. 61.

[56] Marco Ferro, *Dizionario del diritto comune e Veneto*, 2:244–47, 249–58, 278–83.

[57] Stanley Chojnacki, "Patrician Women in Early Renaissance Venice." Chojnacki's study emphasizes, however, the considerable economic rights patrician women retained.

Throughout Europe until well into the seventeenth century, commonwealths and kingdoms were frequently compared in serious political theory to the family, and kings to fathers and husbands.[58] The comparison signified that a ruler had the same obligations to his subjects, and prerogatives over them, that a paterfamilias had over his wife and offspring. King Louis XI, immediately after his 1469 reconciliation with his rebellious brother, Charles, had the ring with which the bishop of Lisieux had married Duke Charles to Normandy broken on an anvil in the presence of the local nobility, thus ending Charles' union with the duchy and dissolving his treasonous dominion.[59] First used in the Middle Ages as a metaphor for the bond between Christ (or the pope) and the Church or between a bishop and his diocese, marriage was gradually adopted by secular rulers to illustrate the nature of the *Corpus Reipublicae mysticum.*[60] The marriage metaphor was fairly common among secular princes by the end of the thirteenth century, when it seems the Venetians started to apply the idea to their own political situation. The most comprehensive medieval discourse on the marriage metaphor was by Lucas de Penna, a Neapolitan jurist who wrote a commentary on the Justinian code around the middle of the fourteenth century. He emphasized the contractural obligations of a moral and political marriage between a prince and his people, a union that was the same as the marriage between a bishop and his flock and that united the metaphorical spouses: "The Prince is in the state, and the state is the Prince."[61] Matrimony was a consensual union, and thus the prince and *res*

[58] Michael Walzer, *The Revolution of the Saints,* pp. 183–98.

[59] Johan Huizinga, *The Waning of the Middle Ages,* p. 234.

[60] For what follows see Ernst H. Kantorowicz, *The King's Two Bodies,* pp. 207–32; idem, "Mysteries of State." In Florence the archbishop married the abbess of San Pier Maggiore as part of his formal entry into the city to take possession of his episcopal seat. "Et la sposò invece della chiesa Florentina mettendoli nel dito annulare uno Diamante di pregio di scudi 200." Archivio di Stato, Florence (hereafter ASF), Peruzzi Medici 234, inserto 3, fol. 176, entry dated 15 May 1567. Also see ASF, Corp. Relig. Sopp., Montalve di Ripoli: S. Pier Maggiore, 323 (CRIA 7287), last foglio in the box. These references were kindly brought to my attention by Professor David R. Edward Wright.

[61] Quoted in Kantorowicz, *The King's Two Bodies,* p. 214.

publica agreed to their relationship; but the agreement, like that of marriage, was permanently binding. Divorce or rebellion was not possible.

The Venetians did not interpret the metaphorical marriage in quite the same way as did Lucas de Penna. In one respect the difference was a matter of emphasis, and in another a corollary of a political distinction peculiar to Venice. In espousing the sea the doge was marrying the subjects of the Venetian maritime colonies and establishing that he was the *padrone* of the sea lanes, but he was most certainly not espousing the people of Venice. The Sensa was an imperial rite, not a constitutional definition of the doge's powers over or within the *res publica*. In accord with the interpretation of Lucas de Penna, however, the Venetian version of the metaphor made perfectly good use of the notion of matrimonial consent, since there was tremendous propagandistic merit in the idea that conquered subjects had somehow agreed to their conquest but were forever barred from changing their minds.

The political distinction peculiar to Venice was that the doge's rights as a prince were strictly limited. The doge, serving as the representative of the *res publica*, could quite harmlessly symbolize what the Venetians wished to be, the domineering husband of their colonies; but in Venice proper he was the groom to only a few carefully specified institutions, over which he retained rights of patronage. The doge had the privilege, for example, of using the ring of Saint Mark to "marry" each new abbess of Santa Maria Nuova in Gerusalemme (or delle Vergini) as a confirmation of her election and of his patronage of the convent. This marriage, as did the Sensa, originated in the thirteenth century. In 1224, Ugolino, bishop of Ostia, who later became Pope Gregory IX, went to Venice as the legate of Pope Honorius III in order to ask for aid against Emperor Frederick II. During his stay Ugolino persuaded Doge Pietro Ziani to erect a chapel in memory of a church dedicated to the Virgin that the Saracens had destroyed in Jerusalem. In complying with the request, Ziani built a church and an adjoining convent for Augustinian nuns and confirmed his patronage rights over them by "marrying" the abbess. The rite eventually fell under

the all-embracing blanket of the legend of Pope Alexander III:
by the sixteenth century Pietro Ziani had been confused with
Sebastiano Ziani and Frederick II with Frederick I Barbarossa,
so that Alexander III rather than Ugolino was normally given
credit for encouraging the foundation of the monastery and
introducing the marriage ceremony.[62] The monastic nuptials
and the crediting of their origin to Pope Alexander, of course,
closely paralleled the Sensa and signified a similar relationship:
the husband was to be *padrone* of the wife.

This interpretation of the marriage of the sea as a demonstration of mastery eventually brought some embarrassment to
Venetians sensitive to the delicate nuances of European diplomacy. By the last few decades of the sixteenth century, the
Adriatic was no longer a Venetian lake, but a sea lane increasingly threatened by Uskok, Barbary, Maltese, Florentine, Spanish, and English pirates.[63] By the eighteenth century the marriage of the sea was at best a quaint anachronism, at worst a
joke: as the pun went, the Sensa was *senza sensa*. An anonymous *History of the Venetian Wars with the Ottomans* written
in the last quarter of the sixteenth century diligently attempted
to prove that Venice was neither an aggressive nor a tyrannical
power—La Serenissima had had to fight wars and maintain
control over the sea lanes purely as a defensive measure. Nor
did it own the sea: "It is true that the sea is common to all."[64]
This perspective led the author to a thoroughly unpretentious
interpretation of the marriage of the sea: it was merely a joyful

[62] Pope Alexander III: "O' Ziano per mia auctorità queste dò desponsatione
de duplicata fede son di ti, e li toi Successori intendano, che in tal possesso con
l'Anello di San Marcho faci tal cerimonia in memoria del divo evangelista
Marcho el qual hà facto questo Benedetto Ordine, et regula confirmata per San
Pietro Apostolo alla Sacra ancorche sia là seconda disponsatione de Saphyro in
memoria, che lui, et li altri Prencipi usasseno questo in perpetuum nella
proprietate Sancti Petri confirmata ad perpetuam rei memoriam, et sigilla-
tam." MCV, Cod. Gradenigo, no. 214, fol. 2r. Also see MCV, MS Venier, P.D.
517b, under heading "Visite alle monache de Santa Maria delle Virgine";
Doglioni, *Le cose notabili,* p. 264; Michiel, *Le origine delle feste veneziane,*
1:69–99; Giuseppe Tassini, *Curiosità veneziane,* p. 766; Cicogna, *Delle inscri-
zione veneziane,* 5:5–7.

[63] Alberto Tenenti, *Piracy and the Decline of Venice, 1580–1615.*

[64] BMV, MS Italiano VII, 11 (8378), fol. 483v.

commemoration of the victory of the Venetians over Barbarossa's fleet.[65]

Others concentrated on the pacificatory and consecratory aspects of the *benedictio*. Although works such as Semusovio's poem tended to use descriptions of the ceremony as indirect praise for Venetian constitutional and mercantile practices, such works often suppressed elements that implied dominion and instead pictured the Sensa as an attempt to quell storms at sea.[66] Marriage-of-the-sea rites found elsewhere, such as those performed at Cervia (a small fishing village near Ravenna), where since 1446 the archbishop of Ravenna had married the sea with his pastoral ring, were largely religious in nature and indeed signified the pacification of the often violent sea.[67] The idea that the Sensa had consecrated the sea as a holy shrine was also common in Venice. One of the testaments most revealing of this attitude is the will of Andrea Donà, written before he sailed in 1570 as captain of a galley in the Turkish wars. To him the acme of patriotic service would have been a death at sea.

> In the name of my Lord God, on Saturday, May 13, 1570, I, Andrea Donado . . . commander of a galley of the fleet which will go out to defend the fatherland in this war which Sultan Selim of Turkey has treacherously begun, [am writing this will] because it may be that God in His mercy will give me the grace during this undertaking to die, and with my death to wash away some of the many sins I have committed against His majesty. I go forth firmly resolved to sacrifice my life for the fatherland if I have the opportunity. . . . There is no reason for me to discuss my burial because I hope my Lord God will grant that we fight with the ships of that treacherous treaty-

[65] "Che la Republica nelle sue Vittorie contro nemici sia solita di far allegrezze ne fà fede la sollennità annuale che nel giorno dell'ascensione di nostro Signore fà di sposar il mare in memoria della Vittoria ottennuta over l'Armata di Federico Barbarossa primo Imperatore persecutore d'Alessandro III come s'è detto, e finalmente sforzato adimandar perdono à questa di trionfato et i piedi dell pontefice davanti la porta maggiore della chiesa di San Marco in Venetia." Ibid.

[66] Biliński, "Venezia nelle peregrinazioni polacche," pp. 263, 271–72.

[67] V. Trojani di Nerfa, *Sagre, feste e riti*, pp. 128–30.

breaker and that it will please Him on that day to accept the sacrifice of my life in remission of my sins. Then the sea itself will be my honorable and glorious sepulcher and monument.[68]

In the late sixteenth century there seem to have been two differing interpretations of the Sensa based, in fact, on the formal division of the ceremony into a *desponsatio* and a *benedictio:* one view jingoistically upheld the dominion of Venice over the sea, the other more humbly envisioned the rite as a religious supplication. One advocate of the former viewpoint went so far as to deny completely that the Sensa was intended to consecrate the sea for those who died without receiving extreme unction.[69] There is little evidence to help determine what, if any, political interest or faction these differing interpretations served, but they may well reflect two common concerns of late sixteenth-century Venetian patricians: one was to re-assert Venetian authority in a period of growing foreign encroachment upon the traditional Venetian sphere of influence, and the other was to reaffirm in accord with post-Tridentine principles the orthodoxy and religious fervor of the city.[70] The two views were not necessarily mutually exclusive, but they led to the emphasis of dissimilar parts of the Sensa.

Like any ritual, the Sensa undoubtedly pointed to certain attitudes and social relationships of which the Venetians themselves were unconscious. It is the historian's task to uncover, if possible, these mentalities and structures. Among modern interpretations of the marriage, that of Gina Fasoli is most perceptive. She argues that it was, on the one hand, a hydromantic rite, consistent with the practices usual at the beginning of a reign, the embarking of an expedition, or the turning to a new year in a king's tenure, when a ring or symbolic object was thrown into a river, lake, or sea. In this sense, the Sensa was a prognostication, an attempt to forecast the future by the dis-

---

[68] ASV, Testamenti notarili, 1262, III, 37. As cited and translated (but with slight changes in punctuation) by James Cushman Davis, *A Venetian Family and its Fortune, 1500–1900,* p. 13.

[69] Bardi, *Delle cose notabili,* pp. 40ff.

[70] Muir, "Images of Power"; Grendler, *The Roman Inquisition.*

covery of an omen; and there are, indeed, numerous examples in Venetian lore of meterological events, mistakes or accidents in the ceremonies, or dramatic news from abroad interpreted as omens for good or evil.[71] On the other hand, she notes that it was also a rite of possession, symbolized by a mystic marriage, and suggests that the sexual conception of the doge's relationship to the sea can be traced in the shift from the neuter gender of *mare* in Latin to the feminine gender of *la mar* in Venetian dialect.[72] Without abusing the evidence one could, however, offer a considerably more extensive interpretation of the rite.

The marriage of the sea was a Venetian version of a spring fertility festival. The usual goals of agrarian fertility rites—safeguarding the fecundity of women and crops—were transformed by the Venetian rites to serve maritime and mercantile needs: the rites ensured the safety of sailors at sea, expressed political and commercial hegemony, established a trade fair for the crowds, and invoked, through a mystical marriage, continued prosperity. At the moment of their occurrence such fertility rites characteristically contribute to social cohesion and unanimity within the community.[73] But there is a danger that the exuberance of the festival—the drinking, the crowds, and the opportunity to let off steam—could lead to violence and civil disturbances, hardly signs of communal stability. For this eventuality the Council of Ten was always prepared, and its policing was quite successful; for never did the excesses of a Sensa festival lead to social revolt.[74] Many of the European festivals

[71] Auguries of evil were seen when the doge's umbrella was accidently broken in a procession. Sanuto, *I diarii*, 19:333. A similar incident occurred in 1572. "Onde fù giudicato da ogn'uno infelice auguriò e principalm[en]te dal Doge." MCV, Cod. Cicogna 2991/1.16, fol. 1v.

[72] Fasoli, "Liturgia e cerimoniale ducale," pp. 274–75.

[73] Cf. the comments on rites of violence in Bercé, *Fête et révolte*, pp. 52–53.

[74] An order of the Council of Ten dated 1365 reads "Quod pro bona custodia civitatis nostrae pro festo Ascensionis ad quod veniunt multae, et infinitae personae, et gentes, Committatur Dominis de Nocte, quod ultra custodes solitos accipiant alios quinque custodes pro qualibet pro vigilia, et pro die Ascensionis cum illo soldo, cum quo melius poterunt pro bono communis. Et similiter committatur Capitibus Sexteriorum, ut bona custodia fiat." ASV, Consiglio dei Dieci, miscellanea cod. 1, called "Magnus" (1310–1618), p. 32.

permitted activity that on other occasions would be proscribed, and there was often a delicate balance between actions that affirmed social control and those that rejected it; in Venice, however, the Sensa always seemed to advance public order.

The Sensa, as well, had a spatial aspect that reveals certain perceptual habits of the Venetians. The ceremony took place within the context of a ritual voyage, a miniature expedition abroad, in which the doge as the captain of Venice sailed from the secure haven of the city's center, the hospice of Saint Mark, to the periphery of Venetian communal space, where the known waters of the lagoon met the unknown and unpredictable waves of the sea. By following the route along which goods moved and conquerors sailed, the water-procession described the axis of the Venetian economic and imperial world and affirmed that what lay beyond the lagoon was subject to those who came from within it. The route duplicated the one taken by the old fisherman who rowed Saint Mark, Saint George, and Saint Nicholas out to repulse the demons besieging Venice at its very gate, the opening in the Lido Islands. Saint Mark stood at one pole of this processional axis, at the fixed sacral, political, and economic center of the empire; and at the opposite pole was Saint Nicholas, a gatekeeper and beacon, who looked outward and guarded the "walls" of the city just as he guided Venice's first line of defense, the fleet.[75] Saint Nicholas was the last succor for the departing sailor, the saint into whose hands men placed themselves and their ships as they left the safety of Saint Mark's harbor. Saint Nicholas, as we have seen in the previous chapter, was the patron saint most dedicated to fecundity; so it was no accident that the participants in the fertility rite of the Sensa made a detour to pray at his church on the Lido.

The Sensa also deprived the sea of its frightening demeanor by feminizing it. The men who sailed abroad could most easily imagine the sea as a female archetype: unpredictable, fickle, sometimes violent, other times passive; but assuredly she could

[75] Cf. Victor Turner, "The Center Out There." Although it was published too late to be considered in this study, a more extensive discussion of these issues may be found in Victor Turner and Edith Turner, *Image and Pilgrimage in Christian Culture.*

be mastered by the resolute male. The Sensa revealed two profound psychological habits of belief: that natural forces could
be comprehended by personifying them, and that through understanding these forces one could better control them, or at
least predict their influences. And in symbolizing sexual conquest the processional movement took full advantage of the
female metaphor. Through the marriage each year at the beginning of the sailing season and through the subsequent voyages
that consummated the union, the sea was deprived of her mystery; men now "knew" her.[76]

Spatial analysis of the Sensa reveals that the opening in the
Lido Islands was a focus of particular symbolic attention. Here
the two worlds, Venetian and non-Venetian, met; here Venice
was most vulnerable and the outer world most subject to Venetian influence; here Saint Nicholas presided, and here male and
female metaphorically joined. In this symbolic sense the passage was binomial and two-sided; it was the entrance to Venice
and conversely the exit to the sea. This pairing of meanings
permeated the entire ceremony by juxtaposing actual or ima-
gistic opposites: Venice and the beyond, the doge and the sea,
male and female, the doge and the patriarch, secular and ecclesiastical authority, Saint Mark and Saint Nicholas, inside the
lagoon and outside it, holy water and sea water, blessed and
unblessed, humanity and nature, the living and the dead, the
mortal and the immortal, above the surface and below it, the
profane and the consecrated, land and sea, us and them.
Throughout the ritual these pairs were joined in numerous
ways, but they were most obviously fused when they symbolically met at the gap in the Lido or were united by the iconographic image of the ring. With the ring token, devoutly believed to be a papal gift, the entire complex of images, symbols,
inferences, legends, sacred mysteries, and legal precepts were

[76] One might ask whether the conspicuous public parade of courtesans at the
marriage-of-the-sea ritual reflected this fertility image. Sir Henry Wotton
reported that the 1617 Ascension solemnity ". . . hath this year been celebrated here with a very poor show of *gondole*, by reason of a decree in Senate
against the courtesans, that none of them shall be rowed *con due remi*; a
decree made at the suit of all the gentlewomen, who before were indistinguish-
able abroad from those baggaes." Smith, *Sir Henry Wotton*, 2:114.

united. With this ring "We espouse thee, O sea, as a sign of true and perpetual dominion." The circular ring, a shape without ends or poles or parts, wedded potentially conflicting opposites, reduced duality to unity, and brought harmony to a divided world.

THE GIFTS of Pope Alexander III and the marriage of the sea were the principal legendary and ritualistic components of the imperial myth of Venice. They helped to transform the amorphous Venetian sense of primacy and saintly favor into a precise political conception of sovereignty over the lagoon and of colonial prerogatives over the subject lands. These principles found echoes, as we shall see, in many other Venetian rites, but the Sensa was primarily outward looking; it existed largely because the Venetians had to explain themselves to foreigners. How then did the Venetians explain themselves to themselves? To answer this question one must turn to the rituals that reveal the social relations within the city itself, the Festival of the Marys and Giovedì Grasso.

FOUR

TWELVE WOODEN MARYS
AND A FAT THURSDAY:
A SERENE SOCIETY

THE DOGE'S ANNUAL VISIT TO SANTA MARIA FORMOSA

During carnival every Venetian, whatever his or her social station, had a chance not only to witness but to participate in festive civic rituals. These included, most notably, the parish celebration at Santa Maria Formosa and the city-wide frolics on Giovedì Grasso. Carnival sported many irrepressibly popular activities, but the Venetian government carefully watched and often supervised these amusements in its ever-present anxiety to secure and extend its authority. The history of the festive rites associated with Santa Maria Formosa is tortuously complex; yet, in its complexity, this history best reveals the interplay between popular and elite institutions in Venetian society and, ultimately, the triumph of the government in diverting popular festivities toward a political end.

In the fifteenth and sixteenth centuries it was generally believed that the annual ceremonies at the church of Santa Maria Formosa had begun in the tenth century as a celebration of a victory over pirates. An anonymous chronicle composed at the end of the fifteenth century, perhaps the most detailed account of the legend, claims that since "ancient times" on January 31, the day of the Transfer of Saint Mark, the prince and commune gave dowries to and sponsored weddings for twelve deserving but poor young girls in a ceremony conducted by the bishop at his cathedral of San Pietro di Castello.[1] One year a group of

---

[1] The chronicle was once falsely believed to have been written by Daniele Barbaro. The account is published by Iacopo Morelli, *Delle solennità e pompe nuziali già usate presso li Veneziani*, in his *Operette*, 1:130–34. Cf. "Matricola de' Casselleri," cited and discussed in G. B. Galicciolli, *Storie e memorie venete profane ed ecclesiastiche*, 6:3, 5–7; G. Monticolo, "La costituzione del

Triestine pirates, tempted by the girls, their dowries, and the gems with which the prince adorned them for the occasion, stole their way into the cathedral; after attacking and wounding or killing many of the assembled worshippers, the pirates fled the cathedral with the bejeweled brides and their dowry boxes, escaping aboard boats they had hidden outside.[2] Quickly assembling a fleet, the Venetian menfolk pursued them to a small port near Caorle—to this day called the Porto delle Donzelle— where the Triestines had anchored to divide the spoils. First to board the pirate craft, the *casseleri* (either cabinetmakers or carpenters) of the parish of Santa Maria Formosa fought valiantly, killed all the Triestines, threw the corpses without ceremony into the sea, and burned the ships.[3] Returning with brides, dowries, and treasures intact, the *casseleri* won honors for the victory, which occurred on February 2, the day of the Purification of the Virgin, or Candlemas. To reward the *casseleri* the doge agreed that he and his successors would visit Santa Maria Formosa each year for vespers on the eve of the Purification and for mass on the feast day itself.

The Santa Maria Formosa chronicle is a legend that explained a pre-existing ritual. The earliest sources that describe the

Doge Pietro Polani (febbraio 1143, 1142 more veneto) circa la processo scolarum," p. 37 in extract; Jacopo Filiasi, *Memorie storiche de' Veneti primi e secondi*, 6:63–69; Fabio Mutinelli, *Annali urbani di Venezia dall'anno 810 al 12 maggio 1797*, pp. 22–24; BMV, MS Italiano VII, 519 (8438), fol. 46v; BMV, MS Italiano VII, 794 (8503), fols. 53v–54r; Giovanni Battista Pace, "Ceremoniale Magnum, sive raccolta universale di tutte le ceremonie spettanti alla Ducal Regia Capella di San Marco, 1678," BMV, MS Italiano VII, 1269 (9573), fol. 20v; Sacchi, *Delle condizione degli italiani ne' tempi municipali*, p. 19; Tassini, *Feste, spettacoli*, p. 9, n. 1; Sansovino, *Venetia*, 1663, pp. 493–94; Michiel, *Le origine delle feste veneziane*, 1:139–45; Silvio Tramontin, "Una pagina di folklore religioso veneziano antico," pp. 411–12.

[2] In the accounts the date of the attack varies from 836 to 943. Giovanni Musolino, "Culto mariano," p. 257; Pace del Friuli, *La festa delle Marie descritta in un poemetto elegiaco*, 1843, p. 23; Pace del Friuli's poem is also published in Flaminio Corner, *Ecclesiae Venetae*, 3:303–8; BMV, MS Italiano VII, 519 (8438), fol. 46v. Some sources say the pirates were Istrians or Narentans. Monticolo, "La costituzione del Doge Pietro Polani," p. 37; Mutinelli, *Annali urbani di Venezia*, pp. 22–24.

[3] On the meaning of the word *casseleri* see Gallicciolli, *Storie e memorie venete*, 6:8; Mutinelli, *Annali urbani di Venezia*, pp. 22–24.

doge's ceremonial visit—the Altinate chronicle, the chronicles of John the Deacon and Martin da Canal, and the constitution of Doge Pietro Polani—make no mention of this piracy; the first intimations of the legend are in the late thirteenth-century chronicle of Marco, which reports that the annual visit to Santa Maria Formosa commemorated the defeat of a legendary Istrian pirate named Gaiolus.[4] The mid-tenth century, the period when Gaiolus was reputedly active, witnessed the initial commercial expansion of Venice into Istria and occasional expeditions against the Narentans and the Slavs, but there are no recorded incidents of provocations or attacks on Venice itself that might have provided a historical basis for the legend.[5] One must assume that the account was an accumulative fabrication that, beginning with the chronicle of Marco, explained the origin of the Festival of the Twelve Marys. The story had, nevertheless, a tremendous impact on Venetian literature and mythology. It was frequently retold in fifteenth- and sixteenth-century chronicles, and in the late seventeenth century Cesare Tebaldi attempted to transform the story into a Venetian-dialect epic in his *Venezia in cuna co le novizze liberae*. In the eighteenth century Emmanuele de Azevedo compared the Venetian legend to the Roman story of the rape of the Sabine women, thereby elevating a local tradition to the status of literary myth.[6]

The rape of the Venetian and of the Sabine women are both myths concerned with the problem of preserving group fertility. In both stories brides were protected or obtained through the communal, military efforts of men; but the Venetian version was the Sabine myth stood on its head. Told from a point of view similar to that of the Sabine men, the Venetian account emphasized the protective, peaceful, inward-looking order provided by a strong, cohesive community; whereas the Roman

[4] BMV, MS Italiano XI, 124 (6802), fols. 37r–38v. This passage was published by Angelo Zon in *Archivio storico italiano* 8 (1845):266–67. Cf. Tramontin, "Una pagina di folklore," p. 412.

[5] Roberto Cessi, *Venezia ducale*, 1:309–18.

[6] "Quid iactas, o Roma, olim repuisse puellos / Ac furto potuisse frui? melioribus ausis / Nobilis Urbs hebetes poterat docuisse Sabinos / Qua patriae iura expediat ratione tueri." Quoted in Antonio Pilot, "Il ratto delle 'novizze' veneziane," p. 13. Filiasi also made a comparison between the Venetian story and the rape of the Sabine women. *Memorie storiche de' Veneti*, 6:63.

fable lauded the necessarily aggressive, outward-looking attitude of a band of warriors. In the Venetian story the culprits were vaguely the same as the subjects in Istria and Dalmatia, who were reduced to their proper subordinate place by the marriage of the sea; and as did the interpretation of the Sensa, the pirate story characterized Venetian expeditions as purely defensive and just reprisals for the plunderings of others. But, unlike the marriage of the sea, the rituals associated with this piracy legend did not paint Venetian imperial goals; they sketched the outlines of a strong community preoccupied with maintaining domestic peace and tranquillity and perfectly capable of defending itself without any external intervention, worldly or divine.[7]

There was, however, another way of looking at the legend. In his 1354 chronicle Lorenzo de Monaco argued that the Marian rites, dating from ancient times, began from a purely religious desire to honor the Virgin; but as the rites grew in ostentation and pomp they aroused the jealousy of foreigners, who raided the church in an attempt to steal the gold and jewels displayed on the occasion.[8] The rape story was, by this account, just one episode in the annual observance of the cult of the Madonna. The rites glorified the Virgin, not Venetian valor. Another fourteenth-century source, discounting the part played by the *casseleri*, claimed that the ducal visit to Santa Maria Formosa was established solely because the famous victory had occurred on the day of the Purification of the Virgin and because this church was at the time the only one in Venice dedicated to Mary.[9] The veneration of the Virgin was undoubtedly a major feature of the rites, but, especially in the mid-four-

[7] Victor Turner contrasts earth and fertility cults, which create ritual bonds among the members of a group and which emphasize shared values, to ancestral and political cults, which divide, classify, and distinguish different groups and which emphasize selfish or sectional interests and values. Turner, "The Center Out There," p. 207. The marriage cult in Venice clearly falls into the former classification.

[8] Lorenzo d'Monaco, *Chronicon de rebus venetis* . . ., p. 12. Cf. Galliciolli, *Storie e memorie venete*, 6:4–5; Filiasi, *Memorie storiche de' Veneti*, 6:69–70; Tramontin, "Una pagina di folklore," pp. 412–13.

[9] Galliciolli, *Storie e memorie venete*, 6:9.

teenth century, her adoration was nearly overwhelmed by the bacchanalian preoccupations of the populace. Lorenzo de Monaco probably wished to reassert the Marian nature of the feast,[10] and in so doing he voiced yet another common Venetian precept: the city had long shown a special fondness for the Madonna.

The Venetians, indeed, assiduously venerated the Virgin Mary. Her cult was so popular and so ancient that, like many other cities, Venice was often identified as the city of the Virgin. The day of the Annunciation, March 25, marked the legendary foundation of the city in 421; a sixth-century native of Venetia, Venantius Fortunatus, wrote the matins and lauds sung on her feast days; the seventh-century cathedral at Torcello was named in her honor; Paulinus of Aquileia (died 802) wrote one of the earliest defenses of Mary's divine motherhood against the claims of adoptionists; and after a tremendous increase in hymns and prayers to Mary in the eleventh century, the Litany of Venice, so called because of its long-standing use in San Marco, was matched in popularity in Europe only by that of Loreto.[11]

The Purification of the Virgin, one of the four major Marian feasts, was Byzantine in origin; introduced in Rome no later than the first half of the seventh century, it replaced the feast of the Presentation of Christ in the Temple, which had long before amalgamated and replaced the pagan Feast of Lights (February 1) and Lupercalia (February 15). Both pagan Roman feasts had generative implications: the former was a highly evolved fire ceremony in which a procession of blazing torches lighted the way for the return of a goddess from the underworld and the rebirth of nature; at Lupercalia two male youths, stripped to their loincloths, ran about the Palatine Hill striking with strips of goat and dog hide all they encountered, but especially women, who were thereby made fertile and guaranteed an easy delivery. Livy, in fact, reported that the principal purpose of the Lupercalia was to remedy barrenness in females. In the long transformation from pagan to Christ-centered to Mar-

---

[10] Cf. Del Friuli, *La festa delle Marie*, p. 17.
[11] Musolino, "Culto mariano," p. 241; Hilda Graef, *Mary*, 1:130, 174, 232.

ian rite, Candlemas retained its associations with lustration, fire symbolism, and fertility. By commemorating Mary's post-partum purification, Candlemas became a celebration of divine motherhood, and in the penitential procession lighted candles pierced the gloom of night just as Mary's holiness, "her incandescent purity," exorcized evil.[12] In Venice, however, images of fertility dominated the holiday, and the penetential elements and light symbolism were not emphasized.

The Venetian legend of the rape of the brides and the Marian lore of Candlemas embodied liturgical, expiatory, historical, and even libertine elements that reveal the rich layers of meaning in the Festival of the Twelve Marys, a grand communal rite matched in splendor only by the marriage of the sea. The festival was peculiarly Venetian and known throughout Italy. Although it was abrogated long before the sixteenth century, this tantalizingly ephemeral ritual did not disappear from the collective memory, since it was kept alive in folklore and in a vestigial ducal ceremony.[13]

Medieval Venetian women considered the Festival of the Twelve Marys their own. It was celebrated from at least the mid-twelfth century, when it was first mentioned, to 1379, when it was formally abolished.[14] The festival lasted for eight continuous days beginning on the day of the Conversion of Saint Paul (January 25) and ending on Candlemas (February 2), a period with numerous formal banquets in patrician palaces, frequent social gatherings of women, regattas, and popular sports and games—the *ludi mariani*.[15] Chosen each year by the principle of rotation, two *contrade* (formal divisions of neighborhoods) sponsored the festival, and financial responsibility

---

[12] Graef, *Mary*, 1:48–49, 142–43, 202; Marina Warner, *Alone of All Her Sex*, pp. 66–67, 106; James, *Seasonal Feasts and Festivals*, pp. 177–80, 232–34; *The Catholic Encyclopedia*, s.v. "Candelmas"; Cross, ed., *The Oxford Dictionary of the Christian Church*, p. 226.

[13] On the fame of the festival see Giorgio Padoan, "Sulla novella veneziana del 'Decameron' (IV 2)," 1979, p. 20. On the memory of the festival in the sixteenth century see Sansovino, *Venetia*, 1663, p. 406.

[14] For a discussion of the sources and a bibliography of the literature on the festival see Tramontin, "Una pagina di folklore," pp. 402, 416, n. 73.

[15] Ibid., pp. 402–3; Filiasi, *Memorie storiche de' Veneti*, 6:70, 75; Morelli, *Operette*, 1:133.

fell on these *contrade's* richest noble families, who opened their palaces for visits and 'supplied the charitable offerings distributed on the occasion.[16] The formal rituals began on January 30, the eve of the feast of the Transfer of Saint Mark, when a company of young men from one of the designated *contrade* rowed from their parish to the Ducal Palace, debarked at the Molo (see map), handed out little flags to a group of urchins who crowded around them, and walked around the Piazza in a procession that included trumpet-players, the *contrada's* priests, and servants carrying trays piled high with sweets (*calisons*), bottles of wine, and silver or gold cups. From Piazza San Marco the procession members, singing sacred hymns, made their way to the church of Santa Maria Formosa, where the young men distributed their gifts to the large number of poor young girls who had gathered there. The second designated *contrada* followed shortly with a similar procession and made its own contribution to the wedding feasts of these prospective brides.[17] The first element of the festival was, thus, a charitable and moralistic act in which the rich contributed to the poor by providing dowries and the *contrade* supported the institution of the family by encouraging marriages.

On the following day the ceremonies were even more solemnly religious and more overtly Marian.[18] The two *contrade* formed processions in Piazza San Marco, as on the previous evening. The first consisted of the youths and adult men (*li damosiaus et li homes d'aage*) of one *contrada*, who, as they debarked, distributed five hundred flags to the assembled little children (*petis enfans*) and who carried a hundred silver crosses; bringing up the rear were musicians, priests, and four men

[16] The *contrade* corresponded to the parishes and were paired as early as 1207 into thirty territorial units called the *trentacie*, which preceded the more modern grouping into *sestieri*. Canal, *Les estoires de Venise*, p. 252; Tramontin, "Una pagina di folklore," p. 402, n. 7. An early fourteenth-century decree declared that the two designated *contrade* must begin preparation one month in advance of January 31. Del Friuli, *La festa delle Marie*, pp. 25–26.

[17] Canal, *Les estoires de Venise*, pp. 252–54; Tramontin, "Una pagina di folklore," p. 403; Musolino, "Culto mariano," p. 258.

[18] This account of the events of January 31 has been taken from Canal, *Les estoires de Venise*, pp. 254–58. Cf. Tramontin, "Una pagina di folklore," pp. 404–5, and Musolino, "Culto mariano," pp. 258–59.

shouldering a throne upon which sat a priest dressed as the Virgin Mary. Three priests broke away from the procession, climbed up on a platform placed in front of the doge and assembled dignitaries, and sang a laud to the doge:

> Christ conquers, Christ reigns, Christ commands: To Our Lord _____ and _____ by the grace of God the illustrious doge of Venice, Dalmatia, and Croatia, and ruler of a quarter and half a quarter of the empire of Romania [Byzantium], good health, fame, long life and victory; may Saint Mark help thee.[19]

The doge responded by throwing coins to the priests, who then rejoined the procession. After the priest impersonating the Virgin paid his respects to the doge, the procession of the first *contrada* moved on to Santa Maria Formosa to await that of the second, which was identical to the first save only that the second *contrada's* priest impersonated the Angel Gabriel. When the two processions met at Santa Maria Formosa the two enthroned priests re-enacted the Annunciation as reported in Luke 1:28–38.[20]

It had been the custom in Venice for parish priests to solemnize on the afternoon of January 31, all betrothals of the previous year. This mass celebration explains the significance of the Annunciation play, for Mary was the bride's model and guide, the paragon of motherhood, and God's consort who had been mystically wed at the Annunciation.[21] The Annunciation

---

[19] "Criste vince, Criste regne, Criste inpere: nostre signor Ranier Gen, Des grace inclit dus de Venise, Dalmace et Groace, et dominator quarte part et demi de tot l'enpire de Romanie, sauvement, honor, vie et victoire: saint Marc, tu le aïe!" Canal, *Les estoires de Venise*, p. 254. Cf. Peyer, *Stadt und Stadtpatron*, pp. 63–67.

[20] Canal, *Les estoires de Venise*, pp. 254–56; Tramontin, "Una pagina di folklore," p. 405; Musolino, "Culto mariano," pp. 258–59. The dramatic behavior of the priests impersonating Mary and the angel is prescribed in ASV, Maggior Consiglio, deliberazioni, "Libro d'oro," P. IV, 2 January 1328, m.v., fol. 30r. Elsewhere, on the day of the Purification of the Virgin, the priests impersonated Simon, Joseph, and Mary in a dramatization of Luke 2:22–38. James, *Seasonal Feasts and Festivals*, p. 262.

[21] Unfortunately there is no direct evidence from the period stating all marriages were celebrated on this day; the information comes from later sources

play was certainly more suitable for the Venetian festival than a re-enactment of the Purification, which was performed elsewhere on this occasion. Up to this point the dominant elements of the feast, as we have traced them, were the singing of the liturgical office, the performance of a sacred drama, and the homage paid to the doge.

After the play the members of the processions returned to their *contrade,* where began a far more peculiar ritual. In each of the two *contrade* six nobles or rich citizens opened their houses to the public; displayed inside each was a wooden effigy of Mary dressed in golden robes and adorned with pearls, precious stones, and a gleaming crown.[22] The married ladies and

---

but is consistent with the rites as they were reported by contemporaries. Sanuto, *Le vite dei dogi,* pp. 127–29. Cf. Tramontin, "Una pagina di folklore," p. 413, n. 51.

[22] At first the obligation to open one's house to visitors was distributed by lot to six houses in each of the two *contrade.* ASV, Maggior Consiglio, deliberazioni, "Liber tractus," 13 January 1273, m.v., fol. 21v. The privilege was so onerous that in 1289 only noble families or, if there were an insufficient number of them in the *contrada,* rich *cittadini* were obliged to cover the expenses of the festival; the Quarantia reserved the right to decide who was most qualified. ASV, Maggior Consiglio, deliberazioni, "Liber zaneta," 15 January 1288, m.v., fol. 55r. Cf. Tramontin, "Una pagina di folklore," p. 406, n. 16 and Del Friuli, *La festa delle Marie,* pp. 25–26. Filiasi cites an unidentified source to the effect that there was once a parish-wide tax to support the festival. *Memorie storiche de' Veneti,* 6:73.
    Ever since the fifteenth century, historians of the festival have differed about whether the Marys were live women or effigies. One argument is that the Marys were at first twelve wooden effigies representing the twelve brides abducted by the pirates and that later the twelve most beautiful girls in the city replaced the effigies. Filiasi, *Memorie storiche de' Veneti,* 6:71–72; Mutinelli, *Annali urbani di Venezia,* pp. 22–24; Isa Moro, *I dogi di Venezia,* pp. 7–14. The opposite point of view is that the Marys were at first live women later replaced by wooden statues, possibly to protect the women from public scandal. Michiel, *Le origine delle feste veneziane,* 1:133–57; Sacchi, *Delle condizione degli italiani ne' tempi municipali,* pp. 19–20; Cicogna's notes to Del Friuli, *La festa delle Marie,* pp. 24–25. In Del Friuli's description itself, p. 17, and in Morelli, *Operette,* 1:133, the Marys are wooden effigies. Gallicciolli has a very different account of the festival and says merely that at times the Marys were alive and at other times they were wood. *Storie e memorie venete,* 6:10–11. The extant sources from the period when the Marys festival was still celebrated are sometimes ambiguous but on the whole support the generalization that the Marys were always wooden effigies. These contem-

their maiden daughters entered in their finest clothes and sat quietly chatting while the men stood, drinking wine "in quantity." The following day the visiting and drinking continued,

porary sources are those published in Monticolo, "La costituzione del Doge Pietro Polani"; Canal, *Les estoires de Venise;* Del Friuli, *La festa delle Marie;* and the ASV legislation. This conclusion agrees with that of Tramontin, "Una pagina di folklore," pp. 415–16. At one point in a comparable festive use of female effigies, the peasants' observance of Ascension Day in Transylvania, the richly dressed straw effigy was stripped of its ornaments and clothing, which were then put on a live girl who was led singing through the streets of her village. James, *Seasonal Feasts and Festivals,* pp. 219–20. This practice suggests the possibility that there was a similar switch from effigy to live girl in the Venetian festival, but there is no direct evidence to support such a hypothesis.

Why there were *twelve* Marys is unclear. The explanation that they symbolize the twelve brides abducted by pirates is unlikely, since the pirate legend appears in the sources much later than the Twelve Marys Festival. The only other example I have been able to discover of an association between the number twelve and Mary is in her Crown of Twelve Stars derived from the twelve stars in Apocalypse 12:1. Saint Bernard, Saint Albert, Thomas à Kempis, and others interpreted these twelve stars in various ways. Donald Attwater, *A Dictionary of Mary,* p. 57. Pietro di Giovanni Olivi interpreted the twelve stars in Mary's crown as a symbol of her twelve victories over temptations. Petrus Ioannis Olivi, *Quaestiones quatuor de Domina,* pp. 23–44. (Kenneth Pennington kindly passed on this reference to me.) Most likely the twelve Marys were merely a local manifestation of the widespread fascination with the mystic properties of the number twelve, because there is no evidence to connect the crowns worn by the Marys directly with the Crown of Twelve Stars, nor are there any precise descriptions of the crowns they did wear. The crowns and other jewels of the Marys were kept in the treasury of San Marco, and the procurators were authorized to lend them out each year for the festival. ASV, Maggior Consiglio, deliberazioni, "Liber comunis primus," 4 January 1277 and 25 January 1271, m.v., fol. 2r; Tramontin, "Una pagina di folklore," p. 405, n. 14; Musolino, "Culto mariano," p. 260; Del Friuli, *La festa delle Marie,* p. 25; Gallicciolli, *Storie e memorie venete,* 6:13. Some three quarters of a century after the abolition of the festival, the crowns and jewels of the Marys were used to decorate the high altar of San Marco for principal feast days. Dolfin, "Cronica di Venezia," BMV, MS Italiano VII, 794 (8503), fol. 54r. In 1506 an English traveler saw the "xii crownes of fynew golde, and xii pectorales" still in the treasury of San Marco. *The Pylgrymage of Sir Richard Guylforde to the Holy Land, A.D. 1506,* p. 7. Tramontin says the crowns remained in the treasury until 1797. "Una pagina di folklore," p. 405. Richard Trexler has noted that silver, gold, and precious stones were understood to foster pious devotion by creating a setting that encouraged reverence. "Ritual Behavior," pp. 129–30.

and in the evening the doge accompanied the priests impersonating Mary and Gabriel to hear vespers chanted in Santa Maria Formosa.

The festival culminated on Candlemas proper with a series of ceremonies linked by an extensive water-procession (see map). Early in the morning two boats took a priest, a deacon, and a subdeacon from Santa Maria Formosa to assist in the mass and blessing of candles at the episcopal church of San Pietro di Castello. In the meantime the two *contrade* in charge prepared six boats (*scaule* or *scole*) decorated with tapestries and bunting; one was for forty armed men, a second for priests and the bishop, and the other four each carried three of the Mary statues attended by a group of women and girls. The water-borne cortege formed by these six craft and the hundreds of private ones that came to watch rowed first to San Pietro, where the bishop blessed the boats containing the Marys and then boarded the priests' boat; next the water-procession, consisting now of the six *contrade* boats, the two from Santa Maria Formosa, and two additional ones representing the *contrade* scheduled to sponsor the festival the following year, rowed to the Molo, where the entire company debarked to enter San Marco.[23] In the basilica the *primicerio* presided over a second mass during which candles were again blessed and distributed and after which the water-cortege, this time with the doge's boat added, was reformed.[24] The procession rowed up the Grand Canal to the canal alongside the Fondaco dei Tedeschi (before 1250 it went as far as Santi Apostoli), then down a smaller canal to Santa Maria Formosa, where a third mass was sung to complete the *processio scolarum* and the religious rites. Banquets and popular games, however, continued for days.[25]

[23] On the role of the doge at this point see Tramontin, "Una pagina di folklore," p. 408, n. 28.

[24] Since the procession had to navigate a relatively narrow back canal, it is doubtful that the doge's great ceremonial gallery, the Bucintoro, was used on this occasion. The Bucintoro, however, is specifically mentioned in the chronicle of Marco. Monticolo, "La costituzione del Doge Pietro Polani," p. 133.

[25] This description has been synthesized from several sources: "La costituzione del Doge Pietro Polani," and ASV, Archivio della Mensa Patriarcale, busta 21, fol. 9r, both published in ibid., pp. 124–28, 131–33; ASV, Maggior

IN ITS ORGANIZATION by *contrade* this festival was without parallel among medieval Venetian celebrations. The *contrade* were not only responsible for its financing, planning, and execution, but also the residents of each *contrada* took considerable pride in their efforts and attempted to eclipse their competitors in sumptuous display; there is some evidence that the *contrade* youths spent the eight days parading their Mary effigies around the city in fancily decorated boats, challenging and mocking the other *contradaioli*, and thus revealing an inter-*contrade* rivalry rooted in a strong emotional identification with the parish church and neighborhood territory.[26] The early growth of Venice had probably encouraged parish-consciousness, since most parishes had originally been self-sufficient nuclei isolated on the more than sixty-seven islands that constituted the Realtine city. Each had its own rich and influential families, patron saint, special feasts, customs, and defined border. The *contradaioli* had considerable autonomy over local affairs; they elected their own captain and selected a parish priest, subject only to the confirmation of the bishop and later the patriarch.[27] In Venice the church was, thus, parochially grounded, and the urban structure consisted of a conglomeration of semi-autonomous communities, each serving as a microcosm of the city as a whole.

In a modern anthropological study of Siena the similar constituent *contrade* have been shown to function as independent "city-states," each perceived by the *contradaioli* as the true *patria*, providing an identity in the face of which all other social divisions disappear. And in Siena the *contrade* emblems have

---

Consiglio, deliberazioni, "Liber primus pactorum," fol. 134r; Canal, *Les estoires de Venise*, p. 258; and Del Friuli, *La festa delle Marie,* pp. 17–20. The description agrees closely with the similar efforts at synthesis in Tramontin, "Una pagina di folklore," pp. 406–10, and Musolino, "Culto mariano," pp. 259–60.

[26] Filiasi, *Memorie storiche de' Veneti*, 6:74. Since Filiasi incorrectly assumes that the Marys were alive and that the parading about was a kind of beauty contest, one must treat his account with caution.

[27] Saverio Muratori, *Studi per una operante storia urbana di Venezia*, 1:42; Eugenio Miozzi, *Venezia nei secoli*, 1:111–57; Lane, *Venice*, pp. 11–12; Howard, *Jacopo Sansovino*, pp. 62–63.

an almost totemic significance.[28] This kind of extreme parochialism can create what Erik Erikson has called "pseudo-specia-
tion"; that is to say, by investing individuals with a group
identity through participation in rituals and by excluding as
inhuman, immoral, or at least disloyal all endeavors not sanctioned by the group, such parishes, like tribes and secret societies, behave as if they constituted a separate species of beings.[29]
In medieval Italy *contrade* frequently functioned in this way. In
forming the Santa Maria Formosa visit around processions of
contradaioli, the Venetians revealed an inclination, reinforced
by the urban geography, to conceive of their civic world as the
sum of constituent parishes. The identification with one's *contrada*, however, does not seem to have been quite as pervasive
or all-inclusive in Venice as elsewhere in Italy, particularly in
Siena or Florence, where the *contrade* and *gonfaloni* retained a
far greater judicial and administrative significance. In addition
to this relative weakness, *contrada* identification in Venice may
have been declining absolutely by the fourteenth century as it
was being replaced by the ascendent magnetism of the centralized city.[30]

At the Festival of the Marys the two participating *contrade*
and the parish church of Santa Maria Formosa became the poles
of a special processional route. The first two processions, on the
eve and day of the Transfer of Saint Mark, joined to the cult
centers of Saint Mark and the Virgin all sixty *contrade* of Ven-
jce, symbolized by the designated pair. The *contrade's* distribution of wedding gifts at Santa Maria Formosa discloses that
the parishes were a major source of public alms and that the
parish organization was necessary to provide charity on such a

[28] Alan Dundes and Alessandro Falassi, *La Terra in Piazza*, pp. 12–35. For
other studies critical of their interpretation see Alice Pomponio Logan, "The
Palio of Siena," and Sydel Silverman, "On the Uses of History in Anthropology."

[29] Erikson, "Ontogeny of Ritualization in Man," in Huxley, ed., *A Discussion on Ritualization*, pp. 337–50.

[30] William M. Bowsky, "The Anatomy of Rebellion in Fourteenth-Century
Siena," pp. 234–35; Trexler, "Ritual Behavior," p. 144, n. 62, and idem,
"Ritual in Florence," p. 221; Dale Kent, *The Rise of the Medici*, pp. 62–63;
John M. Najemy, "Guild Republicanism in Trecento Florence," p. 68.

large scale. Parish priests performed the liturgical drama and celebrated the marriages. Although the *contrade* paid formal obeisance to the superior authority of the doge, the doge's participation was by no means as stellar as it was on so many other feast days.

At the procession on Candlemas (see map) the route changed to link a different combination of ceremonial "centers."[31] The procession went from the ecclesiastical center at San Pietro di Castello to the political center at San Marco and to the Marian center at Santa Maria Formosa; it eliminated the spatial significance of the *contrade,* which were not included in the processional route. The *contradaioli* continued to participate, however, and the inclusion of two boats representing the *contrade* that would march the following year established temporal continuity from one year to the next. The *contrade* thus played an important if somewhat equivocal role in these processions: they were necessary to organize the festivities, to provide the charitable gifts, and to harbor the wooden Marys—just as they sheltered the human brides—but, as we shall see, as processional groups the *contrade* were resolutely pushed aside in the late fourteenth century the better to display the centralization and unity of the Venetian commonwealth.

The twelve wooden Marys were, of course, the symbolic centerpieces of the entire festival. The accounts agreed that these statues represented the Madonna herself, especially her attributes of purity and innocence and her ability to command the devotion of and render consolation to the Venetian populace.[32] Pace del Friuli saw the entire festival as an adoration of Mary, and the jewelry and golden dresses of the effigies as signs of the supreme power of virginity.[33] The Annunciation drama, the processions to Santa Maria Formosa, and the distribution of white candles at each of the three masses on February 2 also contributed to the Marian character of the event.

[31] On the concept of ritual centers see Turner, "The Center Out There."

[32] Filiasi, *Memorie storiche de' Veneti,* 6:69; Monticolo, "La costituzione del Doge Pietro Polani," p. 37; Musolino, "Culto mariano," pp. 259–60; Tramontin, "Una pagina di folklore," p. 413.

[33] Del Friuli, *La festa delle Marie,* pp. 19–20.

Women and girls watched over the processions, and their presence implied that the specific objective of the festival was to exalt a particular ideal of femininity to which all women were expected to conform. Throughout the festival, sex and social roles and, surprisingly, age groups were precisely differentiated. In the water-procession on February 2, four boats carried the Marys and their female attendants, one a band of forty soldiers, one an assembly of priests, two the ecclesiastics of Santa Maria Formosa, and two the young men from the next year's *contrade*. Besides depicting the participants in the legendary rescue of the Venetian brides, these boats, in which the men and women were clearly segregated, exposed the constituent social groups of medieval Venetian society: women appeared in their role as virginal daughters, devoted spouses, and pious mothers; men were grouped in the three estates of those who prayed, those who fought, and those who labored.[34] One also sees a society divided into precise age groups. The females were always described as "women and girls," that is, those who had married and those who were still maidens; female status depended on marital state, which in Italian society was often a function of age, since women who were unmarried by the time they were in their middle twenties usually disappeared from the social world into a convent. Males likewise were precisely differentiated according to age groups: on the first evening young men (presumably those who had not yet married) gave flags, perhaps symbols of manhood, to little boys. At the January 31 procession youths and adult men again gave flags to little boys and were followed in the procession by older boys,

---

[34] Although there is a remarkable similarity between these ritual groupings and the legendary rescue of the abducted brides, the appearance during the fifteenth century of the full legend—after the Festival of the Twelve Marys had in fact died out—tempts one to suggest that the legend itself was a late rationalization created to explain a ritual that had lost its original significance. If this were the case, then the four boats of women and the boat of forty soldiers may never have symbolized the participants in the rape story; they may have merely represented the different social orders. Alternately the soldiers may have originally been in the procession to guard the jewels and gold on display.

possibly adolescents, bearing crosses.[35] These divisions of the male community may well have been based on stages in sexual maturity; but, even without knowing precisely the exact generations these groupings contained, one can still be impressed by the precision of the age differentiation, something often assumed to be a distinguishing characteristic of a more modern society.[36]

In other ways the Festival of the Marys paraphrased the peculiar status of women in trecento Venetian society. In two recent articles Stanley Chojnacki has shown that women, especially patrician ladies, had a distinctive and important social and economic influence that contributed to the harmony and stability of Venetian society.[37] In a patriarchal regime such as that of Venice, a complex of attitudes, legal precepts, and rules of inheritance served to protect the patriline as the foundation of society. In Venice a woman had a "curious status": she was exiled from the patriline when she received her dowry—in theory her share of the patrimony—so that the absence of an obligatory orientation toward her paternal kin permitted her to mediate between the two patrilines allied through her in marriage. Thus, women contributed, in particular, to the strength and stability of the patriciate by bonding together various patrician lineages. Moreover, through their ability to make be-

[35] I have assumed here that females were significantly younger than males at first marriage. Although there are no figures published for trecento Venice, David Herlihy has argued that Venetian demographic history probably paralleled Verona's experience, and he has discovered an average age difference of seven years between Veronese spouses in 1424. The age difference was significant, but considerably less extreme than the thirteen years characteristic of early quattrocento Florence. "The Population of Verona," pp. 111–13; Herlihy and Klapisch-Zuber, *Les Toscans et leurs familles*, pp. 393–419. One should be cautious about such an assumption, however, since in twelfth- and thirteenth-century Genoa aristocratic males and females both married in their teens, whereas the sons of artisans usually waited until their mid-twenties to find a teen-age bride. In Genoa, thus, the age at first marriage was class-specific. Diane Owen Hughes, "Urban Growth and Family Structure in Medieval Genoa."

[36] Philippe Ariès, *Centuries of Childhood.*

[37] Stanley Chojnacki, "Dowries and Kinsmen in Early Renaissance Venice," and idem, "Patrician Women." His thesis contrasts with that of Bartolomeo Cecchetti, "La donna nel medioevo a Venezia."

quests, dispose of their own dowries in their wills, and invest independently in business, women were able to exert psychological pressure on their male kin and to express personal preferences without regard to lineage; in their last testaments women showed strong attachments to other women and a desire to strengthen the economic position of their daughters and female relatives. In view of the considerable economic independence of Venetian women, it would be a mistake to view the Festival of the Marys as a patriarchal or misogynous imposition on a group of passive females. Although the notion that outward beauty is the distinguishing characteristic of women governed the festive images, the festival was clearly a major event for women, in which social ties other than those of kinship or marriage could be established or confirmed and in which women could pay homage to their paragon and protector, taking advantage of the opportunity to dominate Venetian society, at least for a moment. In this sense, the Marys' festival was an integral part of the carnival season, during which numerous restrictive social roles were temporarily abandoned.

If the Festival of the Marys was such a vital expression of the medieval social order in Venice, as has been argued here, why then was it abolished? The immediate cause was the War of Chioggia with Genoa (1379–81), during which financial demands on the fisc were so high—one estimate is that through forced levies the government absorbed about one quarter of all the private wealth in Venice—that all superfluous expenses had to be reduced.[38] The festival was suspended temporarily in 1379, and after the war it was reintroduced only in a completely altered form.[39] The pressures of war, however, merely provided the opportunity to reform a festival that had long aggravated officialdom. The Festival of the Twelve Marys was on the one hand far too costly, for competition among the *contrade* meant that each year greater and greater sums were spent to provision banquets, to decorate palaces and boats with precious tapestries, gold, and silver, and to adorn the womenfolk with pearls, gems,

[38] The estimate is in Chojnacki, "Dowries and Kinsmen," p. 574.
[39] Dandolo, *Chronicon venetum*, col. 448; BMV, MS Italiano VII, 794 (8503), fol. 54r; BMV, MS Italiano VII, 519 (8438), fol. 46v.

and fine fabrics; on the other hand the constant parties and revelries often degenerated, according to the more prudish writers, into bacchanalian orgies. The festival had become an occasion when devotion mixed with intemperance, gravity with puerility, and reverence with lechery. Women were released on this occasion from their normal seclusion, and they took proper revenge by walking about in public and chatting, perhaps flirting, with strange men; one complaint was that the men spent more time contemplating the parades of women than the processions of sacred images.

Throughout the early fourteenth century the Senate repeatedly and vainly passed laws designed to eliminate the popular disorders and irreverences: there were orders to the Council of Ten to watch out for suspicious-looking foreigners, to prevent brawls between the *contrade* members, and to guard against stabbings and murders; a 1339 law made it illegal to throw turnips or apples at the Marys; boatmen were often tempted to row jauntily away from the procession, making their own parade up the Grand Canal, even when the penalty for doing so was exile, confiscation, and excommunication; others ignored all social deference and raced past the doge's boat in the water-procession, to the shocked indignation of the noble rulers.[40] In 1379 the government gave up trying to control things and abolished the whole mess. Clearly the major problem lay in the tension that was inevitably created by the celebration of a solemn Marian feast in the midst of the carnival season—Mary and Bacchus were distinctly incompatible mates. Thereafter, Candlemas was reduced to the status of a parish feast; the doge attended the rites in Santa Maria Formosa, but the festival was no longer the occasion for competition among *contrade*. The day for major reverences to Mary and the performance of sacred dramas shifted to the feast of the Presentation of the Virgin (November 21), which was introduced in Venice in 1369–70 by Philippe de Mézières, who had seen the Presentation

[40] Del Friuli, *La festa delle Marie*, pp. 25–26; Monaco, *Chronicon de rebus venetis*, col. 448; Gallicciolli, *Storie e memorie venete*, 6:15; Filiasi, *Memorie storiche de' Veneti*, 6:70–77; Musolino, "Culto mariano," p. 260; Tramontin, "Una pagina di folklore," pp. 409–10.

celebrated in the East and wished to see it established in the Western Church.[41]

In other ways not explicitly mentioned at the time, the Festival of the Marys had become, by the late fourteenth century and from the point of view of the government, anachronistic. The very necessity to offer a historical or legendary justification for the rite reveals a spreading uncertainty about just what this junket of wooden women was supposed to signify. There are other possible explanations for its demise, but the research on this period is yet insufficient for anything more secure than some educated questions: What was the influence of the mendicant orders on the reform of the festival? Was there a renewed reverence for the Virgin in the late fourteenth century? Had the position of women changed in some subtle way? We can be more certain that from the fourteenth to sixteenth centuries the administration of public charity was gradually transferred from the parishes to the Scuole Grandi, which eventually became the mediating institutions in Venice between the rich and poor.[42] This transformation discloses an altered conception of the charitable function from a ritual one, in which the giving of alms was a regularized, mechanical, and liturgical gesture, to an institutional one, in which the creation of organized, permanent services for the poor was a matter of public policy. Similarly, the abolition of the festival and the preceding legislation reveal that the government was growing increasingly anxious about the implications of *contrade* participation. Competition among constituent neighborhoods could either reinforce the communal order by directing potentially disruptive energies into ritualized patterns or lead to communal disorder by encouraging violence and disrespect for authority. It appears that the Festival of the Marys had allowed the *contrade* rivalries to threaten domestic harmony and, potentially, the patrician regime itself, which during wartime was especially wary of challenges to its authority. In the succeeding decades the *contrade* were replaced as competitive organizations by other cor-

[41] Karl Young, "Philippe de Mézière's Dramatic Office for the Presentation of the Virgin," and James, *Seasonal Feasts and Festivals*, pp. 363–64.

[42] Pullan, *Rich and Poor in Venice*, pp. 33–187.

porate entities such as the guilds or the Compagnie delle Calze or the large-scale divisions of the *popolani*, the Castellani and Nicolotti, who occasionally met in an organized combat for the possession of a bridge.

In the Santa Maria Formosa ceremonies that replaced the Festival of the Marys, the government not only abolished *contrada* participation but redesigned the entire spatial pattern of the procession so that it linked the political center at San Marco solely to the Marian center at Santa Maria Formosa, thereby enhancing the established state Catholicism and detracting from the ritual significance of the parishes. The various changes in the routes of the Candlemas processions also chronicled changes in the administration of religious services: in earliest times the episcopal church in Castello accommodated the religious needs of the populace; then, as the city grew, the sacraments and marriages, to the extent that nuptials were under church control at all, became a parochial responsibility; finally, with political centralization the parochial functions were reduced, and reverence turned toward Piazza San Marco, from which henceforward all mystical and magical power emanated. Changes in processional routes followed these transformations only schematically and fitfully, since the administrative changes were not *événements* but gradual movements. By the Renaissance period all processional paths led to and from the Piazza; San Marco was no longer just a stopping-off place, but the unchallenged center of attention. Against the mystical majesty and political superiority of San Marco, the parishes could hardly compete.[43]

Vanished but not forgotten, the Festival of the Marys was remembered throughout the Renaissance in numerous historical accounts, and it was remembered every year as the predecessor to the ducal procession to Santa Maria Formosa.[44] In the

[43] The decline of the *contrade* as foci of identity may also have been caused by the disruptions in population created by the Black Death and ensuing epidemics. With the high mortality among long-established residents and their replacement by immigrants from the mainland, it is conceivable that local ties of kinship and association were so disrupted that people sought to identify with a less personal but more stable entity such as the republic.

[44] Sanuto, *Le vite dei dogi*, pp. 127–29; Sansovino, *Venetia*, 1663, pp. 494–

reformed festival on February 1, the doge and Signoria walked in procession—all boats were eliminated—from the basilica toward Santa Maria Formosa; at the parish border, the doge was obliged to drop several copper coins (called *bianci*), minted especially for the occasion, on a white cloth; at the church the parish priest thanked the doge for coming, performed the divine services, offered the dignitaries refreshments of wine and oranges, and gave the doge a straw hat decorated with the arms of the pope, patriarch, doge, and parish priest himself.[45] A revised legend of the rape of the Venetian brides explained these gifts by saying that after the *casseleri* returned triumphant from their rescue of the maidens the doge asked the *casseleri* to name a reward, and they responded with a request for an annual ducal procession to their parish church. The doge objected that it might rain or that he might be thirsty; so the *casseleri* promised to provide him with a hat to protect his head and with wine and oranges to assuage his thirst. These gifts and, in fact, the whole ceremonial role of the doge on this occasion postdate the abolition of the Festival of the Marys in 1379; before then the bishop made an offering of coins to the parishioners of Santa Maria Formosa on the last day of the festival, but otherwise there was little resemblance between the two festivals.[46] On Candlemas proper, attention shifted entirely to San Marco and to the liturgical offices in which the doge again assumed his paternal role of distributing candles to the Scuole Grandi members, monks, priests, and priors of the hospitals.[47] The elaborate evocations of *contrade* loyalties, marriage, and the idealized images of womankind had been dis-

---

95; Bardi, *Delle cose notabili*, p. 27. Cf. Michiel, *Le origine delle feste veneziane*, 1:133–57; Tassini, *Feste, spettacoli*, pp. 9–14.

[45] Sanuto, *Le vite dei dogi*, p. 89; ASV, Collegio Cerimoniali 1, fol. 9v; BMV, MS Latin III, 172 (2276), fols. 53v–54r; MCV, MS Venier P.D. 517b, under heading "Febraro." Cf. Filiasi, *Memorie storiche de' Veneti*, 6:74–75. In 1534, when the parish priest complained that the financial burden of providing refreshments for all the dignitaries was too great, the requirement was dropped. MCV, Cod. Cicogna 2991/5–6, fols. 3r–4r.

[46] On the bishop's gift of coins see Monticolo, "La costituzione del Doge Pietro Polani," p. 133.

[47] Sanuto, *Le vite dei dogi*, p. 90; MCV, MS Venier P.D. 517b, under heading "Febraro."

placed by the more sober political assertion of ducal pre-
eminence; all this seemed to say that the patrician regime
would not tolerate civil strife, even if it were found only in the
form of neighborhood rivalries. In addition, the celebration of
Candlemas was fully protected from unseemly incursions of
carnival revelries, which were now held predominantly on
Giovedì Grasso.

GIOVEDÌ GRASSO AND THE CARNIVAL SEASON

In January 1507, the serious-minded faculty at the University
of Padua decided to lecture through the carnival season and
thereby to eliminate the liturgically unnecessary but customary
vacation, hoping perhaps to save their students from folly and
from the beckoning festivities of nearby Venice. That hope was
a mistake. The students rioted, smashing the classroom benches
and beating any tutors who dared to discourse on Aristotle or
Galen.[48] Carnival was a time to be seriously playful and gaily
disrespectful, a fact these students fully appreciated, as did
most everyone else save the unredeemably prudish or those
obliged to care for public safety and morality. The students of
course did not want to miss the fun; but their riot reveals more
than disappointment, for in attacking their mentors and destroying the seats of their labor they were themselves partaking
in the liberation of carnival, exercising their wills against their
masters, turning the world upside down in a way they would
rarely attempt at other times of the year. Everywhere during
carnival misrule ruled.

In Venice the carnival season lasted from the feast of Saint
Stephen (December 26) to the first day of Lent, during which
time there were numerous popular entertainments, such as bull
chases and human pyramids; comedies were produced and fireworks displayed; and the alleys and squares came alive with
drinking, feasting, masquerading, and fighting.[49] In characteristically Venetian fashion, when the government could not lead

[48] Sanuto, I diarii, 6:534.

[49] For general descriptions see Molmenti, La storia di Venezia, pp. 55–84,
287–328; Tassini, Feste, spettacoli, pp. 23–28, 35–40, 64–69, 122–27;
Bianca Tamassia Mazzarotto, Le feste veneziane, pp. 31–36, 103–25.

the masses, it was not far behind them; during carnival the patricians tried to bridle excesses by remaining vigilant against the worst threats to the civic peace and public morality, but they also tippled from the carnival cup themselves by sponsoring the most stupendous and entertaining shows. Throughout carnival, but especially on Giovedì Grasso, noble rulers and plebian subjects played games with authority: they asserted and parodied the republic's sovereignty, ducal processions displayed a hierarchical structure that popular ones inverted, and the lords of the nightwatch went out in a show of force but ignored much of what they saw. What did these games mean? Did they serve the much-vaunted social harmony of Venice, or are they evidence that Venice was not as serene as it pretended?

Renaissance writers were themselves insecure about the dangers and significance of carnival. They knew, of course, that this was a period to make merry before the rigors of Lent and that an entertained people ought to be more easily pacified, but they wondered whether the rabble might learn dangerous habits of disobedience during carnival. Did jestful disrespect encourage open rebellion and vengeful reaction? Elsewhere it sometimes did. In Romans in 1580 a group of artisans in a carnival masquerade threatened to eat the rich, who were thereby provoked to attack and massacre the paraders.[50] At Issoudun in 1562 officials arrested a group of Catholics who planned a ghastly Mardi Gras drama calling for thirteen pilgrims, thirteen reapers, thirteen wine-harvesters, and thirteen tax-collectors in a gruesome demonstration against the Huguenots.[51] Throughout the French wars of religion, ritual events including carnival were the most frequent occasion for religious riots and, in fact, became the most likely forum in which to express genuine dissatisfaction and revolutionary sentiments.[52] By the nineteenth century political demonstrations relied heavily on traditional *fête* forms, and the rowdiness and status in-

[50] Emmanuel Le Roy Ladurie, *The Peasants of Languedoc*, pp. 192–97.

[51] Natalie Zemon Davis, "The Rites of Violence," p. 74.

[52] Ibid., pp. 70–75. For Janine Estebe's criticisms of the Davis study and Professor Davis's response, see *Past and Present* 67 (1975): 127–35. For a general analysis of the transition in France of festival occasions into occasions for revolts see Bercé, *Fête et révolte*, pp. 55–92.

versions of carnival itself came to be understood normally as a threat to government.[53]

In the more common cases, where carnival disorder did not lead to open revolt, as was true in Renaissance Venice, scholars have interpreted disorder as a protector of certain communal values and as an explicator of the political and religious hierarchy. How this theory works in actuality is a matter of disagreement. Victor Turner and Roger Caillous emphasize that the ritual inversion of the social hierarchy and the apparent festival disorders actually become organizing principles for social relationships that are not contractually defined; rituals produce communal coherence and buttress the social structure.[54] As Turner explains, absurdity, paradox, extravagance, and illicit behavior in the context of ritual provide an emotional release to hierarchically bound individuals. The ritual release also demonstrates, by isolating such behavior from normal everyday life, that the social hierarchy is predictable and eternal. Inverting a hierarchical order affirms hierarchy as a principle of social organization, and an inferior's mimicking of the behavior of a superior asserts the stability and reasonableness of a hierarchical social relationship. As well as strengthening the social structure, rites of status reversal restore a sense of *communitas*, for they renew personal contact between individuals whom the social ladder sets apart.[55] In somewhat the same way, Keith Thomas posits the pre-industrial carnival as a safety-valve for a highly structured, hierarchical society; carnival was essentially an apolitical activity that periodically reduced social tensions and underscored a "pre-industrial sense of time," that is to say, time that was ritualistic and cyclic, bound as was work to a seasonal calendar.[56]

More suggestive is an argument that sees carnival and in fact

[53] Robert J. Bezucha, "Popular Festivity and Politics During the Second Republic," paper presented to the Davis Seminar, Princeton University, 3 October 1975.

[54] Turner, *The Ritual Process*, pp. 167–68; Roger Caillois, *Les jeux et les hommes*, pp. 171–72. Cf. Turner, "The Center Out There."

[55] Turner, *The Ritual Process*, pp. 176–78. Cf. Natalie Zemon Davis, "The Reasons of Misrule," pp. 48–49.

[56] Keith Thomas, "Work and Leisure in Pre-Industrial Society," pp. 53–54.

all popular festivities during the Renaissance as possessing a logic and structure all their own. Carnival helped to transform society, not just to reinforce hierarchy; by offering the "people" an experience of utopia, it was a built-in mechanism of social reform. Mikhail Bakhtin sees carnival as a kind of psychic redemption effected by the dramatization of destruction, death, rebirth, and renewal. "Carnival . . . did liberate human consciousness and permit a new outlook, but at the same time it implied no nihilism; it had a positive character because it disclosed the abundant material principle, change and becoming, the irresistible triumph of the new immortal people."[57] It did this by permitting the people to organize themselves "in their own way" as a carnival crowd, a concrete collectivity in which the individual became an inseparable part of the human mass. "In this whole the individual body ceases to a certain extent to be itself; it is possible, so to say, to exchange bodies, to be renewed (through change of costume and mask). At the same time the people become aware of their sensual, material bodily unity and community."[58] By permitting such a collectivity to coalesce, "Popular-festive forms look into the future. They present the victory of this future, of the golden age, over the past. This is the victory of all the people's material abundance, freedom, equality, brotherhood. The victory of the future is ensured by the people's immortality."[59] By suspending the authority of the Church and state, popular festivities enacted a utopian truth in real life; and, according to Bakhtin, the influence of carnival was particularly strong during the Renaissance. The "carnivalization" of consciousness, philosophy, and literature was a progressive step in the relentless historical liberation of mankind.[60]

Natalie Davis is equally convinced that popular festivities and rites of status reversal were the product of a distinctively popular culture, but she is far less mechanical in analyzing their social and political effects: "Rather than being a mere 'safety

[57] Bakhtin, *Rabelais and His World*, p. 274. His discussion of carnival is in the chapter entitled "Popular-festive Forms," pp. 196–277.

[58] Ibid., p. 255.

[59] Ibid., p. 256.

[60] Cf. ibid., p. 273.

valve,' deflecting attention from social reality, festive life can on the one hand perpetuate certain values of the community, even guarantee its survival, and on the other hand, criticize political order. Misrule can have its own rigour and can also decipher king and state."[61] Davis emphasizes that carnival forms reveal the social creativity of the inarticulate and that such forms were no less varied and dependent on the circumstances of a particular time and place than were the products of elite culture. From her point of view there can be no universal interpretation, like Bakhtin's view, of popular carnivals. To Davis, festive rituals had a peculiar logic that was independent of any social function they performed; they translated and interpreted the social world into a popular vocabulary.

From this theoretical excursion we return to Venice, where on Giovedì Grasso, as at the Festival of the Marys, popular festive forms mingled with governmental rituals. As was usual in Venice, the rites were explained by a quasi-official legend that, in this case, illustrated a principle of interest to the ruling class. During the twelfth century the patriarch of Aquileia and the patriarch of Grado, a puppet of the Venetians, were locked in deadly conflict over the ecclesiastical jurisdiction of western Dalmatia, which, according to the patriarch of Grado, Pope Adrian IV conceded to him in 1155. Taking advantage of the Venetian involvement in a war with Padua and Ferrara, Patriarch Ulrich of Aquileia attacked Grado in 1162 and forced Patriarch Enrico Dandolo to flee to Venice. Doge Vitale II Michiel counterattacked, captured Ulrich, and destroyed a number of his Friulian castles. After the intercession of Pope Alexander III—the Venetians' much favored patron—Doge Michiel released his captives on condition that the patriarch of Aquileia would henceforth send the doge an annual tribute on Giovedì Grasso, consisting of one bull, twelve pigs, and 300 loaves of bread; the animals would then be slaughtered in public view as a reminder of the defeat of the patriarch and the twelve Friulian canons and lords who had supported him.[62] The patriarchs sent

---

[61] N. Davis, "The Reasons of Misrule," p. 41.

[62] Michiel, *Le origine delle feste veneziane*, 2:37–41; Tassini, *Feste, spettacoli*, p. 23; Tamassia Mazzarotto, *Le feste veneziane*, pp. 31–32. Cf. "Percioche havendo Ulrico Patriarca d'Aquilea mosse l'armi contra la Rep. vinto, & preso

their tribute regularly until 1420, when their temporal domain was abolished; but the symbolic slaughter had become so popular that the government found it necessary to continue it with animals provided from the public purse.[63]

In the rites performed on the morning of Giovedì Grasso the government itself, at least until the reform of 1525, participated in a comic burlesque in which carnival festivity caricatured the serious implications of the defeat of the patriarch of Aquileia. First, before an assembly consisting of the doge, foreign ambassadors, and the scarlet-clad members of the Signoria, a *giudice del proprio* (judge for civil cases in the first instance) solemnly and formally condemned the bull and twelve pigs to a sentence of death.[64] The dignitaries then marched in a procession, from which the ducal *trionfi* were specifically excluded, to the Piazzetta in front of the Ducal Palace, where public executions generally took place, in order to watch the guildsmen of the *fabri* chase the animals around the Piazzetta, capture them, and decapitate them. The large crowd in attendance laughed and chanted in derision of the symbolic captives. After the guildsmen butchered the pigs and divided the meat, the doge and dignitaries retired to the Senate Hall in the Ducal Palace, where they watched the usually solemn senators, also dressed in scarlet, wield clubs to smash miniature wooden castles built for the occasion as representations of the Friulian fortresses destroyed after the defeat of the patriarch.[65]

---

in una giornata: fu instituto per legge irrevocabile sotto gravissime pene, che in memoria perpetua di tanta vittoria, si facesse ogni anno la predetta festa." Sansovino, *Venetia*, 1663, p. 406. See also BMV, MS Italiano VII, 519 (8438), fol. 57v; MCV, Cod. Cicogna 2991/124, fols. 2r–3r. A slightly different interpretation of the origin reads, "per memoria di semitis prestato a Santa Chiesa repetendola ogni Anno per dar esempio à successori à non degenerare delle gloriose attioni de loro Antenati." In "Historia delle guerre de Venetiani con Ottomani," BMV, MS Italiano VII, 11 (8378), fol. 483v. MS dated in the last quarter of the sixteenth century.

[63] Tassini, *Feste, spettacoli*, pp. 23–24.

[64] The only other occasions on which the Signoria wore scarlet were Palm Sunday and Christmas Eve. MCV, MS Venier, P.D. 517b, under heading "Domenica di Carnivale."

[65] On the absence of the *trionfi* in the procession see MCV, MS Venier, P.D. 517b, under heading "Avertimenti generali." On the scarlet dress see under

By the early sixteenth century these bloody and brutal rites began to appear ridiculous to the republic's more sophisticated elders, who instituted a series of reforms. In 1509 the doge ceased to give the butchered pork to the senators and instead offered it as alms for the monasteries and prisons.[66] But the most thoroughgoing reform came in a decree of the Council of Ten dated February 17, 1525.[67] The document betrays the government's attitude toward public ceremony, particularly toward carnival, in an interesting way. The legislation emanated from the Council of Ten, the body charged with matters of state security, rather than from the Collegio of the Senate, which normally handled ceremonial details and answered questions of precedence. The reform of Giovedì Grasso was a matter for the highest councils of government and an object of contention, for in fact the measure passed by the narrow margin of eight to six. The act referred to a previous reform of 1521 that had eliminated, for purposes of decorum and for the merit of the Signoria, the giudice del proprio's announcement of the sentence against the animals and the senators' castle smashing; but the act also noted that the "idiocy" of decapitating the pigs brought solace to the populace. In view of the popularity of the event, the Council of Ten pledged to spend thirty ducats from the Ten's own treasury on the ritual, but ordered that the twelve pigs be replaced by one bull, which the fabri would then

---

heading "Ceremonie che si usano nelle solennità mobili del Ser[enissi]mo Prencipe di Venetia." This last section mentions the 1591 carnival in which all the guilds participated. The fabri earned the right to decapitate the animals because of the valor they displayed in the war against the Patriarch Ulrich. Canal, Les estoires de Venise, pp. 260–62; BMV, MS Italiano VII, 519 (8438), fol. 57v; Sansovino, Venetia, 1663, p. 406; Michiel, Le origine delle feste veneziane, 2:41–45; Tassini, Feste, spettacoli, p. 23; Tamassia Mazzarotto, Le feste veneziane, p. 32.

[66] Giovanni Battista Pace, "Ceremoniale Magnum, sive raccolta universale di tutte le ceremonie spettanti alla ducal regia capella di San Marco, 1678," BMV, MS Italiano VII, 1269 (9573), fol. 23v. Martin da Canal, "La cronique des Venetiens," Archivio storico italiano, 1st series, 8(1845):745, n. 311. This is the first published edition of Canal's Les estoires de Venise.

[67] ASV, Consiglio dei Dieci, parti misti, registro 47, fol. 192r–v. Dated 1524, m.v. Cf. Michiel, Le origine delle feste veneziane, 2:45.

decapitate for the pleasure of the crowds.[68] The elder patricians would thus be relieved of participation in such a dishonorable and degrading spectacle, and the *popolani* would still have their show.

Sansovino later reported that Doge Andrea Gritti (1523–38) was the moving force behind this reform. "In the opinion of prince Gritti such a custom, which had become utterly ridiculous, even if it had been properly instituted by the ancient fathers, was to be thrown out, leaving only the festival in the Piazza, the pageants, and the decapitation of the bull by the guildsmen of the fabri."[69] One of Gritti's major preoccupations during his dogeship was to elevate the republic's *nobiltà* through reforming the annual ducal ritual and restructuring and re-embellishing the ceremonial spaces of the Piazzetta of the Ducal Palace and Piazza San Marco. To this end he encouraged governmental patronage of the best artists; it was Gritti who brought to Venice Adrian Willaert, the composer; Jacopo Sansovino, the architect; and Pietro Aretino, the poet.[70] Sansovino cleared away the shacks of butchers and salami-sellers who had infested the Piazzetta and the Piazza, and he built the famed Marciana Library, the Procuratoria Nuova, the Mint, and the Loggetta at the base of the Bell Tower, thereby magnifying the splendor of the setting for state ceremonies.[71] Gritti wished to replace the popular and vulgar elements of carnival with more noble entertainments such as comedies, ballets, masquerades, fireworks, and pageants.

[68] Usually the Council of Ten spent fifty ducats each year on Giovedì Grasso. Sanuto, *I diarii*, 44:171.

[69] "Il quale uso, parendo al Principe Gritti, che fosse ridicolo affatto, se bene ordinato da gli antichi Padri, fu del tutto levato via, restando solamente la festa in piazza, del solaro, & del tagliar la testa altoro, che tocca all'arte de fabri." Sansovino, *Venetia*, 1663, p. 406. Cf. "Io la sento molto biasimar come debile, e di poca importa[n]za, e molti dicono, che si doverebbe levare: nondimeno ella hà il suo principo, & si celebra per antica memoria di una vittoria recevuta da questi Signoria. . . ." Doglioni, *Le cose notabile*, p. 44.

[70] E. Rosand, "Music in the Myth," pp. 518–19; Howard, *Jacopo Sansovino*, p. 4; Muir, "Images of Power."

[71] Howard, *Jacopo Sansovino*, pp. 10–16 and passim.

In the following centuries the festival remained an important governmental concern. In 1550 the Council of Ten transferred responsibility for supervision of the festival to the Rason Vecchie, which was limited at that time to a budget of 100 ducats.[72] The officers of the Rason Vecchie co-ordinated public and private expenditures, organized special entertainments, and selected the best plans for festive decorations and pageants from proposals submitted by artists, who were often of highest renown.[73] The official disgust with the popular festivities and the concerted attempts to enhance the aristocratic bearing of the republic, revealed first by Gritti and the Council of Ten and later by the institutional commitment of the Rason Vecchie, disclose the widening cultural separation so evident in the last three-quarters of the sixteenth century between many of the Venetian nobles and the lower classes. During this same period the government reinvigorated its concern for the public appearance of the regime.[74] Yet, the best efforts of Gritti and his colleagues were insufficient to suppress completely the Rabelaisian entertainments demanded not only by the masses but by the younger nobles as well. Sanuto reported that at the carnival two years after the reform the squires of the doge decapitated five pigs, and a butcher swung a sword to a bull; pigs and bulls were slaughtered "as usual" again in 1528, 1529, and 1530.[75] The reforms were at least partially ignored.

Besides the official rites that recalled the victory over the patriarch of Aquileia, Venetian carnival boasted a mélange of activities that included chivalric sports, imitations of ancient Roman entertainments, and popular festive forms. The government was always concerned about these entertainments, but

[72] ASV, Rason Vecchie, busta 1, fol. 1142, and busta 3, fol. 169v. Cf. MCV, Cod. Cicogna, 2991/125, fol. 4r. The date of 1594 given in Tassini is incorrect. The transer of control was in 1549 m.v. *Feste, spettacoli,* p. 24, n. 1.

[73] There are, unfortunately, no extant sixteenth-century proposals, as there are for the seventeenth and eighteenth centuries. See ASV, Rason Vecchie, buste 225 and 226. Antonio Pellanda published one of the seventeenth-century proposals from busta 226 in *A Giacinto de' Mitri nel giorno faustissimo del suo matrimonio colla gentile Signora Erminia Bolliana,* pp. 19–21. Also see his *Festa del Giovedì Grasso (Sei documenti di storia veneziana).*

[74] These ideas are more fully developed in Muir, "Images of Power."

[75] Sanuto, *I diarii,* 44:171, 46:611, 49:422, 54:295.

6. Giacomo Franco, *Giovedì Grasso Celebrations in Memory of the Victory of the Republic over the Patriarch of Aquileia in Friuli.*

only irregularly involved in them; they were organized in a variety of ways. On one occasion the Signoria gave Doge Andrea Gritti's son, Pelegrin, 100 ducats to build a pageant stage (soler) in the middle of Piazza San Marco.[76] On another a lawyer named Luca Donà wrote a dramatic burlesque and masquerade held in Campo Santa Maria Formosa.[77] On Giovedì Grasso in 1517, to express their joy for having reached an accord with the emperor over trading rights in Trieste, the German merchants of the Fondaco dei Tedeschi (see map) sponsored jousts, bull chases, battles between dogs and a bear, a transvestite ballet, and an allegorical pageant in the courtyard of their warehouse.[78]

More typically, during carnivals in the early sixteenth century a herald or buffoon organized and participated in the festivities. In northern Europe by the fifteenth century, the office of herald had lost its association with the *joculatores* of the twelfth and thirteenth centuries and had become the preserve of educated clerks, whose responsibilities were less those of court fools and more those of chancellery officials in charge of the very serious matters of diplomatic and political ceremony.[79] The Venetians had a similar heraldic official, a master of ceremonies (discussed in the next chapter), but in sixteenth-century Venice the term "herald" itself retained the original connotations of buffoonery.[80] In this office, Venetians were decades behind Florentine practice. At a 1520 carnival masquerade in the *sestiere* of Cannaregio, a herald "who put things in order" opened the dramas by delivering a letter to the "lord" of the carnival and then danced away.[81] The herald organized matters

[76] Ibid., 46:611.

[77] Ibid., 19:441.

[78] Ibid., 23:583.

[79] On the office of herald see the excellent discussion by Richard C. Trexler, *The Libro Cerimoniale of the Florentine Republic*, pp. 13–31; on the Florentine heralds see pp. 33–46.

[80] In 1530 "heralds" were described as presenting a "momarie buffonesca." Lionello Venturi, "Le compagnie della calza (sec. XV–XVI)," 17:178.

[81] "Poi, a hore 3 di note, vene l'araldo di la muraria grande, qual si messe in ordene a do di la muraria grande, qual si messe in ordene a la chiesia di Canarejo fata per Marco Tonin insegna ballar, la qual costò ducati 300, che vene con assa' torzi da numero 40 portati per famegii et li compagni per tre la

on this occasion but was also a performer in a mummery that
was bawdy and irreverent.

Venetians depended on specialists for the organization of
many carnival festivities. During the 1510s Zuan Polo, an im-
provisator and quick-change artist, was a favorite buffoon who
wrote and acted in mini-comedies performed between the acts
of plays.[82] In 1517 he fell off a horse in a comic joust and hurt
his leg, ending his part in the games.[83] One Zuan Cosaza appeared several times either mounted on a horse for jousts or as
the captain of soldiers in mock battles, but it is unclear whether
he was a professional buffoon or merely an expert horseman.[84]
Marco Tonin was much admired as a ballet master in charge of
masquerades during the 1520s; in 1527 the crowds scorned a
master named Cherea, who had been put in charge of the Giovedì Grasso preparations, when he failed to come up to the high
standards Tonin had established.[85] Carnival in Venice was to
some degree a calculated affair, a civic drama directed by experts
who may have borrowed from a popular cultural tradition, but
who were themselves beholden to their sponsors.

The Compagnie delle Calze, the festive companies formed by
young nobles to plan parties and pageants, provide decorations,
and perform comedies, were the primary institutions for organizing noble carnival activities. The young dandies in these compagnie uniformed themselves by adopting distinctive multi-col-

compagnava. Et il signor Zuane Cosaza, è di dita compagnia, a cavallo da
capitanio armigero, facendo far largo a tutti, vene sopra 3 cavali marani portati
da' fachini tre mumi vestiti per excelentia, come si consuetava di far, et in
questi era l'araldo con la letera al signor quando doveva venir la muraria, e con
gran fuogi artificiali ne l'andar sul soler. Poi tornato indrio esso araldo, fu
balato sopra dito soler, et a hore 4 vene la muraria acompagnata da li torzi, *ut
supra*, che fu bel veder." Sanuto, *I diarii*, 28:254.

[82] Ibid., 19:443; Venturi, "Le compagnie della calza," 17:221–22.

[83] Sanuto, *I diarii*, 23:583.

[84] Ibid., 19:441, 28:254.

[85] ". . . zorno deputato a far la caza sopra la piaza di S. Marco, perchè fu
preso in Conseio di X dar ogni anno ducati 50 per far la festa, Cherea tolse tal
cargo." After describing the masquerade, Sanuto reported, ". . . siché fo bru-
tissima festa et da tutti biasemato Cherea. Quella di l'altro anno che fece
maistro Tonin con cari etc. fo assà meglio: concludo che fu cosa bruttissima."
Ibid., 44:171–72. On Tonin as a dance-master see ibid., 28:254. Tonin died in
1530. Ibid., 52:599.

ored, tight-fitting hose that covered the whole leg, as can be seen in Carpaccio's *Legend of Saint Ursula* and in the background of Gentile Bellini's *Procession in Piazza San Marco of the Scuola Grande San Giovanni Evangelista*.[86] There were some twenty-three *compagnie* chartered as proper Compagnie delle Calze between 1487 and 1565, but there were similar corporations in the early fifteenth century, numerous unofficial ones or ones that did not use hosiery to identify themselves in the sixteenth century, and occasional ad hoc *compagnie* after 1565.[87]

As with the Festival of the Twelve Marys, in the fourteenth century the *contrade* and guild societies (*scuole artigiane*) organized festival games and processions; but increasingly during the fifteenth century the nobility sought to regulate private as well as public entertainments, and the Compagnie delle Calze provided the institutional device for such regulation. Although the *compagnie* were themselves private corporations, they eventually fell under the supervision of the Council of Ten: the Council limited each *compagnie* to twenty-five members in 1494 (a decree which was often ignored), licensed new ones, and used them to entertain visiting dignitaries; but occasionally the Ten made minor concessions to the *compagnie* such as allowing members to hold parties in Piazza San Marco or loaning

---

[86] Michelangelo Muraro, "Vittore Carpaccio o il teatro in pittura." The founders of the Trionfanti in 1516 were twenty years of age. Sanuto, *I diarii*, 21:436.

[87] Venturi, "Le compagnie della calza," 16:161–221, 17:140–233. During his lifetime Sanuto reported that he had known of thirty-four *campagnie* of young nobles. *I diarii*, 58:184–85. Sansovino said there had been forty-three *compagnie* up to 1562. *Venetia*, 1604, fol. 273v. Some argued that the *compagnie* first appeared in 1400 in order to celebrate the election of Doge Michele Steno. Sansovino, *Venetia*, 1604, fol. 273v, and MCV, Cod. Cicogna, 3278/24, fol. 13r. Elsewhere (fol. 34r) the same MS reports that the *campagnie* dated from the establishment of the first dogeship, were originally military in nature, and were designed to maintain the peace and to protect the public welfare. The military function of the *compagnie* is echoed in Bernardo Giustiniani, *Historie cronologiche dell'origine degl'ordine militari e di tutte le religioni cavalleresche infino ad hora instituite nel mondo . . .*, p. 107. The theory of the military origin of the *compagnie* is probably false, but is understandable in light of the sixteenth-century Venetian attempts to magnify the nobility of the patriciate.

the Hall of the Great Council for the performance of a comedy.[88]

The Ten occasionally recoiled, however, from allowing the young too much liberty: in 1527 the Ten ordered that the pageant stages for Giovedì Grasso, built in Piazza San Marco by an unidentified group of young nobles, be torn down, forcing the would-be party-goers to come before the Council to plead their case;[89] in 1529 the Floridi were denied permission to have a private carnival party in Piazza San Marco;[90] and sumptuary laws were repeatedly passed to limit the costs of banquets and clothing and to keep unmarried girls away from the *compagnie* parties.[91] Nonetheless, the *compagnie* regularly looked to the Council of Ten for subsidies for pageants and protection from destructive rivalries; in 1533 the Cortesi went to the Ten to complain that somebody had damaged their pageant floats and painted defamatory slogans on the walls of buildings.[92]

The *compagnie*, usually incorporated for a fixed period of less than a year, consisted of about twenty members who each contributed an initiation fee—fifty ducats in the case of the Sempiterni, founded in 1541—and who elected a prior or lord to direct their festivities. The sixteenth-century *compagnie* developed complex organizational structures that included counselors and hired hands such as a secretary, chamberlain, chaplain, and occasionally a poet, architect, or painter.[93] Besides

[88] Venturi, "Le compagnie della calza," 16:203–17.

[89] Sanuto, *I diarii*, 44:169.

[90] Venturi, "Le campagnie della calza," 16:217.

[91] Ibid., 16:217–21. Sanuto disapproved of the "shamefully" wasteful and expensive costumes of the men and women at the parties the *compagnie* sponsored during carnival. *I diarii*, 19:418.

[92] "A dolersi de dolfini roti a le loro barche et parole scrite sopra li muri in suo vituperio, pregando volesseno dar taia per il Conseio di X, et loro offeriscono dil suo dar a chi manifesterà ducati 200." Sanuto, *I diarii*, 58:189.

[93] Venturi, "Le compagnie della calza," 17:141–42; Sansovino, *Venetia*, 1604, fol. 273v. The *capitoli* of the Sempiterni (1541) are published in Giustiniani, *Historie*, pp. 111–13. The *capitoli* of the Modesti are in MCV, Cod. Cicogna, 3278/24, fols. 25r–29r. Without giving a source, Maria Teresa Muraro says that each year the *compagnie* appointed a poet, architect, and painter. "Le lieu des spectacles (publics ou privés) à Venise au XVᵉ et au XVIᵉ siècles," p. 85, n. 1. None of the sources I have been able to find mention these annual appointments as a characteristic of all the *compagnie*.

initiation parties, which were often magnificent and which were important occasions for artistic patronage, the members sponsored *feste* whenever one of them married, and they organized pageants and dramas for carnival.[94] The Compagnie delle Calze provided festive services for their members and for the republic, gave valuable experience in management and planning to young nobles, harnessed youthful energies to a socially useful end, and probably gave license to a limited amount of supervised courtship. The *compagnie* were similar to many other youth groups, from the *brigate* of Boccaccio's Florence to modern college fraternities, in the sense that the associations were temporary, like youth itself; they occupied young males with the details of social and festive life in preparation for marriage and adult responsibilities.[95] *Compagnie* members, however, sometimes established long-lasting ties that later took the form of political alliances or, at least, mutual regard.[96] *Compagnia* association was extrafamilial and outside the patrilineal concerns that dominated the nobles' social and political consciousness.

During the late fifteenth century and the first half of the sixteenth, no organization surpassed the Compagnie delle Calze in the enthusiastic preparation of carnival festivities. The *compagnie* provided bulls and pigs to be chased and slaughtered in Piazza San Marco and elsewhere.[97] They sponsored masquer-

[94] For a summary of the festive activities of many of the *compagnie* see Venturi, "Le compagnie della calza," 17:141–233. The initiation ceremony of the Sempiterni and Titian's role as designer of the festive décor is described in Giustiniani, *Historie*, pp. 114–15. The founding of the Fedeli of 1459 and of the Concordi of 1489 is noted in MCV, Cod. Cicogna 2991/II.3, fol. 1r; of the Contenti of 1504 in Sanuto, *I diarii*, 6:99; of the Immortali of 1507 in ibid., 7:169; of the Trionfanti of 1516 in ibid., 21:436; of the Valarosi of 1524 in ibid., 36:282–83; of the Reali and the Floridi of 1529 in ibid., 50:431–32, 436–38; and of the Cortesi of 1533 in ibid., 58:182–83.

[95] On the function of youth groups in Florence as ritual "saviors" of society see Trexler, "Ritual in Florence: Adolescence."

[96] At the election of Doge Antonio Grimani, Sanuto commented that "Questo Doxe fo Compagno dil Doxe defonto [Leonardo Loredan]; ha mexi 22 manco di lui; la qual compagnia si chiamava *Solenni*, di quali è vivi *solum* 5 con lui." *I diarii*, 30:484.

[97] Ibid., 15:501, 19:418, 28:254, 44:171. Sanuto notes in 1504 that it was unusual to have a festival in Campo San Polo: "cossa inusitata far in campi." Ibid., 5:739. Later it was more common.

ades, ballets, banquets, and fireworks displays,[98] built pageant devices and stages, adorned boats with marine monsters and serpents,[99] and hired daredevils, usually Turks, to walk on ropes strung from the bell tower in Piazza San Marco to boats in the lagoon;[100] sometimes they gouged the public with high prices for admission to their shows.[101] In all, the most significant and memorable contribution of the *compagnie* was their support of drama, with performances ranging from *momaria* (allegorical pantomimes enacted on boats or *soleri*) to restorations of comedies by Plautus and Terence.[102] They were as well major sponsors of Ruzante, whose irreverent comedies about loutish peasants (*alla villanesca* and *alla vilota*) were perfect carnival vehicles.[103] The famous Sempiterni, who had hired Titian for their initiation festival, commissioned Aretino to write *Talanta* and brought Vasari to Venice to design the scenery for the play's first performance at the carnival of 1542.[104] The *compagnie* members themselves acted in these comedies, which were proverbially lascivious.[105] The age of the *compagnie*

[98] Ibid., 1:886, 15:501, 28:248. Other *compagnia*-like festivals for which no sponsor is named are described in ibid., 6:297, 13:489, 15:522.

[99] Ibid., 28:254.

[100] The Accesi paid a Turkish tight-rope walker 100 ducats in 1564. "Cronaca Agostini di Venezia," MCV, Cod. Cicogna 2853, fol. 126v.

[101] Sanuto, *I diarii*, 44:171.

[102] Ludovico Zorzi, "Elementi per la visualizzazione della scena veneta prima del Palladio," pp. 35–36. Cf. Sansovino, *Venetia*, 1604, fols. 273v–74r, 301v. The dramatic *momaria* is discussed by Venturi, "Le compagnie della calza," 17:224–26. For a description of a typical *momaria* see Sanuto, *I diarii*, 13:483. At the carnivals of 1515 and 1520 at least three *compagnie* were active at the same time in presenting comedies. Ibid., 19:418, 28:253–56. In 1515 at least two comedies by Plautus were staged. Ibid., 19:443–44. Plautus's *Aulularia* was recited during carnival in 1517. Ibid., 23:598. In 1520 the Trionfanti performed *Adelphoe* by Terence. Ibid., 28:256.

[103] Plays by Ruzante or by Ruzante and Menato are mentioned in Sanuto, *I diarii*, 28:255, 29:536–37, 35:393. The account in vol. 28 is published separately as *Narrazione della feste solenne data in Venezia dalla compagnia della calza nel MDXX adi XIII febraio per l'accettazione di tre socii*. See also Venturi, "Le compagnie della calza," 17:220–21.

[104] Vittorio Rossi, *Fra i compagni Sempiterni*, p. 8. Cf. Juergen Schulz, "Vasari at Venice."

[105] Sanuto described a comedy presented in 1515 in the courtyard of the Mint: "Poi preparato uno loco bellissimo, fu fato per una compagnia nova ditta

members, the comedies they produced, and the burlesque allusions to sexuality found in the *momarie* reflect one of the dominant themes of all carnival festivity: the celebration of renewal and liberation, of youthfulness and fertility, and the denigration of the impotence of the elderly, the worn, the established.

Carnival pageants, sponsored either by Compagnie delle Calze members or others and staged in various *campi* throughout Venice, unfurled the various cultural traditions that characterized Renaissance Venice. Chivalric conceits and neoclassical iconography were mixed with popular and carnivalesque allusions to sexuality, death, and rebirth. Early sixteenth-century Venetians felt no aesthetic discordance between Gothic and Renaissance imagery, and there was no dialectical opposition between the elite and popular origins of the various festive forms. In 1520, for example, the Compagnia degli Immortali sponsored an evening *festa* in front of Ca' Foscari on the Fondamenta San Simeone (see map). After a preliminary bull chase, the *momaria* began as a dancing herald presented to the lord of the festival a letter, which was presumably a program of the performance. Zuan Cosaza paraded around as an armed captain; two knights jousted with lances; then various actors, dressed as Laocoön with a serpent around his neck, a Trojan, an idol, and a king and his daughter, pantomimed the fall of Troy. The pageant ended with a devil emerging from a ball of fire, which ultimately consumed the set.[106] In Piazza San Marco in 1528, fourteen pageant cars included actors dressed as Neptune, Mars, Mercury, and the Sun, all mounted on marine horses; Jupiter accompanied by eight other unidentified gods; and Hercules, who pantomimed his labors.[107]

More common were droll allegories of death and regeneration. In 1515, between the acts of Plautus' *Miles Gloriosus* performed in the courtyard of Ca' Pesaro by the Immortali, the buffoon Zuan Polo and his assistants presented a short farce. It

---

i Ortolani, una bellissima comedia recitata da loro, cosa nova ma un poco lassiva." *I diarii,* 19:434.

[106] Ibid., 28:253–56. Cf. 26:503, and Iulio Faroldo, *Annali veneti,* fol. 38v.

[107] Sanuto, *I diarii,* 46:611–12.

opened with a scene of a flaming Hell peopled by actors in blackface. A God of Love was carried into Hell where he met the castrato Domenico Taiacalze, who was singing; a chorus of castrati then emerged from Hell singing and dancing. After this musical interlude, nymphs entered on a triumphal car chanting and beating time with hammers on an anvil disguised as a heart. (The evening must have been a tremendous success, for Sanuto reported that hardly anyone showed up in the Senate the next morning.)[108]

The hammer-and-anvil image was used again at the carnival of 1529, but this time in a more explicitly sexual way. Sanuto carefully noted that the female roles on this occasion were performed by "real women." The *momaria* began with four wild men (*homeni salvadegi*) fighting with their women, who were eventually overpowered and dragged away; young men entered and fought the wild men, but were captured; the young men returned from offstage to shoot the wild men with arquebuses and then carried in an anvil around which they danced as they kept time by beating it with hammers. Eventually a little boy and little girl emerged from under the anvil and danced "most excellently." The pageant continued with a battle between young women and wild women and ended happily when the young women, holding a gigantic arrow, tied up the wild men, and the young men bound the wild women.[109] This battle of the sexes, with its allegorical triumph of civilization over nature and the sexual hammer-and-anvil dance that produced a new generation, was indeed crude but explicit and typically carnivalesque in its imagery of regeneration through violence.

Birth and death images were found in a variety of pageant allegories. In 1517, after eight men dressed as women danced a ballet, triumphal cars entered upon which appeared a God of Love, nymphs, and their lovers all dancing. The lovers made sacrifices to the God of Love, the nymphs gave birth, and all were buried without even an interruption of the dance![110]

[108] Ibid., 19:443.
[109] Ibid., 49:422.
[110] ". . . Far sacrificii, parturir et sepulture sempre balando. . . ." Ibid., 23:583.

Sometimes regeneration images were more dignified, as in 1527 when a pageant compared the old world (a turning globe with an old man in it) to a new world (a globe containing a boy dressed as an angel). After an oration by the boy angel on the faults of the old world, the first globe was burned, leaving the new world triumphant.[111] At other times regeneration images were simply lewd, as in 1518 when a petty trader dressed as an old man walked around during the *festa* in Campo San Polo (see map) showing off to the women watching from palace windows a cage containing a statue of Priapus with a huge erect phallus.[112] Occasionally sensual by-play was directed against the virtuous pretensions of the religiously devout. At the 1530 Giovedì Grasso celebration, a tableau vivant depicted six pilgrims who were first tempted by a devil and then by a beautiful woman laden with riches; in the end they were unable to resist her, threw off their habits, and thus stripped (*spogliati*) danced as they beat time with their pilgrims' staffs. After they left, two live horses pulled in a pageant car containing five nymphs followed by peasants adorned with jewels on their heads. The nymphs, identified as famous courtesan ballerinas from Ferrara, danced alone and then with the bizarre peasants. That evening at a Ducal Palace banquet for the foreign ambassadors, Doge Andrea Gritti (again the carnival reformer) stopped the recitation of an eclogue because dirty words figured in it.[113] So went much of carnival, the annual breaking out of the sensual and prohibited from the prison of conformist social life. Although many outlandish inversions of the normal, such as bejeweled peasants, appeared during carnival, the dominant imagery was one of death and reproduction; sexual parodies were most common of all, revealing not only the liberation achieved through ribaldry but the habit, still popular in the sixteenth century, of celebrating marriages at carnival time.[114]

The examples above portray a carnival in which much was a calculated drama, bawdy and disrespectful perhaps, but planned

[111] Ibid., 44:171–72.

[112] "Et *accidit*, che uno bazarioto vestito da vechio, havia una cheba con uno priapo dentro; stava benissimo, l'andava monstrando a le done." Ibid., 25:216.

[113] Ibid., 54:296.

[114] Ibid., 19:393–94, 23:598, 28:248.

to be so; and if the authorities did not entirely approve, at least
they tolerated most of it. In some respects, though, such a
picture is misleading. Much that took place during carnival was
spontaneous, accidental, violent, or outside of the acceptable
limits set by the government. Some pageant displays were just
too crude and insufficiently entertaining, as was the case when
in 1518 the Signoria ordered a disappointing display torn
down.[115] At other times the exuberance of the occasion led to
accidents: someone was killed in Campo San Geremia in 1513,
a sixteen-year-old girl died at Santa Maria Zubenigo in 1518,
and in 1530 a bull attacked and killed the seventy-two-year-old
notary, Antonio Beneto.[116]

Masquerades gave malefactors and criminals special opportunities. In 1518, near the church of San Zulian, a man masquerading as a Slovenian surprised Vicenzo da Molin and his
cousin Domenico while they were walking home for lunch; the
masked man wounded Domenico, and when Vicenzo fell while
trying to run away, he was clubbed to death; in the ensuing
chase the culprit escaped through a house on the Calle del
Paradiso. The confusion created by so many wandering about
the city in masquerade made the search for the murderer extremely difficult; the authorities brought in for questioning a
Tuscan costumed as a peasant, but he revealed nothing.[117]
Masks also allowed prostitutes dressed as men to ply their trade
more covertly than usual, and these violations of the public
peace and morality led to occasional prohibitions against wearing masks during carnival time.[118] Such lapses in the public
order were what one would expect in a large city like Venice at
festive times, but, whatever their cause, none of these incidents
had distinctly political overtones; the Venetian carnival never
became the Venetian revolution. Marin Sanuto's diaries, upon

[115] Ibid., 25:215–16.

[116] Ibid., 15:501, 25:215–16, 54:296–97.

[117] Suspicion eventually fell on one Marco Michiel, banished for six years
for a previous attack, and a warrant was issued for his arrest. Ibid., 25:217–
18.

[118] Ibid., 6:297, 7:751. After the death of Doge Marin Grimani in 1605,
masquerades were prohibited during carnival in order to discourage outbreaks
of violence. Smith, *Sir Henry Wotton*, 1:343.

which this discussion has been largely based, covered the difficult years during the War of the League of Cambrai when foreign powers came closest to threatening the independence of Venice and the survival of the patrician regime; but never during this period did carnival, the occasion when domestic political violence and revolutionary sentiments might be most likely to burst forth, produce anything resembling the religious riots in France during the last half of the century.[119]

The expression during carnival of popular political attitudes came in a rather different form. In his account of the carnival of 1533 Sanuto described a mock procession of *popolani*.

> There were many people walking about in masquerade, among whom were some persons dressed in ducal sleeves of scarlet silk and in velvet hoods. One of them had a gold chain [around his neck] like the grand chancellor, and others dressed as commanders or carried trombones and cornets before them as a sign that here marched the Signoria. However, in my opinion it was not very well done.[120]

This clownish imitation of an official procession, in which the masqueraders dared go only so far as to caricature the *cittadine* grand chancellor and not the noble doge, was hardly revolutionary and not even very satirical. At most it might be interpreted as a ritual of status reversal, in which persons of low rank affect the style of their social superiors and in so doing temporarily invert a hierarchy they normally accept.[121] This burlesque procession occurred in public, but the perpetrators were probably able to preserve their anonymity by wearing masks.[122] It was nothing like the direct, personal role reversal that slaves in

---

[119] N. Davis, "The Rites of Violence," pp. 72–73.

[120] "Fo assà mascare per la terra, tra le qual erano alcuni con manege dogal di scarlato, e seda e becheti di veludo, et una havia una coladena d'oro come il canzelier grando davanti, e altri vestiti da comandadori, altri con trombe e pifari davanti in segno che va la Signoria, che per mia oppinion non fo ben fatto." Sanuto, *I diarii*, 57:548.

[121] Cf. Turner, *The Ritual Process*, pp. 167–68, and Le Roy Ladurie, *The Peasants of Languedoc*, pp. 207–10.

[122] On the significance of anonymity in satrical mimicry see Goffman, *The Presentation of Self*, pp. 171–72.

ancient Rome enjoyed during Saturnalia, when they wore badges of freedom and their masters' clothes and had their owners serve them at table.[123] The Venetian *popolani* were neither slaves nor disciplined subordinates like the enlisted sailors in the British Royal Navy, who are served Christmas dinner by their officers; the Venetian hierarchy was real enough and rigid enough to engender rather mild role reversals, but there is little evidence of any aggressive popular antipathy to the regime expressed during the carnival celebrations.

All the carnival images discussed here turned everyday society on its head. Most masqueraders identified themselves ritually or dramatically with their social opposites: *popolani* dressed themselves as officials, nobles as peasants, men as women, harlots as men; likewise, destruction led to birth and sex to death; the old became young and the decrepit potent. Carnival was always topsy-turvy but never mindless; there were no mobs, and any violence was usually the idiosyncratic act of an individual. Even in its most abandoned moments the crowd behaved in a structured fashion, following patterns sometimes adopted from other places and other times, such as when Troy burned and knights jousted, but usually derived from a rich local tradition.[124] The mimicry was playful, but it was serious play and just as socially important and useful as productive work, and psychologically perhaps more valuable.[125]

The authorities tolerated and sometimes supported even the most orgiastic and sadistic displays: if not the government itself, then the semi-private noble organizations sponsored the lascivious comedies and pantomimes and provided the pigs and bulls for slaughter.[126] Some of the best clues for an interpretation of Venetian carnival sadism can be found in Bakhtin's explication of Rabelais. Carnival, which according to some etymologists comes from *carne levare*, meaning the putting away of flesh as food, preceded the Lenten abstinence from meat, and

---

[123] James, *Seasonal Feasts and Festivals*, p. 176.

[124] Cf. Bakhtin, *Rabelais and His World*, pp. 217–19, and N. Davis, "The Rites of Violence," p. 91.

[125] Cf. Thomas, "Work and Leisure," pp. 51–52.

[126] Cf. comments by Lawrence Stone on ibid., p. 65.

thus carnival offered a last chance to eat meat.[127] But the pi
and bulls were not just butchered for meat; they were chase
perhaps tortured, and ceremoniously decapitated while t
spectators laughed. What was so funny? Bakhtin sees in su
abuse the ambivalence of carnival: a thrashing becomes prais
and pain is transformed into joy. He cites as example the Fren
peasants' custom during carnival of leading through town an
they had decorated with ribbons. "The ox was to be slaug
tered, it was to be a carnivalesque victim. It was a king,
procreator, symbolizing the city's fertility; at the same time,
was the sacrificial meat, to be chopped up for sausages ai
patés."[128] A practical, seasonal chore became a festive image
regeneration. Elsewhere Bakhtin extends his interpretation
the thrashings and slaughters characteristic of carnival.

> . . . [those] killed, rent, beaten, chased, abused, cursed,
> derided . . . are representatives of the old world but also
> of that two-bodied world that gives birth in death. By
> cutting off and discarding the old dying body, the umbilical
> cord of the new youthful world is simultaneously broken.
> The Rabelaisian images fix the very moment of this trans-
> fer which contains the two poles. Every blow dealt to the
> old helps the new to be born. The caesarian operation kills
> the mother but delivers the child. The representatives of
> the old but generating world are beaten and abused. There-
> fore, the punishment is transformed into festive laughter.[129]

Death and abuse are thus erotic and life-giving.

The Venetians dealt their blows to the old world in a varie
of festive and pageant forms. Most striking is the indigeno
interpretation of the slaughter of the pigs and bull and t
senators' smashing of miniature castles as a ritual re-enactme
of the Venetian victory over the patriarch of Aquileia and h

---

[127] On the etymology of carnival see the *Oxford English Dictionary*, 2:1
Professor Kenneth Pennington pointed out to me that Boccaccio frequer
punned *carne levare* to mean the male erection. Such a double entendre
course, suits quite well the many layers of meanings, many ribald, commoi
Venetian carnival images.

[128] Bakhtin, *Rabelais and His World*, p. 202.

[129] Ibid., p. 206.

Friulian allies. With each swing of the executioner's sword and senators' clubs, Venice destroyed its historical parent-city of Aquileia, killing the mother so the child could live, crushing the old so the new would prosper. What could reveal more convincingly the Venetian habit of turning all festivity, solemn religious rites or popular games, toward a political end? And conversely, what could illustrate more concretely how a carnivalesque attitude infiltrated even the most sober political circles than the ambivalence of the government toward the ritual pig slaughter in the years after the 1525 reforms? The Council of Ten and Doge Gritti, so obviously repelled by the spectacle, could not stamp it out, nor did they always act as if they wanted to. Their alternating repulsion and attraction to Giovedì Grasso mirrored the ambiguity of carnival itself.

The dichotomy between the old and the young in carnival probably parodied, as well, certain social realities of Renaissance Italian life. In their massive study of Tuscan households David Herlihy and Christiane Klapisch-Zuber have explored the implications of the social fact that brides were invariably many years younger than their husbands and that because of superior wealth older men could consistently out-compete young men for wives. This led to the coupling of dried up, wrinkled old men with fresh young beauties, a situation that was ritually redressed in the absurd caricatures of randy old men so commonly found in carnival pageants.[130] Through organizations like the Compagnie delle Calze, the unmarried young men had primary responsibility for the carnival *feste,* and they took advantage of their opportunities. Natalie Davis has shown that in French peasant communities carnival frolics and other forms of misrule were inevitably the responsibility of unmarried youths who formed bands that cut across class lines. When these misrulers appeared in cities, however, each band tended to represent a neighborhood, occupational, or class grouping; they became confirmations of social exclusivity rather than communal unity.[131] The Venetian case affirms this view. Not only were the *compagnie* manned exclusively by nobles, but all the members

---

[130] Herlihy and Klapisch-Zuber, *Les Toscans et leurs familles,* pp. 607–8.
[131] N. Davis, "The Reasons of Misrule," pp. 49–74.

were often from the same *sestiere*. [132] Social differentiation was everywhere; persons inevitably were identified as either belonging to or mocking a particular social group—young girls, old men, nobles, peasants, barterers, senators, foreigners, barbarians, or the civilized. [133]

[132] Sanuto, *I diarii*, 28:253–56.

[133] One of Boccaccio's best-known satires on the Venetians, the story of Frate Alberto (*Decameron*, fourth day, second tale), parodied the Festival of the Twelve Marys and Giovedì Grasso. The central deception in the story has numerous literary sources and parallels, but the setting and details are entirely Venetian. A wicked and vice-ridden man from Imola, Berto della Massa, moved to Venice, disguised himself as a minor friar, and pretended to be a great preacher and popular confessor named Alberto. Beguiled by the vain and beautiful but stunningly simple-minded young wife of a traveling merchant, Frate Alberto tricked her to believe that the Angel Gabriel had fallen in love with her and wished to make nocturnal visits to her bed while inhabiting the body of Frate Alberto. Dressed in an angel's wings, Frate Alberto visited her many times. But Madonna Lisetta gossiped too much; her cousins heard about the angelic visitor and surprised the lovers one night. Naked, Frate Alberto escaped by jumping into the Grand Canal and found refuge in the house of a goodman who was just about to leave for the day. After hearing rumors of the previous night's events, the goodman returned to his house and convinced Frate Alberto that his only hope for escape was to disguise himself as a wild man of the woods or as a bear and be led about by another, since there was a festival on that day in Piazza San Marco during which the citizens appeared in masquerade to attend a pig hunt. Unwilling, but too afraid to resist, Frate Alberto allowed the man to smear honey all over him, cover him with feathers, put a chain around his neck, and mask his face. The man gave Alberto a large stick and two huge dogs and sent a message to the Rialto that the Angel Gabriel would soon appear in Piazza San Marco. The man led his wild man of the woods to a column in the Piazza; then, in front of the gathering crowd, he unmasked the false friar and shouted, "Gentlemen, since the pig has not come to the hunt, and since the hunt is off, I do not wish you to have come in vain, and so I wish you to see the Angel Gabriel who came down from Heaven to earth during the night to console the Venetian ladies." Recognizing Frate Alberto, the crowd shouted insults against him and threw filth in his face until some of the other friars from his convent arrived, bound him up, and threw him in prison, where he soon died.

The story has many local details and uses Venetian dialect, and one can assume that Boccaccio witnessed a Venetian carnival and the Festival of the Twelve Marys, possibly during a visit in 1346 or 1347. The details of the pig hunt and the masquerade of a wild man of the woods are unmistakable, and one might argue that Frate Alberto's masquerade as the Angel Gabriel was an irreverent allusion to the Annunciation masque on Candlemas Eve, during which a priest dressed as Gabriel and another as the Virgin. The beatings,

A SERENE SOCIETY

Carnival had no single meaning, but multiple meanings that undoubtedly evolved. Nor did carnival have a simple, single purpose; rather, it provided a cyclic commentary on the entire social order, symbolically redressing grievances in one case and reinforcing class distinctions in another. Two aspects that made it distinctively Venetian were the general popular acceptance—whether reluctant or enthusiastic is unknown—of the social and political status quo, and the direct involvement of the government in the interpretation and control of carnival imagery. The general acquiescence to such control contributed importantly to Venice's reputation for social harmony and to the notion of a widespread popular allegiance to the patrician republic. As Machiavelli observed, men more often judge by appearances than by reality. The vision of Venetian social life presented by ritual was vivid: Venice was La Serenissima.

---

maskings, and sexual game are carnivalesque. Boccaccio's tale itself burlesques the ironic Venetian mixture of the Annunciation drama about virginity with the libertine, grotesque, boisterous images of Giovedì Grasso. He used this carnival story to demonstrate that the Venetians had trouble distinguishing appearances from realities.

After reading this chapter Kenneth Pennington noticed the similarity between Boccaccio's tale and the Venetian carnival and kindly pointed out to me the parallel. For the antecedents to this story see Giovanni Boccaccio, *Tutte le opere*, 4:1211, n. 1, and A. C. Lee, *The Decameron*, pp. 123–35. Also see Erich Auerbach, *Mimesis*, pp. 177–203. The connection between the Festival of the Marys, carnival, and the Boccaccio tale is fully worked out in Padoan, "Sulla novella veneziana del 'Decameron.' "

PART THREE

GOVERNMENT
BY RITUAL

By viewing the ceremonial ordinances of a prince,
we know the character of his government.
— Master of Meng, China, fourth century B.C.

In pompous ceremonies a secret of government
doth much consist.
— Spaniard, sixteenth century A.D.

FIVE

A REPUBLIC OF PROCESSIONS

From Theory to Practice

Aristotle defined the citizen as he who both rules and is ruled. His definition quite accurately describes the theoretical status of the Venetian patricians, who inherited political rights through membership in the Great Council; and so it was no accident that humanists who wrote about Venetian government, as did Gasparo Contarini, thought that the Venetian constitution epitomized Aristotelian ideas. Not only were the Venetians able to maintain a reasonably stable class of patrician citizens who were both rulers and the ruled, but they were also able to reconcile, in theory at least, the principles of a hierarchic and hereditary political order with the republican ideals of equality among these patricians. Although the contrasts among symbols of princely authority, ideals of equality, and realities of oligarchy produced considerable structural tensions within the Venetian commonwealth, these tensions were contained within a constitutional and ceremonial framework and did not create the same kind of ideological fissure between hierarchism and republicanism found in early fifteenth-century Florence.[1] In Venice republicanism was, if anything, the ideology of a ruling class, whereas hierarchy was the structural principle of government. In the unwritten constitution, which was republican in that it guaranteed to all patricians citizenship, the right to vote, and the opportunity to seek elected office, there was a hierarchical ordering of offices that bequeathed to the holders of the most elevated posts a special distinction. There was some ideological opposition between the two principles, but the conflict was never sufficiently severe during the sixteenth century to upset

[1] Baron, *Crisis of the Early Renaissance*, passim, and Pocock, *The Machiavellian Moment*, especially pp. 53–54.

constitutional harmony entirely. Minor adjustments had to be made from time to time, but the issues were never quite as stark as they were in troubled sixteenth-century Florence, where there were only antithetical alternatives—either the republic or the Medici princes.

One of the ways the Venetians may have achieved this constitutional stability was through a pious, intensely conservative adherence to inherited ritual and legend, a habit that rendered the political order both mystical and sanctified. The Venetian "political theology" was not without parallel—indeed all sovereign powers have an inherent sacredness[2]—but it did have a peculiarly Venetian character. As we have seen in chapter 2, the primary figure of political authority in Venice, the doge, enhanced his prestige by claiming for himself the patronage of Saint Mark and exercised a personal discipline over the ecclesiastical establishment.[3] Furthermore, early Venetian humanists subordinated all values, including the theological virtues of Faith, Hope, and Charity, to the republic. Giovanni Caldiera, the fifteenth-century *cittadine* humanist, saw the republic as a rigid hierarchy that was the "living repository of all excellence." In Caldiera's writings, "Republican virtues are identified with divine virtues, and God and the State, patriotism and religion, are metaphorically fused."[4] Neither hierarchy and republicanism nor patriotism and faith were in any way opposed in his thought, nor did they serve as the contrasting theses in a dialectical process. Humanists like Caldiera codified the political and religious mythology already apparent in Venetian ceremonies, which by their very nature emphasized communal cohesion as opposed to ideological disagreement, and political sacredness rather than secular power struggles.[5] Under different conditions this codification might have emptied the cere-

[2] "A world wholly demystified is a world wholly depoliticized." Clifford Geertz, "Centers, Kings, and Charisma," p. 168; also see pp. 151–52. Cf. Ernst H. Kantorowicz, "Deus per Naturam, Deus per Gratiam."

[3] Cf. Olimpia Aureggi Ariatta, "Influssi delle relazioni col Levante sul diritto ecclesiastico della repubblica veneta," pp. 214–15.

[4] King, "Personal, Domestic, and Republican Values," p. 565 and passim.

[5] The fifteenth-century Florentines similarly strove to show in their ceremonies a "boundlessly stable inner state." Trexler, *The Libro Cerimoniale*, pp. 63–64.

monies of their potential to comment spontaneously on recent events, but the ceremonies never totally degenerated to political vapidity.

In Renaissance Europe ceremonies were in broadest terms an expression of the world order and more narrowly a formulation of political rules that usually appeared in written theory much later.[6] Civic ceremonies thus provided a continuous discourse on the constitutional order. In Venice a rather large group of ceremonial specialists recorded and watched over the text of this constitutional commentary. In the middle of the sixteenth century the ceremonial officials fell into two groups, one consisting of laymen attached to the Ducal Palace and the other of priests or lay assistants working in the basilica. The political supervisor of official ceremonies was one of the five *savii di terraferma* who were patrician administrators elected to the Collegio of the Senate.[7] None of the incumbents held office long enough or frequently enough to acquire any particular expertise in ceremonial matters; as *savii*, they were charged to make sure that the ducal ceremonies produced the desired political effect. The *savii* had to rely continually on the services of others, such as the master of ceremonies (*maestro cerimoniale*), who was one of the palace retainers bearing the title of cavalier of the doge.[8] The master performed many of the functions associated with his office: he was, for example, in charge of informing the Scuole Grandi members and friars of their responsibilities for each procession;[9] in the records of the last thirty years of the sixteenth century, one Gironimo Lippomano appeared again and again as a herald who orchestrated diplomatic meetings in the Collegio;[10] another cavalier, named Salustio Gnicchi, wrote up a ceremonial book in 1590, a task which reveals that the office was not just honorific.[11] The cavalier was

---

[6] Cf. ibid., p. 25, and Lawrence M. Bryant, *"Parlementaire* Political Theory in the Parisian Royal Entry Ceremony," p. 15.

[7] Mosto, *L'Archivio di Stato*, 1:22.

[8] Andrea da Mosto, *I dogi di Venezia nella vita pubblica e privata*, p. lix.

[9] BMV, MS Latin III, 172 (2276), fol. 63v.

[10] ASV, Collegio Cerimoniale 1, passim.

[11] "Ceremoniali delle uscite di casa delli Principi di Venetia scritto in tempo del Ser[enissi]mo Paschale Cicogna da Salustio Gnicchi suo cavallarie." MCV,

assisted by the grand captain, who informed the scuole piccoli and parishes of their obligations for any major procession and who organized the various captains of the guards (*cappi de guardie*) to control the crowds.[12] In addition, the Council of Ten charged a chancellery secretary with keeping a book of ceremonies that would provide an official account of the visits of "princes and other personages" and that would be kept in the *secreta* of the Collegio, where it could be easily consulted.[13] All physical props necessary for ceremonies—canopies, bleachers, stages, and boats—were maintained and stored by the office of the Rason Vecchie.[14]

In addition to this extensive corps of ceremonial specialists attached to the Ducal Palace, San Marco had its own cadre of ritual officials; indeed all the canons and servants of the basilica in some sense had liturgical ceremonial responsibilities. Of interest here is the master of the choir, sometimes also called the master of ceremonies, who personally accompanied all ducal processions and took care of liturgical details.[15] Like the chan-

---

MS Donà delle Rose, 132/6. Cf. Trexler, *The Libro Cerimoniale*, p. 18, n. 25; p. 19, n. 28.

[12] BMV, MS Latin III, 172 (2276), fol. 63v. The captain of the guard was considered to be the chief plebian magistrate: "Di quì è che si suol dir volgarmente, che trà Nobili il maggior è il Doge, tra i Cittadini il Cancellier Grande, e'tra la plebe minuta il Capitano Grande." Bardi, *Delle cose notabili*, p. 31.

[13] There were ". . . due Cancellieri chiamati Ducali, & Inferiori, & un Cancelliero, che è quasi Maestro delle ceremonie nelle sue [the doge's] andate in trionfo." Sansovino, *Venetia*, 1604, fol. 314r. Paulo Pera in his introductory note to the official *Libro Cerimoniale* compiled in 1593 identified himself as a "secretario, come Deputato al carico delle ceremoniale per occasion di venute de Prenicpe et altri personaggi. . . ." He kept two books—ASV, Collegio Cerimoniale 1 and 2—that are virtually identical. The early sections were copied from ASV, Regina Margherita, B-14, series LXXVI, n. 6 (formerly catalogued as ex Brera 277). Cf. Regina Margherita, fols. 31r–32v, with Collegio Cerimoniale, fols. 1r–4v. The Collegio Cerimoniale books are in six volumes covering the period from the beginning of the sixteenth century to 1729. Cf. J. B. Lorenzi, ed., *Monumenti per servire alla storia del palazzo ducale di Venezia*, doc. 711.

[14] Mosto, *I dogi di Venezia*, p. xxxvi; ASV, Rason Vecchie, buste 219, 223, 225, 226.

[15] BMV, MS Latin III, 172 (2276), fols. 63v, 116r; ASV, Collegio Cerimoniale 1, fol. 75r; 2, fol. 58v; 3, fol. 3v; MCV, Cod. Cicogna 1295, p. 13. Venetians

cellery secretary in the Collegio, he was obliged to keep a descriptive book of ceremonies, which combined an *ordo* of prayers, hymns, and anthems used for various feasts and a directory prescribing how the *ordo* was to be performed.[16] The ceremonial functions of the secular and ecclesiastical officials were not divided into political and religious categories, for in Venice matters political were not easily distinguished from those religious. Instead the officials were in charge of different ceremonial territories: questions of diplomatic procedure that arose when visitors or ambassadors entered the Ducal Palace concerned the palace magistrates, whereas the master of the choir was obliged to look after liturgical matters in the basilica. Nonetheless, these concerns often intersected, and it was not unusual for the cavalier of the doge to worry about how the Scuole Grandi and the friars would appear, or for the master of the choir to bother himself with questions of precedence. In the mid-sixteenth century Venice boasted a large, specialized ceremonial bureaucracy that testified to the importance of ritual matters in Venetian society as well as to the extent of political centralization.

THE DUCAL PROCESSION

One can best see the hierarchic conception of the republic in an analysis of the ducal procession. The procession, a subject of much legislation and a charge of the ceremonial specialists, created in its ranking of officials a constitutional ideal for Venice that existed nowhere else, neither in visual nor even in written

---

used the term *maestro cerimoniale* rather loosely; at various times the cavalier of the doge, the chancellery secretary, and the *maestro di coro* were each called *maestri cerimoniali.* On the multiple functions of the *maestro di coro* or *capella* of San Marco, see E. Rosand, "Music in the Myth."

[16] A "Libro ordinum Ecclesiae sancti Marci editorum in MCCCVII," which is no longer extant, is cited in ASV, Collegio Cerimoniale 1, fol. 10r. In 1562 Bartolomeo Bonifacio, the *maestro di coro* of San Marco, compiled the "Rituum ecclesiasticorum cerimoniale . . . ," BMV, MS Latin III, 172 (2276). To replace it Giovanni Battista Pace wrote in 1678 the "Ceremoniale Magnum," MCV, Cod. Cicogna 1295. On the general types of ceremonial books see Richard A. Jackson, "A Little-Known Description of Charles IX's Coronation," p. 290, n. 7.

form; in effect, the ducal procession was the constitution. Changes in processional order were, hence, grave matters. The relative constancy of the ducal procession during the sixteenth century reveals an institutional continuity, and yet at the same time it hides a less attractive struggle for power among the patrician families.

In the procession, position was everything.[17] First to emerge from the portals of the Ducal Palace were eight standard-bearers (see figure 7 and table) walking two abreast and carrying the colored silk banners, each emblazoned with the Lion of Saint Mark (discussed in chapter three). Commanders (*commandatori* or *precones*) walking two by two were second. These men, who are mentioned only in the late sixteenth-century descriptions, were low-ranking judicial officials who had the conspicuous public duty of publishing the decisions of the courts and announcing edicts. Behind them walked six musicians, whose long silver trumpets, sometimes bearing silk banners stamped with the ducal crown and the doge's family crest, were carried on the shoulders of small boys.[18] Then came the squires of the visiting ambassadors, preceding the ducal squires and cavalier, who was followed by another group of instrumentalists, these playing a silver sackbut and five cornets.[19] Minor *cittadini* officials came next: prison clerks and captains, stewards of the doge, and notaries of the Great Council. The six canons of San Marco usually appeared in the following position, and they were ahead of the patriarch, who walked only in

[17] Ducal processions were called an "andar in trionfo." Sansovino, *Venetia*, 1604, fol. 330r.

[18] The first four of the following sources, which were all used to compile this description of the ducal processions, mention the hanging banners: Canal, *Les estoires de Venise*, pp. 246–48; Sanuto, *Le vite dei dogi*, pp. 91–92; ASV, Collegio Cerimoniale 1, fols. 7v–8r; BMV, MS Latin III, 172 (2276), fol. 52v; Sansovino, *Venetia*, 1604, fol. 330r–v. The most useable of the many pictoral sources is an engraving by Matteo Pagan, *The Procession of the Doge on Palm Sunday* (plate 7 herein). There are a number of minor discrepancies in the processional order described by these sources, but no signs of significant changes. In two sources the commanders appear in front of the trumpet-bearers instead of behind them. Sansovino, *Venetia*, 1604, fol. 330r–v, and the Pagan engraving.

[19] Cf. Curt Sachs, *The History of Musical Instruments*, pp. 323–29.

ducal processions held on the most solemn religious holidays.
Next came the doge's personal chaplain or an acolyte holding a
white candle in a silver candelabrum; on certain occasions a
squire, carrying the jeweled coronation crown of the doge on a
gold platter, followed the candle-bearer.[20] The ducal and sena-
torial secretaries, the inferior curial chancellors, and the grand
chancellor completed the contingent of *cittadini* officials who
comprised the first segment of the procession.[21]

Three persons walking abreast led the second segment: on
the left a squire supported on his shoulder a gold faldstool, the
symbolic throne of the doges; on the far right another squire
held the gold foot-cushion of the doge; and between these two
squires walked the *ballotino,* a young boy chosen to handle the
ballots at elections. The doge himself, flanked by the two most
prestigious foreign ambassadors resident in Venice (usually the
papal nuncio and the imperial orator), followed this symbolic
group. Behind the doge a patrician held an elaborate, gold-cloth
umbrella over the doge's head. The umbrella-bearer was usually
one of the cavaliers of the doge or, if one were not available, a
procurator.[22] Behind him followed the other ambassadors. Then
came the sword-bearer. He and the companion who walked
beside him were chosen especially by the doge for each procession and were typically nobles about to be sent abroad as a
podestà or *capitano del terraferma* or *del mar.*[23]

The third segment of the procession consisted of the most
important noble office-holders, each placed according to the
rank of his office. At the head of this group, one of the *giudici
del proprio* walked on the right side of the senior ducal counselor. They preceded the other counselors, who were paired
with the procurators; then came the heads of the Quarantia al

[20] Unlike most others, Sansovino placed the candle-bearer before the six
canons of San Marco. *Venetia,* 1604, fol. 330v.

[21] If the grand chancellor were unavailable, he was replaced by one of the
holders of the upper secretarial posts. ASV, Collegio Cerimoniale 1, fol. 75r;
MCV, MS Venier, P.D. 517b, under heading "avertimenti generali."

[22] Such was the case at a procession of 1583 mentioned in MCV, Cod.
Cicogna 1295, fol. 423.

[23] Sansovino, *Venetia,* 1604, fol. 330v. There are literally hundreds of examples in Sanuto, *I diarii;* for some see 2:257; 3:72, 96; 5:17, 23, 795; 6:116,
274, 275, 290, 326, 331, 341, 353, 516, 542; 8:72.

Criminale (the chief criminal court), the sons and brothers of the doge, the *savii grandi*, the *avogadori di comun* (state attornies), the heads of the Council of Ten, the censors (officials who after 1517 were charged with investigating alleged electoral violations), the *savii di terraferma*, the *savii agli ordini* (the *savii* were the members of the Collegio of the Senate), the cavaliers of San Marco (Venice's only knightly order), and the members of the Senate.[24]

The foregoing list presents the necessary participants and rankings for a ducal procession, but sometimes only a portion of the procession appeared, and sometimes there were additions to it. On minor saints' days the doge heard mass in San Marco accompanied by only the Signoria, a group comprised of the ducal counselors and the heads of the Quarantia, but for major festive events members of the Scuole Grandi and piccoli, orders of ecclesiastics, and even foreign pilgrims were appended to this core group.

As can be seen from this listing, the procession displayed office-holders and symbols. The office-holders marched in the procession not as individuals who boasted certain qualities but as possessors of particular titles or dignities, most of which were not permanent acquisitions but rather temporary designations.[25] The procession was a ranking by status rather than a sorting of persons, and the fundamental principle of cleavage was one of class: the officials were divided into two separate hierarchies, fore and aft of the doge; the chancellery servants of the *cittadine* class (commanders, notaries, secretaries, and the grand chancellor) walked in front of the doge; and the noble magistrates were ranked behind him.

The most significant change in the ducal procession from the thirteenth to sixteenth centuries was the delineation and segregation of *cittadini* and noble hierarchies. In Martin da Canal's

---

[24] Mosto, *L'Archivio di Stato*, 1:28; MCV, Cod. Cicogna, 2991/18, fol. 6r; and MCV, MS Venier, P.D. 517b, under heading "modo di caminare collegialmente." On the place of the relatives of the doge in the procession see ASV, Collegio Cerimoniale 1, fol. 8r.

[25] Richard Trexler argues that at Florentine diplomatic receptions the titles of the participants rather than their "intentional or internal attitudes" determined how they would behave. *The Libro Cerimoniale*, p. 62.

The Ducal Procession

Segment I

Standard-bearers
Commanders
Trumpeters
Squires of the doge
Cavalier of the doge
Sackbut player
Cornet players
Prison clerks
Prison captains
Stewards of the doge
Notaries of the Great Council
Canons of San Marco*
Patriarch*
Chaplain or acolyte carrying the white candle
Squire carrying the coronation crown*
Secretaries of the doge and Senate
Inferior curial chancellors
Grand chancellor

Segment II

Squire with throne	Ballotino	Squire with cushion
Ambassador	Doge	Ambassador
	Umbrella-bearer	
	Ambassadors	
Podestà or Capitano del Mar or Terraferma		Sword-bearer

Segment III

Senior ducal counselor	Giudice del proprio
Ducal counselors	Procurators of San Marco

Heads of the Quarantia al Criminale
Sons and brothers of the doge
Savii grandi
Avogadori di comun
Heads of the Council of Ten
Censors
Savii di terraferma
Savii agli ordini
Cavaliers
Senators

---

*Participation depended on the occasion

Trumpeters   Commanders   Eight standard-bearers

7A, B, C, D Matteo Pagan, *The Procession of the Doge on the Palm Sunday.* There are discrepancies between this engraving of the ducal procession and the processional order required by the official ceremonial legislation (see the accompanying table). Aesthetic considerations—the need for a balance among the figures, the desire to space out the instrumentalists and the symbol-bearers, and the requirement to avoid the crowding of three figures walking abreast—led Pagan to alter the processional order. An arrow shows where the grand chancellor would actually have been—at the end of Segment 1.

SEGMENT I

Canons of
San Marco

Squires of
the doge

Cavalier of
the doge

Musicians

Retainers of the
foreign ambassadors

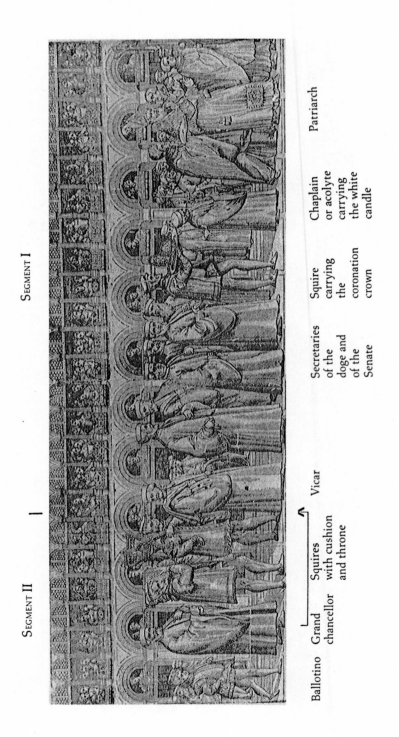

Segment I

Segment II

Patriarch

Chaplain or acolyte carrying the white candle

Squire carrying the coronation crown

Secretaries of the doge and of the Senate

Vicar

Squires with cushion and throne

Grand chancellor

Ballotino

Segment II

Segment III

The Signoria   Sword-bearer   Ambassadors   Umbrella-bearer   Doge

thirteenth-century description of the ducal procession, both nobles and citizens walked in an undifferentiated crowd behind the doge;[26] but after the so-called closing of the Great Council in 1297, an act that defined the political rights and membership of the ruling patriciate, class differentiation became increasingly important to Venetians, and it was eventually reflected in the arrangement of the ducal procession.[27] Important to Contarini's explanation of Venetian class harmony was the doctrine that the special dignities granted to the *cittadini* compensated for their lack of formal political power, and the most conspicuous of these dignities was the position of the *cittadini* officials in the ducal procession.[28] In an age that perceived processional rankings and ceremonial precedence as authentic indicators of social realities, Contarini's views made good sense. Perhaps most influential, then, in producing the Renaissance myth of Venice was the appearance of the ducal procession, which suggested both a broad social participation in the government and a general acceptance of it, an appearance that contrasted with the princely and courtly image of most other states.

The last segment of the procession consisted of a ranking of noble magistrates that descended from the ducal counselors and procurators of San Marco to the members of the Senate. The processional rankings corresponded rather closely to both the legal distribution of authority and the positions of actual power within Venetian government. Under law the head of state in the absence of the doge was the group of magistrates in the

---

[26] "Et aprés monsignor li dus s'en vont les gentis homes de Venise, et maint preudomes dou peuple." Canal, *Les estoires de Venise*, p. 246; in the 1845 ed. see pp. 560 and 741, n. 287. In the 1204 mosaics in Saint Clement's chapel in San Marco, the only differentiation is among "pontifices, clerus, populus, dux." Schramm, *Herrschaftszeichen und Staatssymbolik*, p. 866.

[27] Lane, "The Enlargement of the Great Council." Cf. Stanley Chojnacki, "In Search of the Venetian Patriciate."

[28] Contarini is not entirely consistent on the importance of class differentiation in Venice. Although he emphasizes the compensations given to the *cittadini* in many passages, in one place he seems to deny that Venice had a class structure at all: "The Venetians will not allow among their citizens any other difference, then [sic] only of age, because from thence never sprang any sedition or contention!" *De magistratibus et republica Venetorum*, English version, p. 34. For an example of the manifold ceremonial distinctions made according to age in Venice see ASV, Collegio Cerimoniale 1, fol. 93v.

Signoria, and consequently these officials followed closely behind the doge, ambassadors, and ducal symbols.[29] The inner circle of oligarchs who wielded most of the power in Venice consisted of the doge, his six counselors, the procurators of San Marco, the *savii grandi*, the members of the Council of Ten (and until 1583 the members of the Zonta of the Ten), and the five resident ambassadors posted to Rome, Vienna, Madrid, Paris, and Constantinople.[30] Thus, of the first nine processional ranks after the doge's sword-bearer, members of the inner political circle held five; the other four positions went to senior judicial officials and to the family of the doge. The *podestà* or *capitano del terraferma* or *del mar* who carried the doge's sword was probably a member of this ruling oligarchy as well. The participation of the Senate contingent, which consisted of sixty regular and sixty supplementary (Zonta) members or of some portion of the senators, was optional and depended on the degree of pomp called for by the occasion.[31] The Senate, as the

[29] Definitions of the Signoria: "La Seigneurie de Venise se peult entendre par troys manieres: la premiere est que la Seigneurie de Venise est entendue pour toute la chose publique de Venise et pour tout l'estat des Venissiens; la 2ᵉ est que la Seigneurie de Venise est entendue pour tout le colliege duquel se traicte de present; la 3ᵉ est que la Seigneurie de Venise est entendue seulement pour le Duc et ses conseillers et chefz de Quarante." *Traité du gouvernement*, p. 272.

[30] There were about thirty members of this inner circle. Grendler, *The Roman Inquisition*, p. 43, and Lowry, "Reform of the Council," pp. 307–10. Lane defines the inner circle as consisting of ". . . the sixteen men holding the positions of doge, Ducal Councillors, Savii Grandi, and Chiefs of the Ten. . . . The rest of the Ten, the Savii di Terra Ferma, the three Heads of the Forty, and the three State Attorneys [*avogadori di comun*] were on the outer edge of the inner circle." *Venice*, pp. 256–57. James Davis adds to these lists "the governers of the leading cities and islands, the members of a few principal Senate committees, and a few naval offices." This meant that there were sixty essential posts to be filled at any one time. "Adding to these another forty men who might have been temporarily inactive because their terms of office had expired, or they were sick, traveling, or attending to business affairs, the total goes up to about 100." *The Decline of the Venetian Nobility*, p. 23.

[31] For evidence of the grand chancellor inviting the senators to a procession see Sanuto, *I diarii*, 24:173. Since nearly all important magistrates were entitled to attend Senate meetings in an ex officio capacity, the Senate could consist of as many as 220 members. Contarini, *De magistratibus et republica Venetorum*, p. 63; English version, p. 66. For processions some portion, such as half the Senate and half the Zonta, were obliged to attend. Sanuto, *I diarii*, 24:637; MCV, Cod. Cicogna 2991/117, fol. 7r.

principal legislative body, included in its number nearly all of the older, politically successful patricians, so that when the senators walked in a ducal procession, the entire political hierarchy of Venice was presented.[32]

More than anything else this precise and rigid ranking of magistrates distinguished the Venetian procession. Since at least the fourteenth century the patricians had shown an almost fanatical concern to define the processional rankings and to uphold ceremonial decorum and solemnity.[33] Such a preoccupation reveals a desire to prevent factional strife by forcing a constitutional mold upon the teeming passions of political life; placing officials into a processional hierarchy implied that the only legitimate way to pursue political power was through election to office. In addition, the liturgical context in which processions were formed sanctified this hierarchical arrangement. Pietro Casolo, a Milanese pilgrim returning from the Holy Land who witnessed an All Saints' Day procession in 1494, observed in its hierarchical precision a reflection of social and political harmony absent elsewhere.

They all walked two and two, as I said, after the Doge in perfect order. This is very different from the practices I have witnessed at many courts, both ecclesiastical and secular, where the moment the Prince has passed all go pell-mell (as we say in our tongue *a rubo*) and without any order. In Venice, both before and behind the Doge, everyone goes in the best order imaginable.[34]

[32] "The whole manner of the commonwealths government belongeth to the senate." Contarini, *De magistratibus et republica Venetorum*, p. 65; English version, p. 68.

[33] For examples see ASV, Maggior Consiglio, deliberazioni, "Libro d'oro," P. IV, fol. 9r– v (21 July 1327) and fol. 202r– v (19 April 1355); ASV, Consiglio dei Dieci, miscellanea cod. 1, "Magnus," p. 40 (16 December 1377).

[34] "Dreto al Duce con uno ordine contrario a li ordini de molti corti ho veduto io, et ecclesiastiche e mondane, le quali subito sii passato el principe vanno catervatim e senz'altro ordine (se dice in lingua nostra vanno a rubo [he was Milanese]), e quivi inante e dreto si si va tanto ordinatamente quanto si possa dire." Casolo, *Viaggio a Gerusalemme*, p. 108; in English translation, p. 338. Good order in processions was not as peculiarly Venetian as Casolo thought. Several Florentine propitiatory processions were described as eminating from God and miraculous because of the perfect order displayed in them. Trexler, "Ritual Behavior," p. 144, n. 77.

In their public facade, at least, the Venetians were able to convince themselves and some others that Venice was a city of singular serenity, as free from class strife and political turmoil as the processions seemed to be free from disorder and disobedience.

Casolo's testimony about the near-miraculous good order of the Venetian procession he witnessed can be rebutted, however, with numerous incidents recorded in Venetian sources of turmoil, laxity, and even disinterest. The Scuole Grandi members were notorious for joining processions late, often in improper attire, and for involving themselves in shoving matches over precedence with the *batuti* of other Scuole.[35] On one embarrassing occasion the Carità showed up for a celebratory procession mistakenly carrying the arms of the Holy League rather than those of France.[36] Friars, monks, priests, and even the patriarch were no better, and the government was frequently called upon to resolve conflicts and confirm the rules of priority among the ecclesiastics.[37] Political rivalries, personal jealousies, and perhaps sincere ideological differences over the proper hi-

[35] Sanuto, *I diarii*, 11:679, 27:193; MCV, Cod. Cicogna, 2991/113–14, fol. 7r; ASV, Inquisitori et revisori sopra le Scuole Grandi, capitolare 1, fols. 8v–9r, 25r–27v, 33r–v, 78v–79v, 83v–84v, 116v. The Inquisitori records are cited extensively in Pullan, *Rich and Poor in Venice*, pp. 52ff, 82ff. The *maestro di coro* of San Marco organized the ecclesiastics and Scuole Grandi members who arrived late to a procession according to this rule of precedence: "Ordinate, si inferiores primi; maiores vero postremi." BMV, MS Latin III, 172 (2276), fol. 17r.

[36] "Le scuole è mal ad ordine, et quela di la Carità havia arme de la liga et non di Franza, che fo notado da mi, cosa che non dovevano far." Sanuto, *I diarii*, 53:312.

[37] An act in 1502 established the processional placement of the religious groups. Sansovino, *Venetia*, 1604, fol. 339r–v. Supplemental legislation reveals, however, that problems recurred throughout the sixteenth century. A dispute between the Observant and Conventual Franciscans had to be resolved in 1517. Sanuto, *I diarii*, 24:476–77. In 1522 and 1530 further controversies required the re-enactment of a law that cited the precedents established by a 1319 decree. MCV, Cod. Cicogna, 2991/17, fols. 1r–2v. In 1553 a system of rotation was established for the nine congregations of priests. BMV, MS Latin III, 172 (2276), fol. 55r. In 1575, when the patriarch was invited to the funeral of a grand chancellor, the patriarch said he would come, but asked the Signoria to determine his seating position in advance to avoid struggles over precedence. ASV, Collegio Cerimoniale 1, fol. 45v.

erarchy of offices fueled passionate arguments over the proper processional arrangement of the noble magistrates; as anyone familiar with the behavior in Renaissance courts knows, ceremonial rankings were matters of great political and often personal concern.[38]

Despite these recurring infractions, the Venetians chose not to follow the solution invented for King Arthur when the Round Table eliminated combats for pride of place among his knights, but instead to pursue ever more single-mindedly the hierarchical organization of society as dictated by the leaders of the patrician regime. Evidence of disputes over precedence might be interpreted in two ways: either they signify an underlying political turmoil that contradicted the serenity of the processional image, or they reveal not so much a lack of concern for the image of the republic as the overwhelming importance Renaissance Venetians granted the concept of ceremonial primacy. There undoubtedly was political conflict in Venice; but it is most important that such conflict occurred within an established ceremonial and institutional context, so that political and social ambition found expression in the pursuit of office or perhaps in the redefinition of an office already held, but not in the overt repudiation of the hierarchical conception of society. In addition, the recurring governmental efforts during the sixteenth century to enforce order through legislation, decree, and arbitration of disputes disclose the growing willingness of the ruling elite to use the apparatus of government still more effectively to extend its authority and to promulgate its idea of the proper arrangement of the commonwealth. The contentious attitude of some Scuole Grandi members toward ceremonial behavior may not be so much an indication of their repudiation of the republic or their indifference to it—Venetians after all were as human as anyone else and as prone to laziness and selfishness as others—as it is of the sometimes monomaniacal concern of the regime to eliminate all sources of scandal, to

[38] For examples of such disputes see Sanuto, *I diarii*, 34:239; MCV, MS Venier, P.D. 517b, under heading "Decembre"; MCV, Cod. Cicogna, 2991/1 8, fol. 4r. For an example of the nobles' indifference to a proper show of respect for the marquis of Mantua see Sanuto, *I diarii*, 24:268, 292–94.

control, to order, and to regiment.

In the middle of the procession walked the doge. Before him the *cittadini* civil servants ranked themselves in an ascending order of prestige, from the beginning of the procession to the grand chancellor; after him the noble magistrates walked in a descending order of status. Hierarchies of rank thus moved inward, from the periphery to the center. In many of the processions discussed by anthropologists, the most important elements appear in the middle; the core of meaning and the center of society are at the heart of the procession.[39] At each side of the doge, accompanying him as equals, were ambassadors, who legally stood in place of their own sovereigns and spoke their princes' wills. The processional nucleus symbolized sovereignty, and a Venetian conception of sovereignty at that, for the doge, in accord with the legend of the gifts of Pope Alexander III, walked in equality with representatives of the pope and emperor; and from the doge, the sovereign font, all authority flowed, coursing its way down through the hierarchy of assembled magistrates.

A comparison of Venetian with Florentine processions is illuminating. In both cities processions displayed the political and ecclesiastical order according to a fixed linear ranking, they revealed an evident age and sex differentiation (although in Venice women appeared in processions far less frequently than in Florence), and they relied on the same organizational principles for both propitiatory and celebratory functions. In Venice, however, there was a far more rigid separation of the classes than was evident in Florence, and in the Florentine procession no individual similar to the doge became the visual, ceremonial, and structural center of the procession. In Venice the doge and assembled magistrates were the essence of the procession, and their pre-eminence reveals its overwhelmingly political nature; without the doge the entire character of the procession would have been transmuted from a full-fledged assembly of the Venetian social order to a mere collection of clerics and a congregation. The Florentines in their processions treated the Sig-

---

[39] Cf. Geertz, "Centers, Kings, and Charisma," p. 159, and Dundes and Falassi, *La Terra in Piazza*, p. 105.

noria—the representatives of the political establishment—as if
it were a sacred object, a living votive image perhaps; but it was
still a mere adjunct to the procession, fetched from the Palazzo
Vecchio as if it were some relic picked up when the cortege
passed a shrine. Although both Florentine and Venetian processions recognized the sacredness of secular authorities and did
much to establish a political theology consonant with their republican traditions, the doge provided the Venetians with a
mystical and holy image that was no mere relic, but a living
being who had been elected and made sacred through the political system.[40] Without a doge, the Florentines tended to search
in various places for a sacred central symbol; at different times
adolescents, miraculous images, a range of charismatic or fash-
ionable clerics, and eventually the Medici fed the Florentines'
appetite. The Venetians, on the other hand, seemed satisfied
with their traditional doge. In such deep structural differences
one begins to see the foundations for the contrasting destinies
of the two great Renaissance republics.

In addition to officials the procession displayed the ducal
trionfi, which were scattered through the first part of the
procession and grouped around the doge at the core. Regarding
the *trionfi* Sansovino remarked, "When walking in triumph
and with solemnity [the doge] carries with him, among others,
seven things worthy of consideration, which show us his pre-
eminence. These things he received from the first princes of the
world, that is, from the popes and emperors."[41] These seven

[40] On Florentine processions see Trexler, "Ritual Behavior," especially pp.
132–33, and idem, "Ritual in Florence: Adolescence," especially
pp. 233, 262. Members of the Genoese *alberghi*—the great family clans—
required household retainers and kinsmen to appear assembled together,
bearing the arms and insignia of the clan as proof of group strength, whenever a ceremony brought notables together in the presence of the doge.
Jacques Heers, *Family Clans in the Middle Ages*, p. 226. No such ceremonial
representation of clans occurred in Venetian ritual. The only exception might
be at the dogaressa's coronation, but then only the doge's and dogaressa's
families had opportunities for public display.

[41] "Andando adunque in trionfo, & con solennità, porta con lui fra l'altre,
sette cose degne di consideratione, & dimerstratrici della sua molta eccellenza. Le quali egli hebbe da i primi Prencipi del mondo, cioè da i Pontefici,
& da gli Imperatori." Sansovino, *Venetia*, 1604, fol. 321r–v.

trionfi—the banners, musical instruments, candle, cushion, faldstool, umbrella, ànd sword—were closely identified with the ducal office, and most of them had no significance when separated from it. If a doge were unable to participate in a scheduled procession because of illness or some other cause, the candle, cushion, seat, and umbrella were not displayed; if either the doge or the *giudice del proprio* were absent, the sword was not carried. When the doge was not present and his place taken by the vice-doge (one of the ducal counselors), only the eight standards and the musical instruments, those symbols carried at the beginning of the procession at some distance from the doge, appeared.[42] Except for the instruments, to which the Venetians attached no special significance, and the banners, under which any Venetian commander fought, the *trionfi* symbolized attributes of the doge's authority. As we saw in chapter three, all of the *trionfi* except the faldstool and cushion were interpreted in light of the legend of the donation of Pope Alexander III and understood to signify Venice's devotion to the Roman Church, the doge's rank as a prince equal to popes and emperors, Saint Mark's patronage of Venetian soldiers, and the government's dedication to the principles of justice (a principle echoed by the presence of the commanders in the first part of the procession). The ducal office was the repository of these gifts and the institutional link between present politics and distinguished deeds of the past.

Although the faldstool and cushion were not usually included among the gifts of Pope Alexander, they were given a similar interpretation.[43] Like the sword, both were probably derived from the insignia of Byzantine officialdom and appeared in Ven-

[42] ASV, Collegio Cerimoniale 1, fol. 9v; BMV, MS Latin III, 172 (2276), fol. 54r; MCV, MS Venier, P.D. 517b, under heading "avertimenti generali" and "Primo giorno di quadragesima"; for examples of doges absent from processions see Sanuto, *I diarii*, 14:145, 157; 18:372; 20:141. In contrast to the interpretation offered here—that the standards were military insignia associated with the doge or with any other military captain—Staale Sinding-Larsen identifies the banners as signs of the presence of the Signoria. *Christ in the Council Hall*, p. 165.

[43] Sansovino added the faldstool to the list of papal gifts. *Venetia*, 1604, fol. 322v. Bardi depicts a scene where Pope Alexander III gave Doge Ziani a "seat" and golden gloves. *Dichiaratione di tutte le istorie*, fol. 39r.

ice at least as early as the tenth century. In the sixteenth century Sansovino claimed that the faldstool or throne indicated the stability, steadfastness (*fermezza*), dignity, and pre-eminence of the ducal authority, and it reminded the *popolani* of the respect they owed to their lord—when the prince was seated the subject stood. The foot cushion, Sansovino remarked, implied a state of repose, a fit symbol for the peacefulness of life under the ducal republic.[44]

Between the squires who held the faldstool and cushion walked the *ballotino*, who was not actually an office-holder but a living symbol for the impartial electoral system that elevated the doge and all other magistrates. His office began when he was a young boy, supposedly free of political ambition, and he was responsible for drawing ballots out of the electoral urns during the meetings of the Great Council. The choice of a young boy to represent the entire electoral process suggests that Venetians saw youth as an untainted state, a period of innocence from which the society as a whole could draw a continually renewed guarantee that elections would be carried on without corruption. With the display of the *ballotino*, Venetian adults borrowed virtue from youth, and this virtue was turned toward a specific political end—an act which compares, interestingly enough, with Savonarola's use of a youth corps to refresh the morals of Florentine society.[45] The participation of youths in the ducal procession dated from at least the thirteenth century, for Martin da Canal reported that youths carried the ducal umbrella, faldstool, and cushion; but there seems to have been no necessary connotation of youthful innocence then, as there was with the *ballotino* in the sixteenth century.[46] The *ballotino*, walking between the faldstool- and cushion-bearing squires, centered, as it were, the symbolic triad, which heralded the princely dignity, electoral honesty, and peacefulness of the Venetian polity.

[44] Sansovino, *Venetia*, 1604, fol. 322r; Pertusi, "Quedam regalia insignia," pp. 82–83; Peyer, *Stadt und Stadtpatron*, p. 63.

[45] Trexler, "Ritual in Florence: Adolescence."

[46] "Si vait aprés lui un damoisau qui porte une unbrele de dras a or sur son chief, et devant lui porte un damoisau un faudestoire mult biau et un autre damoisau porte un coissin covert de dras a or: et toutevoie vait aprés lui s'espee et la porte un gentil home." Canal, *Les estoires de Venise*, pp. 6–8.

A REPUBLIC OF PROCESSIONS

The final objects of symbolic value in the procession were the doge's head-gear, consisting of his crown, the *corno* or *berretta*, and his white linen skull-cap, the *camauro*. The doge wore his *corno* for all ceremonial occasions, and in the Holy Week processions a squire carried a bejewelled coronation crown on a gold platter.[47] The doge's embroidered crown probably derived from either the *skiadion* worn by Byzantine dignitaries or the imperial *kamelaukion* used in Constantinople after the ninth century. By the time of Doge Jacopo Tiepolo (1229–49), when the crown's characteristic peak appeared, the *corno* had become the principal insigne of the dogeship, and it specifically connoted Venetian independence from the Byzantine Empire. Venetians consciously imitated Byzantine fashions, especially during the period after the Latin conquest of Constantinople in 1204, as a means of establishing their own imperial iconography and bruiting their own recently enhanced authority.[48] The *camauro* appeared in Venice also during the late thirteenth century; but it was not at first considered to be a particular attribute of the doge, for it was worn by numerous officials. By the fifteenth century, however, it had become a ducal symbol with which the doges were invested at their coronations.

The doges were not anointed at their coronations; yet Sansovino reported that the skull-cap reminded men of the holy oil with which Christian kings were consecrated at their coronations, and he added that the *camauro* resembled the *fascia* used by ancient kings as a crown.[49] For his interpretation Sansovino apparently borrowed more from the political theories and coronation practices current in Western Europe in his time than from a distinctly Venetian tradition; in the West the central

---

[47] Sansovino, *Venetia*, 1604, fol. 315v; the crown on a platter can be seen in the engraving by Matteo Pagan (plate 7 herein).

[48] Pertusi, "Quedam regalia insignia," pp. 83–86; Schramm, *Herrschaftszeichen und Staatssymbolik*, p. 865; Fasoli, "Liturgia e cerimoniale ducale," p. 272; M. J. Armingaud, *Venise et le Bas-Empire*, pp. 311, 433. Venetian imitation of Byzantine fashions during the thirteenth century is discussed at length in Demus, *The Church of San Marco*, passim.

[49] The *camauro* was ". . . quasi come insegna di persona sacra, rappresentandosi con quella, una certa memoria del santo olio, col quale s'ungono alcuni Re Christiani, non altrimenti che se questo Prencipe fosse uno del corpo loro." Sansovino, *Venetia*, 1604, fol. 315v. Cf. Pertusi, "Quedam regalia insignia," pp. 86–87.

feature of an inauguration was the king's anointment, which sanctified the monarch, delineated the strict separation of his kingship from his mortal personality, and transformed government into a *mysterium* administered by a king-highpriest. The sovereign's acts, according to this theory of royal "pontifical-ism," were divinely ordained and justified. But as Mediterranean peoples, Venetians were unlikely to value olive oil as did northern Europeans, for whom the olive was a luxury whose very scarceness gave it a charismatic value; so in Venice such oil never became a "natural symbol," nor was it ever associated with the divine sanction of political authority as it was in the north.[50] Among the northern monarchies, crowns were often interpreted as symbols that recalled the act of anointment, and in this sense the crown bestowed on its wearer a holy dignity;[51] it was probably this idea, alien though it was to Venetian ritual, that Sansovino borrowed to explain the doge's *camauro*. The fact that he did so reveals, it would seem, that by the sixteenth century Venetian symbolic forms had been severed completely from their Byzantine roots and interpreted in a new way. Meaning was in the mind of the beholder, and the beholders had changed.

Besides the six canons of San Marco, who served the doge's sacramental needs in the basilica, the sole ecclesiastic to appear in the ducal procession was the patriarch, and he was invited only for Holy Week and a few other major feasts.[52] The patriarch was always a member of one of the most distinguished patrician families and was thus a prominent Venetian, not a foreign representative of the Church of Rome. He walked, however, next to the bearer of the white candle, the symbol of Venice's adherence to the true faith, and among the *cittadini* who preceded the doge, rather than among the patrician office-holders. The canons and patriarch were included not so much because they were exalted ecclesiastics, men of rank comparable

[50] Kantorowicz, "Mysteries of State"; Janet L. Nelson, "Symbols in Context," pp. 108–110, 118–19. Cf. Douglas, *Natural Symbols*.

[51] Bak, "Medieval Symbology of the State," p. 62.

[52] The occasions when the six canons and the patriarch were invited to participate in the procession are listed in BMV, MS Latin III, 172 (2276). The relevant passage is published in the introduction to Canal, *Les estoires de Venise*, p. cccxxiii.

to the ambassadors or senators, but because they celebrated the liturgical rites at the end of the procession and because the government wished its piety ever advertised. Sansovino reported that the canons were included ". . . because it has always been the custom of this Most Christian Republic to couple temporal things with religion."[53] The canons marched less as office-holders, men who occupied a niche in the hierarchy, than as symbols, much like the *ballotino*, of certain values with which the government wished to be identified. Since the doge had been linked to the cult of Saint Mark for so long, it is unlikely that the Venetian procession was ever exclusively ecclesiastical; at any rate, by the sixteenth century the political dimension of the processional arrangement was clearly ascendant over the ecclesiastical.

The ducal procession usually began at the Ducal Palace, wove around the periphery of Piazza San Marco, and ended in the basilica. On occasion the paraders went afterward on foot or by boat to another site, usually a church, for a special commemoration, but the normal ritual territory was the centrally located Piazza (see map). Piazza San Marco was, in fact, enlarged and embellished at various times to be more suitable for processions, thereby showing both the power of the republic to redesign the cityscape to suit its own purposes and the central importance of the ducal procession in Venetian public life. The procession, with its display of ducal authority and of the hierarchical order of the republic, visually and physically linked the government palace with Saint Mark's tomb and, depending on the occasion, with other cult centers. The Venetian conception of ritual space was perhaps unusually dramatic—the splendor of the Piazza remains unmatched—but it was not without parallel. In numerous societies the ritual topography, the spatial distribution of sacred sites, coexists with the centers of political power.[54] In Venice the primary religious and political sites were spatially contiguous and, by means of the procession, ritually integrated. As indicated by the demise of the Festival of the Marys in 1379 and the concern of Doge Gritti in the 1520s and 1530s for refurbishing the Piazza, from the fourteenth to six-

---

[53] Sansovino, *Venetia*, 1604, fol. 330v.
[54] Turner, "The Center Out There," p. 206.

8. Cesare Vecellio, *Procession in Piazza San Marco.*

teenth centurie there was a growing concentration of interest
in Venice's ritual centér, at the expense of the periphery.

A comparison with Florence is again instructive. Venetian
civic space was far more geographically concentrated than that
of Florence. In the Arno city there was no single sacred turf,
and in fact there was no "holy land" at all; but there were a
variety of ritual centers—convents, churches, and government
buildings—that were joined on feast days when processions
transformed city streets into *viae sacrae*.[55] On some occasions
the Venetians used their canals and dark alleys to similar effect;
but'in Florence there was no place, neither the Piazza della
Signoria nor the Piazza del Duomo, that compared with the
intense, introspective covergence of Venetian ritual space at the
Ducal Palace, the basilica, and Piazza San Marco.

THE DUCAL PROCESSION had, in summary, hierarchic, symbolic,
and spatial aspects. Besides illustrating the symbiosis of the
religious and political organs of authority, the origins of Venetian independence, and the harmony of Venetian society, the
procession created a paradigmatic arrangement of the Venetian
constitution and social structure. To those who, like Gasparo
Contarini, were acquainted with the Aristotelian division of
political societies into democracies, aristocracies, and monarchies, the processional arrangement of nobles, higher magistrates, and the doge seemed to confirm the hypothesis that the
Venetian commonwealth mixed these forms of government.
The sixteenth-century idealization of the Venetian republic was
thus in accord with its processional order, the most commonly
seen image of the Venetian polity. This order emphasized a
continuity of institutionalized offices transcending any particular office-holder, it trumpeted the sovereignty of the doge,
and it propagandized the loyalty supposedly nurtured among
the unenfranchised through the distribution of special honors.
More than merely reinforcing the ideology of Venice, the ducal
processions helped create that ideology by serving as a conscious, visible synthesis of the parts of society: each symbol or
person in the procession corresponded to a specific principle or
institution; placed together and set in motion, they were the
narrative outline for the myth of Venetian republicanism.

[55] Trexler, "Ritual Behavior," especially pp. 125–28.

SIX

THE RITUAL OCCASION

ANNUAL OBSERVANCES

By the end of the sixteenth century, the doge and the Signoria members participated in about sixteen annual processions, although in four of these the ducal *trionfi* were not displayed. There had been a marked increase in the number of obligatory processions since the beginning of the century and, especially after the 1540s, a remarkable extension of pageantry display in connection with the ducal processions. Consequently, solemn processional observances were becoming, if anything, a more popular and more important characteristic of Venetian life. In its public ceremonies the Renaissance did not usher in a more secular and rational, less mystical and ritualistic view of things; nor did the Erasmian and Protestant intolerance for collective liturgical observances find as many sympathetic spirits in Venice as one might have expected.

The ceremonial year fell roughly into two parts: from All Saints' Day in early November until Pentecost and Corpus Christi in May or June, the great cycles of feasts devoted to the life and ministry of Christ—Christmas, Lent, Easter, the Ascension, and the Annunciation—preoccupied Christians almost everywhere; after Corpus Christi until autumn, however, the relative infrequency of major feasts left the Venetians room for more specialized devotions to the saints and to commemorations of their own history.[1]

Besides the great events of Christian history, the most common occasions for feast days in Venice were events in Venetian history. These events were overwhelmingly political in nature, and many commemorated victory in war, the achievement that more than any other enhanced a government's image at home and abroad. In recelebrating victories, the government not only

[1] Cf. Emmanuel Le Roy Ladurie, *Montaillou*, p. 279.

paid homage to the saint under whose protection the victory had occurred and not only remembered the dead, but also reasserted the effectiveness of the leadership, renewed social bonds by reviving patriotism, and reidentified a despised enemy against whom the populace could unite.

The crusades provided numerous examples of Venetian valor abroad. Doge Domenico Michiel's successes of 1125, which gained as booty the body of Saint Isidore and the marble columns placed around San Marco, were immortalized by the doge and Signoria's annual visit to the chapel of Saint Isidore in the basilica. Likewise, the doge's participation in a mass celebrated on December 6 in the chapel of Saint Nicholas in the Ducal Palace recalled, as we have seen, Doge Enrico Dandolo's 1204 conquest of Constantinople.[2] Paeans to past victories crowded the liturgical calendar during the campaigning months of July and August. On the days dedicated to Saint Martial (July 1), Mary Magdalene (July 22), and the beheading of Saint John the Baptist (August 29), special masses in San Marco observed various fourteenth-century victories over Genoa.[3] And the elaborate July 17 procession of secular and ecclesiastical officials and members of the Scuole Grandi to the parish church of Santa Marina marked the recovery of Padua in 1509 from the troops of the League of Cambrai.[4]

[2] Michiel, Le origine delle feste veneziane, 2:101–37, 139–91; MCV, MS Venier, P.D. 517b, under heading "Decembre."

[3] Copies of the original legislation for the Saint Martial celebration are in MCV, Cod. Cicogna 2043, fol. 13, and Cod. Cicogna 2991/10, fol. 9r. Besides the victory against the Genoese and their Carrara allies that marked the recovery of Chioggia in 1379–80, the ceremonies celebrated the recovery of the bastion of Zara from the Hungarians and the defeat of the Turkish fleet off the coast of Asia Minor that occurred the same year. Sanuto, Le vite dei dogi, p. 88; ASV, Collegio Cerimoniale 1, fol. 11r–v; Michiel, Le origine delle feste veneziane, 4:153–222; Sansovino, Venetia, 1663, p. 523. On the day of Saint Mary Magdalene see Sansovino, Venetia, 1663, p. 524. On the beheading of Saint John the Baptist commemoration see Sansovino, Venetia, 1663, pp. 523–24, and Michiel, Le origine delle feste veneziane, 2:243–55.

[4] Copies of the original legislation are in MCV, Cod. Cicogna 2043, fol. 74, and MCV, Cod. Cicogna 2991/10, fol. 1r. On the ceremonies see Sanuto, Le vite dei dogi, p. 88; ASV, Collegio Cerimoniale 1, fol. 9r; Sansovino, Venetia, 1663, pp. 503–504; and Michiel, Le origine delle feste veneziane, 5:24–132. Cf. BMV, MS Latin III, 172 (2276), fol. 53v; MCV, MS Venier, P.D. 517b,

Other than the festivities associated with the legendary Venetian defeat of the fleet of Emperor Frederick Barbarossa, the most popular victory celebration came to be the feast of Saint Justina on October 7, when Venice recalled its famous 1571 triumph over the Turks at Lepanto. Since 1499, when the Venetians lost at Zonchio, the Turks had made a relentless assault on Venetian positions in the eastern Mediterranean. As a whole, the allied Catholic campaign of 1571 was by no means successful, and Venice soon after gave up its claims to Cyprus; yet the Venetians grasped at the psychological victory they had won at Lepanto. A tremendous outpouring of patriotic enthusiasm swept the city after the news arrived, and the government, determined to prolong the memory of this confirmation of Venetian naval strength and to promote future triumphs through ritual petition, declared a permanent *festum solemnis* to be held on October 7.[5] On that day the doge, accompanied by various dignitaries, went to hear mass at the church of Santa Giustina (see map) and returned to San Marco to review a procession of Scuole Grandi members and regular and secular clergy before the processioners themselves went to Santa Giustina.[6] Commemorations of victories, then, characteristically included a ducal procession, celebratory masses, and often a visit to the local shrine of the saint on whose feast day the victory had occurred.

Other annual feasts had a more strongly supplicatory character. During the plague that decimated Venice between 1575 and 1577, the Senate decreed, as a promise to God, that it would build a church to the Redeemer and conduct an annual procession there as soon as the plague passed.[7] To honor their

under heading "Luglio"; MCV, MS P.D. 396c/III, fol. 847; and MCV, Cod. Cicogna 2043c, fols. 74r–76v. Doglioni misattributed the origin of the annual procession to an order of Andrea Gritti. *Le cose notabile*, pp. 46–47.

[5] E. H. Gombrich, "Celebrations in Venice of the Holy League and of the Victory of Lepanto."

[6] Sansovino, *Venetia*, 1663, p. 514; MCV, MS Venier, P.D. 517b, under heading "Ottobre."

[7] ASV, Collegio Cerimoniale 1, fols. 47v–51v, 59v–60r; MCV, Cod. Cicogna, 2043, fols. 94–99; Rocco Benedetti and Mutio Lumina, *Raguaglio minutissimo del successo della peste di Venetia, con gli casi occorsi, provisioni fatte, & altri particolari, infino alla liberatione di essa. Et la relatione partico-*

PARAFRASI POETICA
SOPRA ALCVNI SALMI
DI DAVID PROFETA,

Molto accommodate per render gratie à
Dio della vittoria donata al Chri-
stianesmo contra Turchi,

Accioche le nostre allegrezze sieno veramente
Christiane, e grate a sua Diuina Maestà.

IN VENETIA,
Appresso Nicolò Beuilacqua.
M D LXXI.

9. Frontispiece of a pamphlet containing poetic paraphrases of the Psalms
of David, published in Venice in 1571 in honor of the Holy League's victory
at Lepanto against the Turks. The central medallion shows the lion of Saint
Mark guided by the hand of God.

pledge the senators hired Palladio to design the austere Capu-
chin church of Redentore on the island of the Giudecca (see
map) and in 1577 they inaugurated an immense procession to
be repeated each year on the third Sunday in July. After an
early morning visit to Redentore, the doge, seated in Piazza
San Marco, reviewed the passing of Scuole Grandi members,
monks, friars, congregations of priests, and thousands of lay
penitents, who then walked to Redentore across a temporary
bridge of boats. In the late sixteenth century, when most Venetians still remembered the depredations of the plague, this
procession attracted enormous crowds and was a favorite occasion for the display of precious liturgical objects and relics,
especially by the Scuola Grande di San Rocco, whose patron
was reputed to help victims of the plague.[8] Since there were no
similar annual events dating from the period after the first
ravage of the Black Death in 1348, one is tempted to attribute
the penitential processions that went to Redentore and to Santa
Maria della Salute (see map), inaugurated after the 1630 plague,
to the pious preoccupations of the Catholic Reformation.[9] The
plagues of the sixteenth century were particularly savage—between 1575 and 1577 some thirty percent of the Venetian populace died—but hardly unprecedented.[10] If the visits and be-
quests to Redentore and Salute are indications, devotional
processions were on the rise during the Catholic Reformation.
The ritual view of the world was hardly in decline.

Several observances of events in Venetian history emphasized
the limits of the doge's authority and the futility of revolutionary attempts to alter the established distribution of political
responsibilities; some even obliged the doge to participate in

---

lare della publicata liberatione, con le solenni e devote pompe, Tivoli, 1577, in
BMV, Misc. 2421/2; Mutio Lumina, La liberazione di Vinegia al molto magn.
et. eccell. sign. il signor G.F., Venice, 1577, in BMV, Misc. 2380/21.

[8] Sansovino, Venetia, 1663, p. 513; Michiel, Le origine delle feste veneziane,
4:45–59.

[9] When plague attacked Venice during the 1630s, the Senate again promised
to build a church and to conduct an annual procession. The result was Long-
hena's Madonna della Salute and a procession in November. Sansovino, Venetia, 1663, p. 525; Michiel, Le origine delle feste veneziane, 5:3–23.

[10] Pullan, Rich and Poor in Venice, p. 315.

formal condemnations of past abuses of ducal power and disruptions of civic concord. Chapter 3 cites the example of the doge's annual penance on the Sunday of the Apostles, which he did in conformity with a twelfth-century pledge made to the pope after a doge had dismantled the church of San Geminiano. At terce the doge had to cross Piazza San Marco to the rebuilt San Geminiano, light a candle at the high altar, and, as he returned, listen to the priest of San Geminiano chastise him for the presumption of his predecessor.[11] Despite the indignity of the obligation, no doge attempted to eliminate it.

More politically pointed were the ceremonies on the feasts of Saint Vitus and Saint Isidore. The observance on Saint Vitus's Day was directed against anyone disgruntled with the regime. For more than half a century after the closing of the Great Council in 1297, political feelings remained volatile; there were major conspiracies against the government in 1310, 1328, and 1355. Two dissatisfied gentlemen, Marco Querini and Baiamonto Tiepolo, led the 1310 conspiracy against Doge Pietro Gradenigo in an attempt to make Tiepolo the lord of Venice on the pattern established in Padua, Verona, and Milan. Doge Gradenigo's loyal followers thwarted an armed attack on the Ducal Palace, killed Querini, and sent Tiepolo into exile. In response to this attempted coup the Great Council established a committee of public safety, the Council of Ten, which investigated the conspiracy and ordered an annual ducal procession for Saint Vitus's Day (June 15), the anniversary of the attack, so that God would be thanked for the preservation of domestic peace.[12] The lengthy procession, which included the doge and magistrates, the clerical congregations, friars, monks, and Scuole Grandi members, traveled from San Marco to the parish church of San Vito (see map). As an expression of his thanks to the saint, the doge gave San Vito's parish priest twelve large candles, one of the most costly obligatory offerings of the cere-

[11] See chapter 3, n. 20.
[12] Descriptions of the conspiracy are in Lane, *Venice*, pp. 114–17, and Cicogna, *Delle inscrizioni veneziane*, 3:28–40. The original decree instituting the annual procession is in ASV, Consiglio dei Dieci, miscellanea cod. 1, "Magnus," p. 7 (27 June 1310). Cf. Sansovino, *Venetia*, 1663, p. 502, and Michiel, *Le origine delle feste veneziane*, 1:48–87.

monial year.[13] By ritualizing the defeat of the Tiepolo conspir-
ators, the procession hallowed the republican polity, honored
Saint Vitus for his intercession, and insured against future conspiracies through prayer and candle offerings.

The procession of the feast of Saint Isidore more specifically
denounced an overly ambitious doge. Doge Marin Falier led the
last fourteenth-century conspiracy of any magnitude against
the republican government; in the wake of a humiliating defeat
at the hands of the Genoese, he plotted with some rich but
disfranchised families to strengthen Venice by establishing a
despotism. On April 15, 1355, before the rebels could rally for
an attack, the Council of Ten discovered the plot and within a
few days tried and executed the traitors, including Doge Falier.[14] In subsequent years the government transformed the annual April 16 procession to hear mass in the Saint Isidore chapel
in San Marco, already established as a memorial to Doge Domenico Michiel's triumphs in the crusades, into a ritual re-
enactment of the funeral of the disgraced Doge Falier.[15] The
ducal symbols, banners, and musicians were excluded from the
procession, and members of the Scuole Grandi carried candles
held upside down.[16] The procession was somber and admoni-
tory: plots similar to Doge Falier's would come to a similar end.
A few weeks after Falier's execution Petrarch explained in a
letter the significance of the event and offered some advice to

[13] Sanuto, Le vite dei dogi, p. 87; BMV, MS Latin III, 172 (2276), fol. 53v;
and ASV, Collegio Cerimoniale 1, fol. 9r. All these sources speak of the doge
passing over a temporary bridge to get to San Vito. Both editions of Sansovino
speak of the doge normally traveling to the church by boat. Venetia, 1604, fol.
339r, and 1663, p. 503. Cf. MCV, MS Venier, P.D. 517b, under heading
"Giugno." The candles cost 100 lire and were paid for by the office of the
Rason Vecchie. BMV, MS Latin III, 172 (2276), fol. 53r–v.

[14] Lane, Venice, pp. 181–83; Vittorio Lazzarini, "Marino Falier."

[15] Michiel, Le origine delle feste veneziane, 2:101–37. Saint Isidore was one
of several military protectors of Venice. Tramontin, "I santi dei mosaici marciani," p. 142.

[16] Sansovino, Venetia, 1604, fols. 343v–44r; 1663, pp. 510–11; MCV, MS
Venier, P.D., 517b, under heading "Aprile." Giustina Renier Michiel, who lived
in the generation that witnessed the demise of the republic, wrote that the
ceremonies reminded Venetians that they should never abandon the spirit of
vendetta and that above all they should love the republic. Le origine delle feste
veneziane, 3:147–73.

Falier's successors: "Those who are for a time doges I would warn to study the image this sets before their eyes, that they may see as in a mirror that they are leaders not lords, nay not even leaders, but honored servants of the state."[17] Year after year, century after century, the Saint Isidore procession resurrected this advice for the instruction of every succeeding doge.

Political themes were found even in the most sacred liturgical feasts, such as those of Holy Week and Easter. Throughout the week the doge dominated the rites. On Palm Sunday he and other magistrates carried gold-leaf palm branches around Piazza San Marco in a re-enactment of Christ's entry into Jerusalem, and during the week there were several ducal processions to receive indulgences or to view holy relics.[18] At each stage in the dramatization of Christ's last days the doge himself impersonated Christ.[19]

On Good Friday bells were muted, San Marco was festooned in mourning, and the processioners wore black. In the middle of the day's procession, beneath a funeral baldachin, members of the Scuola Grande di San Marco carried a coffin containing the body of Christ in the form of the Consecrated Host; after mass in the basilica the officiating cleric took the Host from the processional coffin and placed it in the ciborium. Approaching the high altar, the doge removed his signet ring and handed it to the grand chancellor, who in turn gave it to the vicar; the door of the ciborium closed, the vicar sealed it with the ducal signet. The choir chanted, "I have buried the Lord, and the door of the tomb has been sealed."[20]

[17] Quoted in Lane, Venice, p. 181.

[18] On Palm Sunday see ASV, Collegio Cerimoniale 1, fol. 46r–v. On Holy Wednesday the doge visited San Giovanni and on Holy Thursday San Giacomo di Rialto to receive special indulgences. On Thursday evening there was a procession of Scuole Grandi members, who entered San Marco to view a relic of the blood of Christ. MCV, MS Venier, P.D. 517b, under heading "Settimana Santa"; Sansovino, Venetia, 1604, fol. 348r–v, 1663, pp. 519–20; Doglioni, Le cose notabili, pp. 72–73.

[19] Silverman witnessed the Holy Week in Montecastello in 1961 and reports that the public re-enactment of the death of Christ was so intensely followed and realistic that people ". . . speak of the events in the present tense, as if they were taking place anew every year." Three Bells of Civilization, p. 150.

[20] "Sepulto Domino, signatum est monumentum ad Ostium monumenti." Sansovino, Venetia, 1663, p. 521. Cf. MCV, MS Venier, P.D. 517b, under

THE RITUAL OCCASION

The refulgent scene on Easter morning contrasted with the somber Good Friday. In San Marco the choir and doge's throne were now decorated with rich brocades, the jeweled side of the *pala d'oro* was turned out to the congregation, the greatest treasures of the basilica were placed on the high altar and the black robes of the doge and Signoria replaced with golden silks. To begin the rites, canons of San Marco met the doge in the Ducal Palace, where they gave him a tall paschal candle and then accompanied him in a procession to the door of San Marco, which they found closed. The vicar knocked at the door, and four singers inside asked, "Whom do you seek in the tomb of Christ?" The vicar outside answered, "The crucified Jesus of Nazareth, O angel of Heaven." From inside came, "He is not here; for he has risen, just as he said. So proclaim the news again and again, for he is risen." With the singing of an "Alleluia" the doors opened, the procession entered, and the doge approached the high altar. The vicar opened the ciborium by breaking the ducal seal, and, having found the tabernacle empty, he announced that "Christ has risen." After the chorus responded with a "Deo Gratias," the vicar repeated his proclamation of Christ's resurrection and received a "kiss of joy" from the doge. The kiss was passed from magistrate to magistrate down the entire governmental hierarchy to the youngest senator. Then mass was sung, and the doge confessed before receiving communion.[21]

---

heading "Settimana Santa"; Michiel, *Le origine delle feste veneziane*, 3:3–13. That evening each parish repeated the candle procession, while the churches and many private homes were illuminated by torches. Sanuto, *I diarii*, 27:194. There were no processions on Saturday, and the altars were stripped bare as a sign of mourning; the doge and his counselors, however, attended a blessing of the baptismal font in the chapel of the Baptist in San Marco. Sansovino, *Venetia*, 1604, fol. 349v; 1663, p. 521.

[21] "Quem quaeritis in sepulcro Christicolae?" "Iesum Nazaremum crucifixum, o Coelicolae." "Non est hic; surrexit, sicut praedixerat. Ite, nunciate, quia surrexit, dicentes." "Surrexit Christus." Sansovino, *Venetia*, 1604, fol. 350r; 1663, pp. 521–22. See also MCV, MS Venier, P.D. 517b, under heading "Settimana Santa." The entire Easter text from BMV, MS Latin III, 172 (2276), is published in Canal, *Les estoires de Venise*, pp. cccxviii-cccxxiii. Normally the doge confessed by climbing up to the pulpit; Doge Andrea Gritti, however, refused to do so: "Serenissimus autem dux dominus Andreas Griti nollebat ascendere in pulpitum, sed residebat in sua sede in choro." Canal, *Les estoires*

THE RITUAL OCCASION

The rituals on this most holy of Christian occasions were a collage of religious and profane motifs. The vicar's act of placing the doge's blazon on the ciborium and the doge's role in the "Quem quaeritis" drama affirmed that even the greatest mysteries, such as the resurrection, had to be illustrated in a worldly way and that individuals, especially politically powerful ones, sought to share in the sacred power of the Host.[22] The unbroken ducal seal on the ciborium lent human validation to the divine miracle; conversely, the liturgical kiss, passed from magistrate to magistrate, put a divine countenance on the human social order; and, most specifically, the doge's conspicuous dramatic and ritual role vouched for governmental supervision of matters ecclesiastical and confirmed the holy nature of his office.

The sacred sources of secular authority were even more conspicuous at the vespers procession to the church and monastery of San Zaccaria (see map). According to the most popular of several legends regarding the origin of the visit, Pope Benedict III found refuge in Venice in 855 (during the tenure of Augustina Morosini as abbess of the Benedictine convent of San Zaccaria), while he was fleeing from his rival, the anti-pope Anastasius III (shades of Alexander III). Gratified by the grace and piety shown him by the abbess, Benedict is said to have sent the nuns, after he returned to Rome, a number of precious relics, an annual indulgence for visitors to the convent, and a jeweled crown. When Doge Pietro Tradonico later came with the crowds of common people to show his devotion to the holy gifts and to obtain the indulgence, Abbess Morosini gave him the jeweled crown, which became the first *corno ducale*. After a rival faction murdered Doge Tradonico on September 13, 864,

---

de Venise, p. cccxx. In the thirteenth-century source for the Easter services, there is no mention of the *Quem quaeritis* drama. Canal, *Les estoires de Venise*, p. 248. Normally in a *Quem quaeritis* drama, priests would re-enact the confrontation between the Marys and the angel at the entrance to Christ's tomb. James, *Seasonal Feasts and Festivals*, pp. 246–47.

[22] Trexler, "Ritual Behavior," pp. 130–31. Fasoli argues that the Easter rite in Venice was unparalleled, but it is unclear what she means by this since both the "Quem quaeritis" play and the placing of blazons on liturgical objects were known elsewhere. "Liturgia e cerimoniale ducale," p. 284.

while he was walking in a procession to San Zaccaria, an annual memorial visit was established for all future doges; but after Doge Vital II Michiel was also murdered under similar circumstances in 1172, the visit was moved from September to vespers on Easter Sunday.[23]

The Venetians of the sixteenth century relished this legend because it created, as did the story of Pope Alexander III's donations, an interpretation of the origins of the crown consistent with the ideals of Venetian sovereignty and independence. The doges, as a result of their piety, obtained the crown at least indirectly from a pope; the legend thus provided the doge with a source of legitimacy other than that derived from his Byzantine provincial titles. In fact, the legend obscured the actual history of the crown, which probably was Byzantine in origin. Like the legend of Pope Alexander III, the Abbess Morosini story was markedly pro-papal, veiling in myth the historical fact that secular rulers borrowed much of their political imagery from pontifical sources; but unlike the Alexandrine legend, the story included a nun as a mediator between pope and doge. One should not make too much of this female mediation, however, since the procession to San Zaccaria may have actually begun as a partial compensation to the convent for lands lost in the expansion of Piazza San Marco, and the legend was probably a late rationalization for the role of the abbess in a preexisting ritual. But it did allow the doge and thus, symbolically, the republic to be touched by the prayerful seclusion and special sacredness of the convent.[24]

[23] Michiel, *Le origine delle feste veneziane*, 1:123–33; Tassini, *Feste, spettacoli*, p. 77. Cf. Sansovino, *Venetia*, 1663, pp. 84, 495. Besides this legend Sansovino offered two other theories about the origin of the visits, one of which was derived from the tradition that between 809 and 827 either Doge Agnello Particiaco or his son Giustiniano made an addition to the convent, endowed it with the relics of Saint Zaccarius that the Particiaci had received from the Byzantine Emperor Leo V, and instituted the annual ducal visit. Sansovino, *Venetia*, 1663, p. 82. Cf. Cicogna, *Delle inscrizioni veneziane*, 2:105, and Sanuto, *Le vite dei dogi*, p. 90. Sansovino's other theory, based on the trecento chronicle of Doge Andrea Dandolo, was that the annual visit began in the late thirteenth century as partial compensation to the convent for its loss of land to the expanded Piazza San Marco. In one place Sansovino supported this last theory, but in another he claimed that it was impossible to judge among the three theories. *Venetia*, 1663, pp. 84, 495.

[24] Cf. Trexler, "Ritual Behavior," p. 126.

The procession to San Zaccaria consisted of the doge, magistrates, *trionfi*, a squire carrying the jeweled ducal coronation crown on a gold tray, and canons from San Marco, who came to sing vespers "according to the rite of our church of Saint Mark." The doge knelt to pray on a gold cloth spread out at the entrance to the convent church, heard vespers, and made a candle offering.[25]

For all of these annual observances, the cardinal ritual component was the ducal procession; it became a structural device around which clustered various dramatic, narrative, or symbolic accessories. None of these examples, however, quite matched Corpus Christi, the consummate annual procession by land.

CORPUS CHRISTI

During the sixteenth century the procession for Corpus Christi assembled tableaux vivants, the characteristic Venetian pageant device, and turned religious drama to a political end.[26] In 1264 Pope Urban IV made formal the feast of Corpus Christi at the instigation of Saint Juliana of Liège, a nun devoted to the cult of the Eucharist. The feast soon became one of the most popular in Europe, and Saint Thomas Aquinas himself wrote liturgical services for it.[27] In a 1295 decree the Great Council established the solemnity in Venice and in 1407 added to the liturgy a procession of the Host, declaring the procession to be "for the

[25] "Secundum ritum ecclesiae nostrae sancti Marci." BMV, MS Latin III, 172 (2276), fol. 52v, published in Canal, *Les estoires de Venise*, pp. cccxx-cccxxi. Canal's description is on p. 248. See also Sanuto, *Le vite dei dogi*, p. 90; ASV, Collegio Cerimoniale 1, fol. 8r; Sansovino, *Venetia*, 1604, fol. 350v; 1663, pp. 495–96. A mention of tableaux vivants in the procession of 1618 appears in Giovanni Carlos Sivos, "Dose di Venetia," IV, BMV, MS Italiano VII, 121–22 (8862–63), fol. 103. Cf. Michiel, *Le origine delle feste veneziane*, 1:129–31.

[26] Examples of recent studies on Corpus Christi elsewhere include Francis George Very, *The Spanish Corpus Christi Procession*, and James F. Hay, "On the Relationship of the Corpus Christi Plays to the Corpus Christi Procession at York."

[27] F. L. Cross, ed., *The Oxford Dictionary of the Christian Church*, s.v. "Feast of Corpus Christi." *The Catholic Encyclopedia*, s.v. "Orvieto," and James, *Seasonal Feasts and Festivals*, pp. 257–58. Tamassia Mazzarotto accepts the unjustified tradition that the Corpus Christi feast was prompted by the Miracle of Bolsena. *Le feste veneziane*, p. 165.

reverence of our glorious Lord Jesus Christ and for the honor of the fatherland."[28]

Corpus Christi attracted thousands of spectators from Venice and the *terraferma* to watch a sumptuous parade under a canopy of white cloth erected in the Piazza for the event.[29] The ceremonies began when the doge entered San Marco, confessed to the patriarch, and took his seat in the choir, in front of rows of magistrates and senators, to watch the formidably long procession (in 1506 it took more than five hours to pass through the basilica), which consisted of Scuole Grandi members, guildsmen, members of the scuole piccoli dedicated to the Eucharist, the regulars, and congregations of seculars.[30] These groups formed a lengthy preamble to the ducal procession itself, which on this occasion included both the patriarch, who carried a tabernacle containing the Host, and the senators, who were each paired with a foreign pilgrim bound for the Holy Land.[31] The composition of the procession was distinctive in two ways: it gave a place to nearly every corporate body in Venice, and it associated the regime with the support of pilgrimages. At the end of the fifteenth century, the Milanese pilgrim Pietro Casolo was impressed by the order and solemnity of the Corpus Christi procession in which he participated on the eve of his embarkation for Jerusalem.

> A great silence was maintained, more than I have ever observed on similar occasions, even in seating so many Venetian gentlemen; every sound could be heard. One single person appeared to me to direct everything, and he was

[28] "Pro reverentia gloriosi Jesu Christi Domini Nostri et honore Patriae." MCV, Cod. Cicogna 2043, fol. 17. On the 1295 decree see Sansovino, *Venetia*, 1663, p. 511, and Michiel, *Le origine delle feste veneziane*, 1:129.

[29] On the crowds see Doglioni, *Le cose notabili*, p. 72. The Senate obligated the *arte lane* in an act of 30 December 1454 to provide the cloth for the canopy as a contribution to the procession. MCV, Cod. Cicogna 2143, fols. 37–39.

[30] A twenty-five lire fine was imposed on groups that were asked to attend but failed to appear. BMV, MS Latin III, 172 (2276), fol. 63v.

[31] Sanuto, *I diarii*, 7:555, 24:348, 56:286. Casolo, *Viaggio a Gerusalemme*, pp. 15–19. In the eighteenth century, when there no longer were pilgrims making the voyage to the Holy Land, men from the pool of local poor walked with the senators. Michiel, *Le origine delle feste veneziane*, 1:141.

obeyed by everyone without protest. This filled me with astonishment, because I had never seen such perfect obedience at similar spectacles elsewhere.[32]

For Casolo, at least, the Venetian Corpus Christi procession disclosed a singular preoccupation with ceremonial precision and social control.

Besides its comprehensiveness, the Corpus Christi promenade was novel in that it created an opportunity for the development of pageantry. Before the sixteenth century, portable tableaux employing either live actors or groups of wooden or plaster statues were rare if not unknown. In the fifteenth century the scuole members and priests carried gilded and bejeweled reliquaries, sometimes so large that four or more men were required to support them; but allegorical or dramatic tableaux were infrequent before the first decade of the sixteenth century.[33] In a brief note about the Corpus Christi procession of 1506, Sanuto says that it was most beautiful because the scuole had prepared many "demonstrations and floats."[34] This was perhaps the first or at least one of the earliest pageants, as

[32] "Uno grande silentio se tene, e più che mai vedeti tenere a simili spectaculi, etiam in lo assetar tanti zentilhomini veneziani, ita che ogni cosa potete intendere. E uno solo a me pariva governasse ogni cosa, el qual senza resistentia era da ogni homo obedito. E da questo pigliai grande admiratione, perchè non vidi mai tanta obedientia a tali spectaculi." Casolo, *Viaggio a Gerusalemme*, p. 16; English trans., p. 147. There were, of course, occasions when things did not work as smoothly as they did for Casolo. See ASV, Inquisitori et revisori sopra le Scuole Grandi, capitolare 1, fols. 101v–102r, 127r–v.

[33] In the particularly sumptuous procession of 1440, which also celebrated a Venetian victory, there were no pageant scenes of any kind. MCV, Cod. Cicogna 2043, fols. 25–27. The same is true for the processions of 1468 and 1495. MCV, Cod. Cicogna 2991/11, fols. 13r–24r.

[34] "Fu fato una bellissima precessione, le scuole a rogata si feno honor, con molte demonstration et soleri. . . ." Sanuto, *I diarii*, 6:350. By 1510 pageant floats were considered normal, as Sanuto revealed when he commented about a procession that lacked them: "La procession ferial, non soleri ni anzoli chome li anni passati." *I diarii*, 10:460; cf. 12:243. The procession on Palm Sunday, 1495, to celebrate the signing of a league against Charles VIII of France had allegorical chariots and floats, but I do not know whether such pageant devices were used on Corpus Christi at this early date. Philippe de Commynes, *Mémoires*, 3:126–33.

opposed to mere processions. Sanuto and other Venetians failed to record any details of this cortege, but a member of the entourage of Sir Richard Guylforde, an Englishman on his way to the Holy Land, was more specific.

The other feeste was on Corporis Xpi day, where was the most solempne procession that ever I sawe. There went Pagentis of ye olde lawe and the newe, joynynge togyther the fygures of the blessyd sacrament in suche noumbre and soo apte and convenyent for that feeste y^t it wold make any man joyous to se it. And ouer that it was a grete marueyle [marvel] to se the grete noumbre of relygyous folkes, and of scoles that we call bretherhed e or felysshyps, with theyr deuyses [devices], whiche all bare lyghte of wondre goodly facyon, and bytwene euery of the pagentis went lytell children of bothe kyndes, gloryously and rychely dressyd, berynge [bearing] in their hande in riche cuppes or other vessaylles some pleasau[n]t floures or other well smellynge or riche stuffe, dressed as aungelles to odorne the sayde processyon. The forme and maner therof excedyd all other that euer I sawe so moche that I can not wryte it. The Duke sat in seynt Markes churche in ryght hyghe estate, with all the Seygnyourye [Signoria], and all the pylgrymes were present. The Duke thus sythynge [sitting], the sayde p[ro]cessyon come by hym, and bygganne to passe by aboute .vii. of the cloke, and it was passed .xii. or the sayde procession myght come oones [once] aboute, passynge by as fast as they myght goo but one tyme. There was greate honoure done to the Pylgrymes, for we all moste and leste wente all there nexte the Duke in the sayd processyon, before all the lardes and other estate, with lyghte also in our handes of wexe, of the fresshest formynge [forming], yeuen [given] unto us by the mynysters of the sayde processyon.[35]

Although it is unclear from this passage whether the "fygures of the blessyd sacrament" were merely liturgical objects or some kind of representational device, the account does mention

[35] *The Pylgrymage of Sir Richard Guylforde*, pp. 8–9.

some proper pageantry consisting of biblical scenes and of little boys and girls impersonating angels.

The Scuole Grandi, especially San Rocco, which specialized in themes concerning the Old Testament and the Church Fathers, took the lead in devising tableaux vivants.[36] For the 1532 Corpus Christi procession the San Rocco members provided one float adorned with silver liturgical objects and three with Old Testament tableaux; they dressed twelve members as patriarchs, built a wheel (a wheel of Fortune?) with six children turning on it, and arranged themselves in thirty-three pairs to carry shining silver-plate—all in an overt exhibition of wealth and of the divine blessings such wealth implied, but displayed, of course, as a means of magnifying the honor rendered to God. The other scuole merely sent cadres of children dressed as angels. But the friars of San Giovanni e Paolo were better prepared: they built a float on which two naked children depicted Adam and Eve, and others, probably adults, represented Christ and the four orders of friars; behind them came a boat laden with silver and inscribed with the legend *pro fide et patria*.[37]

By the time Sansovino compiled his famous *Venetia città nobilissima et singolare* (first published in 1581), pageantry had reached its apogee. According to Sansovino, the Scuole Grandi members in a characteristic Corpus Christi pageant appeared "With so much greater solemnity [than the other processioners] because they all are pompously turned out with decorated robes, with silver-plate, with relics in their hands, and with scenes on platforms so rare and beautiful that it is a worthy thing to see."[38] Long practice in displaying relics, rich liturgical

---

[36] A record of the increasingly more sophisticated and complex displays can be traced in Sanuto, *I diarii*, 14:306, 16:303–4, 18:271, 20:274–75, 24:347–48, 25:437, 27:405, 30:281, 34:238, 36:369, 39:77, 41:414, 45:356, 50:374, 58:315. Cf. BMV, MS Latin III, 172 (2276), fols. 16v–17r, and Doglioni, *Le cose notabili*, p. 72.

[37] Sanuto, *I diarii*, 56:285–86. A Greek ambassador criticized similar scenes from the Old Testament at the procession of 1525 with the words, "non elle scritte? che bisogna portarle?" Sanuto, *I diarii*, 39:78. On the significance of children in Renaissance dramatic productions see Trexler, "Ritual in Florence: Adolescence," pp. 227, 231–32.

[38] "Con assai maggior solennità; imperoche tutti compariscono pomposamente con ornamenti di abiti, con Argentarie, con Reliquie in mano, con

10. Giacomo Franco, *The Procession of Corpus Christi.*

objects, and didactic tableaux at the Corpus Christi pageants had given the Venetians such a repetoire of splendid scenic displays for other pageantry events, such as carnival or the visits of foreign dignitaries, that Venice's civic reputation flourished accordingly.

The full propagandistic potential of Corpus Christi was realized during the famous interdict of Pope Paul V against Venice in 1606–7. The Venetians largely ignored the pope's prohibition against celebrating the sacraments, and the government banned the circulation of the papal decree, on pain of death. While Fra Paolo Sarpi turned a defense of the republic's position into a stirring and influential treatise justifying the independence of secular authorities from papal interference, the Scuole Grandi and loyal clergy indoctrinated the Venetian populace

rappresentationi sopra palchi, così rare, e belle, ch'è una cosa degna à vedere." Sansovino, *Venetia*, 1663, p. 512.

about the infamy of, the pope and the righteousness of the
government's opposition. In May 1606, the government ex-
pressly commanded that the Corpus Christi procession be held
in defiance of the pope.[39] Corpus Christi gave the regime an
unparalleled opportunity both to affirm the Venetians' loyalty
to the government's policy and to proselytize through pageantry; the resulting procession was so striking that the sympathetic English ambassador, Sir Henry Wotton, acclaimed it
". . . the most sumptuous procession that ever had been seen
here. . . ."[40] The congregations of secular priests, most of the
orders of the regulars, and the Scuole Grandi showed up for the
procession, the latter having prepared tableaux that, according
to the euphemism of the day, had ". . . some scenes which
alluded to the reasonable claims of the republic against the
pope."[41] In particular, several tableaux invoked the notion of
the separation of ecclesiastical and political authorities: in one
tableau a scuola member dressed as Christ stood above a Latin
motto that quoted Mark 12:17, "Render to Caesar the things
that are Caesar's, and to God the things that are God's"; on
another, God ordained Moses and Aaron with the priesthood;
and on a third, Christ chided his Apostles to remember that
their priesthood required them to superintend matters spiritual
but did not permit them to meddle in the affairs of kings, who
properly ruled over the temporal concerns of mankind. Other
floats exhibited traditional Venetian political images such as the
. bearded doge, portrayed by a youngster who humbly knelt to
receive Saint Mark's blessing, and the woman personifying Venice, dressed as a queen seated upon the backs of two lions, who

[39] Bouwsma, *Venice and Republican Liberty*, pp. 417–82; Pullan, *Rich and
Poor in Venice*, pp. 55–62; A. D. Wright, "Why the *Venetian* Interdict?"
Enrico Cornet, ed., "Paolo V e la republica veneta nuova serie di documenti
(MDCV–MDCVII) tratti dalle deliberazioni secrete (Roma) del Consiglio dei
Dieci," 5:60–61.

[40] Smith, *Sir Henry Wotton*, 1:350; "Relazione dell'interdetto di Paolo V,"
ASV, Consultori in jure, E. 537, fol. 23v, as printed in Gaetano Cozzi, "Paolo
Sarpi tra il cattolico Philippe Canaye de Fresnes e il calvinista Isaac Casaubon," *Bollettino dell'Istituto di Storia della Società e dello Stato Veneziano* 1
(1959):105.

[41] "Alcune rappresentationi che alludevano alla pretentione ragionevole
della Republica con il Papa." "Relazione dell'interdetto di Paolo V," p. 105.

pledged her constancy to Faith. Some friars sponsored the most inflammatory float, which consisted of a collapsing church (*chiesa cadente*) supported by the doge, who was assisted by Saint Dominic and Saint Francis. On either side of the church stood other friars holding broad swords emblazoned with the motto "Viva il Dose." This tableau in particular outraged the Jesuit spy, Giacomo Lambertengo, who in a letter to one of his fellows referred to it as a "spettacolo miserabile."[42]

The procession signaled a diplomatic triumph. Some nine days earlier, when the Signoria had walked in the Pentecost procession without any foreign ambassadors accompanying it, there had been anxiety that Venice had been abandoned by its friends; but, to the delight of the crowds, on Corpus Christi both the French and the imperial ambassadors made a belated appearance.[43] Ambassador Wotton observed that

> The reasons of this extraordinary solemnity were two, as I conceive it. First, to contain the people in good order with superstition, the foolish band of obedience. Secondly, to let the Pope know (who wanteth not intelligencers) that notwithstanding his interdict, they had friars enough and other clergymen to furnish out the day.[44]

The Corpus Christi demonstration apparently achieved these ends and also helped to turn hesitant diplomats and foreign monarchs toward at least a passive support of the Venetian cause. The pageants show, as do Sarpi's writings, the Venetians' stratagem of transforming their own isolated dispute with the pope into a cause célèbre, a pivotal defense of secular prerogatives against ecclesiastical usurpations. And at the forefront of that defense was the Corpus Christi pageant.

---

[42] Ibid. The Lambertengo description of the last float is published in "L'interdetto di Venezia del 1606 e i Gesuiti: Silloge di documenti con introduzione," p. 223. The scriptural passages were recorded by Wotton. Smith, *Sir Henry Wotton*, 1:350. Cf. Pullan, *Rich and Poor in Venice*, pp. 59–60.

[43] "Relazione dell'interdetto di Paolo V," pp. 105–6.

[44] Smith, *Sir Henry Wotton*, 1:350.

THE RITUAL OCCASION

Special Observances

A mere list of the occasions for special processions and ceremonies could chronicle the Venetians' own perception of their
contemporary history during the late Quattrocento and the
Cinquecento. The significant demanded ritual. Through its
power to arrange ritual life, the government attempted to im-
press its own political concerns on the cosmos by restructuring
time, which was still in the Renaissance a comparatively flexible
dimension defined by the saints' feasts and the office hours of
the Church rather than by the inexorable mechanisms of the
modern age. The length of an hour in Renaissance Venice, for
example, varied according to the season; so time was truly
relative. In addition to the liturgical divisions of the Church,
the republic, in response to communal concerns, apportioned
time into its various components of festive and ferial days.[45]

Special observances in Venice may be categorized into five
types according to the function and structure of the processions
formed for the occasion. Some received a foreign emissary or
prince; some celebrated an event or paid homage to God, depending on the military, political, or natural circumstances,
such as a victory, declaration of peace, plague, or earthquake;
a fourth sort of procession announced the secular patronage of
sacred shrines and marked important events in the Church.
And in a fifth, convicted criminals were transported for mutilation or execution and publicly denounced in a judicial procession. The processions formed on all these occasions were at the
same time outward- and inward-directed; they appealed to a
foreigner's vanity or to God's grace, structured society in a
ritual way, and focused the attention of the populace on a particular problem or event. But the structure of the procession
differed according to circumstance. For the arrival of an ambassador or the visit of a prince, the cortege consisted of officials
ranked according to the pattern established in the ducal procession, and thus it emphasized hierarchy and noble privilege. For

---

[45] Cf. "Clearly, time was no more exempt from social authentification than
object." Trexler, "Ritual Behavior," p. 139.

more somber events, such as the appearance of plague, hierarchy was de-emphasized in favor of a communal march akin to a pilgrimage; social ranking never entirely disappeared in these communal pilgrimages, but the "limnal" experience produced by the mass evocation of divine aid tended to overshadow social differences.[46]

Except for public executions, diplomatic affairs and foreign visitors occasioned by far the greatest number of special ceremonies. Of the 337 nonliturgical ceremonies listed between 1556 and 1607 in the *Libro Cerimoniale* of the Collegio, 171, or nearly fifty-one percent, were receptions for ambassadors or papal nuncios. Eighteen percent (61 occasions) were formal entrances for visiting royalty or distinguished nobility. Some 39 celebratory and propitiatory processions in response to victories, treaties, leagues, jubilees, or plagues accounted for about twelve percent of the total, and the remaining nineteen percent consisted of 33 receptions for high-ranking ecclesiastics—cardinals, bishops, and abbots primarily—26 state funerals, 6 elections for doges (3 were not recorded), and the coronation of one dogaressa (one was not noted).[47]

The most common ceremonial situation, then, was the arrival of an ambassador, a nuncio, or an emissary of a foreign state. On these occasions each action on the part of the representatives of the Venetian republic was a carefully calculated gesture that recognized the distinctive office of the foreigner. Richard Trexler has defined the ceremonial frame of mind in regard to the Florentine diplomatic reception: "The systematic mode of ceremonial perception presumed that the title or dignity of each visitor determined a fixed behavior by the receptionists and a fixed gift. The quality of each *persona* and not his intentional or internal attitude, was what mattered: the visitor could not demand more nor the commune give less."[48] As in Florence, one of the principal purposes of keeping a *Libro Cerimoniale* in Venice was to record the customary ceremonies due

[46] On limnality and pilgrimages see Turner, "The Center Out There," and V. Turner and E. Turner, *Image and Pilgrimage.*

[47] ASV, Collegio Cerimoniale 1, fols. 23r–149r.

[48] Trexler, *The Libro Cerimoniale,* p. 62.

a visitor of any given station. How far out in the lagoon must
the senators (and how many senators) go to greet an arriving
guest? Should the doge take off his crown, arise from his seat,
or descend from the dias in the Collegio to meet an ambassador?
How costly should be the gold chain normally given as a token
to an ambassador? What were the Venetian magistrates to wear
at the meeting? These were critical ceremonial questions, and
the seriousness with which they were asked discloses the depth
of meaning imputed to the formal behavior, the deportment,
and even the mien of officials. Indeed, the careful formulation
of ceremonial actions maintained the communal face, which
served as a mask or, to expand the metaphor, a kind of resplen-
dent shield for the living commune that protected it from
threatening foreign intrusions into the psychic and social inte-
rior.

Sir Henry Wotton described how this elaborately artificial
ceremonial face appeared to an arriving ambassador. To him and
his compatriots the Venetian diplomatic reception was sometimes a rather tedious theatrical contrivance, but at other times
it included a communication that, properly deciphered, revealed
much about Venetian policy. When he arrived in 1616 for his
second tour of duty as an ambassador to Venice, Wotton reported that he first spent a few days moving into a new residence, ". . . which done, I must signify, according to the custom of the place, that I will be in some of their little islands at
a certain hour, and there they will come to receive me."[49] Six
years before, when Sir Dudley Carleton replaced Sir Henry
after Wotton's first tour as ambassador, Carleton complained
about his own reception on a cold and stormy November day,
saying that "to go out from home purposely to be brought
thither again" was a bit silly.[50]

But more often ambassadors took receptions quite seriously.
Wotton could not hide his concern about Venetian intentions
when the Cardinal Joyeuse, a special envoy from Henry IV sent

[49] Smith, *Sir Henry Wotton*, 2:96. When he arrived for his third stay as
ambassador, Wotton's reception was at San Giorgio Maggiore. Smith, *Sir
Henry Wotton*, 2:203.

[50] Ibid., 1:499, n. 2.

to preside over the formal revocation in 1607 of the papal interdict against the republic, enjoyed what was obviously an exceptional welcome.

> He was met three miles off at one of their islands by some
> threescore, all senators, in their best robes, with the
> barges of the Prince, whereas other ambassadors are com-
> monly received in gondolas. . . .[51]

In another letter Wotton continued,

> The Cardinal Joyeuse arrived here yesterday was seven-
> night [sic], in quality of ambassador extraordinary from
> the French King, and on the morning following he had
> audience as a Cardinal, the Prince with his assistants in
> College descending three rooms to meet him; and so, lead-
> ing him up on his left hand, between himself and the
> ordinary French ambassador, he placed him on an equal
> form appointed for that purpose, before the regal seat, in
> the same order as he had led him, and brought him after-
> wards down to the last stairhead of the place. On Sunday
> he was revisited by the Prince; on Tuesday he had his first
> private hearing in the College, as others, but conveyed
> thither through the secret lodgings of the Prince, without
> rumour, or the appearance of almost so much as a French
> lacquey in the palace—which silent and mysterious car-
> riage (so contrary to that nation) is thought to have been
> affected, either to increase opinion of the business, or to
> be (as they have been in all the rest) directly opposite to
> the Spanish ostentation.[52]

Movement, placement, gesture, seating, and demeanor por-
tended to Wotton a disturbing diplomatic reversal in his efforts
to separate Venice from France and Rome.

Most of these ceremonial acts derived their significance from
who performed them and *where* they occurred; the participants' ranking and the setting were the primary variables in
diplomatic ceremonies, and it is in this sense that they con-

[51] Ibid., 1:377.
[52] Ibid., 1:379–80.

trasted with liturgical rituals, in which the participants and spatial movements remained relatively fixed from event to event. The various settings for diplomatic receptions were, however, far from arbitrary, for they were plotted as a sequence according to their distance from the ducal throne in the Collegio: the farther away from that center a visitor was greeted and the higher the rank of the welcoming magistrates sent, the greater the honor. The least that could be offered (besides refusing to receive someone) was a nod from the doge, who left his crown on his head and remained seated; the most was to have the doge himself meet the visitor at the confines of the lagoon—the figurative terminus of communal space—as Alvise I Mocenigo did for Henry III in 1574.[53] To define precisely all the variables in the ceremonies of diplomacy in Venice would require another entire study. Short of that, one might note that diplomatic ceremony took place in a spatial dimension that was in many ways distinct from the ritual area of the civic liturgy: the center was the Hall of the Collegio, rather than San Marco, and the processional territory involved a hierarchy of islands in the lagoon rather than Piazza San Marco and the routes to the churches visited on saints' days.

When it came to measuring the city against the outside world, the focus of ceremonial activity in Venice shifted dramatically. At a diplomatic reception the Venetians' communally centered world confronted the preconceptions of another society, often with uncomfortable results. Each participant in a diplomatic encounter generated numerous highly charged political and personal relationships. By carefully establishing precedence and by formalizing gestures, ceremonies tended to make these relationships predictable and thus to reduce the likelihood of personal feuding or political miscalculation. Sometimes, however, ceremonies failed, and the result was an endless string of quarrels over rank and honor. Ambassadors, especially those of France and Spain, often wrangled over ceremonial precedence and frequently refused to join a procession or social gathering

---

[53] Pier di Nolhac and Angelo Solerti, *Il viaggio in Italia di Enrico III re di Francia e le feste a Venezia, Ferrara, Mantova, e Torino.*

11. Andrea Michieli, called "il Vicentino," *Visit of King Henry III to Venice in 1574.*

when participation meant ceding place to a rival orator.[54] Sometimes a foreigner might refuse to grant pride of place to a Venetian official; the nuncio, for example, haggled interminably with the patriarch.[55] When possible, the Signoria mediated such disputes as at the funeral of Doge Alvise I Mocenigo, when the French ambassador demanded that he displace the patriarch in the procession; the Signoria placated the ambassador only by convincing him of the antiquity of the custom.[56]

[54] Examples of precedence disputes among ambassadors can be found in Sanuto, *I diarii*, 2:85, 4:589, 5:38, 7:75, 34:134, 49:422. The bitter rows between the French and Spanish ambassadors culminated in 1558, when each submitted memorials to the Signoria, which decided in favor of France; henceforth the Spanish envoy refused to participate in any procession where the French ambassador appeared. "Cronaca Agostini di Venezia," MCV, Cod. Cicogna 2853, fols. 108v–109v; MCV, MS P.D. 250c, vol. 3 (XXIV), fols. 4r–5r; MCV, MS P.D. 396c, vol. 2, fol. 97; BMV, MS Latin III, 172 (2276), fol. 88r.

[55] On disputes between the patriarch and the nuncio see BMV, MS Italiano VII, 708 (7899), pt. 1, p. 29; MCV, Cod. Cicogna, 3281, IV, p. 25.

[56] ASV, Collegio Cerimoniale 1, fol. 54v.

These clashes were, of course, common everywhere and divulged that, as ever, 'the preservation of order in a tension-ridden world was extremely difficult, whatever the idyllic decorum that diplomatic ceremonies might prescribe.

The ceremonial problems created by the visits of foreign princes were similar to those of ambassadors, but the presence of a sovereign in person, instead of just his diplomatic representative, magnified the significance of every act and gesture. The meeting of a head of state with the republican magistrates often warped the normal organization of Venetian ceremonies. For instance, the doge's princely aspect became even more regal. In addition, the desires of the visitor were taken into consideration. During the visit of Henry III in 1574, the rules prohibiting the doge from having private audiences with foreigners were relaxed, and the Venetians had to change their festive schedule more than once in order to satisfy the caprice of France's dissolute young king. A comparison of the traditional Venetian attitude toward visitors with the view dominant in Florence during the late Trecento and early Quattrocento is revealing. From as early as 1347 Venice confidently welcomed a long line of emperors, kings, popes, dukes, and other princes and saw those visits as enhancements of its own communal reputation; in contrast, from the appearance of the Black Death until 1419 the Florentines barred distinguished outsiders, fearing that a great prince might establish himself as lord of Florence, that princes would exacerbate factional discord, and that other states might be wary about Florence's friendship.[57] Could there be a more telling comparison to explain the contrasting reputations of Venice and Florence for civic stability?

More consistent with the ceremonial practices found at the annual festivals were those processions that celebrated a military victory or success abroad. Petrarch enthusiastically described a procession he witnessed in 1361 that marked the repression of a revolt against the Venetian garrison on Crete.[58]

[57] Princes who visited Venice are listed in "Memorie del passaggio per lo stato veneto di principi e soggetti esteri, 1347–1773," BMV, MS Italiano VII, 164 (7306). On Florence see Brucker, *Early Renaissance Florence*, pp. 297–99.

[58] Michiel, *Le origine delle feste veneziane*, 2:193–241; Petrarch, *Letters*, book IV/3.

During the late fourteenth and early fifteenth centuries, the Genoese wars prompted numerous triumphs,[59] but not all victory processions during the fifteenth century were celebratory. A solemn procession of 1449 recognizing a recent peace with Milan had all the devotional elements—legions of Scuole Grandi members, friars, and congregations of seculars carrying relics and sacred images—of a procession organized during a communal crisis; in contrast, one exulting over a naval victory off the Dalmatian coast in 1495 excluded the confraternities and religious and consisted solely of orders of magistrates and foreign ambassadors.[60] The theoretical distinction between a celebration and a propitiation often broke down in practice.

At the arrival of joyful news, Venetians had several possible ceremonial responses at their command, and they did not act as if there were an automatic or rigid ritual reaction to any given occurance. Some victories, especially those against the infidels, stimulated charitable acts in addition to processions, as was the case in the summer of 1469, when a procession described as "solemn, but not in supplication" preceded the distribution of alms; a year later a victory over the Turks activated a procession, a call for universal prayers, and an offering by the government of 300 ducats in alms.[61] A peace with Hungary in 1485 inspired jousts and carnival games; the victories in September 1494 and April 1500 against the Turks excited crowds of banner-waving *popolani* youths, who chanted "Marco, Marco," and who marched in seemingly spontaneous parades.[62] Venetians, indeed, enjoyed the diversity of their ceremonies.[63]

The variations in ceremonies permit one to follow, to some extent at least, the course of communal and governmental attitudes during periods of sustained trouble such as the years of

[59] Romanin, *Storia documentata di Venezia*, 4:10 and 3:292.

[60] MCV, Cod. Cicogna, 2043, fol. 28; MCV, Cod. Cicogna 2991/15–6, fol. 1v. On the distinction between celebratory and propitiative processions in Florence see Trexler, "Ritual in Florence: Adolescence," p. 221.

[61] "Solemnus, nec non suplicationes." MCV, Cod. Cicogna 2043, pp. 63–64.

[62] Dolfin, "Cronica di Venezia," BMV, MS Italiano VII, 794 (8503), fol. 177v; Priuli, *I diarii*, 2d ed., 1:180; Sanuto, *I diarii*, 3:222–23.

[63] Cf. Trexler, *The Libro Cerimoniale*, p. 60.

the War of the League of Cambrai. Upon the lifting of the papal interdict against the republic in 1510, the government, in an attempt to restore flagging morale, declared that there be processions in Venice and in the subject towns of the *terraferma*. When the monks of San Giorgio and San Nicolò al Lido, who had left the city in order to observe the interdict, reappeared in the procession, the Venetian crowds abused them, calling the Benedictines "fratachioni" and accusing them of stealing relics and precious liturgical objects.[64] Again, despite a recent defeat at Ravenna during the same struggle, the doge and 'Signoria were so overjoyed when they heard news of the defection of Genoa and the emperor from the league that they ordered processions be held all over the city.[65] Developments in October 1511, the following spring, and in May 1513 animated the Scuole Grandi on each occasion to put together allegorical tableaux vivants that propagandized the republic's cause and praised its friends, but these jubilant processions did not preclude the charitable grants and solemnly religious mofits common in the previous century. At the 1511 procession, a sacred iconography was employed to help define Venice's position in the latest diplomatic realignment. The members of the Scuola Grande di San Rocco built a tableau with statues depicting Justice, Saint Roch, Saint Mark, and a woman dressed as Venice holding a dove representing the Holy Spirit; they were accom-

[64] "Quali veneno con apparati et arzenti, ma da tutti erano molestati dicendo: vui seti tornati fratachioni, questi non è tutti li arzenti ni reliquie etc." Sanuto, *I diarii*, 10:16; also see 10:7–8, 17. Cf. MCV, Cod. Cicogna, 2991/ı.15, fol. 11. This response to the end of the interdict in 1510 contrasted with the resolution of the 1607 interdict, when every care was taken to act as if there had never been one. Cardinal Joyeuse, acting as papal legate, supervised the ceremonial end of the interdict and the resumption of normal liturgical services: "From the College he goeth to the Church di Castello, whereof he seemeth to have made choice, for being the Patriarch's parish, having been by precise order excluded from celebrating the mass in the Cathedral Church of St. Mark, and wheresoever without intervention of the Signory, without music, without noise of bells, or of artillery at the elevation, without any form of benediction or absolution, except the ordinary of the missal *benedicat nolus Deus*, & c., finally without any public note of gladness or thankfulness, or so much as acknowledgement on their parts here." Smith, *Sir Henry Wotton*, 1:390–91.

[65] Pietro Marcello, *Vite de'prencipi di Vinegia*, p. 291.

panied by two kings on horseback (the kings of Spain and England, who had recently joined the Venetian cause), and by a ship with a sign reading "nolite timere, cessavit ventus." Venice's remaining enemy, the king of France, faced a flaming ball representing Amor Dei, and beside him stood the pope with a placard questioning why France had denied the true faith.[66] To oppose Venice was to become God's enemy. Finally, celebration and propitiation were neither opposing nor contrasting alternatives, but complementary approaches to the ever-present ritual and practical problems of reinvigorating the social order and placating God.

During the sixteenth century, policy decisions, popular fads, and traditional ties of affection led Venetians to recognize a number of events with processions: the birth of a son to King Francis I in 1518, a new league in 1537, the peace of Cateau-Cambrésis in 1559, the victory of Catholic forces over the Huguenots in 1563, the Catholic victory over the Turks at Lepanto in 1571, the league between France and Spain in 1598, and the elections of new popes.[67] These ceremonies achieved powerful

[66] Sanuto, *I diarii*, 13:79–80, 95–96, 100, 127, 128, 130–49; 14:226, 228, 230–31, 257, 259–60; 16:284–90. To announce a new league in September 1515, the Signoria gave 500 ducats in alms to the poorer monasteries and 2,000 ducats for bread to poor mariners. MCV, Cod. Cicogna 2848, fol. 199r.

[67] The ducal procession for the anti-Turkish league of 1537 was by papal command, and the Senate ordered that in addition there be processions in each parish. MCV, Cod. Cicogna 2043, fol. 82; MCV, 2991/I.23, fol. 10r. Other important processions of the period celebrating new leagues included the following: 1495 in Priuli, *I diarii*, 2d ed., 1:115; 25 March 1499 and 30 May 1501 in Sanuto, *I diarii*, 2:547–49 and 4:40; 22 May 1514 in Alovise Borghe, "Cronaca," MCV, Cod. Cicogna, 2814, fol. 7v; 26 August 1514 in Marcantonio Michiel, "Diarii," MCV, Cod. Cicogna 2848, fol. 124r–v; 18 January 1517 in Sanuto, *I diarii*, 23:485, 488–89; 15 August 1523 in Sanuto, *I diarii*, 34:363–65, and MCV, Cod. Cicogna 3281, IV, p. 30; 8 July 1526 in Sanuto, *I diarii*, 42:40, 56–60, 62–79; and 1 January 1530 in MCV, MS, P.D. 396c III, p. 786, and Sanuto, *I diarii*, 52:435–36. In 1530 the government sponsored special services designed to promote the recovery of the French king's children held hostage by Charles V since 1526. Sanuto, *I diarii*, 25:292–99, 53:552; ASV, Collegio Cerimoniale 1, fol. 10v. On the peace of Cateau-Cambrésis celebrations see BMV, MS Latin III, 172 (2276), fol. 89r; MCV, Cod. Cicogna 2853, fol. 110. On the celebrations of the victories over the Huguenots see BMV, MS Latin III, 172 (2276), fol. 95v. The Venetians sponsored an elaborate pageant on 2 July 1571 to celebrate the formation of

effects, not only by giving a political shape to masses of people but also by reordering civic space and time. Piazza San Marco stood ever ready to be transformed into a great theater for political drama; a feast day selected one particular event from the uninterrupted flow of time, isolated it, hallowed it, and gave it a special historical significance that served some immediate political or communal purpose. The leaders could, by these means, praise or exploit the deeds of others, associate themselves or Venice itself with the success of an ally, or flatter a foreign power; they could even refuse to recognize an event by ómitting a ceremonial observance. They were conscious of the eyes around them and deliberately used ceremony for a calculated effect. In his account of the celebration of an anti-Turkish league in 1495, for example, the French ambassador, Philippe de Commynes, noted that the Turkish envoy watched the procession from the window of the Procuratoria and that the Venetians ". . . wanted him to see the festival."[68]

When the diplomats failed and war was the result, Renaissance Italians responded with ritual invocations as well as military force. In his analysis of the ritual setting in Florence, Richard Trexler has noted that acts with identical goals were often performed at the same moment—for instance, masses were said in hopes of obtaining divine aid in battle at the same time the attack was launched—not only because it was believed

the league with the pope and Spain. BMV, MS Italiano VII, 69 (8438), fol. ‛330v–31v. *Cerimoni e fatte nella publicatione della lega fatta in Venetia, con la dechiaratione di solari & altre cose come legendo inendereti*, n.p., n.d. in BMV, Misc. 167/40. Celebrations of the victory of the league at Lepanto on 7 October 1571 lasted through the carnival season. Gombrich, "Celebrations." On the processions of 1598 see Francesco da Molino, "Compendio . . . delle cose . . . che sucederanno in mio tempo si della Republica Venetiana, e' di Venetia mia patria . . .," BMV, MS Italiano VII, 533 (8812), pp. 76–82. (Molino copied the account written by G. B. V., *Relationi della solenne processione fatta in Venetia l'anno 1598 adi 26 Luglio . . .*, Vicenza, 1598, in BMV, Misc. 1226/2); and Giovanni Luigi Collini, *Esplicatione dei carri trionfali fatti nella processione per la pace, tra Franza, e Spagna, dalla Scola di S. Teodoro il dì 26 Luglio 1598*, Venice, 1598, in BMV, Misc. 180/10. The deaths of the popes were also marked with state ceremony. ASV, Collegio Cerimoniale 1, fols. 10v, 118r, 120v, 122r; Sanuto, *I diarii*, 33:415, 416; 16:38.

[68] Commynes, *Mémoires*, 2:424.

that the divine powers would be more receptive but also because
these acts each had their own *telos,* or inherent direction; when
two actions, one ritualistic and the other military, were performed simultaneously they created a direct sympathy that
itself caused the desired result.[69]

The propensity to perform a ritual and a political act either
at the same moment or on the same day can be illustrated in
Venice by the long history of the republic's attempts to obtain
the canonization of Lorenzo Giustiniani (died 1456), the first
bishop of Venice to bear the title of patriarch. The case also
reveals the extent to which the Venetians relied on ritual to
influence politics in Rome. The agitation for Giustiniani's canonization began in 1472, when Sixtus IV beatified him and
commenced the official investigation for canonization.[70] In April
1519 the republic sent a legate to the court of Leo X to further
Giustiniani's case; in co-ordination with the legate, the patriarch ordered that all shops be closed on May 10 and that processions and masses be held to invoke God's support for the legate's
plea.[71] The legate, one presumes, obtained an appointment for
a simultaneous hearing in Rome. In 1524 the patriarch again
ordered a procession to Giustiniani's tomb.[72] Clement VII, Sixtus V, and Clement VIII each made minor concessions, but the
canonization trial fell into abeyance until 1613, when the republic asked that the case be reopened.[73] During the fierce
plagues of 1630 the Senate, in an attempt to expedite Giustiniani's canonization, ordered the doge and Signoria to make an
annual pilgrimage to his tomb on January 8.[74] After two centuries of political and ritual pressure the trial was completed in
1690 and Giustiniani made a saint in 1727.[75] The prime mover

[69] Trexler, "Ritual Behavior," pp. 135–36.

[70] Giuseppe Cappelletti, *Storia della chiesa di Venezia dalla sua fondazione
sino ai nostri giorni,* 1:411–12; *Bibliotheca sanctorum,* s.v. "Lorenzo Giustiniano, protopatriarca di Venezia, santo."

[71] Sanuto, *I diarii,* 27:139, 264.

[72] Ibid., 36:507–8.

[73] Cappelletti, *Storia,* 1:412.

[74] Ibid., pp. 412–14; MCV, Cod. Cicogna 2043, fol. 132; BMV, MS Latin
III, 172 (2276), fols. 54r–55r.

[75] Cappelletti, *Storia,* 1:414.

in this long struggle was the Senate, which, often aided by the patriarch, repeatedly commanded the dual approach of combining political cajoling in Rome with pious supplications at home.

Certain events demanded, in addition, abject prostration. Parish processions, mass prayers, and governmental charity were tried again and again during the late fifteenth and early sixteenth centuries to counter the Turkish onslaught; in the summer of 1500 seven days were set aside for such prayers and processions.[76] Too much rain or too little, earthquakes, and plagues also incited pious implorations for divine intercession. In several processions designed to influence the weather during the spring and early summer of 1528, supplicants carried a miraculous image of the Madonna, which by August, Sanuto reported, had worked a miracle.[77] Occasionally, popular fears outstripped official efforts to assuage them, and penitents organized their own processions (some involving Scuole Grandi members) in which little children appeared dressed as angels and banners and relics were displayed; or, as happened in 1511, the populace themselves demanded that the government entreat the Virgin's aid by parading her image.[78] Unlike the more political ceremonies, which emphasized social distinctions, group-crisis rites bound the community together as one: various specialized sources of ritual protection and mystical power, whether a venerated painting of Mary or children as representatives of social innocence, were summoned for extraordinary service to supplement the efforts of the institutionalized ritual protectors—the priests who celebrated masses, the monks and confraternity members who prayed, and the magistrates who formed processions.[79]

Because they were so ruinous and long-lasting, plagues in particular impelled the entire community to ritual action. In

[76] Priuli, I diarii, 2d ed., 1:129; Pietro Bembo, Della historia vinitiana, fol. 59r. See also Sanuto, I diarii, 37:602, 612–13.

[77] Sanuto, I diarii, 48:275, 353. For other examples of processions designed to influence the weather see Sanuto, I diarii, 6:185, 38:271, 47:178. For other examples of the use of miraculous images in processions see Sanuto, I diarii, 12:79–84, 87, 98, and ASV, Collegio Cerimoniale 1, fol. 77r. Cf. Richard Trexler, "Florentine Religious Experience."

[78] Sanuto, I diarii, 12:174.

[79] Cf. Trexler, "Ritual in Florence: Adolescence," pp. 232–33.

desperation the Venetians were willing to go to extraordinary lengths. During the 1575–77 plague, the Senate commanded all religious houses to pray continuously, organized frequent mass processions, and, as we have seen, promised God through legislative decree that in return for his abating the pestilence, the state would finance a new church dedicated to the Redeemer and inaugurate an annual communal procession. The Senate ". . . was resolved to nothing other than ending the plague with the usual processions and praying to the great God that he would take them into his holy hand."[80]

When the government acted as a secular patron of the Venetian church and validated ecclesiastical actions, it established the republic's reputation for pious devotion and, just as importantly, secured a phylacteric guardian. In 1514 the Collegio organized an official procession in the Piazza in order to display a rib of Saint Stephen newly acquired in Montenegro.[81] On the occasion of the dedication of a new church, there was often a devotional procession: in 1506 a special bridge was built to permit a procession honoring the laying of the first stone of the new monastery of Santa Maria Zobenigo, and there were three processions between 1506 and 1530 to San Salvatore while it was being rebuilt (see map).[82] The doge always witnessed the installation of a new patriarch or new canons of San Marco, and the assembled magistrates honored a Pisani when he received a cardinal's hat in 1517.[83] The Venetian regime was always preoccupied with the details of an essentially ritualistic piety, and there never was a sense that the secular government and the sacred Church were entities with radically differing objectives. In ritual matters the only important distinction was be-

[80] ". . . fu risoluto non farne altro, ma s'attendesse ad estinguer la peste con le solite processioni, con pregar il grande Iddio che vi mettesse la sua S. mano." Benedetti and Lumina, *Raguaglio minutissimo della peste*, no pagination. Cf. Lumina, *La liberazione di Vinegia*, in BMV, 2380/21, and ASV, Collegio Cerimoniale 1, fols. 47v–60v. On processions during earlier plagues see MCV, Cod. Cicogna 2043, fols. 46–47, 58–59.

[81] Sanuto, *I diarii*, 18:413.

[82] Ibid., 6:307, 496; 46:289; 53:72. For other processions to new churches see MCV, Cod. Cicogna 2853, vol. 2, fol. 143v; ASV, Collegio Cerimoniale 1, fols. 84v–85r, 112v.

[83] Sanuto, *I diarii*, 7:611, 24:585–87.

tween the two bureaucracies, which may have had different functions but which shared similar points of view and loyalties. The secular bureaucracy employed processions, as well, to bind the peripheral parishes and shrines more tightly to the central authority of the republic.

A rejection of the majestic, sacred authority of the republic, most notoriously seen in crimes and acts of treason, also called for a calculated ritual response. But only sometimes. There were many crimes the Venetian magistrates wanted hushed up; those persons condemned by the Inquisition, for example, were quietly drowned in the dead of night, and the Council of Ten cloaked its proceedings in secrecy. Other miscreants became public examples, and an essential part of their punishment was a public humiliation, mutilation, or execution through which the judicial councils ritually reasserted their authority, redressed private wrongs with public actions, freed the community of its collective guilt, brought vengeance upon a violator of the communal order, and reaffirmed the government's guarantee to provide a stable, harmonious society that guarded citizens against criminals.[84]

Least stringent was a public humiliation, sometimes seen as sufficient punishment in and of itself and sometimes enforced as a prelude to banishment. Typically, a malefactor would be obliged to wear a crown painted with devils and to stand all day on a stage erected between the two Columns of Justice in the Piazzetta next to the Ducal Palace (see map). In the early Cinquecento, this penalty was inflicted on a foreign lawyer who falsely obtained power of attorney, a procuress for homosexuals, a priest's concubine who had borne him children, and two old women accused of witchcraft.[85] Such a punishment constituted a loss of face—a public destruction of reputation or of one's *bella figura*—and reveals the essential principle of Venetian ritual justice. This principle might be described as the law of the "conservation of justice"; that is to say, a wrong-doer who took something away from society repaid this loss by giv-

[84] Parts of this interpretation follow Guido Ruggiero, "Law and Punishment in Early Renaissance Venice," pp. 251–52.

[85] Sanuto, *I diarii*, 18:63, 25:190–91, 57:104–5, 26:360–61.

ing up something in return. Liars, immodest women, and witches marred the *figura* of the city and had to suffer a loss of their own *figura* in order to re-establish the civic reputation.

More serious misdeeds required a greater repayment than the loss of face. The government reserved mutilation, sometimes followed by execution, for lower-class persons who in the eyes of society had committed the foulest crimes, who earned their living with their hands, and who had no property worth confiscating. Mutilation and execution were carried out with great public solemnity and were ritualized through a judicial procession. The condemned was first transported to the scene of the crime, where the offending member, usually a hand, was cut off, or an eye gouged out. The severed hand was often hung around the criminal's neck to be displayed while he or she was transported to the Columns of Justice for execution. All during the procession and at each stopping point a herald proclaimed the condemned person's crime.[86] A penalty for crimes of violence, mutilation was also commonly meted out to those who had committed even relatively minor crimes against the state: in 1514 the Council of Ten ordered that in public view on a stage in the Piazzetta an eye be gouged out and a hand cut off of a collector of the wine tax who had made false seals, and in 1518 the Ten proclaimed that a counterfeiter, who had already lost an eye for his offense, must lose a hand after he had been caught in violation of his banishment.[87] An act that hurt the good name of the state was more severely and more publicly punished than a merely private wrong.

The most gruesome punishments were reserved for those guilty of multiple violations of the public morality and order. In 1506 a widowed prostitute who had lived "domestically" in the parish of Santa Sofia with a smith attacked him one night while he slept, stabbed him in the chest, and threw boiling oil in his face. After taking two sacks of money, his purse, and some belts and clothing, she set his bed afire and left. The fire consumed the house and threatened neighboring dwellings. After apprehending and trying her, the Quarantia Criminale

[86] Ruggiero, "Law and Punishment," p. 251.
[87] Sanuto, *I diarii*, 18:44, 25:190.

ordered that "She be transported along the Grand Canal on a float [see map], as usual, as far as Santa Croce; she should disembark at *Corpus Domini*, where she will be taken on a litter by land to Santa Sofia, and there [at the scene of the crime] a hand will be cut off; then she will be taken to San Marco, also by land, and between the two columns she will be whipped and then decapitated; her head is to be hung up at San Giorgio [Maggiore], and the body is to be burned."[88] The severance of the prostitute's hand at the spot where she murdered her lover followed a common judicial procedure of transforming the offending member into a ritual object, thereby cleansing the scene of the crime of the pollution that remained. This cleansing was akin to an exorcism; the devil's instrument, the hand, was destroyed, thus eliminating the chance that such evil would reoccur at this spot. Such mutilation was thus far more than an attempt to make an example of the sinner: it compensated society for a loss of order, which the judicial procession from the republic's prisons to the scene of the crime and then to the Columns of Justice re-established. The judicial procession retied the bond between the various parts of the city and the central power and, in this case, proclaimed that the justice of the republic reached into even the remotest corners of the city.

The Venetian judiciary felt most obliged to order a ritual cleansing of the republic after traitors had been apprehended; this was especially true for those captured during the tense years of the War of the League of Cambrai, when the loyalty of the mainland subjects was repeatedly tested and when the Venetian government found demonstrations of the swiftness of its vengeance most necessary. Great public executions were the centerpiece of a policy that used the formal apparatus of justice to enforce political loyalty. Seditious nobles, however, were exempted from the undignified dismemberment imposed on commoners before execution and instead suffered confiscation of

[88] "La sia conduta per canal grando su uno soler, *juxta* il solito, fin a Santa †, dismonti al *Corpus Domini*, dove sopra uno altro soler sia menata per terra fino a Santa Sophia, e ivi al loco li sia tajà una man, poi conduta a San Marco, pur per terra, e in mezo le do colone sia descopata e poi tajà la testa, la qual sia apichata a San Zorzi, et il corpo sia brusato; et cussì fo exequito." Ibid., 6:289.

their property and goods. After the 1509 capitulation of Padua to the troops of the League of Cambrai, four Paduan notables, convicted of rebellion by the Council of Ten, were led to the gallows in the Piazzetta, allowed to make a final public statement to the huge crowd present, and then simply hung without a whipping or mutilation.[89] The rebellious clergy fared less well. In 1514 a treasonous Friulian priest convicted by the Council of Ten and the vicar of the patriarch for "having committed many evils and deeds against God and his Signoria" was first publicly divested of his ecclesiastical office through a ritual reversal of his investiture: he was stripped of his vestments one by one, in a ceremony similar to the one in which Shakespeare's King Richard II gives up his royal garments and crown to Bolingbroke. Thus despoiled of his clerical status, the seditious priest then suffered a horrible end. When no papal briefs arrived to support the suspension of his sentence, the Council of Ten ordered that punishment be carried out without delay: "Today in Piazza San Marco the priest in question is to be whipped on a stage, then hung by a foot and left suspended from the gallows for a day; then immediately he is to be hung [by the neck] from the gallows."[90] During the execution proceedings Marin Sanuto happened to be passing by in a gondola, and, seeing the crowds gathered in the Piazza, he debarked to record a description of the priest's execution.

> Today at the hour of 23, this priest with his habit removed, but dressed in white stockings and a jacket and habit of the Scuola [di San Fantan] was brought out on a stage. He kissed the crucifix of the Scuola and crossed himself and all the while the friar next to him encouraged him to remember Christ for the salvation of his soul. The executioner took the whip in his right hand and beat the priest, who fell upon the stage, and then the executioner gave him more than four additional great blows. Believing he was dead, they tied a cord to his foot to pull him up to the

[89] Ibid., 9:358–59.

[90] "Ch' el dito prete ozi in piaza de San Marco fusse sopra uno soler discopato, poi apichato per uno pe' et star debbi su la forca per uno zorno, poi apichato, su una forcha; e fo mandato a far la forca subito." Ibid., 18:47.

top of the gallows in order to hang him there, but it was hard work pulling him up, and they struggled for more than half an hour with the help of three men who climbed to the top of the gallows. When finally he was tied up, it was evident that the priest was not yet dead since he moved his legs; hence all who were near by began to throw stones at his face and body, and thus it went whenever he showed signs of life; it went on this way until the end, until after the hour of 24 when he died; so I believe he suffered a cruel death as he deserved from his misdeeds, the ruin of the fatherland. . . , and thus his life ended as he deserved.[91]

The priest's severe whipping and prolonged suspension were certainly designed to make an example of him, especially since anti-Venetian handbills had been spread about the streets during the night after his arrest. Obviously he had supporters in the city. But the execution was more importantly a communal act of purification accomplished by amputating an infectious member from the body politic. The populace's seemingly spontaneous brutality in stoning the hapless cleric is not so much an indication of the blood-thirst of the Venetian mob as it is of the people's readiness to participate in a collective rite. By directing violent emotions through ritual toward the service of a socially useful end, the republic maintained its authority and furthered its reputation for justice.

---

[91] "Hor, a hore 23, fo mandato esso prete con l'abito fu preso, calze bianche e indosso uno zipon et l'abito di la Scola e sopra il soler; poi fato basar il Crocefisso di la Scuola et † et sempre il frate lì apresso a ricordarli di Christo per vadagnarli l'anima, fo per il boja datoli di la manara drio la copa e scopato; qual cazete sul soler, et poi esso boja li dete più di 4 altre gran bote; et credendo fusse morto, lì ligono una corda a uno pe' per tirarlo in zima di la forcha e lì apicharlo, e fo gran stento a tirarlo, et steteno più di meza ora, pur fo tirato con ajuto di tre homeni che andono in zima la forca. E ligato, si vete esso prete non esser ancor morto e moveva le gambe; *unde* tutti chi li era apresso comenzono a trarli saxi a la volta di la testa et di la persona, e cussì come li zonzeva, cussì esso monstrava resentirsi; pur tanto li fo trato che a la fin, a hore 24 a più, morite; sichè credo sentisse una crudel morte come merita li soi mensfati, ruina di la patria. . . . Et cussì finì la vita sua come el meritava." Ibid., 18:48.

THE RITUAL OCCASION

THE CEREMONIAL INVOCATION of *communitas* in Venice had diplomatic, celebratory, propitiatory, ecclesiastical, and judicial dimensions. Whether in jubilant assurance or panic-stricken fear, the republic blended spontaneous communal emotions and carefully planned political objectives; during the vibrant ceremonies of the sixteenth century, communal enthusiasms and elite concerns seldom, if ever, came into conflict. Special processions captured certain passing events, made them collective experiences, and turned the collective experience to political ends. Through these special rituals and processions the republic attempted to direct the course of history—such was the hubris of the state.

SEVEN

THE PARADOXICAL PRINCE

THE DOGE AS PRIMUS INTER PARES AND AS PRINCEPS

In the mid-sixteenth century those who visited and wrote about Venice pictured the doges as princes whose quasi-regal pomposity belied their supposed political impotence. Donato Giannotti reported that "The insignia of the Venetian dominion are invested in the person of the doge, since in the republic he alone has the mien of a lord. But though he alone possesses such a dignity, in nothing is he given complete power since not only is he unable to make decisions however insignificant, but also he can do nothing out of the presence of his counselors."[1] An English traveler echoed Giannotti's description: ". . . and though in appearance he seemeth of great estate, yet in every deed his power is but small. He keepeth no house, liveth privately, and is in so much servitude that I have heard some of the Venetians themselves call him an honorable slave."[2] Gasparo Contarini implied that this peculiar status was based on a political compromise: the doge's only administrative function was to act as a moderator among the other magistrates; he was to follow all public issues, direct each subordinate official toward the common good, and rebuke the wayward; he was deprived of any control over policy or patronage, but in compensation he was allowed "an exterior princely honor, dignitie, and royall appearing shew."[3] In short, "He has the bearing of a

---

[1] "Si come noi habbiamo detto nella persona del Doge si posano le supreme insegne dell'imperio Vinitiano. Percioche egli solo apparisce nella Republica Signore. Ma come che solo egli possegga tanta dignita non gli è pero in cosa alcuna potesta intera concessa percio che non solamente non puo determinare alcuna benche picciola cosa, ma etiamdio esseguire sanza la presenza de Consiglieri. . . ." Giannotti, *Libro de la republica de Vinitiani,* fol. 72r. Cf. "Tuttavia non hà auttorità nessuna, se non quanto gli è conceduto dalla legge. Insomma egli è il primo huomo per preminenza che noi habbiamo in questa Città." Bardi, *Delle cose notabili,* p. 116.

[2] Thomas, *The History of Italy,* p. 70.

[3] Contarini, *De magistratibus et republica Venetorum,* p. 43; English version, p. 43.

prince, but in the Senate he is a senator, and in the market-
place a citizen."[4]

This was the Renaissance literary and ideological image of
the doge, an image that invested the person of a single office-
holder with both princely and republican attributes; and in this
image one can see the nexus at which many of the tensions in
Venetian society and politics were revealed and resolved. Just as
struggles over the composition and powers of the Council of
Ten make evident the tension between an oligarchic and a more
broadly based aristocratic regime, so do disagreements over the
nature of the dogeship disclose the more dialectic conflict between monarchical and republican principles of government.
Since scholars have identified Venice as the paragon republic of
the sixteenth century, the practical and ceremonial resolution
of these two principles is important.

The tendency to disperse political power rather than to concentrate it legally in the doge was practical as well as theoretical. It came from the long medieval conflict between the *mi-
nores*, the wealthy *maiores*, and the *duces*, who struggled over
the ducal insignia and powers; Agostino Pertusi and Gina Fasoli
have reoutlined the early history of this conflict.[5] After the fall
of the Ravenna exarchate in the mid-eighth century, the *dux* of
the Veneto, who was formerly subordinate to Ravenna, used
his own forces to stay in power and eventually had his position
confirmed by Constantinople. In the early centuries of this
quasi-independence, the most powerful local families chose the
dux through factional infighting and were often able to establish, through co-regencies, the rudiments of dynastic succession; but no family was able to dominate the selection process
for as long as even three successive generations. By 887 the
political base broadened considerably when a popular assembly

---

[4] "In habitu princeps, in senatu senator, in foro civis." Quoted by Mosto,
I dogi di Venezia, p. xii.

[5] Pertusi, "Quedam regalia insegni," especially pp. 64–80 and 96–121.
For criticisms of Pertusi's approach and chronology see Roberto Cessi, "L'
investitura ducale"; Fasoli, "Comune veneciarum," pp. 475–90; Fasoli, "Liturgia e cerimoniale ducale," pp. 264–69. For a view that links the development of the Venetian ducal insignia to those of the Latin Empire at Constantinople see Schramm, *Herrschaftszeichen und Staatssymbolik*, pp. 859–68.

forced the elderly Doge Giovanni II Particiaco to abdicate, an
act symbolized by his transfer of the insignia of authority—the
sword, scepter (*baculus*), and faldstool—to Pietro I Candiano.
Through electing and deposing doges and suppressing usurpers,
the popular assembly became the de facto sovereign body, and
it legitimated its decisions by investing persons with the emblems of authority inherited from Byzantium.

As ties with Byzantium loosened, the local power-base expanded. By the end of the tenth century Constantinople no
longer claimed any rights over Venice, and the office of the
doge had matured into the repository of legitimate civic authority, an authority epitomized by the ceremonies of election
and investiture. During the eleventh century the populace, assembled at San Nicolò al Lido, acclaimed each new doge, sang
traditional regalistic lauds to him, invested him with a scepter,
and, in imitation of Byzantine imperial or military practices,
made him undergo a ritualistic spoliation, repeat a formula of
acceptance, be carried in a progress on the shoulders of his
soldiers, and distribute coins to the crowd. The object of interest in these rites was the scepter, which, according to the symbolism of the rite, Saint Mark invested directly on the new
doge and which became an insigne of a highly personal authority. The other *maiores*, jealous of the doge's regal prerogatives,
reduced ducal privilege at the election of Pietro Polani in 1130
by replacing the overly personal scepter with the banner of
Saint Mark (*vexillum S. Marcii*) as the symbol of the commune
(unlike the other insignia, the banners were carried in processions even when the doges were absent) and by introducing the
promissione ducale, an oath of office that codified the legal
limitations on ducal initiative. These developments, which finally severed the ducal office from its Byzantine roots, represented what Pertusi has called a great, bloodless revolution;
symbolic and procedural alterations thus signaled a permanent
transfer of power from the doge to the *communis*. The theoretical position of the dogeship was thereby established: thenceforth the doges would be princes without formal powers and
lords without legal vassals; they would be elected for life and
have no dynastic rights; in short, they became in law nothing
more than the *primus inter pares*, but remained in public bear-

ing and dignity (and usually in actual influence) much like a *princeps*.

Once established, however, the balance between the regal investiture of the doge and the actual powers exercised by the commune did not survive unchallenged, nor was it without many ambiguities and anomalies. One of the ways in which changes in the position of the doge may be traced is through examining the formal obligations and restrictions on ducal gift exchanges. Giving, receiving, and repaying in a formal, ceremonial context define a particular social relationship and create a binding contractual obligation among the parties.[6] Such an obligation was particularly characteristic of a great lord, whose ability to be lavishly generous to his subordinates was often what allowed him to acquire, keep, and expand his authority. Early medieval chiefs were expected to be liberal with their followers, and in the Carolingian period, ". . . the bestowal of a few gifts—a horse, arms, jewels—was an almost invariable complement to the gesture of personal submission."[7] Conversely, new vassals were customarily obliged to reciprocate by making a gift in kind or money to their lord as acknowledgment that the vassal's land, for example, was a fief granted by the lord.[8] Tribute to and largess from the doge, likewise, had significant social and political implications.

The Renaissance doges inherited a variety of gift-exchange relationships that were gradually either eliminated or severely circumscribed. Documents from the thirteenth century mention modest tributes due the doge from various corporate groups or geographical centers in the lagoon and Istria.[9] The oldest *promissioni ducali* reveal that the artisans of Venice owed the doge certain well-defined gifts of goods or services: casks of wine, foodstuffs, shoes, gondola transport, and haircuts.[10] But these guild obligations disappeared long before the sixteenth century. In the thirteenth century, according to Martin

[6] Marcel Mauss, *The Gift*, pp. 3, 37–40; Georg Simmel, *The Sociology of Georg Simmel*, pp. 389–92; Huizinga, *Homo Ludens*, pp. 58–63.

[7] Marc Bloch, *Feudal Society*, vol. 1: *The Growth of Ties of Dependence*, p. 163.

[8] Ibid., pp. 205–6.

[9] Canal, *Les estoires de Venise*, p. 8; Fasoli, "Comune veneciarum," p. 494.

[10] Fasoli, "Liturgia e cerimoniale ducale," p. 288.

da Canal, the doge, as the lord of the woods and marshes of the lagoon and its islands, received in tribute each year at Christmas more than 3,000 mallard ducks and capons, which he redistributed to his fellow patricians and the leading citizens (*prudomes dou peuple*). In 1521 the bird tribute was eliminated, but a vestige of the ritual was preserved in the doge's distribution of medallions called *oselle* ("birds" in Venetian dialect), which were specially minted for the occasion.[11] Likewise, by the 1520s every other formal gift to the doge and redistribution of tribute by him had been abolished; the doge's gift of fish to his six counselors ("li vient donés por treusage") on Thursday of Holy Week disappeared, and, as we have seen, in 1509 the doge began to offer the pork butchered on Giovedì Grasso to the monasteries and prisons rather than continuing to give it to his fellow patricians.[12] These reforms were evidently part of the general readjustment of the doge's public image, which was a major concern of the early sixteenth century.

Throughout the sixteenth century the doge retained the right to be personally generous—but only to plebians, never to his fellow patricians. On Palm Sunday he had flocks of pigeons released from the roof of San Marco to be caught by the poor for their Easter dinner, and on Wednesday after Easter "by ancient obligation" he gave a banquet at his own expense for twenty poor but honorable men.[13] These grants were, of course, seen as alms, and it should be remembered that in sociological terms alms and largess establish similar relationships; he who receives is personally obliged and beholden to he who gives.[14] These ceremonial gifts of alms left open an important way for

[11] Canal, *Les estoires de Venise,* in the 1845 ed., pp. 566–67 and p. 742, n. 297. Cf. Mosto, *I dogi di Venezia,* p. xxxvi.

[12] Canal, *Les estoires de Venise,* 1845, pp. 578–79 and p. 725, n. 311.

[13] MCV; MS Venier, P.D. 517b, under headings "Settimana Santa" and "Pasti maggior che fa il Serenissimo Principe di Venetia." On Palm Sunday see also ASV, Collegio Cerimoniale 1, fol. 46r–v; Sansovino, *Venetia,* 1604, fol. 348r; Michiel, *Le origine delle feste veneziane,* 2:3–19.

[14] Mauss, *The Gift,* pp. 15–16. Fasoli argues that all the tributes were given to the state, not to the doge, because, she says, the offerings went into the public treasury. The fact that the doge redistributed the tribute to his fellow patricians indicates, however, that at least until the 1520s the tribute was given to the doge just as it would have been to a lord. Fasoli, "Comune veneciarum," p. 494.

enth-century doges to accumulate lordly powers and to
ance their princely image, at least among the *popolani*; and
some doges, such as Marin Grimani, manipulated popular sentiments against their patrician colleagues. The doges were by
no means completely disabled by their restricted constitutional
status, and some took advantage of whatever loop-holes they
might find in the legalistic wall built around them.

Opportunities for the doge to become involved in a gift-exchange relationship with patricians or foreigners, however,
were carefully controlled. His *promissione ducale* rigorously
prohibited him from giving or receiving gifts from anyone who
was not his own relative.[15] Even the four annual formal banquets hosted by the doge for various office-holders were meant
solely to renew bonds of comradeship among magistrates who
were social equals; the banquets were paid for by an appropri-
ation from the Senate, the guest lists were prescribed by law,
and the gatherings functioned, as Contarini reports, ". . . for
nourishing and maintaining love and good will among the citizens [i.e., patricians]."[16] Conscious of the implications of gift
giving and the obligations with which it encumbered the recip-
ient, the patricians tolerated the doge's habit of giving alms to
the poor, but were hardly willing to subject themselves and
their colleagues to the vassalage implied by accepting the generosity of a lord.

By the sixteenth century virtually every word, gesture, and
act that the doge made in public was subject to legal and ceremonial regulation.[17] He was not able to buy expensive jewels
for festive decorations; he could not own property outside
Venetian territory; after Michele Steno (1400-13), the doge
was prohibited from displaying the ducal insignia outside of the
Ducal Palace; he could not permit anyone to address him as
"My" or "Our Lord," decorate his apartment as he pleased,
receive private persons in offical dress, send official letters or

---

[15] Mosto, *I dogi di Venezia*, p. xxxiv.

[16] Contarini, *De magistratibus et republica Venetorum*, p. 48; English version, p. 48. The four annual banquets were on the feasts of Saint Stephen,
Saint Mark, Saint Vitus, and Ascension. Sansovino, *Venetia*, 1604, fols.
326v–27r; MCV, MS Venier, P.D. 517b, under heading "Pasti maggiore che
fa il Serenissimo Prencipe di Venetia."

[17] Cf. Fasoli, "Liturgia e cerimoniale ducale," p. 262.

open those that arrived, have private audiences with ambassadors, use his influence on behalf of his family, or even have close ties with the guilds.[18] On Trinity Sunday and All Souls' Day he was not allowed to attend services in San Marco, because the votive masses sung on those occasions for the deceased members of one's own family might have had dynastic implications for the doge.[19] Personal memorials of doges (or of any other individual, as a matter of fact) were banned in San Marco, and no doges were buried there after 1354.

Sometimes the doge acted as a lord in various "feudal" ceremonies, but it was clear that these acts merely made formal a decision of the Great Council, Senate, or Council of Ten. After Jacopo Contarini (1275-80), a doge could not himself decide who would receive a fief, a prerogative eventually ceded to the Council of Ten; but, by giving new vassals of the republic a ring, the doge still ritually invested them with their fiefs.[20] During the fifteenth century several *condottieri* were given fiefs on the borders of the *terraferma* dominions, and in return the vassal *condottieri* had to pay annual tributes of candles to the basilica, but they gave nothing to the doge himself.[21] The doge dubbed knights "without public solemnity" in the privacy of his apartments in the Ducal Palace; however, he could do so only for candidates named by the councils.[22]

For offices within the domestic bureaucracy and patrician hierarchy, the doge had few ceremonial rights to transfer or allocate authority. At the solemnization of the Great Council's election of a new grand chancellor, the chancellor, a *cittadine*, kissed the hands not just of the doge but of all the higher magistrates, as a token of submission to his patrician superiors; he also thanked the Great Council, rather than the doge, for the crimson velvet stole given him as an insigne of office.[23] At the swearing-in ceremony for a new procurator of San Marco,

---

[18] Mosto, *I dogi di Venezia*, pp. xxxiii–xxxiv; ASV, Maggior Consiglio, deliberazione, "Libro d'oro," pt. 4, fol. 29v, dated 2 January 1328.

[19] Sinding-Larsen, *Christ in the Council Hall*, p. 209.

[20] Mosto, *I dogi di Venezia*, p. xxxiv; ASV, Collegio Cerimoniale 1, fols. 74r–75r, 93r.

[21] Michael Mallett, "Venice and its Condottieri, 1404–54," p. 129.

[22] Giustiniani, *Histoire*, p. 127.

[23] ASV, Collegio Cerimoniale 1, fol. 83r; Gilbert, "Last Will," pp. 505–6.

the grand chancellor, instead of the doge, placed a crimson stole on the new procurator's shoulders.[24]

The one notable exception to this rule of divorcing the doge from the ceremonial distribution of governmental responsibilities was the consignment of the banner of Saint Mark to a newly elected captain general of the sea. In the early seventeenth century Sir Henry Wotton described the captaincy general in the most weighty terms: "This is the solemnest title they can confer under the princedom, being indeed a kind of a dictatorship, to which they have no charge equivalent on the land, having been content (as it seems) in honour of their situation to give the prerogative of trust to that element [the sea]."[25] The Senate reserved the right to elect the captain general, but the doge himself consigned the emblem of office. After meeting in the Ducal Palace, the doge and newly elected captain general walked to San Marco, where the captain knelt before the high altar upon which a banner of Saint Mark had been placed and before which lay a general's baton. Invoking Saint Mark's name, the patriarch blessed the banner, gave it to the doge (who in turn handed it to the captain general), and in a prescribed prayer asked God to protect the fleet, to vanquish the enemies of Venice, and to bring victory to the patria. After the choir sang a Te Deum, the captain general turned the banner over to the admiral of his fleet, who climbed onto a small wooden platform carried on the shoulders of Arsenal sailors and was paraded around the Piazza, throwing out coins to the crowds. As a sign of his new dignity, the captain general walked beside the doge in the procession that followed. In the company of his admiral, the new general embarked and was rowed to San Nicolò al Lido, where he enjoyed a banquet with other dignitaries of the republic.[26]

[24] MCV, MS P.D. 115b, p. 58.

[25] Smith, Sir Henry Wotton, 2:133.

[26] At the consignment the doge said, "Elegit ti Deus ut dextera tua fines nostros late circum tueri valeas, turbantesque rerum nostrarum securam, et Justitia partam quietaem Divina virtute repellas. Quapropter hoc formidatum hostibus vexillum tibi creditu victor sospes, et in columis patriae sed de feliciter." ASV, Collegio Cerimoniale 1, fol. 16r. Cf. Sansovino, Venetia, 1604, fol. 353v; Sanuto, I diarii, 2:653, 56:376–77. For a different speech, which Leonardo Loredan delivered to Bartolomeo d'Alviano at his consign-

12. Giacomo Franco, *Procession for the Consignment of the Baton to the Captain General of the Sea.*

---

ment in 1513 see ASV, Collegio Cerimoniale 1, fol. 16r–v. Cf. Sanuto, *I diarii,* 16:250–52, and Romanin, *Storia documentata di Venezia,* 5:284. The new captain general himself paid for the decorations and candles for San Marco. BMV, MS Latin III, 172 (2276), fol. 67r. For other examples of consignments to captains general see ASV, Collegio Cerimoniale 1, fols. 128r–29r; BMV, MS Italiano VII, 1233 (9600), fol. 17r–v; MCV, Cod. Cicogna 2853, fol. 132r; Sanuto, *I diarii,* 8:159. The captain-general consignment ceremony served as a model for the governors general of the *terraferma.* BMV, MS Latin III, 172 (2276), fols. 90v, 93v–94r.

The banner of Saint Mark had been, as we have seen, the Venetian battle-colors since at least the eleventh century and was originally invested on the doge by a bishop; later some claimed that Saint Mark himself directly consigned the banner to the doge when the doge discovered the banner already lying on the altar above Saint Mark's tomb.[27] Banners, moreover, could be carried in a procession even when the doge was absent; thus they identified an authority that was in some ways independent of the doge. In the investiture of a captain general, the doge's intermediary role did not necessarily indicate that he was transferring any of his own particular responsibilities to another—the captain general did not stand in place of the doge abroad as a locum tenens—but rather that the doge was simply representing the republic in investing the eternal authority of Saint Mark. The banner-consignment and the admiral's progress around the Piazza interestingly paralleled, as we shall see, elements of the ducal coronation ceremony devised in 1485, so that the ceremonial elevation of the doge that was attempted in the late fifteenth and early sixteenth centuries confused somewhat, perhaps purposely, the significance of the doge's role in the consignment-of-banners ceremony.

The main point, however, is quite clear. When it came to domestic political matters, giving and receiving gifts, or conferring an office on an elected magistrate, the doge's public actions were circumscribed so that there could be no question in anyone's mind that, legally, power in Venice emanated from the councils and, except for a few isolated cases, never from the doge himself.

All of these restrictive legalisms contrasted startlingly, however, with the quasi-mystical and indeed princely aspect of the doge found in the civic liturgy and the annual public rituals, for the internal distribution of political power was quite a different matter from the illustration of sovereign Venetian authority. In most rituals the doge represented the sovereign and corporate *res publica* through his regal bearing, his symbolic

[27] Fasoli argues that in the eleventh century Saint Mark himself was believed to confer the *baculus* directly upon the doge. "Comune veneciarum," p. 489.

central place in the procession, his display of the ducal insignia, and his performance of the leading role in many rites. A minute and cautious supervision of his two contrasting personae, one so humbled and the other so splendid, was in many ways the objective of the ritual by which the doge was obliged to act and live. This was a remarkable arrangement and in fact quite a successful one, for the duality of the dogeship provided an institutional mechanism that might resolve many internal political tensions.

The schism between the doge as an image of authority and as an actual ruler was least evident in his patronage of San Marco. Only the financial trusteeship he shared with the procurators checked his ability to direct the affairs of the basilica. He alone selected the chaplains and nominated the vicar (*primicerio*) for Senate approval, and there remained a closed circle of administrative ties between the doge in his palace and the clerics in their basilica that no outside ecclesiastical or lay power could break.[28] The doge himself, calling the candidate the "defender and true governor of our church and chapel of Saint Mark," invested ecclesiastical office on each new vicar.[29] The doge frequently gave gifts to the canons, paid them for their services, hosted banquets for them, and for major feasts provided the basilica with candles.[30] In addition, the doge had a peculiar role in the liturgical functions of the basilica: he did not remove his crown when he prayed before a sacred image or relic; during the Divine Offices and the masses special prayers were said for his health just as they were for sovereigns elsewhere; on Holy Thursday he, like any emperor or king, performed the Mandatum, the ceremonial washing of feet; and, as

[28] Ibid., p. 496.

[29] "Patronus et Verus Gubernator Ecclesia et Capelle nostra Sancti Marci." ASV, Procuratia de Supra per la Chiesa di S. Marco, busta 86, processo 191, fascicolo 1, documento 2. Oliver Logan kindly brought this reference to my attention. The doge also had a role in the investitures of patriarchs, bishops, abbots, and abbesses. "Statuti antichi dei canonici di S. Marco," in Gallicciolli, *Storie e memorie venete*, 6:91–92. On the doges' confirmation of each new abbess of the convent of Santa Maria delle Vergini see ASV, Collegio Cerimoniale 1, fol. 62r.

[30] "Statuti antichi dei canonici di S. Marco," in Gallicciolli, *Storie e memorie venete*, 6:77, 85, 101–3.

we have seen, he was at the center of all the annual candle exchanges.[31] In many ways, then, the doge appeared to be a sacred person, a kind of civic cleric who performed rituals on behalf of the commune. In Ranulf Higden's *Policronicon* of 1352 the doges were specifically compared to clerics and to kings: "The dukes of the city are in manner like preachers, and no Christian complains of them. They are lords of the Greek Sea as the king of England is lord of the English Sea."[32] But the doge did not, in fact, enjoy the sacral prerogatives of a Byzantine emperor; there is no evidence, for example, that the doges ever received communion in both kinds, and the doge had to pay the canons of San Marco for various services in a manner without precedent in imperial lore.[33] In his religious duties the doge might better be seen as a lay administrator, not fully a superincumbent priest, over the civic cult centered around Saint Mark.[34] He was a quasi-sacred person and enjoyed the sacredness attributed to any political figure of stature, but he was not a miracle-worker, as was any ordained priest or anointed king.

However great the fears of ardent republicans that the doge was an omnipresent threat, always a potential lord, the office was neither abolished nor completely eviscerated, and the doges held on to and even tried to magnify their mystical and princely attributes. Claims that Venice had a special mandate from God, that it was protected by the saints, that it was independent from the Papacy and the Empire, and that all of this was amply proved by history depended on the ability of the republic to assume the attributes of the doge without destroying the office altogether. The result of this assimilation was a ceremonial

[31] Mosto, *I dogi di Venezia*, p. xxxviii. On Holy Thursday see Fasoli, "Liturgia e cerimoniale ducale," p. 283.

[32] Quoted in Parks, *The English Traveler to Italy*, p. 572.

[33] Fasoli, "Liturgia e cerimoniale ducale," pp. 276, 284.

[34] Cf. Ibid., p. 279. Tramontin speculates that two unnamed figures in the mosaics in the atrium of San Marco may represent the last doge and the last pope in a millenarian reference possibly stimulated by Joachite influences. Despite his cult attributes, the doge never became, as far as I have been able to determine, the symbol of a millenarian movement, as other secular rulers did in times of social or political turmoil. "I santi dei mosaici marciani," p. 148. See Marjorie Reeves, *Joachim of Fiore and the Prophetic Future*, pp. 59–82, and Cohn, *The Pursuit of the Millennium*, passim.

dilemma, ~~the most troublesome part of which involved~~ the
transfer of symbolic authority from one doge to another.

THE FUNERAL AND CORONATION OF THE DOGE

[The crucial test of any political order comes when power or
authority is transferred.] In many ancient societies a ruler commanded both secular and religious power or was deified; as a
result, his death caused a crisis of the entire world order, which
could be resolved only by an elaborate ritual reconstruction of
the ties between the society and the gods.[35] Yet the death of a
prince did not jolt Renaissance Europeans with the catastrophe
that struck ancient Egyptians at the death of a pharoah, for
Christianity offered its followers a vision of the cosmos less
troubled by the mortality of secular princes.

A king's death created a problem for most Renaissance prin-
cipalities in that power had to be transferred in an orderly
manner from deceased to successor, and so did legitimacy. Royal
funeral rites in particular tempered the abruptness of the transition by distinguishing the undying nature of rulership from
the mortality of individual rulers. By the death of Francis I, in
1547, the French had developed a funeral ceremony that set the
eternality of kingship apart from the mortality of particular
kings: while mourning over the actual body, the subjects directed oaths of loyalty toward a life-like wax effigy of the deceased king.[36] The ceremonial separation of the "living" effigy
and the corpse symbolized that, despite the death of a king, the
King and the body politic never died. In England, where the
constitutional principle of the "King in Parliament" complicated
the picture, monarchists created the elaborate fiction of the
"King's two bodies," the body politic and the body natural, as
an aid to dynastic continuity.[37] During a royal interregnum
France and England were virtually governed by ceremony, and
the funeral and coronation rituals ensured an orderly dynastic
succession. Other European countries created their own solu-

---

[35] H. Frankfort, "State Festivals in Egypt and Mesopotamia."
[36] Ralph E. Giesey, *The Royal Funeral Ceremony in Renaissance France.*
[37] Kantorowicz, *The King's Two Bodies.*

tions to the same problem: in Hungary, the symbol of undying
rulership became the Crown of Saint Stephen, and in Germany
rulership tended to be identified with the abstract State rather
than with a particular princeship.[38] Besides ensuring continuity,
funeral rites could demonstrate the legitimacy of a particular
succession, an idea of critical importance for upstart rulers like
the grand dukes of Tuscany. At Cosimo I de' Medici's death, in
1574, his son Francesco, in order to confirm his own succession,
transformed his father's funeral into an apotheosis modeled on
the funeral ceremonies of the pagan emperors of Rome, an
apotheosis that identified the parvenu Medici dynasty with the
principle of undying rulership.[39] There were, thus, a variety of
ways in which the death rites of a Renaissance prince might
preserve the impression of continuity in rulership.

In the Venetian republic the funeral and coronation rituals of
the doge not only clarified the distinction between undying
rulership and mortal rulers but also maintained the balance, so
characteristic of Venetian government, between the regal aspect
of the doge and the republican values of the patriciate. The
communal and republican nature of Venetian society meant
that the problems created by a ducal interregnum were of a
different order from those found in a monarchy. Funeral and
coronation ceremonies elsewhere protected dynastic succession;
in Venice, they forestalled it.

The ducal funeral and coronation rites were derived from
traditional Venetian ceremonial forms, but the fifteenth-century magnification of ducal splendor challenged the republican
regime to make a careful distinction between the man and his
office. Beginning perhaps with the famous festivities that accompanied the election of Michele Steno to the dogeship in
1400, most fifteenth-century doges elevated the pomp of their
office: Tommaso Mocenigo (1414–57) paid a fine for recom-
mending the redecoration of the Ducal Palace and then went
ahead with his remodeling plans; Francesco Foscari (1423–57)
introduced the use of the royal "we" when using the first person; and Nicolò Marcello (1473–74) changed the doge's robes

[38] Ibid., p. 446.
[39] Eve Borsook, "Art and Politics at the Medici Court I."

from crimson to gold, ordered a lavish new ceremonial umbrella and foot-cushion made of crimson velvet, and had new
ceremonial trumpets hammered out of silver.[40] The fifteenth-
century humanist Giovanni Caldiera, in a surfeit of hyperbole
that underscored the trend, said the doge was as "splendid as
the sun," the ultimate repository of power, and the prince of
Venice, who consulted councils merely for advice.[41]

Two monuments built in the courtyard of the Ducal Palace
best reveal the tendency toward self-aggrandizement among
late fifteenth-century doges. The first is the Arco Foscari,
begun on a modest scale by Francesco Foscari but transformed
into a grandiose monument to the dogeship by Cristoforo Moro
(1462–71). Debra Pincus interprets the iconography of the
multiple levels of statues on the arch as portraying the doge as
the restorer of the earthly paradise lost by Adam and Eve and
promised anew by the Gospel of Saint Mark.[42] This was certainly a lofty claim for any man who had climbed to the peak
of the Venetian *cursus honorum* through the inevitably unholy
process of electoral politics. The second monument, which was
even more self-congratulatory, faces the Arco Foscari and com-
pletes the complex of triumphal architecture devoted to the
doges: it is the imposing marble staircase now called the Scala
dei Giganti. Commissioned by Doge Marco Barbarigo in 1485
and finished by his brother, Agostino, who succeeded him in
the dogeship, the staircase was designed as the centerpiece for
an elaborate new coronation ceremony begun by Marco Barbarigo. The reliefs on the sides of the staircase were far more
personal than the generalized praise of the dogeship on the
Arco Foscari, and they magnified the heroic Agostino as the
leader of the New Rome. Portraits of Aristotle and Alexander
referred to the combination of wisdom and military prowess
that characterized the ideal ruler; the coats of arms from enemy

[40] M. Muraro, "La scala senza giganti," p. 350; Mosto, *I dogi di Venezia*, p.
xxxiii; Sansovino, *Venetia*, 1604, fol. 316r. Other regulations on the doges'
dress may be found in BMV, MS Italiano VII, 794 (8503), fols. 342v–43r, and
ASV, Maggior Consiglio, deliberazioni, fol. 60r–v, dated 6 November 1485.

[41] Discussed in King, "Personal, Domestic, and Republican Values," pp.
564–68.

[42] Debra Pincus, *The Arco Foscari*, pp. 208–52.

cities recalled the victories of Agostino's reign; and allusion:
the crafts and guilds suggested popular support for his auth
ity. Lastly, symbols of justice and sovereignty surrounded D
Agostino's own portrait and, along with the ten inscription:
his name, claimed for him an elevated, princely status.[43] In
De Bello Gallico Marin Sanuto echoed these themes when
called Agostino Barbarigo "the new Augustus," supposedly
having saved Italy from the invasion of Charles VIII; the p
Ventura di Malgate addressed Barbarigo as the "Prince of
new Rome" and compared him to Ulysses in his astuteness
Brutus in his justice, and to Camillus in achieving milit:
victories.[44] Barbarigo's own tomb eulogized him as a great n
itary hero.[45]

The Barbarigo doges went too far in offending the egalitar
sentiments of the patriciate, and the reputation of Agostino
particular, suffered after his death. In the privacy of his di:
Sanuto accused Agostino Barbarigo of arrogance, greed, sti
borness, and venality, and there were rumors of secret g
from the Marquis of Mantua and the Lord of Rimini. Ag
tino had enraged nearly everyone, as well, by insisting that
visitors kiss his hand and kneel before him.[46] Domenico Mo
sini was so disquieted by and hostile to the self-seeking do;
of the late Quattrocento that he proposed reforms that if (
acted would have amounted to a wholesale dismantling of 1
dogeship as it had come to be known.[47] The Barbarigo do;

[43] M. Muraro, "La scala senza giganti"; Mosto, I dogi di Venezia pp. 2(
64; MCV, Cod. Cicogna 2479, under heading "Agostino Barbarigo."

[44] Quoted in Chambers, The Imperial Age of Venice, pp. 25–26.

[45] Filippo Nani-Mocenigo, "Testamento del Doge Agostino Barbarigo,
241. Doge Barbarigo was described as "homo di grande ingiegno, et di
gular memoria. Il quale ancora per la bolla presentia che egli haveva mostr
in se certa maestà con barba longa, et Canuta la quella cossa lo facev:
presso le persone degno di molta reverentia, al prencipio del suo R[egn
Nicolò Trevisan, "Cronaca veneta dalle origine al 1585," BMV, MS Itali
VII, 519 (8438), fol. 294v, new foliation.

[46] "Che era una meraveja a udir le maledition ognun li dava, per la suɲ
bia, rapacità, tenacità, avaritia era in lui, et aceptar de presenti." Sanut
diarii, 4:113; Mario Brunetti, "Due dogi sotto inchiesta," pp. 289–95; M
Cod. Cicogna 2479, under heading "Agostino Barbarigo"; Mosto, I dog
Venezia, pp. 262–64.

[47] Cozzi, "Authority and the Law," p. 302, and idem, "Domenico Mo
sini."

had extended the fifteenth-century attempt to exalt the doge-ship to a forthright imitation of the mainland princes' use of the arts and public ceremonies in order to realize and exemplify their power and majesty.[48] In the case of Agostino Barbarigo the traditional device for enforcing limitations on the doge's behavior, the review after his death by five "correctors" of the provisions of the next doge's *promissione ducale,* was inade-quate, because the correctors had insufficient authority to in-vestigate the career of a dead doge and to hold his heirs respon-sible for any misdeeds. In response to this situation the Great Council created a new institution that consisted of three "in-quisitors" of the dead doge; the inquisitors examined the charges of abuse of office and levied a fine against the estate of Agostino Barbarigo, an act that represented a reassertion of the republi-can aristocracy over princely authority.[49] After the establish-ment of the board of inquisitors, the abuse of the ducal office for personal gain became more difficult, in theory, because the correctors of the *promissione ducale* carefully defined the ducal position within precise and restricted limits; and abuse of office also became less profitable, since the doge's heirs were made financially responsible for his transgressions.[50] Even as late as 1544 the Barbarigo doges' misdeeds were still being undone; in that year Jacopo Sansovino was commissioned to sculpt two giant marble statues of Mars and Neptune symbolizing the power of the republic on land and sea; these statues were then mounted at the top of the offending stairs to deflect attention from the Barbarigo imagery and to dwarf future doges who were crowned there.[51] Reforms were likewise instituted in the

[48] Cf. Gundersheimer, *Ferrara,* pp. 266–67, also see pp. 201–12.

[49] Brunetti, "Due dogi sotto inchiesta," pp. 286–306; Contarini, *De mag-istratibus et republica Venetorum,* English version, p. 157; ASV, Collegio Cer-imoniale 1, fol. 2v; MCV, Cod. Cicogna 2479, under heading "Agostino Barbarigo." "The Correctors are five of the principal gentlemen of the State in knowledge and merit, being chosen to propose what shall seem fit unto them to be altered in the form of the next election, as time hath discovered this or that inconvenience—and this [is] always the first act after the vacancy. There are also chosen three Inquisitors, who are to censure the carriage of the dead Prince." Smith, *Sir Henry Wotton,* 1:339.

[50] Cozzi, "Authority and the Law," p. 302.

[51] M. Muraro, "La scala senza giganti." On the Mars and Neptune statues, see John Pope-Hennessy, *Italian High Renaissance and Baroque Sculpture,* p.

funeral and coronation ceremonies themselves in an attempt to tighten the republican grip on the doge. Venetian patricians, however, vigorously continued to pursue the dogeship, and incumbents did what they could to ignore the restrictions on the office, so that in tracing the office of the doge through the sixteenth century one can see unfold many of the constitutional and ideological conflicts of the Venetian political drama.

WHEN THE MEMBERS of the Collegio were formally told of the death of a doge, their spokesman was required to announce, "With much displeasure we have heard of the death of the Most Serene Prince, a man of such goodness and piety; however, we shall make another."[52] And to make another is what they proceeded to do. Although as private individuals the members of the Collegio may have shared in the general grief, as official representatives of the interregnum government they were obliged to adopt a cavalier disregard for the political impact of the doge's death. As Lewes Lewkenor noted in his appendix to Contarini's De magistratibus, "There is in the Cittie of Venice no greater alteration at the death of their Duke, then at the death of any other private Gentleman."[53] Venice was indeed distant from Pharaonic Egypt or even from monarchical France.

408, and Howard, *Jacopo Sansovino*, p. 33. Pincus argues that after Doge Agostino Barbarigo there was a general shift away from representing the polity through an iconography of eminent persons. *The Arco Foscari*, pp. 377–83. With only one exception, after 1501 no one appears kneeling in front of a doge in the illuminations for the *capitolari* of the government. Sinding-Larsen, *Christ in the Council Hall*, p. 178.

[52] "Con molto dispiacere avemo sentido la morte del Serenissimo Principe di tanta bontà e pietà; però ne faremo un altro." Quoted in Tamassia Mazzarotto, *Le feste veneziane*, p. 225. Tamassia Mazzarotto does not say when this phrase was first used, and I have found no mention of it in the sixteenth century; it is, however, perfectly consistent with the interregnum practices of the Renaissance. For a bibliography of studies on Renaissance attitudes toward death see Davis, "Study of Popular Religion," p. 326, n. 2.

[53] Contarini, *De magistratibus et republica Venetorum*, English version, pp. 156–57. Lewkenor translated this passage directly from Donato Giannotti: "Percioche la nostra Città piglia quella stessa alteratione della morte del nostro Principe, che piglierebbe di quella di qualunque altro privato Gentil'huomo. Onde in essa non apparisce per tal caso variatione alcuna." *Libro de le republica de Vinitiani*, fol. 63v.

From the moment of a doge's death to the coronation of his
successor, the magistrates had to follow a procedure carefully
prescribed by law and custom in order to guarantee the orderly
transfer of ducal authority.[54] The doge's administrative authority passed to the Signoria, which secluded itself in the Ducal
Palace at the news of his death.[55] As their first act of business
the Signoria members ordered the admiral of the Arsenal and
a contingent of sailors to guard the palace during the interregnum, a practice designed to prevent the populace from sacking
the palace, which they had done as late as the fourteenth century; in the sixteenth century sackings no longer took place,
but the threat of violent interference with the electoral process
or of a forced succession was frequent enough to require security precautions.[56] During the conclave that elected Doge
Girolamo Priuli, in 1559, Girolamo Grimani was a leading con-

[54] Officials were to follow the ceremonial model in ASV, Collegio Cerimoniale 1, fols. 1r–6v. Ceremonial procedures for the canons of San Marco are
listed in BMV, MS Latin III, 172 (2276), fols. 67v–70r. Of special interest
among the numerous other models and descriptions of ducal funerals are
BMV, MS Italiano VII, 1219 (9598), which gives details of most of the sixteenth-century ducal funerals and coronations; "Diario delle cose sequite
doppo la morte del Ser[enissi]mo D. D. Silvestro Valier Doge di Venetia osservate secondo il cerimoniale . . . che se vede in Secreta del 1501 . . . et sopra
li cerimoniale posteriore . . .," BMV, MS Italiano VII, 708 (7899); Sanuto, I
diarii, 30:387–402, for the funeral of Leonardo Loredan, and 34:127–55 for
the funeral of Antonio Grimani. On Venetian funeral practices in general see
Sansovino, Venetia, 1604, fols. 270v–73r.

[55] ASV, Collegio Cerimoniale 1, fols. 1r, 53v; BMV, MS Italiano VII, 1219
(9598), fol. 29r; Sanuto, I diarii, 34:129.

[56] Sansovino, Venetia, 1604, fols. 328v. At the death of a doge his family
had three days to vacate the ducal apartments, and until 1328 the populace
was allowed to sack the apartments. Mosto, I dogi di Venezia, p. xxxvii. Such
spoliations at the death of a prince were common in the early medieval period
and indicated the populace conceived of the polity and the mortal prince as
one and the same. The people of Pavia reportedly told Conrad II (1024–
1039), when he rebuked them for having destroyed the imperial place there,
that they had committed no crime, since the sacking had taken place during
an interregnum. "We served our emperor while he lived; when he died, we
no longer had a sovereign." Cited by Bloch, Feudal Society, vol. 2: Social
Classes and Political Organization, p. 409. The end to the sacking of the ducal
palace in Venice may thus indicate a spread of the concept that the polity was
eternal and separate from the mortal prince.

tender; the *popolani* detested Grimani, ostensibly because he was a hunchback, and they displayed their feelings by pounding on the locked doors of the palace and chanting, "If you make Grimani the doge, we shall throw him to the dogs!"[57] In 1595 the populace surrounded the palace demanding the election of Marin Grimani, who had ingratiated himself to the poor with his generous gifts of bread and alms during a famine.[58] In extreme cases such as these the patrician electors saw imminent danger for themselves and for the public order, and the protest may have had some effect on the outcome; normally, however, the transfer of office—the interregnum rites, the funeral of the deceased doge, and the election of his successor—was a completely patrician affair, and there was no disruptive violence. Sir Henry Wotton's report in 1605 could have described most sixteenth-century interregnum periods: "The State is quiet, rather through good laws than good dispositions."[59]

The initial interregnum rites dissociated the dead doge from the office he had occupied and discouraged dynastic succession by destroying the material symbols of the tie between the man and his ducal authority. The ducal ring was the most multivalent symbol of a particular doge's tenure in office: through the concept of the ring the doge invoked the episcopal authority of Saint Mark and became the mystical husband of the sea; without it he lost his office.[60] After a doge's death a secretary

[57] "Se voi fate Doge il Grimani noi lo daremo a mengiar ai cani!" Quoted by Mosto, *I dogi di Venezia*, p. 330.

[58] "Furono sentiti ali strepiti Popolari in rio di Palazzo, et alle Porte con gridi di voler questo Dose, il che pose qualche pensiero, e pericolo nell Città." BMV, MS Italiano VII, 142 (7147), pp. 339–40.

[59] Smith, *Sir Henry Wotton*, 1:337. After eight days Wotton again reported that "The public is quiet, peradventure through good laws [more] than good dispositions" (p. 339). For the practical administrative procedures of the interregnum see BMV, MS Latin III, 172 (2276), fol. 67v. Paul Grendler notes that the interregnum was a time when politically difficult legislation was often passed. *The Roman Inquisition*, p. 219.

[60] When Doge Agostino Barbarigo asked to abdicate due to ill health, he removed his ducal ring and gave it to his oldest counselor. Brunetti, "Due dogi sotto inchiesta," p. 281, n. 1. Similarly, a grand chancellor in his will asked that his ring be broken at his death. "Voglio praeterea che, separata l'anima dal mio corpo, sia tolto el mio anello da bolla cum el qual sum consueto sigillar, et quello destructo, adeo che cum epso non se possi più sigillar." Gilbert, "Last Will," p. 513.

[handwritten margin notes: "The symbol of his office. Destroys." "His office is a symbol"]

of the Council of Ten solemnly smashed this official gold ring, which was inscribed with the doge's arms, the lion of Saint Mark, and the words *Voluntas Ducis*; the pieces were given to the relatives of the former doge as a sign that their privileges as members of the ducal court had now come to an end.[61] The ceremonial involvement of a secretary of the Council of Ten indicated the importance of this act, for the Ten concerned themselves with the security of the commonwealth, which was in jeopardy unless the privileges of the ducal family were definitively curtailed at the death of the doge. Secretaries likewise broke the stamp for the lead ducal seals, and the mint was ordered to remove the arms of the doge from their coins. The arms of the vice-doge replaced those of the former doge on official seals, ensuring that the ducal authority clearly reverted to the senior elected official of the patrician hierarchy rather than to a member of the ducal family.[62]

On receiving news of the doge's death, the magistrates of the salt works at Chioggia sent two silver emblems to the Signoria. The larger one was inscribed with the name of the former doge and depicted an enthroned and crowned doge with a banner of Saint Mark in his hand; the smaller emblem differed only in the absence of the doge's name. The larger emblem, like the ducal ring and seals, was smashed; the senior ducal counselor kept the smaller emblem and presented it to the new doge after his election.[63] Venetian political thought postulated two kinds of doges.

> In this alone are they [the two kinds of doges] different: that the one is the perpetual head of all, while the other is temporary and governs a single part. Both are equally called the Prince: for being the first, and grandly revered and honored by all, he represents a truely absolute Prince to those who see him in his majesty, with so many orna-

[61] Mosto reports that some documents describe the ring as emblazoned with the words *Voluntas Senatus*. *I dogi di Venezia*, p. xlviii.

[62] ASV, Collegio Cerimoniale 1, fol. 1r. The interregnum seal is described as bearing the lion of Saint Mark and the arms and initials of the vice-doge. Bascapè, "Sigilli della repubblica," p. 101. At the accession of the new doge, the interregnum seal was broken. The vice-doge was elected from among the counselors and was not necessarily the eldest. Mosto, *I dogi di Venezia*, p. xl.

[63] ASV, Collegio Cerimoniale 1, fol. 1v.

ments acquired by means of his valor; but in fact he is tied by the laws in a way that his position is not at all different from the other positions of any magistracy.[64]

Clearly the objective of the rite was similar—to divorce the eternal, regal Doge symbolized by the smaller emblem from the taint of the mortal, magistrate doge symbolized by the broken larger emblem. The greatest political sin of Agostino Barbarigo was his attempt to blur this distinction between man and office and to confuse respect for the dogeship with adulation for himself; to this abuse the republic reacted with a renewed legal and ritual emphasis on the separation at death of the doge from the dogeship. The haste with which Venetians were prone to sever the personality from the office during the century after Agostino Barbarigo contrasted markedly with the contemporary funeral ceremonies of the kings of France or of the grand dukes of Tuscany, in which the ceremonies emphasized not the severance but the preservation beyond death of a particular person in his office.[65]

Although the popularity, financial standing, and testamentary provisions of particular doges controlled the character and ostentation of their funeral ceremonies, the legalistic rites followed a consistent pattern. Most ducal funerals were tributes to well-known and respected political figures; for example, when

[64] "In questo solo sono differenti, che l'uno è capo perpetuo del tutto, & l'altro è temporaneo, & governa una parta sola. Fù medesimamente detto Prencipe; percioche essendo prima, & grandemente riverito, & honorato da tutti, rappresenta nella maestà sua con tanti ornamenti acquistati per via del valore, un Prencipe veramente assoluto, all'altrui vista; ma infatti legato dalle leggi, di modo che non è punto differente da gli altri posti in alcun magistrato." Sansovino, *Venetia*, 1604, fol. 314r. In Tintoretto's *Paradiso* in the Great Council Hall of the Ducal Palace, Christ, dressed in the *corruccio* the doges wore on Holy Thursday, figures as the celestial, eternal doge; the terrestrial, mortal doge, who would have stood in front of the painting, was seen as Christ's vicar. In this manner the conceptual distinction between the doge and the dogeship was ever before the patricians during their political assemblies. Charles de Tolnay, "Il 'Paradiso' del Tintoretto note sull'interpretazione della tela in palazzo ducale," p. 104. For a general discussion of the dual nature of rulership see Kantorowicz, *The King's Two Bodies*.

[65] See Giesey, *The Royal Funeral Ceremony*, and Borsook, "Art and Politics at the Medici Court I."

THE PARADOXICAL PRINCE

Andrea Gritti died in 1538, he was buried with "very great pomp and the grief of the people."[66] Sorrow and deference, however, did not always govern the actions of the *popolani*, who occasionally turned a funeral into a demonstration against the government. The fine ceremonial distinctions devised by an aristocratic regime to ensure that the doge remained merely the first among equals hardly concerned the *popolani*, who tended to see the doge as their prince and their patron, who cheered him vigorously if he was generous and condemned him loudly if he was niggardly. Because the government had failed to provide enough food during times of famine, artisans denounced Antonio Grimani and Pietro Loredan at their funerals, calling them misers, and cheered the Signoria in hopes that the interregnum government would redress these grievances.[67] But the sentiments of the *popolani* were largely incidental to the funeral rites, which were dominated by political themes important to the republican patricians.

The funeral that best exemplified the increased vigilance of the early sixteenth-century patricians against ducal usurpations of the Agostino Barbarigo sort was that of his successor, Leonardo Loredan (1501–21).[68] Dressed in the simple robes of the Scuola Grande of which he was an honorary member, Loredan's body lay in state for three days on a gold-cloth-covered catafalque in the Senate Hall, where relatives, patricians, and other dignitaries came to pay their final respects.[69] The dress of Doge Loredan as a poor penitent contrasted with the fifteenth-century practice (which was resurrected later in the sixteenth cen-

[66] "Grandissima pompa, et dolor del Popolo." "Creazione dei dosi," MCV, MS P.D. 381, under entry "Pietro Lando."

[67] On Grimani, "l'è morta la carestia, viva la Signoria!" Sanuto, *I diarii*, 34:134. On Loredan, "il Dose del mejotto che fa vender el pan de mejo a pistori è morto! Viva S. Marco con la Signoria ch'è morto il Dose della carestia. Le'è morto il Loredan Campanin, che ne faceva mangiar pan col bolletin." Quoted by Mosto, *I dogi di Venezia*, p. 336.

[68] The best account of the funeral is in Sanuto, *I diarii*, 30:387–401.

[69] On some occasions the corpse was replaced with an effigy. The first such use of an effigy was in 1485, when Giovanni Mocenigo died of the plague and had to be buried immediately. Effigies were used sporadically throughout the sixteenth and early seventeenth centuries, usually when the deceased had requested it in his will. Mosto, *I dogi di Venezia*, p. lxv.

tury) of dressing the body in a ceremonial, ermine-trimmed mantle and a gold crown. The arrangement of the ducal symbols around the corpse again emphasized the symbolic separation of the man from his office. Beside the body his survivors placed the ducal crown on the faldstool that was carried in ducal processions; by Loredan's left hand they laid a decorated sword, arranged with the tip pointing toward his head and the hilt toward his feet (opposite from the direction a sword would be normally carried in its scabbard); they fastened the spurs of a knight backward on his feet; and at the foot of the catafalque they set up the ducal escutcheon with the lion of Saint Mark turned inward.[70] The inverted sword, backward spurs, and reversed escutcheon signified that death had aborted the authority of Doge Loredan.

If the ducal authority was neither invested in an effigy nor immediately transferred to a successor, then it must rest temporarily with some group designated to rule during the interregnum. The symbolic gestures prescribed for the interregnum carefully conferred the authority of the eternal dogeship on the Signoria for the duration of the interregnum, and in response the Signoria, which had symbolically become the eternal doge, ignored the obsequies of the mortal doge. During the three days that the body of Doge Loredan lay in state in the Senate Hall, each member of an elected contingent of twenty-eight nobles spent several hours a day in an official vigil over the body;[71] meanwhile, the Signoria remained aloof from the vigil and funeral procession to signify, as Sanuto noted, that although the doge was dead his authority, now invested in the

[70] Sanuto, I diarii, 30:387–401. The sword, spurs, and cushion were not entirely symbols of ducal authority, but rather they indicated a high rank that was not even exclusively noble. For the display of a sword at a procurator/knight's funeral, of a cushion and a sword at a captain general's funeral, and of all three attributes at a grand chancellor's funeral, see Sanuto, I diarii, 45:576, 21:276, 34:363, respectively.

[71] Ibid., 30:390–92. Elsewhere Sanuto states that twenty-two nobles were elected for the vigil (col. 389). For Antonio Grimani's funeral twenty-four nobles were elected. Ibid., 34:128–30. For the funeral of Alvise Mocenigo twenty were chosen. ASV, Collegio Cerimoniale 1, fol. 53v.

Signoria, lived on.[72] Nearly a century later ambassador Wotton explained the significance of the interregnum procedures in remarkably similar terms: "Now, after the publication thereof [that is, the death of the doge], the first care is the ordering of the palace, where the Signory (represented by the Councillors and some others) are during the vacancy to reside in the rooms of the dead Prince; thereby figuratively signifying (as they will have it) the immortality of the Commonwealth."[73] One of the singular attributes of the Venetian polity stemmed from the patriciate's attempt to preserve yet still control the ducal authority in this manner. The result was that Venice could benefit from the best of the princely and republican political alternatives: it could deflect factional discord with the unifying persona of a prince, and it could reduce the dangers of an interregnum by transferring that persona temporarily to the Signoria.

The funeral of Doge Loredan followed the three-day vigil. In the procession from the Ducal Palace to the Dominican church of Santi Giovanni e Paolo (see map), the political character of the ceremonies gave way to the funerary rites of the Church, since the ritual severance of the man from his office was by then complete. Now Venetians could devote themselves to honoring for the last time their most favored citizen. The patriarch, foreign ambassadors, procurators, relatives of the doge, and high ecclesiastical officials sat along the benches in the Senate Hall in order to watch the members of 119 scuole piccole, the 5 Scuole Grandi, the monastic orders, and the 9 clerical congre-

[72] "In segno si è morto il Doxe non è morta la Signoria." Sanuto, *I diarii*, 30:389. Also, "in signal si è morto il Doxe non è pero morta la Signoria." Sanuto, *I diarii*, 30:400.

[73] Smith, *Sir Henry Wotton*, 1:343. The metaphor of the immortality of political institutions was, of course, common in medieval and Renaissance political thought. In the eleventh century Conrad II reportedly said to the Pavians on his way to be crowned emperor in Rome that "The *regnum* stays, if the king dies, as the ship remains, even if the skipper is gone." Quoted in Bak, "Medieval Symbology of the State," p. 61. At the funeral of a king in late fifteenth- and sixteenth-century France, the presidents of the parlements dressed in red mantles to indicate that Justice never dies. Ralph E. Giesey, "The Presidents of Parlement at the Royal Funeral."

gations pass in review.[74] The Signoria was again absent. Members of the Scuola Grande della Misericordia, Loredan's own, walked before the casket, which was carried by sailors from the Arsenal and which displayed the ducal escutcheon in clear disregard of the principles governing the earlier vigil, when the escutcheon was turned backward.[75] From the Senate Hall the patrician magistrates, the diplomats, and the ecclesiastics joined the funeral procession past San Marco, where the pall-bearers stopped and raised the casket nine times, once for each congregation of clerics, as a sign of the doge's authority over the Venetian church.[76] Then the procession moved on to Santi Giovanni e Paolo, where the coffin was placed on an immense catafalque that was covered with black velvet and decorated with the lion of Saint Mark and with two crests of the Loredan family, each crowned by the ducal *corno*.[77] The final rites were purely religious in nature, punctuated by a Latin oration recited by the official historian, Andrea Navagero.[78]

Leonardo Loredan was buried in a plain, unmarked grave that contrasted with the nearby monumental tombs of Doges Michele Steno (died 1413), Tommaso Mocenigo (died 1423), Pasquale Malipiero (died 1462), Nicolò Marcello (died 1474), Pietro Mocenigo (died 1476), and Giovanni Mocenigo (died 1485). It was difficult to say whether this was meant as an example of Loredan's known preference for a simple, personal piety or as a reaction to the pretentions of the late fifteenth-century doges. On Loredan's tomb there was no attempt to preserve some

[74] ASV, Collegio Cerimoniale 1, fols. 1v–2r, and Sanuto, *I diarii*, 30:399–401.

[75] Most doges were honorary members of one of the five major confraternities. See Sanuto, *I diarii*, 34:134, and BMV, MS Latin XIV, 230 (4736), fol. 215r. If a doge were not a member of a confraternity, the task of accompanying his casket fell to the members of the Scuola Grande di San Marco. BMV, MS Italiano VII, 708 (7899), pt. 1, fol. 33.

[76] Fasoli, "Liturgia e cerimoniale ducale," p. 287.

[77] Sanuto, *I diarii*, 30:400. Later in the century an elaborate baldachin, covered with lighted candles, was usually erected above the casket. ASV, Collegio Cerimoniale 1, fol. 54v. The baldachin was probably an imitation of the apotheosis funeral of Charles V, but without the same significance. Francis Yates, "Charles quint et l'idée d'empire."

[78] Sanuto, *I diarii*, 30:400.

visual link between the dead individual and his earthly status as doge; on several of the tombs of his fifteenth-century predecessors, a marble effigy of the doge dressed in his full ducal garb lies atop the sepulcher, and on the monument designed by Pietro Lombardo for Doge Pietro Mocenigo the doge stands as a warrior-hero beneath a triumphal arch. Whatever the reason, the simple grave lacked any visual image of Loredan's status in life as a doge.

Within a day or two of the doge's death, the Great Council was called to elect the inquisitors of the dead doge and the correctors of the *promissione ducale* and to draw lots to determine the ducal electors. As in the case of Agostino Barbarigo, the inquisitors found fault in the conduct of Leonardo Loredan and charged his heirs 1,500 ducats, but this time because he had *not* upheld the dignity of his office with the proper majesty and magnificence.[79] Although the Senate appropriated 3,500 ducats per year to be spent for ducal pomp, the doge was expected to add a considerable personal outlay in order to uphold an exalted ducal bearing.[80] Where Doge Barbarigo had been too liberal, Loredan had been too sparing; doges in general had to follow a narrow path, which was by no means clearly defined in the early sixteenth century, between indecorous frugality and inappropriate splendor; and they were constantly subject to contrary political pressures that tempted or forced them from the ideal course.

The investigations and fines following these two dogeships expose an attempt by the controlling families of the patriciate to redefine the boundaries of ducal power without destroying the impressive features of the figurehead. After consulting specialized commercial, administrative, and legal officials about the *promissione ducale* for Loredan's successor, the five correctors rewrote even more precisely the legal prescription of ducal powers: they enacted provisions directing the doge to preserve,

[79] Lewkenor's additions in the English version of Contarini, *De magistratibus et republica Venetorum*, p. 157. The total fine against his estate for all reasons was 2,700 ducats. Mosto, *I dogi di Venezia*, p. 273. For other accusations against Loredan see Brunetti, "Due dogi sotto inchiesta," pp. 307–28.

[80] Contarini, *De magistratibus et republica Venetorum*, p. 45; English version, pp. 44–45.

honor, and fairly execute the laws; aid other magistrates; meet frequently with the ducal counselors; supervise the collection of taxes; be vigilant in conserving the resources of the lagoon; stimulate operations at the Arsenal; encourage speedy trials; oversee hospitals; fulfill his religious duties; and refuse princely obeisances.[81] By redefining ducal authority, the correctors' examinations of the dogeships of Agostino Barbarigo and Leonardo Loredan helped to preserve and strengthen Venice as a republic at a time when, elsewhere in Italy, princes were ignoring or subverting representative and legislative institutions.

These early sixteenth-century reforms were paradigmatic, but they did not, of course, end all clashes between ducal and republican principles. There were some rather nervous adjustments of ducal imagery in the arts throughout the sixteenth century, and two ducal elections near the turn of the century were particularly troublesome. Wotton's analysis of the campaigning before Leonardo Donà's election in 1606 shows that anxieties about an overbearingly able and ambitious doge were still common in the seventeenth century.

It was notable to hear the arguments that were searched for the exclusion of Donato. His merits were known, his wisdom confessed, and rather indeed amplified than denied by his adversaries; but great understandings were rather to be wished in Princes that are absolute. They had been ruled and swayed by his advice . . . though in a private condition: what would he do when he should be Prince? The Commonwealth in this fashion might come by little and little to the form of a monarchy: for what difference was there in the effect between being subject to one man's counsels and to one man's authority?"[82]

To Wotton, at least, this concern over Donà was prophetic; for some time later, during the papal interdict against Venice, the Englishman described Donà ". . . to be not only the Duke, but the Dictator of the State. . . ."[83] Advocates of a republican Ven-

---

[81] ASV, Collegio Cerimoniale 1, fol. 23r, and Eugenio Musatti, *Storia della promissione ducale*, pp. 217–18.

[82] Smith, *Sir Henry Wotton*, 1:344.

[83] Ibid., p. 354.

ice needed more than the interregnum rites to chasten the ambitions of a lordly doge.

Since as early as the ninth century, Venetians had elected their doges in some fashion. A popular assembly (*arengo*) met on the Lido at San Nicolò to choose the new *dux* until 1172, when this unwieldy and often violent gathering was replaced by a committee of first eleven and then, six years later, forty electors who were probably representatives of the most powerful families. In the mid-thirteenth century the electors added an extra member to their body to prevent ties, thus completing the electoral system that lasted (with a number of minor procedural modifications) until the end of the republic.[84] The Great Council selected the forty-one electors through a complex system that alternated the drawing of lots with balloting in a naive attempt to keep any one faction from dominating the electoral committee. While the voting urns were being set up in the Great Council Hall, the *ballotino*, or voting teller, was "discovered" by a carefully prescribed procedure designed to ensure the selection of someone who was innocent both of political ambition and corruption. According to the law, the youngest of the heads of the Quarantia al Criminale was to walk through the basilica and out the west door; once outside he picked the first boy under fifteen he saw to be the *ballotino*. The *ballotino*'s duties, as we have seen, included drawing lots and ballots from the voting urns and participating in ducal processions as a symbol of the impartial election system.[85] The Great Council spent several days completing the nine steps necessary to select the forty-one electors of the doge.[86] After the electors were

[84] Mosto, *I dogi di Venezia*, pp. xii–xv; Pertusi, "Quedam regalia insignia," pp. 64–80.

[85] Mosto, *I dogi di Venezia*, p. xvi; ASV, Collegio Cerimoniale 1, fols 2v, 5v. Cf. BMV MS Italiano VII, 142 (7147), fols. 338–39.

[86] The selection began with a lottery to choose thirty members of the Great Council, none of whom could be related. The thirty were then reduced by lot to nine; the nine nominated by ballot another group of forty; the forty were reduced again by lot to twelve; the twelve chose by ballot twenty-five; the twenty-five were pared down by lot to nine; the nine elected by ballot forty-five; the forty-five were eliminated by lot to eleven; and, finally, the eleven chose by ballot the forty-one electors of the doge. Mosto, *I dogi di Venezia*, pp. xvi–xxii.

finally chosen, they were cloistered in the Ducal Palace for the duration of their deliberations and forbidden to leave or to communicate with anyone on the outside.

Venetian political panegyrists lauded the mysterious incorruptibility of this system, but their view differed markedly from the realities of electoral politics. Gianmaria Masenetti portrayed faith and justice as directly guiding the forty-one in their deliberations and as preventing the subversion of government by factions.[87] In contrast Wotton, usually the stalwart admirer of things Venetian, described the ducal election as ". . . one of the most intricate and curious forms in the world, consisting of ten several precedent ballotations. Whereupon occurreth a pretty question, what need there was of such a deal of solicitude in choosing a Prince of such limited authority?"[88] Notwithstanding Wotton's unanswered question, the electoral system became, as we have seen, an important component in the myth of Venice. Yet, in spite of the complex selection process and elaborate precautions, the conclaves were ridden with factional discord and electoral intrigues; the poorer nobles were often ready to accept gifts from richer, politically ambitious patricians, as happened in one famous seventeenth-century case in which more than two hundred patricians were involved in a bribery scandal.[89] Furthermore, the forty-one electors, who sometimes met for more than a month, were known to take advantage of their right to provisions at public expense by calling for exotic and costly foods. In the ducal elections, practice contrasted dramatically with ideology, and there were frequent attempts to reduce the burdensome costs of the ducal interim and to modify the electoral system itself.[90] A

[87] Giammaria Masenetti, *Li trionfi et feste solenni che si fanno in la creatione del principe di Vineggia, in ottava rima,* in BMV, Misc. 2405/13.

[88] Smith, *Sir Henry Wotton,* 2:136. Wotton continues to conjecture that the system ". . . was (as the tradition runneth) a monk's invention of the Benedictine order. And in truth the whole mysterious frame therein doth much savour of the cloister." (pp. 136–37)

[89] Mosto, *I dogi di Venezia,* pp. xxv–xxvi.

[90] Ibid. "Disposizione e decreti per limitare le spese del Doge (1521–1795)," ASV, Rason Vecchie, busta 219, especially the papers dated 1521, 1624, 1636, and 1656; also see busta 223, paper dated 1623.

supposedly disinterested reform proposed by Alessandro Zorzi
in 1585 professed the high aim of putting an end to the scandal,
shame, and expenditure occasioned by the procedure then current; he would have had the doge selected entirely by lot and
would have punished electoral tampering by ten years' banishment.[91] Others tried to modify the system to their own advantage. A proposal before the conclave that elected Antonio Grimani in 1521 attempted to bar from candidacy anyone whose
son or brother was a priest, a suggestion that would have eliminated three of the leading contenders for the ducal throne,
who were related to cardinals.[92] These schemes involved procedural but not substantive reforms. The ducal election was one
of the Venetian political processes most subject to self-interest
and factional pressure, and although electoral ceremonies played
an important and probably vital role in the symbolic display of
Venetian political ideology, these ceremonies did not exemplify
the virtues of Venetian government as much as the Venetians'
ability to turn politics to a propagandistic purpose. The purpose
in this case was to portray Venice as a commune without "politics," a city in which human decisions bodied forth the eternal
principles of Justice, not the meaner products of dispute, compromise, or defeat.

WHEN THE ELECTORS reached a final decision, the ringing bells of
San Marco announced the election of a new doge, an event the
popolani viewed as cause for celebration; shops closed, bonfires
were laid, and revelers fell into drunken parades reminiscent of
carnival frolics.[93] The official ceremonies of the coronation oc-

---

[91] MCV, Cod. P.D. 296c, III, fol. 831r–v.

[92] Sanuto, I diarii, 30:395; also see cols. 402–6.

[93] During the celebrations held in 1595 after the election of Marin Grimani
was announced, a crowd filled Piazza San Marco and ripped up the booths
built for the Sensa fair to fuel an enormous bonfire. MCV, Cod. Cicogna
2479, under the heading "Marino Grimani." Doge Grimani so amply rewarded the popolani for their support with gifts of wine, bread, and money
that for months after his coronation his mere appearance would bring cries
of Viva! from the crowds. BMV, MS Italiano VII, 142 (7147), pp. 339–40.
For a copy of a poem celebrating the election see Antonio Pilot, "L'elezione
del Doge Marino Grimani." For the expenses Grimani incurred from his
election gifts see G. Giomo, "Le spese del nobil uomo Marino Grimani nella

three stages, performed in succession on the same
t, the doge was presented to the community and in-
vith the banner of Saint Mark in the basilica; second,
he ... carried around the Piazza while he and his relatives
tossed specially minted coins to the crowds; finally, he was
crowned at the top of the Scala dei Giganti in the courtyard of
the Ducal Palace.[94]

The sixteenth-century coronation ceremonies were primarily
secular, emphasizing the restrictive bonds of the law rather
than the mystical consecration of anointment; and they were
aristocratic, demonstrating the elective power of the Great
Council rather than the approbation of the entire community.
Coronations had changed considerably from those of the eleventh century, when the doge, acclaimed by the popular assembly, entered San Marco barefoot, laid himself prostrate on the
pavement, and humbly thanked God for his election — or even
from those of the thirteenth century, when crowds of *popolani*
tore the new doge's cloak from his back.[95] By temporarily degrading the new doge, his future subjects reversed the social
roles to which they would soon be bound. Rites of status reversal such as these frequently appear in ceremonies designed to
elevate a person to a higher social status or office, and they tend

---

sua elezione a doge di Venezia." An unpopular choice could foster demonstrations against the electors, as was the case at the coronation of Andrea Gritti
in 1523. Sanuto, *I diarii*, 34:158– 59. For demonstrations against Pasquale
Cicogna in 1583 see Mosto, *I dogi di Venezia*, p. 379.

[94] On the ducal coronations in general see Mosto, *I dogi di Venezia*, pp.
xxii– xxxi. For the historical development of the ceremonies see Peyer, *Stadt
und Stadtpatron*, pp. 63– 67. Models followed in the sixteenth century are in
BMV, MS Latin III, 172 (2276), fol. 70r– v, and ASV, Collegio Cerimoniale 1,
fol. 4r– v. Of the many extant descriptions of sixteenth-century coronations,
the most useful are those of Antonio Grimani in Sanuto, *I diarii*, 30:479– 90,
31:7– 11, and of Andrea Gritti in 34:155– 85; of Francesco Donà in MCV,
Cod. P.D. 381, under heading for doge number LXXXII; and of Sebastiano Venier
in ASV, Collegio Cerimoniale 1, fols. 56v– 57r.

[95] Peyer, *Stadt und Stadtpatron*, pp. 64– 65. Cf. Schramm, *Herrschaf-
tszeichen und Staatssymbolik*, p. 560, and Nelson, "Symbols in Context," pp.
101– 4. For additional examples of early coronations see Canal, *Les estoires de
Venise*, pp. 128– 30, 270– 309, 362– 64, and Andrea Marini, *De pompa ducatus
Venetorum*. On the Renaissance myth about this early acclamation system see
Contarini, *De magistratibus et republica Venetorum*, p. 51.

to brace authoritarian social roles by providing an emotional
outlet for those in a subordinate station.[96] Before the Renaissance redefinition of the ducal powers, the doges were in truth
multiplying their own authority when they affected a penitential posture and accepted degradation at the hands of the populace. From the late twelfth century, however, as members of
the richest patrician families gradually accumulated power they
eliminated the vestiges of popular election, just as they restricted the powers of the doge. Rites of status reversal and the
penitential conduct of the new doge eventually disappeared; by
the fifteenth century the final reminder of popular ratification
was erased with the elimination of the phrase, "This is your
doge if he pleases you," which had previously qualified the
presentation of the doge to the populace.[97] The election was by
then a thoroughly patrician affair as much in appearance as in
fact.

Like the other interregnum rites, all sixteenth-century coronations followed the model created by the dogeship of Leonardo Loredan, during which the legal and ceremonial position
of the doge was clarified.[98] The ceremonies began when the
eldest of the forty-one electors presented the new doge to the
populace from the porphyry pulpit on the right side of the nave
of San Marco with these words:

> The Most Serene Prince Our Lord Agostino Barbarigo
> being dead and our Signoria properly wishing to provide a
> successor, has, together with the Senate, elected Our
> Prince, the Most Serene and Excellent Lord Leonardo Lo-
> redan, here present. The virtues and worthy condition of
> whom are such, that through divine grace he will fervently
> strive for the good and conservation of the commonweal
> and of every public, as well as private, interest [and] whose

[96] Turner, *The Ritual Process*, pp. 170–71.

[97] Mosto, *I dogi di Venezia*, p. xxvi. At the election in 1400 there was some
minor pillaging of the private palace of the doge-elect, but this was perhaps
the last example of a popular spoliation of the new doge's property or person.
Mosto, *I dogi di Venezia*, p. xxxvii.

[98] For the coronation model see ASV, Collegio Cerimoniale 1, fol. 4. For the
legislation establishing the coronation ceremony in 1485 see fol. 60r.

assumption signifies joy and consolation to all, so that you
acknowledge him your Prince and leader.[99]

This was a precise statement of the principle of election. Selected through the authority of the administrative and legislative bodies of the republic, the Signoria and the Senate, the
new doge was picked out for his personal virtues (and political
connections) rather than for any right of succession, and his
election was a fait accompli, since the patrician magistrates no
longer bothered to solicit from the populace even informal approval for their decision.

After the electors presented the new doge to the people, he
descended from the pulpit, walked to the high altar containing
the relics of Saint Mark, knelt, and kissed the altar; then he
stood to face the celebrant and with his hand on a missal swore
"To conserve the patrimony and ecclesiastical honor of Saint
Mark in good faith and without fraud."[100] With these words
the newly elected doge obliged himself to protect the endowments and trusts whose income supported the basilica. There
was nothing particularly mystical or sacramental about this; it
was simply a legal oath taken as was usual in the Middle Ages,
by placing one's hand on a sacred object in front of witnesses in
a church.

The conferral of a ducal banner, however, introduced into the
rituals the idea that there was an eternal, mystical source for
the doge's authority. The celebrant took one of the eight cere-

[99] "Essendo defunto el Ser[enissi]mo Principe nostro D[omi]no Augustin
Barbarigo et volendo opportunamente proveder la Sig[nori]a nostra de successor, ha eletto con el Senato suo in Principe n[ost]ro el Ser[enissi]mo et Ecc[el-
lentissi]mo D[omi]no Leonardo Loredano qui presente, le virtu del qual, et
degne condittion, mediante la Divina gratia sono tale, che grandemente se
die spezar el ben, et conservation del stado, et ogni com[m]odità si publica, la
qual assontion a letitia, et consolation de tutti ve è significata, accio quello
voi recognosciate per principe, et Capo vostro." ASV, Collegio Cerimoniale
1, fol. 4r. Other copies of this formula, but with slight variations, are
recorded for the presentation of Antonio Grimani in Sanuto, *I diarii*, 30:481,
and of Sebastiano Venier in ASV, Collegio Cerimoniale 1, fol. 57r. Cf. Sinding-Larsen, *Christ in the Council Hall*, p. 203.

[100] "Statum et honorem ecclesiam Sancti Marci bona fide, et sine fraude
conservare." ASV, Collegio Cerimoniale 1, fol. 4r. Cf. Peyer, *Stadt und Stadtpatron*, p. 67, and Bascapè, "Sigilli della repubblica," pp. 95–96.

monial banners of Saint Mark from the admiral of the Arsenal
and gave it to the doge, saying, "We consign on your serenity
the banner of Saint Mark as a sign of true and perpetual dogeship," to which the doge answered, "I accept."[101] The new doge
completed the rite by personally returning the banner to the
admiral of the Arsenal. Sansovino wrote that the standards
signified an absolute, eternal authority.[102] With the consignment of the banner the new doge accepted custody, for the
duration of his life, of an undying, perfected authority, which
was the source of legitimacy for the entire government. The
rites in San Marco promulgated, as did the breaking of the
silver emblems after a doge's death, the notion that there was a
distinction to be drawn between the eternal authority of the
doge — here symbolized by the banner — and the mortal incumbent. In fact, as the similar investiture of the banner on a
captain general illustrates, the exercise of this authority was
not the exclusive prerogative of the doge.[103]

The second stage of the coronation-day ceremonies consisted
of the doge's procession around Piazza San Marco in front of a
vast crown of *popolani*. The doge, accompanied by two of his
closest relatives and the admiral of the Arsenal (who still held
the banner of Saint Mark), stood on a wooden platform that
Arsenal sailors carried on their shoulders around the Piazza. As
other sailors broke a path through the crowd, the four men on
the platform tossed ducat and half-ducat coins to the crowds,
about which Gasparo Contarini reported, "The people be not
negligent in gathering it [the coins] uppe."[104] Each doge varied

[101] "Consignamus Serenitati vestrae vexillum D. Marci in signum veri et
perpetui ducatus." Peyer, *Stadt und Stadtpatron*, p. 67. There is no mention of
what was said at the consignment-of-the-banners ceremony in ASV, Collegio
Cerimoniale 1, fol. 4r. Cf. Pertusi, "Quedam regalia insignia," p. 90.

[102] On the early use of the banners in Venice, see Pertusi, "Quedam regalia
insignia," pp. 88–91.

[103] There is no indication that the doge was anointed at his coronation. On
the significance of anointing at regal or imperial coronations, see Nelson,
"Symbols in Context," pp. 108–110, and D. M. Nicol, *"Kaiseralbung."*

[104] Contarini, *De magistratibus et republica Venetorum*, p. 59; English version, p. 61. At Alvise Mocenigo's election there were prohibitions against
carrying arms, because the numerous soldiers gathered for the Turkish wars
might have been tempted to riot. MCV, Cod. Cicogna 2479, under heading

the amount of money he gave away, depending on his personal resources and on the tolerance of his patrician contemporaries for ducal display: the *promissione* of Nicolò Marcello (elected 1473) limited him to 100 ducats, and that of Leonardo Donà (elected 1606) prohibited him from giving more than 200.[105] Among the more lavish donors were Andrea Gritti (elected 1523), who tried to offset the unpopularity of his election by spending 400 ducats, and Marin Grimani (elected 1595), who rewarded the dedicated support the *popolani* had given him with ample gifts of money, wine, and bread.[106] Ducal largess was a dangerous custom for the aristocratic republic because it bought personal adulation for the doge, possibly at the expense of loyalty to the republican regime; in the hands of a demagogue like Marin Grimani, who could afford lavish expenditures, the largess rite became another threat to the egalitarian balance of the aristocratic government.

The third stage of the ceremonies consisted of the coronation itself, enacted in the open courtyard of the Ducal Palace. First held in 1485 for Doge Marco Barbarigo, Agostino's predecessor and brother, the public coronation was an innovation that countered the restrictive elements of the traditional coronation by again emulating the splendor of the princes on the Italian mainland.[107] Before the Barbarigo doges, the coronation was a simple procedural rite held in the Senate Hall away from the dangerous crowds of *popolani*, who tended to confuse external pomp with personal power. After the Barbarigos the patricians struggled, fitfully it seems, against this new princely rite; they diminished the majesty of the doge by flanking the coronation

---

"Alvise Mocenigo." At the unpopular election of Nicolò Donà there was slight applause, and while he was carried around the Piazza the *popolani* chanted his competitors' names and refused to pick up the money he gave out. Smith, *Sir Henry Wotton*, 2:138.

[105] Mosto, *I dogi di Venezia*, p. xxviii.

[106] On Gritti, see Sanuto, *I diarii*, 34:458. On Grimani, see Giomo, "Le spese del nobil uomo Marco Grimani." Local tradition attributed the origin of ducal largess to the twelfth-century election of Sebastiano Ziani, the first doge chosen by electors rather than by the popular assembly. Contarini, *De magistratibus et republica Venetorum*, English version, p. 212, and Sanuto, *Le vite dei dogi*, p. 302.

[107] Muraro, "La scala senza giganti."

THE PARADOXICAL PRINCE

13. Giacomo Franco, *Arsenal Sailors Carry the Doge-Elect, His Relatives, and the Admiral, Who Throw out Coins to the Crowd before the Coronation.*

stairs with gigantic statues and by emphasizing the restrictive rites over the investive ones. The new ceremony, however, was never abandoned altogether, and in the hands of some six-teenth-century doges it became a stage for aggrandizement.

The coronation took place immediately after the procession around the Piazza; the new doge climbed the stairs past his forty-one electors to greet his counselors, the grand chancellor, and the heads of the Quarantia al Criminale. The grand chancellor handed the *promissione* document to the eldest counselor, who administered to the new doge an oath of obedience to its provisions. The youngest counselor placed on the doge's head the white skull-cap (*camauro*), over which the eldest counselor put the jeweled crown, saying, "Accept the ducal crown of Venice."[108] From the balcony over the courtyard, the doge repeated the same promise to promote peace, prosperity, and justice that he had made in the basilica. Retiring to the Senate Hall, where he would proclaim this promise for the third time, the doge was formally introduced to the young *ballotino*, who would preside over Great Council elections for the entire reign of the new doge.[109] Although the crown and particularly the *camauro* invested the doge with an aura of spiritual sanctity, reminding Venetians of the sacred origins of their polity and their legendary independence from foreign influence, legal ceremonies dominated the coronation: the oath to obey the *promissione*, the thrice-repeated promise, and the reception of the *ballotino*.

THE INTERREGNUM PROCEDURES and rites that developed after the death of Doge Agostino Barbarigo established the definitive model of ducal powers and authority by reasserting aristocratic control over the office, and, although there were recurring counterpressures against the republicanism of the aristocracy, the paradigm was not effectively altered during the following century. These readjustments in the position of the doge pre-

[108] "Accipe coronam Ducatus Venetiarum." ASV, Collegio Cerimoniale 1, fol. 4v.

[109] For contemporary interpretations of the doge's promise, see Giannotti, *Libro de la republica de Vinitiani*, fol. 71r–v, and *Traité du gouvernement*, p. 257. Cf. Mosto, *I dogi di Venezia*, p. xxx, and Schramm, *Herrschaftszeichen und Staatssymbolik*, pp. 862–63.

ceded by nearly a decade the practical and theoretical reassess-
ments of the institutions of the republic that followed the War
of the League of Cambrai; Gasparo Contarini, the most prominent humanist to participate in that reassessment, echoed the
diminished ceremonial position of the doges in his description
of their impotent pomposity in a government dominated by the
Senate, the Collegio, and the Council of Ten. The reduction of
the doge's formal authority allowed a few wealthy families
(from whom the doges were selected) to concentrate political
power and patronage in their hands after the war and enabled
the Council of Ten to subvert more effectively the traditional
principles of egalitarian justice.[110] The clarification of the doge's
position as *primus inter pares* corresponded to the image of
republicanism that dominated Venetian political thought during
the sixteenth century and perhaps aided the oligarchs by eliminating some of the autonomy of the ducal office, but it did not
leave the doges as powerless figureheads, since the doges were
themselves, for the most part, leaders of the oligarchy, who had
attained the ducal honor as a reward for their success and longevity as politicians.

THE DOGARESSA

As consort of the doge, the dogaressa played several well-estab-
lished social roles. Symbolically, she was to be the paragon of
womankind, the living archetype of the feminine virtues as
seen through the quasi-chivalric code adopted by the Venetian
aristocracy. Historically, she was the patroness both of the social institutions of particular interest to women, such as convents and orphanages, and of the guilds, which for centuries
had looked to her as an advocate and protector. Politically, her
position was equivocal, for, although she was not herself an
elected office-holder, she had certain ceremonial prerogatives
and a queenly dignity that distinguished her own and her husband's families. As was the case with the doge, a funeral and
coronation put the dogaressa at frontstage, thus revealing what
can be discovered about her part in Venetian life, her political

[110] Gilbert, "Venice in the Crisis," p. 290; Cozzi, "Authority and the Law,"
pp. 293–345; and Muir, "Images of Power," pp. 30–33.

functions, and the place of patrician women in the republic.

At the dogaressa's coronation the senators promised that when she died her body would lie in state for three days in the Senate Hall, a promise similar to that given to the doges.[111] The obsequies of the doges provided the pattern for her funeral, which included the display of ducal robes and a smaller version of the doge's crown, a procession of the assembled ambassadors and official hierarchy from the Ducal Palace, and final rites in Santi Giovanni e Paolo. The ceremonies there, however, did not include the signs of aborted authority—the inverted sword and broken seals—that characterized the ducal rites and gave to them such an explicit political content; instead the funeral of a dogaressa emphasized her peculiarly feminine position, which was eulogized in the funeral procession by contingents of nuns, children, and ladies in mourning. The rites for the dogaressa were essentially personal and religious; she had made her own fame through her own qualities and deeds, and there were no critical legal questions requiring a resolution at her death, as there were at her husband's. But her funeral was not entirely without a potential political impact. The funerals celebrated for members of the doge's family were often executed in a very unrepublican, dynastic style, and dogaressas and their children frequently were only too anxious to adopt permanently the privileges extended for only the lifetime of the doge.[112] Like nearly all ceremonies involving the ducal family, the dogaressa's funeral revealed the constant tension between family pride and the formal restrictions on the dogeship, between conspicuous waste and honorable pomp, and between regal adulation and republican decorum.

[111] The funeral of Dogaressa Taddia Michiel Mocenigo in 1479 served as the ceremonial model for those held during the sixteenth century. See ASV, Collegio Cerimoniale 1, fols. 10v–11r, and MCV, Cod. Cicogna 2853, vol. 2, fols. 21v–22v. When Sanuto described the 1519 funeral of a son of the doge, he cited Dogaressa Mocenigo's funeral as a precedent and noted that, for the dogaressa, "fatoli tutti li honorei come si fa a Doxe." *I diarii*, 28:7. For the first sixteenth-century funeral of a dogaressa, that of Zilia Dandolo Priuli in 1566, see MCV, Cod. Cicogna 2853, vol. 2, fols. 134r–135r, and ASV, Collegio Cerimoniale 1, fol. 34r–v. The latter description is published in Lorenzi, ed., *Monumenti*, 1:337–39. For the funeral of Dogaressa Lauredana Marcello Mocenigo in 1577, see ASV, Collegio Cerimoniale 1, fols. 41v–42v.

[112] Note the comments in Sanuto, *I diarii*, 28:7.

The coronation of the dogaressa was a ceremonial extension of the doge's coronation.[113] Although there were only two such coronations in the sixteenth century, they were the occasion for some of the most elaborate pageantry of the Venetian Renaissance. A dogaressa's coronation encompassed two themes, among others, which, if not conflicting, were hardly complementary: the restrictions of the family of the doge as expressed in the *promissione ducale* were the legal sine qua non of the ceremonies, whereas the conspicuous display of the personal riches and, accomplishments of the doge, dogaressa, and their clans dominated the accompanying pageantry.

The coronation of the dogaressa probably began as a princely rite performed by the early *duces,* but by the fifteenth century it had been transformed into a rite of limitation for the ducal family. Molmenti argued that the coronation arose after the reforms of Doge Pietro Gradenigo at the end of the thirteenth century;[114] the description of a similar rite in Martin da Canal's chronicle of 1275, however, suggests that there was a long-standing tradition of honoring the wife of the doge in some formal manner soon after his coronation.[115] The elements of the ceremony, as practiced in the Cinquecento, were definitely established no later than 1329, when the ducal counselors accompanied the wife of Doge Francesco Dandolo to services in San Marco and enthroned her in the Ducal Palace. Afterward she was the hostess at a banquet for members of the guilds.[116] . The dogaressa's ceremonial entry into the Ducal Palace after her husband's coronation was common during the fifteenth century, when there were five distaff coronations; in fact a chronicler of the sixteenth century considered the failure of Doge Nicolò Marcello to honor his mate in this fashion as highly unusual.[117]

[113] Although the formal entrance of the dogaressa into the Ducal Palace was usually referred to as a "coronation" in the Venetian accounts, no act of crowning actually took place.

[114] Pompeo G. Molmenti, *La dogaressa di Venezia,* p. 234.

[115] Canal, *Les estoires de Venise,* pp. 282–304. Cf. Schramm, *Herrschaftszeichen und Staatssymbolik,* p. 867.

[116] Molmenti, *La dogaressa di Venezia,* p. 235.

[117] The fifteenth-century coronations are listed in ibid., pp. 244–77, and Sansovino, *Venetia,* 1604, fols. 274v–75r. The palace entrance of Dea Morosini, the wife of Doge Nicolò Tron, provided the official ceremonial model in

During the first half of the sixteenth century, there were no
dogaressa coronations because the doges were either unmarried
or had become widowers before they were elected doge. So
when Doge Lorenzo Priuli revived the coronation in 1557 for
his wife, Zilia Dandolo, some viewed his action as a welcome
return to an ancient dignity, and others saw it as a burdensome
innovation. The coronation followed the precedents established
in the fifteenth century but went far beyond them in its exal-
tation of the Dandolo and Priuli families: the dogaressa was
dressed in gold, hundreds of noble and *cittadini* women were
entertained, and the guilds were encouraged to spend lavish
sums on their pageant booths built in the Ducal Palace in the
dogaressa's honor.[118] Despite the professed desires of the succeeding ducal families, fortune intervened either through war,

---

ASV, Collegio Cerimoniale 1, fols. 6v–7r. The comment about Nicolò Marcello is found in MCV, Cod. Cicogna 2853, vol. 2, fol. 12r. A considerable
amount of information about the fifteenth-century ingresses can be found in
the anonymous manuscript of the Raccolta Stefani (published as *Il trionfo
della dogaressa di Venezia nel secolo XV* in BMV, Misc. 3193/4.) See also MCV,
MS P.D. 303c/xvi, and BMV, MS Italiano VII, 1233 (9600), fols. 23r–24r,
which is published by Agostino Sagredo, *Sulle consorterie delle arti edificative
in Venezia*, pp. 279–81. Tamassia Mazzarotto is incorrect when she states
that there were only four coronations of dogaresse in the entire history of
the republic. *Le feste veneziane*, p. 223.

[118] On the thirteenth-century guild tributes to the dogaressa, see Canal, *Les
estoires de Venise*, p. 606. On the wives of sixteenth-century doges before
Lorenzo Priuli, see Mosto, *I dogi di Venezia*, pp. 283–321. Sansovino notes
that at first there was some difficulty in discovering exactly what the coronation of a dogaressa entailed, because there had not been one in living memory.
Venetia, 1604, fol. 275v. Not surprisingly, resistance to the Zilia Dandolo
Priuli coronation came from the guildsmen whom the doge had asked to pre-
pare decorations for the Ducal Palace "con ogni miglior modo possibile." Many
excused themselves with complaints that the expense was too burdensome,
and in the end only twenty guilds voluntarily offered to build displays. MCV,
Cod. Cicogna 2853, vol. 2, fols. 104v–108r. For other descriptions see ASV,
Collegio Cerimoniale 1, fols. 28r–30r; BMV, MS Latin III, 172 (2276), fol.
87v; BMV, MS Italiano VII, 519 (8438), fol. 319v; Gregorio Marcello, *Ordine
et progreesso* [sic] *del trionfo fatto l'anno MDLVII alli 19 di settembre, per
l'incoronatione della serenis. Dogaressa Priola*, in BMV, Misc. 200/4; *Il
trionfo et le feste fatte in Venetia nella publica entrata della serenissima dogaressa, moglie dell'illustrissimo signor Lorenzo di Priuli, prencipe di Venetia*, in
MCV, Op. P.D. 2159. Andrea Calmo briefly describes the coronation in his
Lettere, fols. 37r–38r, in BMV, 52.D.248. See also Molmenti, *La dogaressa di
Venezia*, pp. 281–94.

plague, or premature death to prevent any further dogaressa coronations until the end of the century, when the Grimani and Morosini families created the most memorable coronation afforded any dogaressa.[119]

Marin Grimani was elected doge in April 1595 amid the tumultuous rejoicing of the Venetian poor, who had received Grimani bread during a recent famine and who had surrounded the Ducal Palace during the conclave and demanded his election. As a result, some patricians received him with suspicion. Apparently in an attempt to break the momentum produced by Grimani's election, his *promissione* required that he wait at least one year for the coronation of his wife, Morosina Morosini, who was also much beloved by the Venetian people for her philanthropy.[120] When, two years after her husband's election, Dogaressa Grimani finally had her coronation, enthusiasm for the Grimani and Morosini had not abated, and the coronation became a monumental exercise in praise of the ducal families.

Doge Grimani's announcement of his plans for a formal coronation on May 4, 1597, forced many patricians and *popolani* to contribute a substantial amount of time and money to the pageant. The Collegio appointed a master of ceremonies to oversee the preparations and a committee of forty young nobles to provide at their own expense entertainments for the nobility.[121] The guilds bore the burden of decorating the Ducal Palace

---

[119] Molmenti, *La dogaresa di Venezia*, pp. 298–303, and Mosto, *I dogi di Venezia*, pp. 342–59.

[120] Mosto, *I dogi di Venezia*, pp. 386–88; Giovanni Rota, *Lettera nella quale si descrive l'ingresso nel palazzo ducale della serenissima Morosina Morosini Grimani prencipessa di Vinetia . . .* , in the BMV, Misc. 200/8, 9. Republished in the nineteenth century (without exact date) by one "N. N." for the Fosca Papafava-Baglioni nozze. I have used this edition because of the convenience of pagination. Dario Tutio, *Ordine et modo tenuto nell'incoronatione della serenissima Moresina Grimani dogaressa di Venetia. L'anno MDXCVII adi 4 di maggio. Con le feste e giochi fatti*, in BMV, Misc. 200/7; Stringa's additions to Sansovino, *Venetia*, 1604, fol. 280r; BMV, MS Italiano VII, 1818 (9436), fol. 9r–v; Smith, *Sir Henry Wotton*, 1:342–43; F. M. Piave, "Feste fatte in Venezia pella incoronazione della serenissima Dogaressa Morosina Morosini Grimani," p. 11; Doglioni, *Le cose notabili*, pp. 107–33; and Molmenti, *La dogaressa di Venezia*, pp. 305–26.

[121] The master of ceremonies was Salustio Gnicchi, a cavalier of the doge. Rota, *L'ingresso della Morosina Grimani*, p. 8. The young nobles were between twenty-five and thirty-five. The group was similar in organization and respon-

and building pageant booths, but, despite the popularity of the Grimani and Morosini, many of the guilds were less than enthusiastic about their obligation.[122]

Morosina Grimani's coronation began when the ducal counselors, sixty senators, and other magistrates arrived at the doge's private palace to meet the dogaressa. (The law barred the doge from attending.) A cavalier of the doge presented her a copy of the *promissione ducale*, full of all sorts of restrictions on the activities of the doge's relatives;[123] she promised to read it and then for their trouble gave each of the six counselors and the grand chancellor a bag of gold medallions bearing her name and profile. From the palace a vast water-procession of more than two hundred boats carrying the wives of the ambassadors, grand chancellor, and highest magistrates, the doge's children and relatives, the ducal musicians, the *cittadini* and noble magistrates, and four hundred women guests were rowed to the Piazzetta. They debarked, passed through a triumphal arch built for the occasion, and walked to San Marco to hear an oration and Te Deum.[124] Before the dogaressa could enter the Ducal Palace, she had to swear at the high altar to obey the *promissione*. In contrast to the spirit of her oath, however, the

---

sibility to the private Compagnie delle Calze, which disappeared after 1564. The members called themselves a *compagnia* and decided to dress in identical black costumes during the three days of festivities. Tutio, *Incoronatione della Moresina Grimani*, pp. 5, 16; Sansovino, *Venetia*, 1604, fol. 280v.

[122] In spite of Doge Grimani's personal appeal to the guilds for contributions, the *gastaldi* of the five poorest guilds demanded to be released from the obligation. Tutio, *Incoronatione della Moresina Grimani*, p. 4, and Sansovino, *Venetia*, 1604, fol. 280v. Even the more financially secure guilds, such as the grocerymen *(macieri)*, showed some reluctance to comply: a resolution to provide 500 ducats for a coronation display first passed, but was defeated on a second ballot, and finally passed again on a third vote. The sometime reluctance of the guildsmen was warranted because, by the time the festival was over, the guild had spent nearly 3,000 ducats, not 500. MCV, Mariegola, IV, 102, fols. 94v–95v, 97v–98r.

[123] Mosto, *I dogi di Venezia*, pp. xxxvii, lxvi–lxxi.

[124] Rota, *L'ingresso della Morosina Grimani*, pp. 12–15; Tutio, *Incoronatione della Moresina Grimani*, pp. 13–16; Molmenti, *La dogaressa di Venezia*, p. 234. On the four hundred women, both "gentildonne" and "cittadine," see Sansovino, *Venetia*, 1604, fol. 280v. Except for two granddaughters of the doge, who covered themselves with jewels, the ladies adhered to the sumptuary laws by wearing only one string of pearls. Doglioni, *Le cose notabili*, p. 125.

coronation procession was suspiciously similar to a royal progress; for example, two dwarfs, a common accoutrement of a prince's court, walked in front of Morosina Grimani, and the pageantry was so dazzling that the legalistic niceties were no doubt obscured.

Vicenzo Scamozzi, a student of Palladio, had been hired for the occasion to design a grand barge (gran macchina) in which Dogaressa Grimani was rowed on the Grand Canal and on which young noble couples later danced. Decorations on the columned loggia of the macchina included a large Neptune riding the tail of a whale, a globe, and a scene in which Saint Mark himself crowned the kneeling doge and dogaressa, implying that the Saint had personally selected Marin and Morosina Grimani to exercise dominion over the seas of the world.[125]

The triumphal arch even more pointedly exalted the nobility of the two families.[126] Surmounting the arch was a statue of a woman (Venice) holding a staff (authority) and bundles of wheat (prosperity) and surrounded by paintings of the Venetian dominions abroad and on the terraferma. Insignia of the offices and honors obtained by the Grimani and Morosini ancestors — ducal and royal crowns (a Morosini had married a king of Hungary), cardinals' hats, bishops' staffs, a patriarch's cross, a legate's caduceus, and generals' batons — surrounded the arms of the two families. There were pointed references to Doge Grimani's eloquence as a legate to Rome, his renowned generosity as a procurator, his justice as a provincial governor, and the popularity of his election. Fortune pointed to an inscription predicting that Dogaressa Grimani's successors would emulate her prudence and virtue.[127]

Inside the Ducal Palace the guildsmen had erected booths, many of which were merely advertisements for the guild's

[125] Rota, L'ingresso della Morosina Grimani, pp. 16–18, and Tutio, Incoronatione della Moresina Grimani, pp. 5–6. Cf. Lina Padoan Urban, "Teatri e 'teatri del mondo' nella Venezia del Cinquecento," pp. 143–44.

[126] The butchers (macellari) built the arch according to the design of a miniaturist named Bernardo Fogari, who had consulted with a humanist lawyer, Attilio Facio. Piave, "Feste pella Morosina Grimani," p. 50.

[127] Rota, L'ingresso della Morosina Grimani, pp. 21–31; Tutio, Incoronatione della Moresina Grimani, pp. 11–13. Cf. Lina Padoan Urban, "Apparati scenografici nelle feste veneziane cinquecentesche," pp. 152–55.

wares; but some guildsmen, more ambitious or perhaps sycophantic, had designed exhibitions that were overt patriotic or
political allegories. Four of the building guilds (*taliapietre, murari, marengoni,* and *fabri*) combined their efforts to create a
complex of triumphal arches and statues that figuratively enunciated the patriotic ideology of Venice: *Religion* signified that
the republic was founded on true dogma; *Concord* promised
that through unity the republic would last forever; *Intelligence*
showed the wisdom of the government; and *Rectitude* demonstrated how the election system was free from intrigue and
bribery. The tailors (*sarti*) built a Temple of Janus inscribed
with a Latin motto to the effect that the portals of war were
closed, testifying that Doge Grimani had brought peace to Venice; and lastly the painters' guild displayed a huge canvas on
which two angels crowned Dogaressa Grimani.[128] Pageant scenes
such as these transformed the restrictive rites of the coronation
into a court festival. The dogaressa's final act at her entrance
was to sit on the doge's throne in the Senate Hall and thereby
take possession, albeit a very domestic form of possession, of
the Ducal Palace.[129] In the end, the lot of the virtuous Dogaressa Grimani, chosen by Saint Mark for lasting fame, was that
of wife and mistress of the household.

The flattery of pageantry compensated somewhat for the
severe limitations placed on the dogaressa and her family by
the *promissione;* but, despite the growth of such pageantry, the
contractual element of the coronation never disappeared, since
the right to live in the Ducal Palace always included some curtailment of freedom. Underlying the dilemmas so evident in
the doge and dogaressa ceremonies were the ever-present family
factions that so disordered Italian Renaissance society. The
Venetians, however, costumed their social tensions in a lengthy,
on-going drama in which the Venetian condition was continuously re-examined. In Venice, it seems, all the world was indeed a stage, and all the men and women merely players.

[128] Rota, *L'ingresso della Morosina Grimani,* pp. 37–51; Tutio, *Incoronatione della Moresina Grimani,* pp. 6–10. During the coronation of Zilia Dandolo Priuli only one guild had a figurative scene in its display, and that was an
allegory of the donation of Constantine. *Il trionfo nella publica entrata della
dogaressa.*

[129] Cf. Fasoli, "Liturgia e cerimoniale ducale," pp. 289–91.

14. Giacomo Franco, *The Dogaressa aboard the Bucintoro and Accompanied by Other Noble Ladies Goes from Her Palace to the Ducal Palace.*

15. Andrea Michieli, called "il Vicentino," *The Coronation of Dogaressa Morosina Grimani.*

CONCLUSION

Organizing a historical study by topic may have the disadvantage of obscuring the chronological distinctions that historians prize as their special province. This danger is magnified in a study of rituals, which by their very nature often seem more static than dynamic and often express less change than can be shown in other, less tradition-bound forms of human expression. Thus, the chronological patterns discovered in this study ought to be reviewed.

An affective parochialism and a tendency to make political institutions sacred underlay the civic rituals and ideology of Venice and persisted throughout the Middle Ages and the Renaissance. As demonstrated by the attitudes of the modern Venetian grandmothers and their contemporary the Utah dentist, these two mentalities exist in that dimension of time, the very long term, which enables them to survive the pressures of ephemeral events. The specific ceremonial and institutional manifestations of these mentalities in Venice were susceptible to long-term alterations, however, even though the peculiarly Venetian ideas that they embodied—the belief that the city was founded in liberty, the notion of Venice's natural right to an empire, and the special devotion to Saint Mark—remained fixed in the minds of Venetians for centuries. The institution of the doge had a most remarkable longevity: from 742 to 1797 the Venetians counted an almost uninterrupted succession of 118 doges; and such a succession gave substance to the Venetians' claims that theirs was a long-lived republic worthy of imitation.[1] Moreover, the sacral character the doges had acquired through sponsoring the cult of Saint Mark was gradually and somewhat furtively transferred to the republic as a whole, so that the entire complex of patrician institutions became a *corpus mysticum*. The continuity of these ideas and institutions must in part be attributed to a profound Venetian sensitivity for civic history, a sensitivity that contrasts with the virtually complete absence of a historical memory among the four-

[1] Fasoli, "Comune veneciarum," p. 474.

teenth-century shepherds of Montaillou studied by Emmanuel Le Roy Ladurie.[2] These long-term ideas gave the Venetians, in addition, their consciousness of a civic destiny. The two under-lying mentalities, parochialism and the belief in the sacredness of political institutions, did not change: the Venetians merely applied new terms and different metaphors in using these con-ceptual habits to understand and hence to cope with a changing political world.

The intensity of civic passions flamed or smoldered in the short term according to the influence of events. During the fourteenth century, specifically the period from the closing of the Great Council in 1297 to the end of the Genoese wars in 1380, Venetians made numerous adjustments in their ritual: they adopted Western ritual and artistic models at the expense of Byzantine ones; the patriciate suppressed the *contrade* as constituent groups in public ceremonies, as shown by the abo-lition of the Festival of the Twelve Marys; and the government began celebrating its defeat of conspiracies against the regime. The tensions of these eighty-odd years seem to have drawn forth a civic ritual that was organized and directed by lay mag-istrates, that was more republican than ducal, and that was pulled toward the vivid political and religious complex at San Marco. Paling in comparison to San Marco, the individual par-ishes lost much of their public identity.

During the fifteenth century, an essentially stable civic ritual succeeded the turmoil and the numerous alterations in detail that characterized the previous century's rituals. Civic ritual was further refined and institutionalized, but remained un-changed in any major way. As perhaps the most obvious fif-teenth-century development, several doges' attempts to reas-sert the authority of their office set the stage for the climactic ceremonial confrontation between republican and princely ideo-logies that occurred in the sixteenth century.

We have sharpened our focus on the sixteenth century be-cause it was during this epoch that the myth of Venice coalesced into a formal political ideology. At the beginning of the century the oligarchs put up a stout-hearted but in many ways ineffec-

[2] Le Roy Ladurie, *Montaillou*, pp. 281–82.

tive resistance to the growing princely status of the doge; they carefully redefined his image by modifying the interregnum rites, and they limited his opportunities to exchange gifts. After the War of the League of Cambrai, particularly under the influence of Doge Andrea Gritti, Venetian civic rituals were reformed in accordance with the authoritarian priorities of the oligarchy. Transformed under the influences of humanism and neoclassicism and often at the hands of refugees and expatriots from Tuscany and Rome, the important feast days became more and more the occasion for pageantry display. What had been open public space used for many purposes became, if not exclusively, then more frequently, a *via sacra* for civic rituals. The elaboration and embellishment of the settings for the civic rituals continued through the century, and particularly in the last three decades there was a notable leap in the number and frequency of civic rites.

Renaissance Venetians did not repudiate their medieval ritual past, but magnified it. In the hands of the governing patricians who advocated a more powerfully centralized city, the myth of civic freedom and the cult of Saint Mark were magnets to attract parochial sentiment. Although the precise origins of the Venetians' belief in their city's birth as an independent community and in the special patronage of Saint Mark are lost in the "dark" centuries before the end of the first Christian millennium, the idea of a free city under divine protection was so enticing that it survived even the death of the republic. In contrast to the belief that modernity brought a decline in ritual and an accompanying loss of communal unity, the evidence from Venice indicates that the oligarchic regime pursued the supposedly modern goals of centralization, bureaucratic growth, and increased social control through the sophisticated manipulation of ritual and ceremonial forms and the elaboration of popular myths.

The increase in the number and frequency of rites in the sixteenth century meant that the secular bureaucracy in charge of the ceremonies expanded and became more professional; but the secular masters of ceremonies did not necessarily replace the ecclesiastical masters, who also grew in number and in specialized expertise. During the Renaissance, Venice was not further laicized in ritual matters precisely because the ecclesiastical establishment at San Marco had been under the direct control of the doge for centuries. Venetian ceremonies often had the force of law, and this ceremonial legalism did not appear to decline during the Cinquecento in any readily perceivable way.

Civic rituals had also long helped the Venetians to identify their place in the world, as the imperial symbolism in the marriage of the sea reveals. The Venetian empire itself, and the notion that Venetians were born to rule others, probably began on that day in about the year 1000 when Doge Pietro II Orseolo received a saint's banner from the bishop and set sail on his Dalmatian expedition. The elaborate imperial legend of Pope Alexander III's gifts was perhaps deliberately constructed to justify the Venetian conquest of Constantinople in 1204, but it remained a useful rationale for Venetian claims to dominion. During the Cinquecento the patriciate began to use public processions and especially pageantry in a more conscious fashion as a diplomatic device. Although the Venetian empire began to decline somewhat during the sixteenth century, an imperial ethic still persisted until at least the end of the seventeenth century, and it survived in the marriage-of-the-sea ritual until 1797.

Hints about changes in social attitudes can also be discovered in the civic rituals. As one surveys the thirteenth to sixteenth centuries, most obvious is the sharpening of class distinctions. Nobles, *cittadini,* and plebians were separated in rituals, and the first two groups were classified according to an elaborate hierarchy of official precedences. The Venetian republic was becoming more aristocratic, more concerned with class privilege, more socially rigid, and less a *communis* of free citizens. During the same period, individual clans or patrilineal families found it more difficult to assert themselves in public ceremonies; the only significant exceptions were certain ducal families who sought to use the privileges of the dogeship for familial aggrandizement. Families nurtured factions, and from factions grew divisiveness and instability. Although familial interests undoubtedly still influenced Venetian politics, they were not

CONCLUSION

entirely compatible with the interests of an oligarchy of elected officials and hence were suppressed with a strong measure of hierarchical ritual.

Civic rituals also differentiated age groups and the sexes. Youths came increasingly to be seen in Venice, as they had been in late quattrocento Florence, as symbols of innocence; the Venetian image of youth was institutionalized in a peculiar political context, however, to demonstrate the incorruptibility of the electoral system. Youths paid a price for their elevated place in public life; their youthfulness itself was abstracted to represent certain moral qualities, and henceforth they were bound to standards different from those that guided their elders. A state of innocence necessarily implied removal from the corrupting influences of real public life. A superiority in morals meant an inferiority in power. Venice was in fact ruled by an unusually elderly group of men; but old age, in and of itself, did not seem to achieve a particular ritualistic significance outside of carnival lampoons.[3] This fact is revealing. The small group of elderly oligarchs who ran Venice compensated their fellow citizens in the glittering coinage of ceremonial status, and hence they avoided sharing political power, the real currency of government. During carnival, when the social order was inverted, the oligarchs were paid back in ritual burlesque; but their rule was hardly threatened by the jokes of louts.

The status of women is perhaps the most difficult to assess. After the abolition of the Festival of the Twelve Marys in the fourteenth century, Venetian women had far fewer independent roles in public ceremonies. The infrequent coronations of the dogaressas in the fifteenth and sixteenth centuries and the more common receptions for dignitaries still allowed some ceremonial outlet, at least for patrician women; but on these occasions the women themselves, not just wooden effigies, had become the symbolic objects. Forced to watch most events from the safe distance of a palace window, women were more isolated from public life and more removed from public consciousness— less the energetically charitable sisters of the Virgin and more

[3] On the age of the most powerful office-holders, see Robert Finlay, "The Venetian Republic as a Gerontocracy."

the subjects of a chivalric fantasy. The aristocrats' court, with all its social distinctions and elaborate rules of etiquette, had begun to push aside the peoples' commune, with its traditions of equality. As was the case with youth, by the Quattro- and Cinquecento the ceremonial representation of womankind occurred largely in a political and courtly context; women as well had been elevated to an ideal status, and thus reduced to passive subjects of the all-embracing aristocratic republic.

The revision of Venetian civic ritual in the Cinquecento corresponded, finally, to the humanist enunciation of a Venetian republican ideology. The correlation of these two activities was not accidental; both reveal the ruling patricians' desire to impose their own cultural and political proclivities even more effectively on the entire society. An explanation for their success might be found in their ability to enlist the inheritance of local legend and ritual in the service of their own political ends. In doing so, the patricians were able to foster the myth of Venice, which made their city the paragon republic of early modern Europe. Just as the humanists used a cultivated prose invigorated by classical studies to clarify, dissect, and refashion Venetian legends into a coherent history of Venetian political institutions and ideas, so did patrician officials use reformed ceremonies and neoclassical pageants to differentiate, separate, and reclassify Venetian society into a stable, aristocratic republic in which every man, and every woman, knew automatically his or her calling and place. Political writings and civic rituals equally proclaimed a mythic vision of Venice as a sovereign, free city possessed of a perfected social hierarchy and contented class groupings.

Two other Venetian tendencies, those of lauding republicanism and using ceremonies to define and stabilize the legal position of certain magistracies, especially of the doge, were also related. The promulgation of an ideology of republicanism might be seen as an attempt to find an alternative to unifying the republic through the charisma of the doge. The doge was not by any means abandoned, since he was the institutional and symbolic link to so much of the Venetian past, a past that could be adapted to a republican purpose. But the personal charisma of a prince was dangerous to a republic. Hence, republican ideology, in a sense, replaced princely charisma. Although this specific transformation was peculiarly Venetian, it echoed a similar phenomenon Percy Schramm has found in Western European monarchies:

> To write the history of the medieval state is to show how kingship changed from an honour with certain rights and duties to an institution that surpasses the individual. This institution is abstract enough to be transferred at the demise of the father to the son. Its justification derives from faith, law, history and a concept of world order. Having reached this point, it will become apparent that there is something that is common to ruler and people, in which the king is only a carrier of certain defined functions: and that is the state.[4]

The state, then, whether a monarchy or a republic, arose when an abstraction or ideology, in some form, came to replace the peculiar power of individual leaders.

THE DRAMA of the Venetian transformation from a scattering of island settlements to a commune to an imperial state was, in perhaps overly simplified terms, a narration of the changing relationships between urban spaces and sacred figures. Two theaters, the local parish directed by its own saint-protector and the central city led by Saint Mark, competed for the attention of the populace. The form of the two theatricals was ritualistic. The cause of the conflict was family, class, and neighborhood rivalry. The resolution was the victory of the centralized city-republic, governed by a closed patriciate that created a new dramatic form, civic ritual, out of the struggle between parish and city and, henceforth, used civic ritual to exalt the state. And the epilogue to this extravaganza was the myth of Venice.

[4] Schramm, *Der König von Frankreich*, 1:1. I have taken the translation of this passage from Bak, "Medieval Symbology of the State," p. 44.

MANUSCRIPT SOURCES

FLORENCE

Archivio di Stato (ASF)
Corp. Relig. Sopp., Montalve di Ripoli: S. Pier Maggiore, 323
(CRIA 7287).
Peruzzi Medici 234, inserto 3.

PADUA

Biblioteca Universitaria di Padova
MS XVIII sec., segn. 104, "Relatione della famosa entrata in Venetia
di Henrico III Re di Francia, e di Polonia. E dell'agregatione alla
veneta nobilità di Henrico IV. Re di Francia e di Navarra, racolta
da Giuseppe Baldan d'ordine dell'Eccellentissimo Piero Gradenigo,
Savio di Terra Firma, 1732."

SYRACUSE, NEW YORK

Syracuse University Library (SUL)
Ranke MS 69, "Dell'origine et accresimento della città di Venetia et
isole della lagune principiato dell'anno CCCCXXI et molte altre cose
notabili fino l'anno MDLVI."

VENICE

Archivio di Stato (ASV)
Collegio Cerimoniale 1, a collection of descriptions of all ceremonial
occasions and copies of decrees from the Great Council, Senate,
Collegio, and Council of Ten that pertained to state ceremony. It
was begun in 1593 and relied on earlier ceremonial books such as
Regina Margherita, B-14, series LXXVI, no. 6 (formerly catalogued
as Ex Brera 277).
Consiglio dei Dieci, miscellanea codici 1, "Magnus" (1310–1618);
parti misti, registro 47.
Inquisitori et revisori sopra le Scuole Grandi, capitolare 1.
Maggior Consiglio, deliberazioni, "Liber comunis primus"; "Liber
primus pactorum"; "Liber tractus"; "Liber zaneta"; "Libro d'oro."

Procuratia de Supra per la Chiesa di S. Marco, busta 86, processo 191, fascicolo 1; registro 122.

Rason Vecchie, buste 1, 3, 219, 223, 225, and 226.

Scuola Grande di S. Giovanni Evangelista, vol. 3.

Scuola Grande di S. Rocco, seconda consegna, vols. 44, 45.

Biblioteca del Museo Civico Correr (MCV)

Codice Cicogna 1295, "Ceremoniale Magnum," compiled by Giovanni Battista Pace in 1678; 2043; 2043c; 2143; 2479; 2814, "Cronaca," by Alovise Borghe; 2848, "Diarii," by Marcantonio Michiel; 2853, "Cronaca Agostini di Venezia"; 2991; 2992; 3278/23, 24; 3281, IV; 3287.

Codice Gradenigo, no. 214, "Cronica del monastero delle Vergini di Venetia."

MS Donà delle Rose, 132/6, "Ceremoniali delle uscite di casa delli Principi di Venetia scritto in tempo del Serenissimo Paschale Cicogna da Salustio Gnicchi suo cavallarie," dated 24 December 1590.

MS Mariegola, IV, 102.

MS P.D. 115b; 296c, III; 303c/XVI, "Cerimoniali per il giuramento della Dogaressa"; 303c/XXVI, "Festa veneziana del 1530 descritta in una lettera di Vettor Malipiero"; 381; 396c/III; 517b; 606c/III; 701c/II (n. 9), the same as BMV, MS Italiano VII, 1743.

MS Venier, B. V (I); P.D. 517b.

Biblioteca Nazionale Marciana (BMV)

MS Italiano VII, 69 (8438), "Cronaca Veneta"; 121–22 (8862–63), "Dose di Venetia," IV, by Giovanni Carlos Sivos; 142 (7147), "Cronaca Veneti," by Ottavio Caroldo; 164 (7306), "Memorie del passaggio per lo stato veneto di principi e soggetti esteri, 1347–1773"; 519 (8438), "Cronaca veneta dalle origine al 1585"; 553 (8812), "Compendio di me Francesco da Molino de M. Marco delle cose . . . che sucederanno in mio tempo si della Republica Venetiana, e' di Venetia mia patria . . ."; 708 (7899), "Diario delle cose sequite doppo la morte del Serenissimo D. D. Silvestro Valier Doge di Venetia osservate secondo il cerimoniale . . . che si vede in Secreta del 1501 . . . et sopra li cerimoniale posteriore . . ."; 794 (8503), "Cronica di Venezia dall'origine sua fino all'anno 1458," by Giorgio Dolfin; 1219 (9598); 1233 (9600), "Ordine di condurre le dogaresse a Palazzo del Principe"; 1269 (9573), "Ceremoniale Magnum," compiled by Giovanni Battista Pace in 1678; 1723 (8598); 1743 (7802), "Discorsi di precedenza officii e feste,

MANUSCRIPT SOURCES

1597–1794"; 1818 (9436), "Vite de Dosi di Venezia," I-III, by Giovanni Carlos Sivos.

MS Italiano XI, 124 (6802), "Cronaca di Marco."

MS Latin III, 172 (2276), "Rituum ecclesiasticorum cerimoniale . . . ," compiled 1559–64.

MS Latin XIV, 230 (4736).

Microfilm Library of the Fondazione Giorgio Cini

Österreichische Nationalbibliothek, Vienna (ONV)

MS ex Foscarini, codice 6228, b. 2, codice 6229, b. 3, "Diario," by Girolamo Priuli, covering the years 1600–1615.

Biblioteca Ambrosiana, Milan

Codice Ambrosiana Latin Q117 sup., fascicolo 102, "De ritibus et caerimoniis in capella Sancti Marci tractatus."

BIBLIOGRAPHY

PRIMARY SOURCES

Adam, Salimbene de. *Cronica.* Edited by Giuseppe Scalia. Scrittori d'Italia. Bari, 1966.

Alati, Alessandro. *Rime . . . in lode della serenissima principessa di Venetia Moresina Grimani.* Venice, 1597.

Apollonio, Ferdinando. *La peste e il voto del MDLXXVI. Ricordo tratto dalle patrie storie per la centenaria ricorrenza.* Venice, 1876.

[Avanzo, Martiale.] *Aviso della solenniss. e trionfante entrata nella inclita città di Venetia, del valorosissimo, e prudentiss. capitano generale dell'armata della sereniss. republica venetiana, l'illust. S. Sebastian Veniero, benemeritissimo procurator della chiesa di San Marco.* Venice, 1574.

Bardi, Girolamo. *Delle cose notabili della città di Venetia, libri III.* Venice, 1587.

————. *Dichiaratione di tutte le istorie, che si contengono ne i quadri posti novamente nelle sale dello scrutinio, & del gran consiglio, del palagio ducale della serenissima republica di Vinegia.* Venice, 1587.

————. *Vittoria navale ottenuta dalla republica venetiana contra Othone, figliuolo di Federico primo imperadore; per la restitutione di Alessandro terzo, pontefice massimo, venuto à Venetia.* Venice, 1584.

Bembo, Pietro. *Della historia vinitiana.* Venice, 1552.

Benedetti, Rocco. *Le feste et trionfi fatti dalla . . . signoria di Venetia nella . . . venuta di Henrico III. . . .* Florence, 1574.

————. *Ordine e dichiaratione di tutta la mascherata fatta nella città di Venezia la domenica di carnevale 1571 per la gloriosa vittoria contra Turchi.* Venice, 1572.

————. *Ragguaglio delle allegrezze, solennità e feste fatte in Venetia per la felice vittoria.* Venice, 1571.

Benedetti, Rocco, and Lumina, Mutio. *Raguaglio minutissimo del successo della peste di Venetia, con gli casi occorsi, provisioni fatte, & altri particolari, infino alla liberatione di essa. Et la relatione particolare della publicata liberatione, con le solenni e devote pompe.* Tivoli, 1577.

Bertaldo, Jacobo. *Splendor Venetorum civitatis consuetudinem.* Edited by F. Schupfer. N.p., 1901.

Boccaccio, Giovanni. *Tutte le opere.* Edited by Vittore Branca. Vol. 4: *Decameron.* Milan, 1976.

BIBLIOGRAPHY: PRIMARY SOURCES

Botero, Giovanni. *Relatione della republica venetiana.* Venice, 1605.

Brixiensi, Ioanne Planerio Quintiano. *Felicissimi adventus Henrici Galliarum, et Poloniae Regis Christianissimi, et Augustissimi ad urbem Venetam brevissima, ac facillima descriptio. Et rerum memorabilium, quae factae sunt, commemoratio.* Venice, 1574.

Buccio, M. Pietro. *Le coronationi di Polonia, et di Francia del christianiss. re Henrico III. Con le attioni, et successi de' suoi viaggi descritte in dieci giornate.* Padua, 1576. The only known copy is in the Biblioteca del Seminario Vescovile di Padova.

Calmo, Andrea. *Delle lettere di M. Andrea Calmo.* Venice, 1584.

Campanella, Tommaso. *Antiveneti.* Edited by Luigi Firpo. Opuscoli filosofici: Testi e documenti inediti o rari, no. 8. Florence, 1945.

Canal, Martin da. *Les estoires de Venise: Cronaca veneziana in lingua francese dalle origini al 1275.* Edited by Alberto Limentani. Civiltà veneziana fonti e testi, no. 12, 3d series 3. Florence, 1972. Previously published as "La cronique des Veniciens," *Archivio storico italiano,* 1st series 8 (1845).

[Caravia, Alessandro]. *La morte de Giurco e Gnagni.* N.p., n.d.

―――――. *Il sogno dil Caravia.* Venice, 1541.

Casolo, Pietro. *Viaggio a Gerusalemme.* Milan, 1855. Translated and with an introduction by M. Margaret Newett, *Canon Pietro Casola's Pilgrimage to Jerusalem in the Year 1494,* Manchester, 1907.

Cavalcanti, B. *Trattati overo discorsi sopra gli ottimi reggimenti delle repubbliche antiche e moderne. Con un discorso di M. Sebastiano Erizo gentil'huomo vinitiano de' governi civili.* Venice, 1570.

Cerimoni e fatte nella publicatione della lega fatta in Venetia, con la dechiaratione di solari & altre cose come legendo inendereti. N.p., n.d.

Cerimoniale solenne nel giorno dell'ascensione per lo sposalizio del mare che compivasi al doge di Venezia tratto dal codice inedito che serviva di norma all'ultimo cavaliere del doge. Edited by Andrea Battaglia. Venice, 1860.

Cessi, Roberto, ed. *Documenti relativi alla storia di Venezia anteriori al mille.* Testi e documenti di storia e di letteratura latina medioevale, no. 1. Padua, 1940.

Collini, Giovanni Luigi. *Esplicatione dei carri trionfali fatti nella processione per la pace, tra Franza, e Spagna, dalla Scola di S. Teodoro il dì 26 Luglio 1598.* Venice, 1598.

Colonna, Francesco. *Le songe de Poliphile ou Hypnérotomachie.* Translated with an introduction and notes by Claudius Popelin. 2 vols. Paris, 1883.

BIBLIOGRAPHY: PRIMARY SOURCES

Commynes, Philippe de. *Mémoires.* Edited by M. Dupont. 3 vols. Paris, 1840–47.

Contarini, Gasparo. *De magistratibus et republica Venetorum libri quinque.* Venice, 1551. Translated by Lewes Lewkenor, *The Commonwealth and Government of Venice,* London, 1599.

Cornet, Enrico, ed. *Paolo V e la republica veneta, giornale dal 22 ottobre 1605 - 9 giugno 1607.* Vienna, 1859.

————, ed. "Paolo V e la republica veneta nuova serie di documenti (MDCV-MDCVII) tratti dalle deliberazioni secrete (Roma) del Consiglio dei Dieci." *Archivio veneto,* new series 5 (1873):27–96, 222–318; 6 (1873):68–131.

Coryate, Thomas. *Crudities.* Glasgow, 1905.

Dalla Croce, Marsiglio. *L'historia della pubblica et famosa entrata in Venezia del serenissimo Henrico III di Francia et Polonia con la descrizione particolare della pompa, e del numero, et varietà delli bergantine, paleschermi et altri vascelli, con la dechiaratione dell'edificio, et arco fatto al Lido.* Venice, 1574.

Dandolo, Andrea. *Chronicon venetum . . . .* Edited by L. A. Muratori. In Rerum Italicarum Scriptores, vol. 12. Milan, 1728. 2d edition by E. Pastorello, Bologna, 1938.

Del Friuli, Pace. *La festa delle Marie descritta in un poemetto elegiaco.* Edited with annotations and notes by E. Cicogna. Venice 1843. Orginally published by Flaminio Corner, *Ecclesiae venetae* . . . , 3:303–8, Venice, 1749.

Delle accolienze usate dai Veneziani ai principi esteri. Venice, 1840.

Diclich, Don Giovanni, ed. *Rito veneto antico detto patriarchino.* Venice, 1823.

Doglioni, Nicolò. *Le cose notabili et maravigliose della città di Venetia.* Venice, 1692.

Dondi, Jacopo. *Liber partium consilii magnifice comunitatis Padue.* In Vittorio Lazzarini, "Il pretesto documento della fondazione di Venezia e la cronaca del medico Jacopo Dondi," *Atti del Reale Instituto Veneto di Scienze, Lettere ed Arti* 75 (1915–16):1263–77.

Dorron, Claudio. *Narratio rerum memorabilium, quae propter adventum christianissimi invictissimique Henrici III Franciae & Polonia regis, a totius orbis florentissima Venetorum Republica factae sunt.* Venice, 1574.

L'entrata che fece in Venezia l'illustrissimo ed eccelentissimo signor Duca Alfonso II Estense. Ferrara, 1562.

Fantasia composta in laude de Veniesia. Venice, 1582.

BIBLIOGRAPHY: PRIMARY SOURCES

Faroldo, Iulio. *Annali veneti.* Venice, 1577.

Ferrarese, Brandimarte Franconi. *Historia di Papa Alessand. III et di Fedrico Barbarossa imperatore.* Treviso, 1650.

Feste di palazzo et giorni ne' quali sua serenità esce di quello. Venice, n.d.

Foscari, Marco. "Relazion fatta per Marco Foscari nell'eccellentissimo Consiglio di Pregadi della legazione de Fiorenza, con qualche cosa adiuncta da lui nel scrivere essa legazione, 1527." In *Relazioni degli ambasciatori veneti al senato,* vol. 3, pt. 1, pp. 3–98. Edited by Arnaldo Segarizzi. Scrittori d'Italia. Bari, 1916.

Franco, Giacomo. *Habiti d'huomeni et donne venetiane con la processione della serenissima signoria et altri particolari cioè trionfi feste cerimonie publiche della nobilissima città di Venetia.* Venice, 160?. Republished Venice, 1878.

Frangipane, Cornelio. *In laude di Venezia.* Edited with an introduction by E. A. Cicogna. Venice, 1850.

—————. *Per la historia di Papa Alessandro III publica nella sala regia à Roma, & del maggior consiglio à Venetia. Allegatione in iure.* Venice, 1615.

Georgii, Bernardi. *Periocha, in XIIII publicas solennitates in quibus praeter aliquot alias illustriss. princeps Venetus comitantibus senatoribus quotannis in publicum prodit.* Venice, 1559.

Giannotti, Donato. *Libro de la republica de Vinitiani.* Rome, 1542.

Giustiniani, Bernardo. *Historie cronologiche dell'origine degl'ordini militari e di tutte le religioni cavalleresche infino ad hora instituite nel mondo. . . .* Venice, 1692.

Giustiniani, Pietro. *Dell'historie venetiane.* Venice, 1670.

Groto, Luigi [Cieco d'Hadria]. "Oratione . . . al christianissimo re di Francia Enrico terzo nella sua venuta à Vinegia. Recitata da lui in casa Foscari il di 25 di luglio nell'anno 1574." In *Le orationi volgari,* fols. 85v–95r. Venice, 1598.

Gualtieri, Guido. *Relationi della venuta de gli ambasciatori Giaponesi à Roma, fino alla partita di Lisbona. Con una descrittione del lor paese, e costumi, e con le accoglienze fatte loro da tutti i prencipi Christiani, per dove sono passati.* Venice, 1586.

"L'interdetto di Venezia del 1606 e i Gesuiti: Silloge di documenti con introduzione." Edited by Pietro Pirri. *Bibliotheca Instituti Historici S. I.* 14 (1959).

John the Deacon. "La cronaca veneziana del diacono Giovanni." In *Cronache veneziane antichissime,* 1:57–171. Edited by Giovanni Monticolo. Rome, 1890.

BIBLIOGRAPHY: PRIMARY SOURCES

Jonson, Ben. *Volpone*. Edited by Alvin B. Kernan. New Haven, 1962.

Kalendarium Venetum saeculi XI. Edited by Stephano Borgia. Rome, 1773.

Leoni, Benedetto. *Canzone fatta intorno allo stato calamitoso dell'inclita città di Vinetia, nel colmo de' maggiori suoi passati travagli per la peste. Et nuovamente data in luce*. Padua, 1577.

I libri commemoriali della republica di Venezia: Regesti 5. Monumenti storici publicati dalla R. Deputazione Veneta di Storia Patria. Venice, 1901.

Lithgow, William. *The Totall Discourse, of the Rare Adventures, and Painfull Peregrinations of Long Nineteene Yeares Travayles, from Scotland, to the Most Famous Kingdomes in Europe, Asia, and Africa*. London, 1632.

Lorenzi, J. B., ed. *Monumenti per servire alla storia del palazzo ducale di Venezia*. Venice, 1868.

Lucangeli da Bevagna, Nicolò. *Successi del viaggio d'Henrico III christianiss[i]mo re di Francia, e di Polonia, dalla sua partita di Craccovia fino all'arrivo in Turino*. Venice, 1574.

Lumina, Mutio. *La liberazione di Vinegia. . . .* Venice, 1577.

Machiavelli, Niccolò. *Opere*. Edited by Mario Bonfantini. La letteratura italiana, storia e testi, no. 29. Milan, 1954.

——————. *The Prince and the Discourses*. Translated by Luigi Ricci and revised by E. R. P. Vincent. New York, 1950.

Magno, Celio. *Trionfo di Christo per la vittoria contra Turchi, rappresentato al sereniss. prencipe di Venetia, il di di San Stefano*. Venice, 1571. New edition by Ubaldo Angeli, Montelione, 1893.

Manzini Bolognese, Dottore. *Il gloriosissimo apparato fatto dalla serenissima republica venetiana per la venuta, per la dimora, & per la partenza del christianissimo Enrico III re di Francia et di Polonia*. Venice, 1574.

——————. *Le sapientissime et caritative ammonitioni et essortationi del christianissimo re di Francia et di Polonia, fatte alli contumaci suoi nella entrata del potentissimo regno suo di Francia*. Venice, 1574.

Marcello, Gregorio. *Ordine et progreesso [sic] del trionfo fatto l'anno MDLVII alli 19 di settembrio, per l'incoronatione della sereniss. Dogaressa Priola*. Venice, 1597.

Marcello, Pietro. *Vite de' prencipi di Vinegia*. Translated from Latin to Italian by Lodovico Domenichi. Venice, 1558.

Marini, Andrea. *De pompa ducatus Venetorum*. Edited by Arnaldo Segarizzi. Venice, 1903.

BIBLIOGRAPHY: PRIMARY SOURCES

Masenetti (Padovano), Giammaria. *Li trionfi et feste solenni che si fanno in la creatione del principe di Vineggia, in ottava rima.* Padua, 1554.

Menechini, Andrea. *Capitolo nel qual la santiss. religion catholica è introdotta à favellar co' l christianiss. potentissimo, & invitiss. Henrico III gloriosissimo re di Francia, et di Polonia.* Venice, 1574.

Meninus, Octavianus. *In Henrici III galliarum et sarmatiae regis potentissimi ad urbem Venetam adventum.* Venice, 1574.

Michele, Agostino. *Oratione . . . nella coronatione della serenissima prencipessa di Vinegia, Moresina Grimani.* Venice, 1597.

Michiel, Marcantonio. *The Anonimo.* Edited by G. C. Williamson. London, 1903.

Michieli, Adriano Augusto. "Il passaggio di Enrico III di Valois per Treviso nel 1574." In *IV annuario dell'Istituto Tecnico "J. Riccati" di Treviso.* Treviso, 1926.

Mocenigo, Alvise. "Relazione fatta al senato nel giorno 29 luglio 1574 dal Doge Aluigi Mocenigo, de' colloquii da lui tenuti col re Enrico III di Francia e di Polonia, nel tempo del suo soggiorno in Venezia." In *Due documenti inediti di storia veneta del secolo decimosesto.* Edited by Sebastiano Rizzi. Venice, 1842.

Monaco, Lorenzo d'. *Chronicon de rebus venetis. . . .* Edited by L. A. Muratori. In *Rerum Italicarum Scriptores,* appendix to vol. 8. Venice, 1758.

Morandi, Francisci. *De adventu Henrici III regis christianiss. in Venetam urbem.* N.p., n.d.

————. *De Veneto senatu Henricum Valesium regem magnificentiss. post hominum memoriam hospitiis excipiente.* N.p., n.d.

Morosini, Andrea. "Historiarum Venetarum." In *Degli istorici delle cose veneziane i quali hanno scritto per pubblico decreto . . . ,* 6:590–95. Venice, 1718.

Moryson, Fynes. *Itinerary Containing his Ten Yeeres Travell.* London, 1617.

Olivi, Petrus Ioannis. *Quaestiones quatuor de Domina.* Edited by Dionysius Pacetti. Florence, 1954.

Ordine et dechiaratione di tutta la mascherata fatta nella città di Venetia la domenica di carnevale MDLXXI per la gloriosa vittoria contra Turchi. Venice, 1572.

Panvinio, Fra Onofrio. *Comentario dell'uso et ordine de' trionfi antichi.* Venice, 1571.

Paschalicus, Marcus. *Orationes due Marci Paschalici philosophiae et theologiae doctoris. Altera de scientiarum laudibus. Altera vero de Veneta sponsaliorum maris ratione.* Venice, 1548.

Petrarch, Francesco. *Letters.* Selected and translated by Morris Bishop. Bloomington, Indiana, 1966.

Plutarchus. *Plutarch's Lives.* Translated by Bernadotte Perrin. 11 vols. London, 1914–26.

Poggio Bracciolini *In laudem rei publicae Venetorum.* In *Opera omnia,* 2:925–37. Edited by Riccardo Fubini. Turin, 1966.

Porcacchi, Tommaso. *Le attioni d'Arrigo terzo re di Francia et quarto di Polonia descritte in dialogo.* . . . Venice, 1574.

Porto, Luigi da. *Lettere storiche dall'anno 1509 al 1528.* Florence, 1857.

Priuli, Girolamo. *I diarii.* Edited by Arturo Segre et al. In Rerum Italicarum Scriptores, vol. 24. 2d edition, Città di Castello and Bologna, 1912–33.

The Pylgrymage of Sir Richard Guylforde to the Holy Land, A.D. 1506. Edited by Henry Ellis. The Camden Society, no. 51. [London, 1851].

Rappresentatione fatta alla presentia del ser[enissi]mo prencipe di Venetia Nicolo da Ponte, il giorno di S. Marco, l'anno 1579. N.p., n.d.

Rappresentatione fatta avanti il serenissimo prencipe di Venetia Nicolo da Ponte, il giorno di S. Stefano 1580. N.p., n.d.

"Relazione del'interdetto di Paolo V." In Gaetano Cozzi, "Paolo Sarpi tra il cattolico Philippe Canaye de Fresnes e il calvinista Isaac Casaubon," *Bollettino dell'Istituto di Storia della Società e dello Stato Veneziano,* vol. 1 (1959), document 6, pp. 105–6.

Ripa, Cesare. *Nova iconologia.* Padua, 1618.

Rota, Giovanni. *Lettera nella quale si descrive l'ingresso nel palazzo ducale della serenissima Morosina Morosini Grimani prencipessa di Vinetia. Co' la cerimonia della rosa benedetta, mandatale à donare dalla santità di nostro Signore.* Venice, 1597.

Sabellico, Marc Antonio. *Le historie vinitiane.* Venice, 1554.

Sansovino, Francesco. *Concetti politici.* Venice, 1568.

―――――. *Delle orationi recitate a principi di Veneti nella loro creatione da gli ambasciadori di diverse città.* . . . Venice, 1562.

―――――. *Venetia città nobilissima et singolare.* With additions by Giovanni Stringa, Venice, 1604. With additions by Giustiniano Martinioni, Venice, 1663. Reprint with an analytical index by Lino Moretti, Venice, 1968.

Sanuto, Marin. *I diarii.* Edited by Rinaldo Fulin et al. 58 vols. Venice, 1879–1903.

―――――. *Narrazione della festa solenne data in Venezia dalla compagnia della calza nel MDXX adi XIII febraio per l'accettazione di tre socii.* Edited by Giuseppe Beltrami. Venice, 1852.

_____. *Le vite dei dogi.* Edited by Giovanni Monticolo and Giosue Carducci. In Rerum Italicarum Scriptores, vol. 22. 2d. edition, Città di Castello and Bologna, 1900–1902.

Savorgnano, Mario. *La venuta della serenissima Bona Sforza et d'Aragona reina di Polonia et duchessa di Bari nella magnifica città di Padova à ventisette di marzo: Con l'entrata nella inclita città di Vinegia, il di 26 aprile 1556, et la sua partita per Bari.* Venice, 1556.

Silimbergius, Bernardinus Parthenius. *In divi Henrici tertii Galliae, ac Poloniae regis christianissimi, ac felicissimi, ed urbem Venetam adventum.* Venice, 1574.

Squintinio della libertà veneta, nel quale si adducono anche le raggioni dell'Impero Romano sopra la città & signoria di Venetia. Mirandola, 1612. French version, *Examen de la liberté originaire de Venise,* Regensburg, 1677. Authorship has been variously attributed to Mark Welser, Alfonso de la Queva (or Cueva), and Gaspare Scioppio.

Stellae, Antonii. *In funere Ziliae Priulae, inclytae Venetiarum ducis . . . oratio.* Venice, 1566.

Stringa, Giovanni. *Vita di S. Marco evangelista, protettore invitissimo della serenissima republica di Venetia, con la traslatione, & apparitione del sacro suo corpo; fatta nella nobilissima chiesa, al nome suo dedicata.* Venice, 1680.

Tafur, Pero. *Travels and Adventures, 1435–1439.* Edited and translated by Malcolm Letts. London, 1926.

Thomas, William. *The History of Italy (1549).* Edited by George B. Parks. Ithaca, New York, 1963.

Traité du gouvernement de la cité et seigneurie de Venise. In P. M. Perret, *Histoire des relations de la France avec Venise du XIIIe siècle a l'avènement de Charles VIII,* 2:239–304. Paris, 1896.

Le trionfi et feste solenni: Che si fanno in la creatione del principe di Vineggia, in ottava rima. Padua, 1554.

Il trionfo della dogaressa di Venezia nel secolo XV. Edited by Girolamo Oriani. Venice, 1874.

Il trionfo et le feste fatte in Venetia nella publica entrata della serenissima dogaressa, moglie dell'illustrissimo signor Lorenzo di Priuli, prencipe di Venetia. Venice, n.d.

Tutio, Dario. *Ordine et modo tenuto nell'incoronatione della serenissima Moresina Grimani dogaressa di Venetia. L'anno MDXCVII adi 4 di maggio. Con le feste e giochi fatti.* Venice, 1597.

Vecellio, Cesare. *Habiti antichi e moderni di tutto il mondo.* Venice, 1598.

Venetiano, G. B. V. *Relationi della solenne processione fatta in Venetia*

*l'anno 1598 adi 26 luglio de ordine del serenissimo prencipe, &
illustrissima signorie per render gratie à Dio della perpetua pace,
et confederatione stabilita tra il christianiss. rè di Francia, & il
cattolico rè di Spagna. Seguita per opera, & assidue orationi fatte
à sua divina maestà dal beatissimo s.n. Papa Clemente VIII.* Vicenza, 1598.

Venier, Giacomo. *L'ordine tenuto del cl[arissi]mo m. Alvise Grimani
in consignare lo stendardo del generalato all'ill[ustrissi]mo & ecc-
[ellentissi]mo s. Giacomo Foscarini, dignissimo capitanio generale
dell'armata venetiana nella città di Zara con li trionfi, feste, et
cerimonie seguite in tal consignatione.* Venice, 1572.

*Vera et fedele relatione del passaggio della ser[enissi]ma principessa
Margherita d'Austria regina di Spagna. Per lo stato della serenissima signoria di Venetia.* Verona, 1599.

Vergili Maronis, P. *Opera.* Edited by Frederic Arthur Hirtzel. Scrip-
torum Classicorum Bibliotheca Oxoniensis. Oxford, 1900.

Wey, William. *The Itineraries . . . to Jerusalem, A.D. 1458 and A.D.
1462; and to Saint James of Compostella, A.D. 1456.* London,
1857.

Zio, Camillo. *La solennissima entrata dell'illustrissimo & eccellentissimo signor Duca di Ferrara, ne la città di Venetia, cominciando
dalla partita di sua eccellenza da Ferrara, per infino al suo ri-
torno.* Bologna, 1562.

SECONDARY SOURCES

Ackerman, Robert. "Frazer on Myth and Ritual." *Journal of the History of Ideas* 36 (1975):115–34.

_____. "Writing about Writing about Myth." *Journal of the His-
tory of Ideas* 34 (1973):147–55.

Anglo, Sydney. *Spectacle, Pageantry, and Early Tudor Policy.* Oxford,
1969.

Ariatta, Olimpia Aureggi. "Influssi delle relazioni col Levante sul diritto ecclesiastico della repubblica veneta." *Archivio storico lombardo* 95 (1969):214–23.

Ariès, Philippe. *Centuries of Childhood: A Social History of Family
Life.* Translated by Robert Baldick. New York, 1962.

Armingaud, M. J. *Venise et le Bas-Empire.* Paris, 1868.

Ashby, Thomas. *Some Italian Scenes and Festivals.* London, 1929.

Attwater, Donald. *A Dictionary of Mary.* New York, 1956.

Auerbach, Erich. *Mimesis: The Representation of Reality in Western
Literature.* Garden City, New York, 1957.

BIBLIOGRAPHY: SECONDARY SOURCES

Bagnoli, Raffaele. *Festività e tradizioni popolari milanesi.* Rome, 1973.

Baiocchi, Angelo. "Paolo Paruta: Ideologia e politica nel Cinquecento veneziano." *Studi veneziani* 17–18 (1975–76):157–233.

_____. Review of *Venice: The Hinge of Europe, 1080–1797,* by William H. McNeill. *Studi veneziani* 17–18 (1975–76):536–40.

Bak, J. M. "Medieval Symbology of the State: Percy E. Schramm's Contribution." *Viator: Medieval and Renaissance Studies* 4 (1973):33–63.

Bakhtin, Mikhail. *Rabelais and His World.* Translated by Helene Iswolsky. Cambridge, Massachusetts, 1968.

Baldassari, Antonio. *La rosa d'oro che si benedice nella quarta domenica di quaresima dal sommo pontefice.* Venice, 1759.

Barkun, Michael. *Disaster and the Millennium.* New Haven, 1974.

Baron, Hans. *The Crisis of the Early Italian Renaissance: Civic Humanism and Republican Liberty in an Age of Classicism and Tyranny.* New edition, Princeton, 1966.

Bartoli, Daniello. *Opere.* Vols. 17–20: *Dell'istoria della Compagnia di Gesù: Il Giappone seconda parte dell' Asia.* Florence, 1831–32.

Bascapè, Giacomo. "Sigilli della repubblica di Venezia. Le bolle dei dogi. I sigilli di uffici e di magistrature." In *Studi in onore di Amintore Fanfani,* vol. 1: *Antichità e alto medioevo,* pp. 91–103. Milan, 1962.

Becker, Marvin B. "Aspects of Lay Piety in Early Renaissance Florence." In *The Pursuit of Holiness in Late Medieval and Renaissance Religion,* pp. 177–99. Edited by Charles Trinkaus with Heiko A. Oberman. Leiden, 1974.

_____. "An essay on the Quest for Identity in the Early Italian Renaissance." In *Florilegium Historiale: Essays Presented to Wallace K. Ferguson,* pp. 294–312. Edited by J. G. Rowe and W. H. Stockdale. Toronto, 1971.

Bercé, Yves-Marie. *Fête et révolte: Des mentalités populaires du XVIe au XVIIIe siècle, essai.* Paris, 1976.

Berchet, Guglielmo. "La antiche ambasciate Giapponesi in Italia." *Archivio veneto* 13 (1877):245–85; 14 (1877):150–203.

Berenson, Bernard. *The Italian Painters of the Renaissance.* Cleveland, 1957.

Bernoni, Giuseppe. *Leggende fantastiche popolari veneziane.* Venice, 1875.

Biasutti, Guglielmo. *La tradizione marciana aquileiese.* Udine, 1959.

Bibliotheca Sanctorum. Rome, 1969. S.v. "Lorenzo Giustiniano, protopatriarca di Venezia, santo," by Guglielmo di Agresti, and "Teodoro, soldato, santo, martire ad Amasea," by Agostino Amore and Maria Chiara Celletti.

Biliński, Bronisław. "Venezia nelle peregrinazioni polacche del Cinquecento e lo *Sposalizio del mare* di Giovanni Siemuszowski (1565)." In *Italia, Venezia e Polonia tra umanismo e Rinascimento*, pp. 233–90. Edited by Mieczysław Brahmer. Warsaw, 1967.

Bistort, G. *Il magistrato alle pompe nella republica di Venezia: Studio storico.* Miscellanea di storia veneta, 3d series 5. Venice, 1912.

Bloch, Marc. *Feudal Society.* Translated by L. A. Manyon. 2 vols. Chicago, 1961.

————. *The Royal Touch: Sacred Monarchy and Scrofula in England and France.* Translated by J. E. Anderson. London, 1973.

Bognetti, Gian Piero. "Natura, politica e religioni nelle origini di Venezia." In *Le origini di Venezia*, pp. 1–33. N.p., n.d. The volume includes lectures given at the Fondazione Giorgio Cini, Venice, in 1962.

Boiteux, Martine. "Carnaval annexé: Essai de lecture d'une fête romaine." *Annales: E. S. C.* 32 (1977):356–80.

Boito, Camillo, ed. *La basilica di San Marco.* Venice, 1888.

Borsook, Eve. "Art and Politics at the Medici Court I: The Funeral of Cosimo I de' Medici." *Mitteilungen des Kunsthistorischen Institutes in Florenz* 12 (1965–66):31–54.

Bossy, John. "The Counter-Reformation and the People of Catholic Europe." *Past and Present* 47 (1970):51–70.

Boucher, Bruce. "Jacopo Sansovino and the Choir of St. Mark's." *The Burlington Magazine* 118 (1976):552–66.

Bouwsma, William J. *Venice and the Defense of Republican Liberty: Renaissance Values in the Age of the Counter Reformation.* Berkeley, 1968.

————. "Venice and the Political Education of Europe." In *Renaissance Venice*, pp. 445–66. Edited by J. R. Hale. London, 1973.

Bowsky, William M. "The Anatomy of Rebellion in Fourteenth-Century Siena: From Commune to Signory?" In *Violence and Civil Disorder in Italian Cities, 1200–1500*, pp. 229–72. Edited by Lauro Martines. Berkeley, 1972.

————. "The Medieval Commune and Internal Violence: Police Power and Public Safety in Siena, 1287–1355." *American Historical Review* 73 (1967):1–17.

Branca, Vittore. "Ermolao Barbaro and Late Quattrocento Venetian Humanism." In *Renaissance Venice*, pp. 218–43. Edited by J. R. Hale. London, 1973.

Braudel, Fernand. "History and the Social Sciences." In *Economy and*

Society in Early Modern Europe: Essays from Annales, pp. 11–42. Edited by Peter Burke. New York, 1972.

————. "La vita economica di Venezia nel secolo XVI." In *La civiltà veneziana del Rinascimento*, pp. 81–102. Florence, 1958.

Brown, Alison M. "The Humanist Portrait of Cosimo de' Medici Pater Patriae." *Journal of the Warburg and Courtauld Institutes* 24 (1961):186–94.

Brown, Horatio F. *Studies in the History of Venice*. 2 vols. New York, 1907.

Brown, William Archer. "Nicolò da Ponte: The Political Career of a Sixteenth-Century Patrician." Ph.D. dissertation, New York University, 1974.

Brucker, Gene. *The Civic World of Early Renaissance Florence*. Princeton, 1977.

Brunetti, Mario. "La crisi finale della Sacra Lega (1573)." In *Miscellanea in onore di Roberto Cessi*, 2:145–55. Rome, 1958.

————. "Due dogi sotto inchiesta: Agostino Barbarigo e Leonardo Loredan." *Archivio veneto-tridentino* 7 (1925):278–329.

Bryant, Lawrence M. "*Parlementaire* Political Theory in the Parisian Royal Entry Ceremony." *Sixteenth Century Journal* 7 (1976):15–24.

Burckhardt, Jacob. *The Civilization of the Renaissance in Italy*. Translated by S. G. C. Middlemore. New York, 1958.

Burke, Peter. "Oblique Approaches to the History of Popular Culture." In *Approaches to Popular Culture*, pp. 69–84. Edited by C. W. E. Bigsby. London, 1976.

————. "Patrician Culture: Venice and Amsterdam in the Seventeenth Century." *Transactions of the Royal Historical Society*, 5th series 23 (1973):135–52.

————. *Popular Culture in Early Modern Europe*. New York, 1978.

————. *Venice and Amsterdam: A Study of Seventeenth-Century Élites*. London, 1974.

Caillois, Roger. *Les jeux et les hommes*. Paris, 1958.

Candiani, Carlo. "Antiche titoli delle chiese." In *Il culto dei santi a Venezia*, pp. 99–131. Edited by Silvio Tramontin. Biblioteca agiografica veneziana, no. 2. Venice, 1965.

Cappelletti, Giuseppe. *Storia della chiesa di Venezia dalla sua fondazione sino ai nostri giorni*. 6 vols. Venice, 1849–50.

Cappelli, A. *Cronologia, cronografia e calendario perpetuo dal principio dell'era cristiana ai giorni nostri*. Milan, 1930.

Cassa, A. *Funerali, pompe e conviti*. Brescia, 1887.

Castellan, Angel A. "Venecia como modelo de ordenamiento politico en el pensamiento italiano de los siglos xv y xvi." *Anales de historia antigua y medieval* 12 (1963– 65):7– 42.

Castellani, Carlo. *La stampa in Venezia, dalla suo origine alla morte di Aldo Manuzio seniore.* Venice, 1889.

The Catholic Encyclopedia. 1908 edition. S.v. "Calendar," by Herbert Thurston; "Candlemas," by Frederick G. Halweck; and "Orvieto," by W. Benigni.

Cecchetti, Bartolomeo. "La donna nel medioevo a Venezia." *Archivio veneto,* new series 31 (1886):33– 69, 305– 45.

_____. "Gli stendardi della piazza di S. Marco nel 1600, e la bandiera del comune di Venezia nel 1886." *Archivio veneto,* new series 31 (1886):284.

Cessi, Roberto. "L'investitura ducale." *Atti dell'Istituto Veneto di Scienze, Lettere ed Arti* 126 (1967– 68):251– 94.

_____. *Le origini del ducato veneziano.* Naples, n.d.

_____. *Storia della repubblica di Venezia.* 2 vols. Milan, 1968.

_____. *Venezia ducale.* 2 vols. Venice, 1963– 65.

Chabod, Federico. "Venezia nella politica italiana ed europea del Cinquecento." In *La civiltà veneziana del Rinascimento,* pp. 27– 55. Florence, 1958.

Chambers, D. S. *The Imperial Age of Venice, 1380–1580.* London, 1970.

Charanis, Peter. "Coronation and Its Constitutional Significance in the Later Roman Empire." *Byzantion* 15 (1940– 41):49– 66.

Chartrou, Josèphe. *Les entrées solennelles et triomphales à la Renaissance (1485–1551).* Paris, 1928.

Chastel, André. "Le lieu de la fête." In *Les fêtes de la Renaissance,* 1:419– 23. Edited by Jean Jacquot. Paris, 1956.

Chew, Samuel C. "The Allegorical Chariot in English Literature of the Renaissance." In *Essays in Honor of Erwin Panofsky,* pp. 37– 54. Edited by Millard Meiss. New York, 1961.

Chojnacki, Stanley. "Crime, Punishment, and the Trecento Venetian State." In *Violence and Civil Disorder in Italian Cities, 1200– 1500,* pp. 184– 228. Edited by Lauro Martines. Berkeley, 1972.

_____. "Dowries and Kinsmen in Early Renaissance Venice." *The Journal of Interdisciplinary History* 5 (1975):571– 600.

_____. "In Search of the Venetian Patriciate: Families and Factions in the Fourteenth Century." In *Renaissance Venice,* pp. 47– 90. Edited by J. R. Hale. London, 1973.

_____. "Patrician Women in Early Renaissance Venice." *Studies in the Renaissance* 21 (1974):176– 203.

Cicogna, Emmanuele Antonio. *Delle inscrizioni veneziane*. 6 vols. Venice, 1827.

Cochrane, Eric, and Kirshner, Julius. "Deconstructing Lane's *Venice*." *Journal of Modern History* 47 (1975):321–34.

Cohn, Norman. *The Pursuit of the Millennium: Revolutionary Millenarians and Mystical Anarchists of the Middle Ages*. Revised edition, New York, 1970.

Corner, Flaminio. *Ecclesiae Venetae*. . . . Venice, 1745.

Cozzi, Gaetano. "Appunti sul teatro e i teatri a Venezia agli inizi del seicento." *Bollettino dell'Istituto di Storia della Società e dello Stato Veneziano* 1 (1959):187–92.

————. "Authority and the Law in Renaissance Venice." In *Renaissance Venice*, pp. 293–345. Edited by J. R. Hale. London, 1973.

————. "Cultura, politica e religione nella 'pubblica storiografia' veneziana del '500." *Bollettino dell'Istituto di Storia della Società e dello Stato Veneziano* 5–6 (1963–64):215–94.

————. *Il Doge Nicolò Contarini: Ricerche sul patriziato veneziano agli inizi del Seicento*. Venice, 1958.

————. "Domenico Morosini e il *De bene instituta re publica*." *Studi veneziani* 12 (1970):405–58.

————. "Marin Sanudo il giovane: Dalla cronaca alla storia." In *La storiografia veneziana fino al secolo XVI: Aspetti e problemi*, pp. 333–58. Edited by Agostino Pertusi. Florence, 1970.

————. "Paolo Paruta, Paolo Sarpi e la questione della sovranità su Ceneda." *Bollettino dell'Istituto di Storia della Società e dello Stato Veneziano* 4 (1962):176–237.

Cracco, Giorgio. *Società e stato nel medioevo veneziano (secoli XII–XIV)*. Florence, 1967.

Cross, F. L., ed. *The Oxford Dictionary of the Christian Church*. Oxford, 1958.

Darnton, Robert. "Reading, Writing, and Publishing in Eighteenth-Century France: A Case Study in the Sociology of Literature." *Daedalus* 100 (1971):214–56.

Davis, Charles T. "Roman Patriotism and Republican Propaganda: Ptolemy of Lucca and Pope Nicholas III." *Speculum* 50 (1975):411–33.

Davis, James Cushman. *The Decline of the Venetian Nobility as a Ruling Class*. The Johns Hopkins University Studies in Historical and Political Science, series 80, no. 2. Baltimore, 1962.

————. *A Venetian Family and Its Fortune, 1500–1900: The Donà and the Conservation of Their Wealth*. Memoirs of the American

Philosophical Society, no. 106. Philadelphia, 1975.

Davis, Natalie Zemon. "The Reasons of Misrule: Youth Groups and Charivaris in Sixteenth-Century France." *Past and Present* 50 (1971):41–75.

_____. "The Rites of Violence: Religious Riot in Sixteenth-Century France." *Past and Present* 59 (1973):51–91.

_____. *Society and Culture in Early Modern France.* Stanford, 1975.

_____. "Some Tasks and Themes in the Study of Popular Religion." In *The Pursuit of Holiness in Late Medieval and Renaissance Religion,* pp. 307–36. Edited by Charles Trinkaus with Heiko A. Oberman. Leiden, 1974.

Dazzi, Manlio. *Feste e costumi di Venezia.* Venice, n.d.

_____. *Il fiore della lirica veneziana.* 2 vols. Venice, 1956.

De Groot, Adriaan D. *Saint Nicholas: A Psychoanalytic Study of His History and Myth.* New York, 1965.

Delehaye, Hippolyte. *Les légendes greques des saints militaires.* Paris, 1909. Reprint, New York, 1975.

Demus, Otto. *The Church of San Marco in Venice: History, Architecture, Sculpture.* Dumbarton Oaks Studies, no. 6. Washington, 1960.

_____. "A Renascence of Early Christian Art in Thirteenth Century Venice." In *Late Classical and Medieval Studies in Honor of Albert Mathias Friend, Jr.,* pp. 348–61. Edited by Kurt Weitzmann. Princeton, 1955.

Dickens, A. G., ed. *The Courts of Europe: Politics, Patronage and Royalty: 1400–1800.* London, 1977.

Douglas, Mary. *Natural Symbols: Explorations in Cosmology.* New York, 1973.

Dundes, Alan, and Falassi, Alessandro. *La Terra in Piazza: An Interpretation of the Palio of Siena.* Berkeley, 1975.

Ell, Stephen Richard. "Citizenship and Immigration in Venice, 1305 to 1500." Ph.D. dissertation, University of Chicago, 1976.

Endrei, Walter. "Mutation d'une allégorie: L'hiver et la sacrifice du nouvel-an." *Annales: E. S. C.* 21 (1966):982–89.

Epstein, Donald Bernard. *Francesco Sansovino (1523–1583) and Venetian Political Thought.* Ph.D. dissertation, University of Oregon, 1971.

Erdmann, Carl. *The Origin of the Idea of Crusade.* Translated by Marshall W. Baldwin and Walter Goffart. Princeton, 1977.

Estebe, Janine. "The Rites of Violence: Religious Riot in Sixteenth-Century France, a Comment." *Past and Present* 67 (1975):127–30.

Fabre, Daniel. "Le monde du carnaval." *Annales: E. S. C.* 31 (1976):389– 406.

Fasoli, Gina. "Comune veneciarum." In Fasoli, *Scritti di storia medievale*, pp. 473– 97. Edited by F. Bocchi, A. Carile, and A. I. Pini. Bologna, 1974.

———. "La coscienza civica nelle 'laudes civitatum.' " In Fasoli, *Scritti di storia medievale*, pp. 293– 318. Edited by F. Bocchi, A. Carile, and A. I. Pini. Bologna, 1974.

———. "I fondamenti della storiografia veneziana." In Fasoli, *Scritti di storia medievale*, pp. 499– 527. Edited by F. Bocchi, A. Carile, and A. I. Pini. Bologna, 1974.

———. "Liturgia e cerimoniale ducale." In *Venezia e il Levante fino al secolo XV*, 1:261– 95. Edited by Agostino Pertusi. Florence, 1973.

———. "Nascita di un mito." In *Studi storici in onore di Gioacchino Volpe* 1:445– 79. Florence, 1958.

Ferro, Marco. *Dizionario del diritto comune e Veneto.* 2 vols. 2d edition, Venice, 1845– 47.

Fietta, Lorenzo. "Catterina Corner del Dott. Enrico Simonsfeld." *Archivio veneto*, new series 21 (1881):40– 81.

Filiasi, Jacopo. *Memoria sopra il corpo di S. Marco.* Venice, 1813.

———. *Memorie storiche de' Veneti primi e secondi.* 7 vols. Padua, 1811– 14.

Fink, Zera S. *The Classical Republicans: An Essay in the Recovery of a Pattern of Thought in Seventeenth-Century England.* 2d edition, Evanston, Illinois, 1962.

———. "Venice and English Political Thought in the Seventeenth Century." *Modern Philology* 38 (1940– 41):155– 72.

Finlay, Robert. *Politics in Renaissance Venice.* New Brunswick, New Jersey, 1980.

———. "The Venetian Republic as a Gerontocracy: Age and Politics in the Renaissance." *The Journal of Medieval and Renaissance Studies* 8 (1978):157– 78.

———. "Venice, the Po Expedition, and the End of the League of Cambrai, 1509– 1510." *Studies in Modern European History and Culture* 2 (1976):37– 72.

Forster, Kurt W. "Metaphors of Rule: Political Ideology and History in the Portraits of Cosimo I de' Medici." *Mitteilungen des Kunsthistorischen Institutes im Florenz* 15 (1971):65– 90.

Fowler, W. Warde. *The Roman Festivals of the Period of the Republic.* London, 1925.

Francastel, Galienne. "Une peinture anti-hérétique à Venise?" *Annales: E. S. C.* 20 (1965):1– 17.

BIBLIOGRAPHY: SECONDARY SOURCES

Franceschini, Ezio. "La cronachetta di Maestro Jacopo Dondi." *Atti del Reale Istituto Veneto di Scienze, Lettere ed Arti* 99 (1939–40):969–84.

Frankfort, H. "State Festivals in Egypt and Mesopotamia." *Journal of the Warburg and Courtauld Institutes* 15 (1952):1–12.

Gaeta, Franco. "Alcuni considerazioni sul mito di Venezia." *Bibliothèque d'humanisme et Renaissance* 23 (1961):58–75.

Gaignebet, Claude. "Le combat de carnaval et de câreme de P. Bruegel (1559)." *Annales: E. S. C.* 27 (1972):313–45.

————, and Florentin, Marie-Claude. *Le carnaval: Essais de mythologie populaire*. Paris, 1974.

Gallicciolli, G. B. *Storie e memorie venete profane ed ecclesiastiche*. 8 vols. Venice, 1795.

Garosci, Aldo. "La formazione del mito di San Marino." *Rivista storica italiana* 71 (1959):21–47.

Geary, Patrick J. *Furta Sacra: Thefts of Relics in The Central Middle Ages*. Princeton, 1978.

Geertz, Clifford. "Centers, Kings, and Charisma: Reflections on the Symbolics of Power." In *Culture and Its Creators: Essays in Honor of Edward Shils*, pp. 150–71. Edited by Joseph Ben-David and Terry Nichols Clark. Chicago, 1977.

————. *The Interpretation of Cultures*. New York, 1973.

————, ed. *Myth, Symbol, and Culture*. New York, 1971.

Ghinzoni, P. "Federico III imperatore à Venezia (7 al 19 febbraio 1469)," *Archivio veneto*, new series 37 (1889):133–44.

Gianturco, Elio. "Bodin's Conception of the Venetian Constitution and His Critical Rift with Fabio Albergati." *Revue di littérature comparée* 18 (1938):684–95.

Giesey, Ralph E. "The Presidents of Parlement at the Royal Funeral." *Sixteenth Century Journal* 7 (1976):25–34.

————. *The Royal Funeral Ceremony in Renaissance France*. Geneva, 1960.

Gilbert, Creighton. "A Sarasota Note Book: III, Ahasuerus and Henri III." *Arte veneta* 15 (1961):42–45.

Gilbert, Felix. "Bernardo Rucellai and the Orti Oricellari: A Study on the Origin of Modern Political Thought." *Journal of the Warburg and Courtauld Institutes* 12 (1949):101–31.

————. "Biondo, Sabellico, and the Beginnings of Venetian Official Historiography." In *Florilegium Historiale: Essays Presented to Wallace K. Ferguson*, pp. 275–93. Edited by J. G. Rowe and W. H. Stockdale. Toronto, 1971.

————. "The Date of the Composition of Contarini's and Giannotti's

Books on Venice." *Studies in the Renaissance* 14 (1967):172–84.

————. *History: Choice and Commitment.* Cambridge, Massachusetts, 1977.

————. "The Last Will of a Venetian Grand Chancellor." In *Philosophy and Humanism: Renaissance Essays in Honor of Paul Oskar Kristeller,* pp. 502–17. Edited by Edward P. Mahoney. Leiden, 1976.

————. "Machiavelli e Venezia." *Lettere italiane* 21 (1969):389–98.

————. "Religion and Politics in the Thought of Gasparo Contarini." In *Action and Conviction in Early Modern Europe: Essays in Memory of E. H. Harbison,* pp. 90–116. Edited by Theodore K. Rabb and Jerrold E. Seigel. Princeton, 1969.

————. "The Venetian Constitution in Florentine Political Thought." In *Florentine Studies,* pp. 463–500. Edited by Nicolai Rubinstein. London, 1968.

————. "Venetian Diplomacy before Pavia: From Reality to Myth." In *The Diversity of History: Essays in Honour of Sir Herbert Butterfield,* pp. 81–116. Edited by J. H. Elliott and H. G. Koenigsberger. London, n.d.

————. "Venice in the Crisis of the League of Cambrai." In *Renaissance Venice,* pp. 274–92. Edited by J. R. Hale. London, 1973.

Gilmore, Myron P. "Myth and Reality in Venetian Political Theory." In *Renaissance Venice,* pp. 431–43. Edited by J. R. Hale. London, 1973.

Giomo, G. "Le spese del nobil uomo Marino Grimani nella sua elezione a doge di Venezia." *Archivio veneto,* new series 33 (1887):443–54.

Goffman, Erving. *The Presentation of Self in Everyday Life.* Garden City, New York, 1959.

Goldthwaite, Richard A. *Private Wealth in Renaissance Florence: A Study of Four Families.* Princeton, 1968.

Gombrich, E. H. "Celebrations in Venice of the Holy League and of the Victory of Lepanto." In *Studies in Renaissance & Baroque Art Presented to Anthony Blunt on His 60th Birthday,* pp. 62–68. London, n.d.

Goody, Jack. "Religion and Ritual: The Definitional Problem." *The British Journal of Sociology* 12 (1961):142–64.

Graef, Hilda. *Mary: A History of Doctrine and Devotion.* Vol. 1: *From the Beginnings to the Eve of the Reformation.* London, 1963.

Grendler, Paul F. "Francesco Sansovino and Italian Popular History,

BIBLIOGRAPHY: SECONDARY SOURCES

1560–1600." *Studies in the Renaissance* 16 (1969):139–80.
————. "The Roman Inquisition and the Venetian Press, 1540–1605." *The Journal of Modern History* 47 (1975):48–65.
————. *The Roman Inquisition and the Venetian Press, 1540–1605.* Princeton, 1977.
Gundersheimer, Werner L. *Ferrara: The Style of a Renaissance Despotism.* Princeton, 1973.
Hale, J. R. *England and the Italian Renaissance: The Growth of Interest in its History and Art.* London, 1954.
Halkin, François. "Saint Marc dans l'hagiographie byzantine." *Studi veneziani* 12 (1970):29–34.
Halpern, Ben. " 'Myth' and 'Ideology' in Modern Usage." *History and Theory* 1 (1961):129–49.
Hammer, William. "The Concept of the New or Second Rome in the Middle Ages." *Speculum* 19 (1944):50–62.
Hay, James F. "On the Relationship of the Corpus Christi Plays to the Corpus Christi Procession at York." *Modern Philology* 71 (1973):166–68.
Heers, Jacques. *Family Clans in the Middle Ages: A Study of Political and Social Structures in Urban Areas.* Translated by Barry Herbert. Amsterdam, 1977.
————. *Fêtes, jeux et joutes dans les sociétés d'Occident à la fin du moyen âge.* Montreal, 1971.
Herlihy, David. "The Population of Verona in the First Century of Venetian Rule." In *Renaissance Venice,* pp. 91–120. Edited by J. R. Hale. London, 1973.
————, and Klapisch-Zuber, Christiane. *Les Toscans et leurs familles: Une étude du catasto florentin de 1427.* Paris, 1978.
Hermann-Mascard, Nicole. *Les reliques des saints: Formation contumière d'un droit.* Société d'histoire du droit: Collection d'histoire institutionelle et sociale, no. 6. Paris, 1975.
Howard, Deborah. *Jacopo Sansovino: Architecture and Patronage in Renaissance Venice.* New Haven, 1975.
Hughes, Diane Owen. "Urban Growth and Family Structure in Medieval Genoa." *Past and Present* 66 (1975):3–28.
Huizinga, Johan. *Homo Ludens: A Study of the Play-Element in Culture.* Boston, 1950.
————. *The Waning of the Middle Ages.* Garden City, New York, 1954.
Huxley, Sir Julian, ed. *A Discussion on Ritualization of Behaviour in Animals and Man.* Philosophical Transactions of the Royal Soci-

ety of London, series B. no. 251. London, 1966.

Ivanoff, Nicolas. "Henri III a Venise." *Gazette des beaux-arts* 80 (1972):313–30.

Jackson, Richard A. "A Little-Known Description of Charles IX's Coronation." *Renaissance Quarterly* 25 (1972):289–96.

————. "The Sleeping King." *Bibliothèque d'humanisme et Renaissance* 31 (1969):535–39.

James, E. O. *Seasonal Feasts and Festivals*. New York, 1961.

Jones, Charles W. *The Saint Nicholas Liturgy and Its Literary Relationships (Ninth to Twelfth Centuries)*. With an essay on the music by Gilbert Reaney. Berkeley, 1963.

————. *Saint Nicholas of Myra, Bari, and Manhattan: Biography of a Legend*. Chicago, 1978.

Jones, P. J. "Communes and Despots: The City State in Late-Medieval Italy." *Transactions of the Royal Historical Society*, 5th series 15 (1965):71–96.

Kantorowicz, Ernst H. "Deus per Naturam, Deus per Gratiam: A Note on Medieval Political Theology." *The Harvard Theological Review* 45 (1952):253–77. Reprinted in his *Selected Studies*, Locust Valley, New York, 1965.

————. "The 'King's Advent' and the Enigmatic Panels in the Doors of Santa Sabina." *The Art Bulletin* 26 (1944):207–31.

————. *The King's Two Bodies: A Study in Medieval Political Theology*. Princeton, 1957.

————. *Laudes Regiae: A Study in Liturgical Acclamations and Medieval Ruler Worship*. University of California Publications in History, no. 33. Berkeley, 1946.

————. "Mysteries of State: An Absolutist Concept and Its Late Medieval Origins." *The Harvard Theological Review* 48 (1955):65–91. Reprinted in his *Selected Studies*, pp. 381–98, Locust Valley, New York, 1965.

Kent, Dale. "The Florentine *Reggimento* in the Fifteenth Century." *Renaissance Quarterly* 28 (1975):575–638.

————. *The Rise of the Medici: Faction in Florence, 1426–1434*. Oxford, 1978.

Kent, Francis William. *Household and Lineage in Renaissance Florence: The Family Life of the Capponi, Ginori, and Rucellai*. Princeton, 1976.

Kernodle, George R. "Déroulement de la procession dans les temps au espace theâtral dans les fêtes de la Renaissance." In *Les fêtes de la Renaissance*, 1:443–49. Edited by Jean Jacquot. Paris, 1956.

BIBLIOGRAPHY: SECONDARY SOURCES

King, Margaret L. "Personal, Domestic, and Republican Values in the Moral Philosophy of Giovanni Caldiera." *Renaissance Quarterly* 28 (1975):535–74.

Kirshner, Julius. "Civitas Sibi Faciat Civem: Bartolus of Sassoferrato's Doctrine on the Making of a Citizen." *Speculum* 48 (1973):694–713.

Koranyi, Karol. "La costituzione di Venezia nel pensiero politico della Polonia." In *Italia, Venezia e Polonia tra umanesimo e Rinascimento*, pp. 206–14. Edited by Mieczysław Brahmer. Warsaw, 1967.

Labalme, Patricia H. *Bernardo Giustiniani: A Venetian of the Quattrocento.* Rome, 1969.

Lane, Frederic C. "At the Roots of Republicanism." *American Historical Review* 71 (1966):403–20. Reprinted in *Venice and History: The Collected Papers of Frederic C. Lane*, pp. 520–37, Baltimore, 1966.

————. "The Enlargement of the Great Council of Venice." In *Florilegium Historiale: Essays Presented to Wallace K. Ferguson*, pp. 236–74. Edited by J. G. Rowe and W. H. Stockdale. Toronto, 1971.

————. "Medieval Political Ideas and the Venetian Constitution." In *Venice and History: The Collected Papers of Frederic C. Lane*, pp. 285–307. Baltimore, 1966.

————. "Naval Actions and Fleet Organization, 1499–1502." In *Renaissance Venice*, pp. 146–73. Edited by J. R. Hale. London, 1973.

————. *Venice: A Maritime Republic.* Baltimore, 1973.

Lanzoni, Francesco. *Genesi svolgimento e tramonto delle leggende storiche.* Studi e testi, no. 43. Rome, 1925.

Law, John Easton. "Age Qualification and the Venetian Constitution: The Case of the Capello Family." *Papers of the British School at Rome* 39 (1971):125–37.

Lazzarini, Vittorio. "Marino Falier: La congiura." *Archivio veneto* 13 (1897):5–107, 277–374.

————. "Il preteso documento della fondazione di Venezia e la cronaca del medico Jacopo Dondi." *Atti del Reale Istituto Veneto di Scienze, Lettere ed Arti* 75 (1915–16):1263–77.

————. "I titoli dei dogi di Venezia." *Nuovo archivio veneto*, new series 5 (1903):271–313.

Lee, A. C. *The Decameron: Its Sources and Analogues.* London, 1909.

Le Roy Ladurie, Emmanuel. *Montaillou: The Promised Land of Error.* Translated by Barbara Bray. New York, 1978.

————. *The Peasants of Languedoc.* Translated by John Day. Urbana, Illinois, 1974.*

Lévi-Strauss, Claude. *Structural Anthropology.* Garden City, New York, 1967.

Libby, Lester J., Jr. "The Reconquest of Padua in 1509 According to the Diary of Girolamo Priuli." *Renaissance Quarterly* 28 (1975):323–31.

————. "Venetian History and Political Thought after 1509." *Studies in the Renaissance* 20 (1973):7–45.

Lievsay, John Leon. *Venetian Phoenix: Paolo Sarpi and Some of His English Friends (1606–1700).* Lawrence, Kansas, 1973.

Logan, Alice Pomponio. "The Palio of Siena: Performance and Process." *Urban Anthropology* 7 (1978):45–65.

Logan, Oliver. *Culture and Society in Venice, 1470–1790: The Renaissance and Its Heritage.* London, 1972.

Lotz, Wolfgang. "Sixteenth-Century Italian Squares." In Lotz, *Studies in Italian Renaissance Architecture*, pp. 74–116. Cambridge, Massachusetts, 1977.

Lowry, Martin John Clement. "The Reform of the Council of Ten, 1582–3: An Unsettled Problem?" *Studi veneziani* 13 (1971):275–310.

————. "Two Great Venetian Libraries in the Age of Aldus Manutius." *Bulletin of the John Rylands University Library of Manchester* 57 (1974):128–66.

McCleary, Nelson. "Note storiche ed archeologiche sul testo della 'Translatio Sancti Marci.'" *Memorie storiche forogiuliesi* 27–29 (1931–33):223–64.

McNeill, William H. *Venice: The Hinge of Europe, 1081–1797.* Chicago, 1974.

Madden, Sarah Hanley. "The *Lit de Justice* and the Fundamental Law." *Sixteenth Century Journal* 7 (1976):3–14.

Mâle, Emile. *The Gothic Image: Religious Art in France of the Thirteenth Century.* Translated by Dora Nussey. New York, 1958.

Mallett, Michael. "Venice and Its Condottieri, 1404–54." In *Renaissance Venice*, pp. 121–45. Edited by J. R. Hale. London, 1973.

Mandowsky, Erna. *Ricerche intorno all'Iconologia di Cesare Ripa.* Florence, 1939.

Maranini, Giuseppe. *La costituzione di Venezia dopo la serrata del maggior consiglio.* Venice, 1931.

Maretto, Paolo. *Studi per una operante storia urbana di Venezia.* Vol. 2 subtitled: *L'edilizia gotica veneziana.* "Palladio" Rivista di storia dell'architettura. Vicenza, 1960.

Mariani Canova, Giordano. "La decorazione dei documenti ufficiali in Venezia." *Atti dell'Istituto Veneto di Scienze, Lettere ed Arti* 126 (1967–68):319–34.

Marx, Leo. Comments on "The Aging of America," by C. Vann Woodward. *American Historical Review* 82 (1977):595–99.

Mathews, Jane de Hart. "Art and Politics in Cold War America." *American Historical Review* 81 (1976):762–87.

Matteucci, Nicola. "Machiavelli, Harrington, Montesquieu e gli 'ordini' di Venezia." *Il pensiero politico* 3 (1970):337–69.

Mauss, Marcel. *The Gift: Forms and Functions of Exchange in Archaic Society.* New York, 1967.

Medin, Antonio. *La storia della repubblica di Venezia nella poesia.* Milan, 1904.

Meiss, Millard. "Sleep in Venice: Ancient Myths and Renaissance Proclivities." *Proceedings of the American Philosophical Society* 110 (1966):348–62.

Menzies, Lucy. *The Saints in Italy.* London, 1924.

Michiel, Giustina Renier. *Le origine delle feste veneziane.* 6 vols. Milan, 1817. 2d edition, Milan, 1829. Citations are to the first edition.

Miozzi, Eugenio. *Venezia nei secoli.* 2 vols. Venice, 1957.

Molmenti, Pompeo G. *La dogaressa di Venezia.* 2d edition, Turin, 1887.

_____. "Le leggende e i ricordi storici di San Marco." In *La basilica di San Marco*, pp. 7–16. Venice, 1888.

_____, ed. *Sebastiano Veniero dopo la battaglia di Lepanto.* Venice, 1915.

_____. *La storia di Venezia nella vita privata dalle origini alla caduta della repubblica.* 3 vols. 2d edition, Bergamo, 1910–12.

_____. *Venice: Its Individual Growth from the Earliest Beginnings to the Fall of the Republic.* Translated by Horatio F. Brown. 6 vols. Chicago, 1906.

Monticolo, G. "L'apparitio Sancti Marci ed i suoi manoscritti." *Nuovo archivio veneto* 9 (1895):111–77, 475–82.

_____. "La costituzione del Doge Pietro Polani (febbraio 1143, 1142 more veneto) circa la processo scolarum." *Rendiconti di Reale Accademia dei Lincei* 9 (1900):91–133. Reprinted as a separate extract, Rome, 1900.

Moore, Sally F., and Myerhoff, Barbara G., eds. *Secular Ritual.* Amsterdam, 1977.

_____, eds. *Symbol and Politics in Communal Ideology: Cases and Questions.* Ithaca, 1975.

Mor, Carlo Guido. "Aspetti della vita costituzionale veneziana fino alla fine del x secolo." In *Le origini di Venezia*, pp. 121–40. N.p., n.d.

Morelli, Iacopo. *Operette.* 2 vols. Venice, 1820.

Moro, Isa. *I dogi di Venezia: Congiure, eroisimi, torture.* Milan, 1968.

Morsolin, Bernardo. "Un episodio della vita di Carlo Quinto." *Archivio veneto,* new series 27 (1884):293–320.

Mosto, Andrea da. *L'Archivio di Stato di Venezia: Indice generale, storico, descrittivo ed analitico.* 2 vols. Rome, 1937–40.

————. *I dogi di Venezia nella vita pubblica e privata.* Milan, n.d.

Mousnier, Roland. "Le trafic des offices à Venise." *Revue historique de droit français et étranger,* 4th series 30 (1952):552–66.

Mueller, Reinhold C. "Charitable Institutions, the Jewish Community, and Venetian Society. A Discussion of the Recent Volume by Brian Pullan." *Studi veneziani* 14 (1972):37–81.

————. "The Procurators of San Marco in the Thirteenth and Fourteenth Centuries: A Study of the Office as a Financial and Trust Institution." *Studi veneziani* 13 (1971):105–220.

Muir, Edward. "The Doge as *Primus Inter Pares:* Interregnum Rites in Early Sixteenth-Century Venice." In *Essays Presented to Myron P. Gilmore,* 1:145–60. Edited by Sergio Bertelli and Gloria Ramakus. Florence, 1978.

————. "Images of Power: Art and Pageantry in Renaissance Venice." *American Historical Review* 84 (1979):16–52.

Muraro, Maria Teresa. "Le lieu des spectacles (publics ou privés) à Venise au xvᵉ et au xviᵉ siècles." In *Le lieu théâtral à la Renaissance,* pp. 85–93. Edited by Jean Jacquot. Paris, 1964.

Muraro, Michelangelo. "Palladio et l'urbanisme vénitien." In *L'urbanisme de Paris e l'Europe, 1600–1680,* pp. 211–17. Edited by Pierre Francastel. Paris, 1969.

————. "La scala senza giganti." In *Essays in Honor of Erwin Panofsky,* pp. 350–70. Edited by Millard Meiss. New York, 1961.

————. "Venezia: Interpretazione del palazzo ducale." *Studi urbinati di storia, filosofia e letteratura* 45 (1971):1160–93.

————. "Vittore Carpaccio o il teatro in pittura." In *Studi sul teatro veneto fra Rinascimento ed età barocca,* pp. 7–19. Edited by Maria Teresa Muraro. Florence, 1971.

Muratori, Saverio. *Studi per una operante storia urbana di Venezia.* Vol. 1: "Palladio" Rivista di storia dell'architettura. Vicenza, 1959.

Musatti, Eugenio. *La donna in Venezia.* Padua, 1891.

————. *Storia della promissione ducale.* Padua, 1888.

Musolino, Giovanni. "Culto mariano." In *Il culto dei santi a Venezia,* pp. 239–74. Edited by Silvio Tramontin. Biblioteca agiografica veneziana, no. 2. Venice, 1965.

————. "Feste religiose popolari." In *Il culto dei santi a Venezia,* pp.

209–37. Edited by Silvio Tramontin. Biblioteca agiografica veneziana, no. 2. Venice, 1965.

————; Niero, A.; and Tramontin, S. *Santi e beati veneziani: Quaranta profili.* Venice, 1963.

Mutinelli, Fabio. *Annali urbani di Venezia dall'anno 810 al 12 maggio 1797.* Venice, 1841.

————. *Storia arcana ed aneddotica d'Italia raccontata dai veneti ambasciatori.* Venice, 1855.

Najemy, John M. "Guild Republicanism in Trecento Florence: The Successes and Ultimate Failure of Corporate Politics." *American Historical Review* 84 (1979):53–71.

Nani-Mocenigo, Filippo. "Testamento del Doge Agostino Barbarigo." *Nuovo archivio veneto,* new series 17 (1909):234–61.

Nelson, Janet L. "Symbols in Context: Rulers' Inauguration Rituals in Byzantium and the West in the Early Middle Ages." *Studies in Church History* 13 (1977):97–119.

Nerfa, V. Trojani di. *Sagre, feste e riti.* Rome, 1932.

Newett, M. Margaret. "The Sumptuary Laws of Venice in the Fourteenth and Fifteenth Centuries." In *Historical Essays by Members of the Owens College, Manchester, Published in Commemoration of Its Jubilee, 1851–1901,* pp. 245–77. London, n.d.

Nicol, D. M. "*Kaiseralbung.* The Unction of Emperors in Late Byzantine Coronation Ritual." *Byzantine and Modern Greek Studies* 2 (1976):37–52.

Nicoletti, Giuseppe. "Dei banchetti pubblici al tempo della repubblica veneta." *Archivio veneto,* new series 33 (1887):165–69.

————. *Intorno alla acconciatura del capo o calzature delle donne veneziane, sec. XV e XVI.* Venice, 1884.

Niero, Antonio. "Culto dei santi dell'antico testamento." In *Il culto dei santi a Venezia,* pp. 155–80. Edited by Silvio Tramontin. Biblioteca agiografica veneziana, no. 2. Venice, 1965.

————. "Questioni agiografiche su San Marco." *Studi veneziani* 12 (1970):3–27.

————. "Reliquie e corpi di santi." In *Il culto dei santi a Venezia,* pp. 181–208. Edited by Silvio Tramontin. Biblioteca agiografica veneziana, no. 2. Venice, 1965.

————. "I santi patroni." In *Il culto dei santi a Venezia,* pp. 75–98. Edited by Silvio Tramontin. Biblioteca agiografica veneziana, no. 2. Venice, 1965.

Nolhac, Pier di, and Solerti, Angelo. *Il viaggio in Italia di Enrico III re di Francia e le feste a Venezia, Ferrara, Mantova, e Torino.* Turin, 1890.

Olivieri, Achille. " 'Dio' e 'fortuna' nelle *Lettere storiche* di Luigi da Porto." *Studi veneziane* 13 (1971):253–73.

Padoan, Giorgio. "Sulla novella veneziana del 'Decameron' (IV 2)." *Studi sul Boccaccio* 10 (1977–78):170–200. Republished in *Boccaccio, Venezia e il Veneto*, pp. 17–46, edited by Vittore Branca and Giorgio Padoan, Florence, 1979.

Parks, George B. *The English Traveler to Italy.* Rome, 1954.

Pasini, Antonio. "Rito antico e cerimoniale della basilica." In *La basilica di San Marco*, pp. 65–71. Venice, 1888.

Pasqualigo, Cristoforo. *Raccolta di proverbi veneti.* Treviso, 1882.

Pecchioli, Renzo. "Il 'mito' di Venezia e la crisi fiorentina intorno al 1500." *Studi storici* 3 (1962):451–92.

Pellanda, Antonio, ed. *Festa del Giovedì Grasso (Sei documenti di storia veneziana).* Venice, 1879.

————, ed. *A Giacinto de Mitri nel giorno faustissimo del suo matrimonio colla gentile Signora Erminia Bolliana.* Venice, 1878.

Perkinson, Richard H. " 'Volpone' and the Reputation of Venetian Justice." *Modern Language Review* 35 (1940):11–18.

Pertusi, Agostino. "Le fonti greche del 'De gestis, moribus et nobilitate civitatis Venetiarum' di Lorenzo de Monacis cancelliere di Creta (1388–1428)." *Italia medioevale e umanistica* 8 (1965):161–211.

————. "Gli inizi della storiografia umanistica nel Quattrocento." In *La storiografia veneziana fino al secolo XVI: Aspetti e problemi*, pp. 269–332. Edited by Agostino Pertusi. Florence, 1970.

————. "Quedam regalia insignia: ricerche sulle insegne del potere ducale à Venezia durante il medioevo." *Studi veneziani* 7 (1965):3–123.

Peyer, Hans Conrad. *Stadt und Stadtpatron im mittelalterlichen Italien.* Zurich, 1955.

Piave, F. M. "Feste fatte in Venezia pella incoronazione della serenissima Dogaressa Morosina Morosini Grimani." *Emporio artistico letterario* 2 (n.d.):9–13, 49–52.

Pilot, Antonio. "L'elezione del Doge Marino Grimani." *Pagine istriane* 2 (1904):53–59.

————. "Del protestantesimo a Venezia e delle poesie religiose di Celio Magno (1536–1602)." *L'ateneo veneto* 32 (1909):199–233.

————. "Il ratto delle 'novizze' veneziane." *Pagine istriane* 8 (1911):3–16.

Pincus, Debra. *The Arco Foscari: The Building of a Triumphal Gateway in Fifteenth Century Venice.* Outstanding Dissertations in the Fine Arts. New York, 1976.

Piovene, Guido. "Anacronismo della Venezia quattrocentesca." In *La*

BIBLIOGRAPHY: SECONDARY SOURCES

civiltà veneziana del Quattrocento, pp. 3–21. Florence, 1957.

Pocock, J. G. A. *The Machiavellian Moment: Florentine Political Thought and the Atlantic Republican Tradition*. Princeton, 1975.

Pope-Hennessy, John. *Italian High Renaissance and Baroque Sculpture*. 2d edition, London, 1970.

Post, Gaines. *Studies in Medieval Legal Thought: Public Law and the State, 1100–1322*. Princeton, 1964.

Prodi, Paolo. "The Structure and Organization of the Church in Renaissance Venice: Suggestions for Research." In *Renaissance Venice*, pp. 409–30. Edited by J. R. Hale. London, 1973.

Pullan, Brian. "The Occupations and Investments of the Venetian Nobility in the Middle and Late Sixteenth Century." In *Renaissance Venice*, pp. 379–408. Edited by J. R. Hale. London, 1973.

―――――. "Poverty, Charity, and the Reason of State: Some Venetian Examples." *Bollettino dell'Istituto di Storia della Società e dello Stato Veneziano* 2 (1960):17–60.

―――――. *Rich and Poor in Renaissance Venice: The Social Institutions of a Catholic State, to 1620*. Oxford, 1971.

―――――. " 'A Ship with Two Rudders': 'Righetto Marrano' and the Inquisition in Venice." *The Historical Journal* 20 (1977):25–58.

―――――. "The Significance of Venice." *Bulletin of the John Rylands University Library of Manchester* 56 (1974):443–62.

Quarti, Guido Antonio. *La battaglia di Lepanto nei canti popolari dell'epoca*. Milan, 1930.

Queller, Donald E. "The Civic Irresponsibility of the Venetian Nobility." In *Economy, Society, and Government in Medieval Italy: Essays in Memory of Robert L. Reynolds*, pp. 223–36. Edited by David Herlihy, Robert S. Lopez, and Vsevolod Slessarev. Kent, Ohio, 1969.

―――――. "The Development of Ambassadorial *Relazioni*." In *Renaissance Venice*, pp. 174–96. Edited by J. R. Hale. London, 1973.

―――――. *Early Venetian Legislation on Ambassadors*. Geneva, 1966.

Rapp, Richard Tilden. *Industry and Economic Decline in Seventeenth-Century Venice*. Cambridge, Massachusetts, 1976.

Reedy, Gerard. "Mystical Politics: The Imagery of Charles II's Coronation." In *Studies in Change and Revolution: Aspects of English Intellectual History, 1640–1800*, pp. 19–42. Edited by Paul J. Korshin. Menston, Yorkshire, 1972.

Reeves, Marjorie. *Joachim of Fiore and the Prophetic Future*. New York, 1976.

Richardson, H. G. "The Coronation in Medieval England: The Evolution of the Office and the Oath." *Traditio* 16 (1960):111–202.

Robertson, Jean. "Rapports du poète et de l'artiste dans la preparation des cortèges du Lord Maire (Londres 1553–1640)." In *Les fêtes de la Renaissance*, 1:265–78. Edited by Jean Jacquot. Paris, 1956.

Rodgers, Edith Cooperrider. *Discussion of Holidays in the Later Middle Ages*. New York, 1940.

Romanin, Samuele. *Storia documentata di Venezia*. 10 vols. 2d edition, Venice, 1853–61.

Rosand, David. "The Crisis of the Venetian Renaissance Tradition." *L'arte* 11–12 (1970):5–53.

Rosand, Ellen. "Music in the Myth of Venice." *Renaissance Quarterly* 30 (1977):511–37.

Rose, Charles Jerome. "The Evolution of the Image of Venice (1500–1630)." Ph.D. dissertation, Columbia University, 1971.

—————. "Marc [*sic*] Antonio Venier, Renier Zeno and 'The Myth of Venice.' " *The Historian* 36 (1974):479–97.

Ross, James Bruce. "The Emergence of Gasparo Contarini: A Bibliographical Essay." *Church History* 41 (1972):22–45.

—————. "Gasparo Contarini and His Friends." *Studies in the Renaissance* 17 (1970):192–232.

Rossi, Vittorio. "Un aneddoto della storia della riforma a Venezia." In *Scritti varii di erudizione e di critica in onore di Rodolfo Renier*, pp. 839–64. Turin, 1912.

—————. *Fra i compagni Sempiterni*. Padua, 1910.

Rubinstein, Nicolai. "The Beginnings of Political Thought in Florence." *Journal of the Warburg and Courtauld Institutes* 5 (1942):198–227.

—————. "Italian Reactions to Terraferma Expansion in the Fifteenth Century." In *Renaissance Venice*, pp. 197–217. Edited by J. R. Hale. London, 1973.

—————. "Political Ideas in Sienese Art: The Frescoes by Ambrogio Lorenzetti and Taddeo di Bartolo in the Palazzo Pubblico." *Journal of the Warburg and Courtauld Institutes* 21 (1958):179–207.

Ruggiero, Guido. "The Cooperation of Physicians and the State in the Control of Violence in Renaissance Venice." *Journal of the History of Medicine and Allied Sciences* 33 (1978):156–66.

—————. "Law and Punishment in Early Renaissance Venice." *The Journal of Criminal Law and Criminology* 69 (1978):243–56.

—————. "Sexual Criminality in Early Renaissance Venice, 1338–58." *Journal of Social History* 8 (1975):18–37.

Russell, Jeffrey Burton. *The Devil: Perceptions of Evil from Antiquity to Primitive Christianity*. Ithaca, New York, 1977.

Russell-Smith, H. F. *Harrington and His "Oceana": A Study of a 17th*

BIBLIOGRAPHY: SECONDARY SOURCES

Century Utopia and Its Influence in America. New York, 1971.

Sacchi, Defendente. *Delle condizione economica, morale e politica degli italiani ne' tempi municipali. Sulle feste, e sull'origine, stato e decadenza de' municipii italiani nel medio evo.* Milan, 1829.

Sachs, Curt. *The History of Musical Instruments.* New York, 1940.

Sagredo, Agostino. *Sulle consorterie delle arti edificative in Venezia.* Venice, 1856.

Santosuosso, Antonio. "Religious Orthodoxy, Dissent and Suppression in Venice in the 1540s." *Church History* 42 (1973):476–85.

Schramm, Percy Ernst. *Herrschaftszeichen und Staatssymbolik: Beiträge zu ihrer Geschichte vom dritten bis zum sechzehnten Jahrhundert.* Schriften der Monumenta Germaniae Historica, vol. 13, pts.1–3. Stuttgart, 1954–56.

————. *Der König von Frankreich: Das Wesen der Monarchie vom 9 zum 16 Jahrhundert.* Weimar, 1939. Republished Weimar, 1960; also Darmstadt, 1960.

Schulz, Juergen. "Vasari at Venice." *The Burlington Magazine* 103 (1961):500–11.

Schwimmer, Erik. *Exchange in the Social Structure of the Orokawa: Traditional and Emergent Ideologies in the Northern District of Papua.* London, 1973.

Seneca, Fedrico. "Venezia, l'equilibrio politico e la crisi della 'libertà' d'Italia." *Critica storica* 6 (1967):453–69.

Setton, Kenneth M. "Saint George's Head." *Speculum* 48 (1973):1–12.

Silverman, Sydel. "On the Uses of History in Anthropology: The *Palio* of Siena." *American Ethologist* 6 (1979):413–36.

————. *Three Bells of Civilization: The Life of an Italian Hill Town.* New York, 1975.

Simmel, Georg. *The Sociology of Georg Simmel.* Translated, edited, and with an introduction by Kurt H. Wolff. New York, 1950.

Sinding-Larsen, Staale. "The Changes in the Iconography and Composition of Veronese's Allegory of the Battle of Lepanto in the Doge's Palace." *Journal of the Warburg and Courtauld Institutes* 19 (1956):298–302.

————. *Christ in the Council Hall: Studies in the Religious Iconography of the Venetian Republic.* With a contribution by A. Kuhn. Acta ad archaeologiam et artium historiam pertinentia, no. 5. Rome, 1974.

Smith, Logan Pearsall. *The Life and Letters of Sir Henry Wotton.* Oxford, 1907.

Soranzo, Giovanni. "Come fu data e come fu accolta a Venezia la notizia della 'S.te Barthélemy.' " In *Miscellanea in onore di Roberto Cessi*, 2:129–44. Rome, 1958.

Staley, Edgcumbe. *The Dogaressas of Venice (The Wives of the Doges)*. London, 1910.

Starn, Randolph. *Donato Giannotti and His "Epistolae."* Geneva, 1968.

Stella, Aldo "La regolazione delle pubbliche entrate e la crisi politica veneziana del 1582." In *Miscellanea in onore di Roberto Cessi*, 2:157–71. Rome, 1958.

Strayer, Joseph. "France: The Holy Land, the Chosen People, and the Most Christian King." In *Action and Conviction in Early Modern Europe: Essays in Memory of E. H. Harbison*, pp. 3–16. Edited by Theodore K. Rabb and Jerrold E. Seigel. Princeton, 1969.

————. *On the Medieval Origins of the Modern State*. Princeton, 1970.

Sumbert, Samuel L. *The Nuremberg Schembart Carnival*. New York, 1941.

Tafuri, Manfredo. *Jacopo Sansovino e l'architettura del '500 a Venezia*. 2d edition, Padua, 1972.

Tamassia Mazzarotto, Bianca. *Le feste veneziane: i giochi popolari, le cerimonie religiose e di governo*. Florence, 1961.

Tassini, Giuseppe. *Curiosità veneziane*. 5th edition, Venice, 1915.

————. *Feste, spettacoli, divertimenti e piaceri degli antichi veneziani*. 2d edition, Venice, 1961.

Tenenti, Alberto. *Piracy and the Decline of Venice, 1580–1615*. Translated by Janet and Brian Pullan. Berkeley, 1967.

————. "The Sense of Space and Time in the Venetian World of the Fifteenth and Sixteenth Centuries." In *Renaissance Venice*, pp. 17–46. Edited by J. R. Hale. London, 1973.

Thomas, Keith. "Work and Leisure in Pre-Industrial Society." *Past and Present* 29 (1964):50–62.

Thompson, E. P. "Anthropology and the Discipline of Historical Context." *Midland History* 1 (1972):41–55.

Thomson, Rodney M. "An English Eyewitness of the Peace of Venice, 1177." *Speculum* 50 (1975):21–32.

Toderini, Teodoro. *Cerimoniali e feste in occasione di avvenimenti e passaggi nelli stati della repubblica veneta di duchi, arciduchi ed imperatori dell'augustissima casa d'Austria dall'anno 1361 al 1797*. Venice, 1857.

Tolnay, Charles de. "Il 'Paradiso' del Tintoretto note sull'interpretazione della tela in palazzo ducale." *Arte veneta* 24 (1970):103–10.

Tramontin, Silvio. "Breve storia dell'agiografia veneziana." In *Il culto dei santi a Venezia,* pp. 17–40. Edited by Silvio Tramontin. Biblioteca agiografica veneziana, no. 2. Venice, 1965.

─────. "Influsso orientale nel culto dei santi a Venezia fino al secolo xv." In *Venezia e il Levante fino al secolo XV,* 1:801–20. Edited by Agostino Pertusi. Florence, 1973.

─────. "Il 'Kalendarium' veneziano." In *Il culto dei santi a Venezia,* pp. 275–327. Edited by Silvio Tramontin. Biblioteca agiografica veneziana, no. 2. Venice, 1965.

─────. "Una pagina di folklore religioso veneziano antico: La festa de 'Le Marie.' " In *La religiosità popolare nella valle padana,* pp. 401–17. Atti del II convegno di studi sul folklore padano, Modena, 19–20–21 marzo 1965. Modena, 1966.

─────. "Realità e leggenda nei racconti marciani veneti." *Studi veneziani* 12 (1970):35–58.

─────. "San Marco." In *Il culto dei santi a Venezia,* pp. 41–73. Edited by Silvio Tramontin. Biblioteca agiografica veneziana, no. 2. Venice, 1965.

─────. "I santi dei mosaici marciani." In *Il culto dei santi a Venezia,* pp. 133–53. Edited by Silvio Tramontin. Biblioteca agiografica veneziana, no. 2 Venice, 1965.

Trevelyan, George Macaulay. *Manin and the Venetian Revolution of 1848.* Reprint. New York, 1974.

Trexler, Richard C. "Florentine Religious Experience: The Sacred Image." *Studies in the Renaissance* 19 (1972):7–41.

─────. *The Libro Cerimoniale of the Florentine Republic.* Travaux d'humanisme et Renaissance, no. 165. Geneva, 1978.

─────. "Ritual Behavior in Renaissance Florence: The Setting." *Medievalia et Humanistica: Studies in Medieval and Renaissance Culture,* new series 4 (1973):125–44.

─────. "Ritual in Florence: Adolescence and Salvation in the Renaissance." In *The Pursuit of Holiness in Late Medieval and Renaissance Religion,* pp. 200–64. Edited by Charles Trinkaus with Heiko A. Oberman. Leiden, 1974.

Tucci, Ugo. "The Psychology of the Venetian Merchant in the Sixteenth Century." In *Renaissance Venice,* pp. 346–78. Edited by J. R. Hale. London, 1973.

Turner, Victor W. "The Center Out There: Pilgrim's Goal." *History of Religions* 12 (1973):191–230.

─────. *The Ritual Process: Structure and Anti-Structure.* London, 1969.

─────, and Turner, Edith. *Image and Pilgrimage in Christian Culture: Anthropological Perspectives.* New York, 1978.

Ullman, Walter. *Principles of Government and Politics in the Middle Ages*. London, 1961.

Urban, Lina Padoan. "Apparati scenografici nelle feste veneziane cinquecentesche." *Arte veneta* 23 (1969):145–55.

————. "La festa della Sensa nelle arti e nell'iconografia." *Studi veneziani* 10 (1968):291–353.

————. "Teatri e 'teatri del mondo' nella Venezia del Cinquecento." *Arte veneta* 20 (1966):137–46.

Venturi, Lionello. "Le compagnie della calza (sec. xv–xvi)." *Nuovo archivio veneto*, new series 16 (1908) and 17 (1909).

Very, Francis George. *The Spanish Corpus Christi Procession: A Literary and Folkloric Study*. Valencia, 1962.

Walzer, Michael. *The Revolution of the Saints: A Study in the Origins of Radical Politics*. New York, 1974.

Warner, Marina. *Alone of All Her Sex: The Myth and the Cult of the Virgin Mary*. New York, 1967.

Weinstein, Donald. *Ambassador from Venice: Pietro Pasqualigo in Lisbon, 1501*. Minneapolis, 1960.

————. "Critical Issues in the Study of Civic Religion in Renaissance Florence." In *The Pursuit of Holiness in Late Medieval and Renaissance Religion*, pp. 265–70. Edited by Charles Trinkaus with Heiko A. Oberman. Leiden, 1974.

————. *Savonarola and Florence: Prophecy and Patriotism in the Renaissance*. Princeton, 1970.

Wieruszowski, Hélène. "Art and the Commune in the Time of Dante." *Speculum* 19 (1944):14–33.

Wolff, Robert Lee. "The Three Romes: The Migration of an Ideology and the Making of an Autocrat." *Daedalus* 88 (1959):291–311.

Wolters, Wolfgang. "Der Programmentwurf zur Dekoration des Dogenpalastes nach dem Brand vom 20 Dezember 1577." *Mitteilungen des Kunsthistorischen Institutes in Florenz* 12 (1966):271–318.

Woodward, C. Vann. "The Aging of America." *American Historical Review* 82 (1977):583–94.

Woolf, S. J. "Venice and the Terraferma: Problems of the Change from Commercial to Landed Activities." *Bollettino dell'Istituto di Storia della Società e dello Stato Veneziano* 4 (1962):415–441. Reprinted in *Crisis and Change in the Venetian Economy in the Sixteenth and Seventeenth Centuries*, pp. 175–203, edited by Brian Pullan, London, 1968.

Wright, A. D. "Why the *Venetian* Interdict?" *The English Historical Review* 89 (1974):534–50.

Yates, Francis A. "Charles quint et l'idée d'empire." In *Les fêtes de la Renaissance II: Fêtes et cérémonies au temps de Charles quint,* pp. 57–97. Edited by Jean Jacquot. Paris, 1960.

Young, Karl. "Philippe de Mézière's Dramatic Office for the Presentation of the Virgin." *Publications of the Modern Language Association of America* 26 (1911):181–234.

Zenatti, O. "Il poemetto di Pietro de' Natali sulla pace di Venezia tra Alessandro III e Frederico Barbarossa." *Bullettino dell'Istituto Storico Italiano* 26 (1905):105–98.

Zorzi, Ludovico. "Elementi per la visualizzazione della scena veneta prima del Palladio." In *Studi sul teatro veneto fra Rinascimento ed età barocca,* pp. 21–51. Edited by Maria Teresa Muraro. Florence, 1971.

INDEX

acolytes, 112, 191
Adam, Salimbene de, 120
address, forms of, 256, 264
admiral: of the Arsenal, 269, 285; of the fleet, 258, 264
Adrian IV, Pope, 160
Adriatic Sea, 60, 98, 107, 119–25, 128
advent of a king into a city, 115–16
Aegean Sea, 96
Aeneid, 67
Agnadello, Venetian defeat at, 27, 34, 35, 46–47. *See also* Cambrai, War of the League of
Albania, Venetian claims in, 26
Alexander III, Pope, 67, 160; gifts or donation of, 77, 84–85, 90, 102, 103–19, 124, 203, 205, 302
Alexander V, Pope, 113
Alexander the Great, relief of, 269
Alexandria, Egypt, 23, 80–81, 82; calendar of, 77
All Saints' Day, 200, 212
All Souls' Day, 257
alms, *see* charity given in rituals
Altinate chronicle, 137
Alviano, Bartolomeo d', 262n
Amasea, 93
ambassadors: foreign, in Venice, 85, 189, 199, 230, 231, 232–37, 257, 290; place of, in Venetian processions, 191; Venetian, abroad, 110, 199
America and Americans, 23, 54, 55
Anastasius III, anti-pope, 221
Ancona, 105–106, 115
animals as tribute, 255; in rituals, 156, 160–66, 170, 172, 177–78, 180–81n
Annunciation Day, 70, 139, 212; of Mary, 71
anointment, 285n
Antenor, 67

Aquileia, city and patriarch of, 66, 69–70, 77, 79–80, 83, 160, 164, 178–79
Aquinas, Saint Thomas, 223
Aragon, 96
arch, triumphal, 295
Arco Foscari, 265
arengo, see assembly, popular
Aretino, Pietro, 163, 171
Aristotle, 48, 185; relief of, 265
Arsenal sailors, 122, 258, 269, 276, 285. *See also* admiral of the Arsenal
Ascension Day, 105, 119–34, 212, 256n. *See also* marriage of the sea
assembly, popular, 252–53, 279, 283–84, 286n
Athens, 17, 23, 44–45, 73
Attila, 68–70, 72
Augustinians, 127
Austrian occupation of Venice, 69
avogadoria di comun (state attorneys), 28–29, 192
Azevedo, Emmanuele de, 137

Bakhtin, Mikhail, 159–60, 177–78
baldachin, 115
ballets, 163, 166, 171, 173
ballotino (voting teller), 191, 206, 279, 288
banners, 59, 100, 106, 113, 116–18, 120, 121, 141, 149, 253, 260, 284–85, 302; place in procession of, 190, 205
banquets: for foreign ambassadors, 174; official, 146, 170–71, 256, 258, 261, 291; for the poor, 255; private, 169
Barbarigo, Doge Agostino, 265–71, 270n, 272, 277, 278, 283, 286, 288
Barbarigo, Doge Marco, 265, 286
Barbaro, Alvise, 35n

Library of Congress Cataloging in Publication Data

Muir, Edward, 1946–
  Civic ritual in Renaissance Venice.

  Bibliography: p.
  Includes index.
    1. Venice—History—1508–1797. 2. Venice—Festivals, etc. 3. Municipal
ceremonial—Italy—Venice.
  I. Title.
  DG678.235.M83   945′.3105   80–8568
  ISBN 0–691–05325–1

EDWARD MUIR is Assistant Professor of History at Syracuse
University.

Printed in the United States
33953LVS00003B/214-219